Learn Quantum Computing with Python and IBM Quantum Experience

A hands-on introduction to quantum computing and writing your own quantum programs with Python

Robert Loredo

BIRMINGHAM—MUMBAI

Learn Quantum Computing with Python and IBM Quantum Experience

Commissioning Editor: Richa Tripathi
Acquisition Editor: Alok Dhuri
Senior Editor: Rohit Singh
Content Development Editor: Rosal Colaco
Technical Editor: Gaurav Gala
Copy Editor: Safis Editing
Project Coordinator: Deeksha Thakkar
Proofreader: Safis Editing
Indexer: Priyanka Dhadke
Production Designer: Aparna Bhagat

First published: September 2020

Production reference: 1250920

Published by Packt Publishing Ltd.
Livery Place
35 Livery Street
Birmingham
B3 2PB, UK.

ISBN 978-1-83898-100-6

www.packt.com

To my father, Israel, my mother, Sadie, and brother, Pierre; without their support throughout my life I would not have gotten to where I am today.

`Packt.com`

Subscribe to our online digital library for full access to over 7,000 books and videos, as well as industry leading tools to help you plan your personal development and advance your career. For more information, please visit our website.

Why subscribe?

- Spend less time learning and more time coding with practical eBooks and Videos from over 4,000 industry professionals

- Improve your learning with Skill Plans built especially for you

- Get a free eBook or video every month

- Fully searchable for easy access to vital information

- Copy and paste, print, and bookmark content

Did you know that Packt offers eBook versions of every book published, with PDF and ePub files available? You can upgrade to the eBook version at `packt.com` and as a print book customer, you are entitled to a discount on the eBook copy. Get in touch with us at `customercare@packtpub.com` for more details.

At `www.packt.com`, you can also read a collection of free technical articles, sign up for a range of free newsletters, and receive exclusive discounts and offers on Packt books and eBooks.

Contributors

About the author

Robert Loredo is the IBM Quantum Global Technical Ambassador lead with over 20 years' experience in software architecture and engineering. He is also a Qiskit Advocate and Master Inventor who holds over 160 patents and has presented various workshops, lectures, and articles covering quantum computing, artificial intelligence, and bioinformatics world-wide. As an adjunct professor, he has taught cloud computing and software engineering at the Florida International University School of Computer Science. He holds both a bachelor's and a master's degree in Computer and Electrical Engineering from the University of Miami and is currently pursuing his PhD in Computer Science, specializing in Machine Learning and Neuroscience, at Florida International University.

I want to thank Arvind Krishna, Dario Gil, Jay Gambetta, Bob Sutor, Scott Crowder, Anthony Annunziata, Denise Ruffner, Mehdi Bozzo-Rey, Tammy Cornell, Abe Asfaw, Andrew Wack, Bill Minor, Brian Eccles, Brian Ingmanson, Bryce Fuller, Chris Nay, Chris Schnabel, Dan Maynard, Enrique Vargas, Frederik Flöther, Gavin Jones, Hanhee Paik, Hassi Norlen, Heather Cortes, Heather Higgins, Heike Riel, Ingolf Wittman, Ismael Faro, James Weaver, James Wootton, Jeanette (Jamie) Garcia, Jerry Chow, Jody Burks, Jules Murphy, Katie Pizzolato, Ken Wood, Liz Durst, Leron Gil, Luuk Ament, M. Lewis Temares, Mark Ritter, Mei-Ling Shyu, Melissa Turesky, Michele Grossi, Miguel Paredes Quiñones, Miroslav Kubat, Mohammed Abdel-Mottaleb, Muir Kumph, Nick Bronn, Noam Zakay, Paco Martin, Paul Kassebaum, Paul Nation, Pete Martinez, Rafael Nepomechie, Rafael Sotelo, Reuven Lask, Reza Sanatinia, Robert Eades, Rudy Wojtecki, Sarah Sheldon, Stefan Woerner, Suzie Kirschner, Talia Gershon, Walter Riess, and Zaira Nazario for their continued support.

About the reviewer

Michele Grossi is a Technical Architect and Quantum Technical Ambassador who has worked for IBM Italy since 2015 with a focus on problem solving, innovation, and technology.

Born in 1989, he received his MSc degree in Physics from the University of Pavia, where he received a scholarship from the **Istituto Nazionale di Fisica Nucleare (INFN)**. He's an industrial PhD student at the University of Pavia specializing in high energy physics and quantum computing. He is the co-author of several scientific publications, a conference speaker, and a lecturer at various universities. In his current role, Michele collaborates with customers to evaluate the latest technology utilization, ranging from machine learning to quantum computing, and with research institutions, among them IBM Research and CERN.

In 2019, Forbes selected Michele as the top "30 under 30s" brightest young Italian leaders.

Packt is searching for authors like you

If you're interested in becoming an author for Packt, please visit `authors.packtpub.com` and apply today. We have worked with thousands of developers and tech professionals, just like you, to help them share their insight with the global tech community. You can make a general application, apply for a specific hot topic that we are recruiting an author for, or submit your own idea.

Table of Contents

6
Understanding Quantum Logic Gates

Section 3:
Algorithms, Noise, and Other Strange Things in Quantum World

7
Introducing Qiskit and its Elements

8

Programming with Qiskit Terra

9

Monitoring and Optimizing Quantum Circuits

10

Executing Circuits Using Qiskit Aer

11

Mitigating Quantum Errors Using Ignis

12

Learning about Qiskit Aqua

13
Understanding Quantum Algorithms

14
Applying Quantum Algorithms

Appendix A
Resources

Assessments

Other Books You May Enjoy

Index

Preface

IBM Quantum Experience is a platform that enables developers to learn the basics of quantum computing by allowing them to run experiments on a quantum computing simulator and a real device. This book will explain the basic principles of quantum computing, along with one principle of quantum mechanics, entanglement, and the implementation of quantum algorithms and experiments on IBM's quantum processors.

This book provides you with a step-by-step introduction to quantum computing using the **IBM Quantum Experience** platform. You will learn how to build quantum programs on your own, discover early use cases in your business, and help to get your company equipped with quantum computing skills.

You will start working with simple programs that illustrate quantum computing principles and slowly work your way up to more complex programs and algorithms that leverage advanced quantum computing algorithms. As you build on your knowledge, you'll understand the functionality of the IBM Quantum Experience and the various resources it offers.

We'll explore quantum computing principles such as superposition, entanglement, and interference, then we'll become familiar with the contents and layout of the IBM Quantum Experience dashboard.

Then, we'll understand quantum gates and how they operate on qubits and discover the **Quantum Information Science Kit (Qiskit)** and its elements such as Terra and Aer.

We'll then get to grips with quantum algorithms such as Deutsch-Jozsa, Simon, Grover, and Shor's algorithms, and then visualize how to create a quantum circuit and run the algorithms on any of the available quantum computers hosted on the IBM Quantum Experience.

Furthermore, you'll learn the differences between the various quantum computers and the different types of simulators available. Later, you'll explore the basics of quantum hardware, pulse scheduling, quantum volume, and how to analyze and optimize your quantum circuits, all while using the resources available on the IBM Quantum Experience.

By the end of this book, you'll have learned how to build quantum programs on your own and will have gained practical quantum computing skills that you can apply to your research or industry.

Who this book is for

This book is for Python developers who are interested in learning about quantum computing and expanding their abilities to solve classically intractable problems with the help of the IBM Quantum Experience and Qiskit. Some background in computer science, physics, and some linear algebra is required.

What this book covers

Chapter 1, Exploring the IBM Quantum Experience, will be your guide to the IBM Q Experience dashboard. This chapter will describe the layout and what each section in the dashboard means. The dashboard might alter over time, but the basic information should still be available to you.

Chapter 2, Circuit Composer – Creating a Quantum Circuit, will help you learn about Circuit Composer. This chapter will outline the user interface that will assist you in learning about quantum circuits, the qubits, and their gates that are used to perform operations on each qubit.

Chapter 3, Creating Quantum Circuits Using Quantum Lab Notebooks, will help you learn how to create circuits using the Notebook with the latest version of Qiskit already installed on the IBM Quantum Experience. You will learn how to save, import, and leverage existing circuits without having to install anything on your local machine.

Chapter 4, Understanding Basic Quantum Computing Principles, will help you learn about the basic quantum computing principles used by the IBM Quantum systems, particularly, superposition, entanglement, and interference. These three properties, often used together, serve as the base differentiators that separate quantum systems from classical systems.

Chapter 5, Understanding the Quantum Bit (Qubit), will help you learn about the basic fundamental component of a quantum system, the quantum bit or qubit, as it is often called. After reading this chapter, you will understand the basis states of a qubit, how they are measured, and how they can be visualized both mathematically and graphically.

Chapter 6, Understanding Quantum Logic Gates, will help you learn how to perform operations on a qubit. These operations are often referred to as quantum gates. This chapter will enable you, via the IBM Quantum Experience, to get to grips with the operations that each of these quantum gates performs on a qubit and the results of each of those operations. Examples of the quantum principles such as reversibility, which is a core principle for all quantum gates, will be included.

Chapter 7, Introducing Qiskit and its Elements, will help you learn about Qiskit and all of its libraries that can help you develop and implement various quantum computing solutions. Qiskit is composed of four elements, each of which has a specific functionality and role that can be leveraged based on the areas you wish to experiment in. The elements are Terra (Earth), Aer (Air), Ignis (Fire), and Aqua (Water). This chapter will also discuss how to contribute to each of the elements and how to install it locally on your machine.

Chapter 8, Programming with Qiskit Terra, will help you learn about the basic foundational element, Terra. Terra is the base library upon which all the other elements of Qiskit are built. Terra allows a developer to code the base of an algorithm to the specific operator on a qubit. This is analogous to assembly language with just a slightly easier set of library functions. It will also include a section on the Pulse library, which allows you to create pulse schedules to manipulate the quantum qubits via the hardware.

Chapter 9, Monitoring and Optimizing Quantum Circuits, will help you learn how to monitor the job requests sent to either the simulator or the quantum computers on the IBM Quantum Experience. Optimization features will also be covered here to allow you to leverage many of the existing optimization features included in the Qiskit libraries or to create your own custom optimizers.

Chapter 10, Executing Circuits Using Qiskit Aer, will help you learn about Qiskit Aer, a high-performance framework that you will use to simulate your circuits on various optimized simulator backends. You will learn what the differences are between the four various simulators of Qasm, State vector, Unitary, and Pulse, and what functionality each one exhibits. Aer also contains tools you can use to construct noise models, should you need to perform some research to reproduce errors due to noise.

Chapter 11, Mitigating Quantum Errors Using Ignis, will help you learn about the various errors that currently affect experiments on read devices, such as relaxation and decoherence, so you can design quantum error correction codes. You will also learn about readout error mitigation, which is a way to mitigate the readout errors returned from a quantum computer.

Chapter 12, Learning about Qiskit Aqua, will, in essence, pull everything together so that end users such as researchers and developers from the various domains of chemistry, machine learning, finance, optimization, and more can run their computations on a quantum computer system without having to know all the inner workings. Aqua is the tool connected to quantum algorithms that has been created to do just that. You will learn how to extend your classical application to include running a quantum algorithm.

Chapter 13, Understanding Quantum Algorithms, will dig into some basic algorithms using the IBM Quantum Experience Composer. This chapter will start with some simple algorithms that illustrate the advantages of superposition and entanglement, such as Bell's state theorem, and extends into some more common algorithms to solve some problems that illustrate uses of superposition and entanglement such as Deutsch-Josza and a few others, each of which provides some variance to the different algorithm types.

Chapter 14, Applying Quantum Algorithms, describes the various quantum computing properties and algorithms used to create some of the more well-known algorithms such as Quantum Amplitude Estimation, Variational Quantum Eigensolvers, and Shor's algorithm.

Appendix A, Resources, will help you get familiar with all the available resources in the IBM Quantum Experience and Qiskit community. These resources that have been contributed either by the Qiskit open source community, or the IBM Quantum research teams themselves. The information is laid out so anyone with basic to expert-level knowledge can jump in and start learning. There is a full quantum course, textbook, and Slack community that you can connect to in order to extend your learning and collaborate with others.

Assessments contains the answers to the questions asked in the chapters.

To get the most out of this book

You will need to have internet access to connect to the IBM Quantum Experience. Since the IBM Quantum Experience is hosted on the IBM Cloud, you will not need anything more other than a supported browser and to register with the IBM Quantum Experience. Everything else is taken care of on the IBM Quantum Experience.

Software/hardware covered in the book	OS requirements
Latest browser (Firefox, Chrome, Safari)	Windows, Mac OS X, and Linux (any)

If you are using the digital version of this book, we advise you to type the code yourself or access the code via the GitHub repository (link available in the next section). Doing so will help you avoid any potential errors related to the copying and pasting of code.

Download the example code files

You can download the example code files for this book from your account at www.packt.com. If you purchased this book elsewhere, you can visit www.packtpub.com/support and register to have the files emailed directly to you.

You can download the code files by following these steps:

1. Log in or register at www.packt.com.
2. Select the **Support** tab.
3. Click on **Code Downloads**.
4. Enter the name of the book in the **Search** box and follow the onscreen instructions.

Once the file is downloaded, please make sure that you unzip or extract the folder using the latest version of:

*   WinRAR/7-Zip for Windows
*   Zipeg/iZip/UnRarX for Mac
*   7-Zip/PeaZip for Linux

The code bundle for the book is also hosted on GitHub at https://github.com/PacktPublishing/Learn-Quantum-Computing-with-Python-and-IBM-Quantum-Experience. In case there's an update to the code, it will be updated on the existing GitHub repository.

We also have other code bundles from our rich catalog of books and videos available at https://github.com/PacktPublishing/. Check them out!

Code in Action

Code in Action videos for this book can be viewed at https://bit.ly/3o5M80.

Download the color images

We also provide a PDF file that has color images of the screenshots/diagrams used in this book. You can download it here: https://static.packt-cdn.com/downloads/9781838981006_ColorImages.pdf.

Conventions used

There are a number of text conventions used throughout this book.

`Code in text`: Indicates code words in text, database table names, folder names, filenames, file extensions, pathnames, dummy URLs, user input, and Twitter handles. Here is an example: "This will initialize our `t1`, `a`, and `b` parameters, which we will use to generate `T1Fitter`."

A block of code is set as follows:

```
# Initialize the parameters for the T1Fitter, A, T1, and B
param_t1 = t1*1.2
param_a = 1.0
param_b = 0.0
```

Any command-line input or output is written as follows:

```
[[1. 0. 0. ... 0. 0. 0.]
 [0. 1. 0. ... 0. 0. 0.]
 [0. 0. 1. ... 0. 0. 0.]
 ...
 [0. 0. 0. ... 1. 0. 0.]
 [0. 0. 0. ... 0. 1. 0.]
 [0. 0. 0. ... 0. 0. 1.]]
```

Bold: Indicates a new term, an important word, or words that you see onscreen. For example, words in menus or dialog boxes appear in the text like this. Here is an example: "As shown in the following screenshot, **ibmq_qasm_simulator** can run wider circuits than most local machines and has a larger variety of basis gates."

> **Tips or important notes**
> Appear like this.

Get in touch

Feedback from our readers is always welcome.

General feedback: If you have questions about any aspect of this book, mention the book title in the subject of your message and email us at customercare@packtpub.com.

Errata: Although we have taken every care to ensure the accuracy of our content, mistakes do happen. If you have found a mistake in this book, we would be grateful if you would report this to us. Please visit www.packtpub.com/support/errata, selecting your book, clicking on the Errata Submission Form link, and entering the details.

Piracy: If you come across any illegal copies of our works in any form on the Internet, we would be grateful if you would provide us with the location address or website name. Please contact us at copyright@packt.com with a link to the material.

If you are interested in becoming an author: If there is a topic that you have expertise in and you are interested in either writing or contributing to a book, please visit authors.packtpub.com.

Reviews

Please leave a review. Once you have read and used this book, why not leave a review on the site that you purchased it from? Potential readers can then see and use your unbiased opinion to make purchase decisions, we at Packt can understand what you think about our products, and our authors can see your feedback on their book. Thank you!

For more information about Packt, please visit packt.com.

Section 1: Tour of the IBM Quantum Experience (QX)

In this section, we will tour all the features and resources available to you on the IBM Quantum Experience. These will include some educational materials for all levels, information on the many simulators and real devices available to you, and tools that you can use to perform experiments from the many tutorials as you learn, or to simply create experiments on your own.

This section comprises the following chapters:

- *Chapter 1, Exploring the IBM Quantum Experience*
- *Chapter 2, Circuit Composer – Creating a Quantum Circuit*
- *Chapter 3, Creating Quantum Circuits Using Quantum Lab Notebooks*

1
Exploring the IBM Quantum Experience

Quantum computing has been growing in popularity over the past few years, most recently since IBM released the **IBM Quantum Experience (IQX)** back in May 2016. This release was the first of its kind, hosted on the cloud and providing the world with the opportunity to experiment with a quantum computer for free. The IQX includes a user interface that allows anyone to run experiments on both a simulator and on a real quantum computer.

The goal of this chapter is to first introduce you to the IBM Quantum Experience site, specifically the **dashboard**, which contains everything you need in order to run experiments. It also allows you to experiment with existing experiments contributed by other developers from around the world, the benefits of which can help you to understand how others are experimenting, and you can perhaps collaborate with them if the experiments correlate with your own ideas.

This chapter will help you understand what actions and information are available in each view. This includes creating an experiment, running experiments on a simulator or real quantum device, information about your profile, available backends, or pending results to experiments. So, let's get started!

The following topics will be covered in this chapter:

- Navigating the IBM Quantum Experience
- Getting started with IBM Quantum Experience

Technical requirements

Throughout this book, it is expected that you will have some experience in developing with Python and, although it isn't necessary, some basic knowledge of classical and quantum mechanics would help.

Most of the information will be provided with each chapter, so if you do not have knowledge of classical or quantum mechanics, we will cover what you need to know here.

For those of you that do have knowledge, the information here will serve as a refresher. The Python editor used throughout this book is **Jupyter Notebook**. You can, of course, use any Python editor of your choice. This may include **Watson Studio**, **PyCharm**, **Spyder**, **Visual Studio Code**, and so on. Here is the link for the CiA videos: `https://bit.ly/35o5M80`

Here is the source code used throughout this book: `https://github.com/PacktPublishing/Learn-Quantum-Computing-with-Python-and-IBM-Quantum-Experience`.

Navigating the IBM Quantum Experience

As mentioned earlier, the dashboard is your high-level view of what you will normally see once you log in to IQX. It aggregates multiple views that you can see, and this helps you to get an idea as to what machines you have access to and what experiments you have pending, running, or completed.

In this section, we will go through the steps to get registered on IQX. Let's do that in the next section.

Registering to the IBM Quantum Experience

In this section, we will get registered and explain what happens in the background once you sign up to IQX for the first time. This will help you understand what features and configurations are prepared and available to you upon registration.

To register to the IBM Quantum Experience, follow these steps:

1. The first step is to head over to the IBM Quantum Experience site at the following link: `https://quantum-computing.ibm.com/`

2. Sign-in to your account from the login screen, as shown in *Figure 1.1*. Your individual situation will determine how to proceed from there.

    If you already have an account or are already signed in, you can skip this section and move on to the next one.

    If you have not registered, then you can select the login method of your choice from the sign-in screen. As you can see, you can register using various methods, such as with your **IBM ID**, **Google**, **GitHub**, **Twitter**, **LinkedIn**, or by email.

    If you do not have any of the account types listed, then you can simply register for an **IBMid** account and use that to sign in:

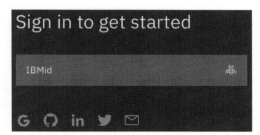

Figure 1.1 – The IBM Quantum Experience sign-in page

3. Once you select the login method of your choice, you will see the login screen for that method. Simply fill out the information, if it's not already there, and select login.

4.   Once signed in, you will land on the **Home** page. This is the first page you will see each time you log in to the IBM Quantum Experience site:

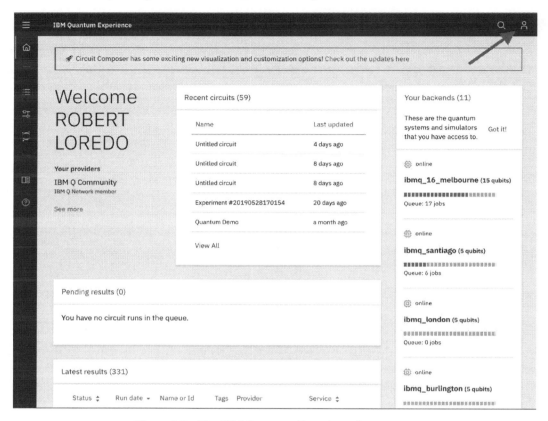

Figure 1.2 – The IBM Quantum Experience home page

Now that you have registered to the IBM Quantum Experience, let's take a quick tour and delve into some features that make up the IQX home page. Let's start by reviewing the home page, specifically the **Personal** profile tab. You can access your personal profile via your avatar, located at the top right of the page (as pointed out in *Figure 1.2*).

Understanding the Personal profile tab

This section explains the profile of the logged-in user. This is helpful if you have multiple accounts and you wish to keep track of them. The provider limits the number of jobs that can be executed or queued on a given device at any one time to a maximum, as specified in the documentation. There are many ways to access all the various quantum devices; those listed in the open group will see all freely available quantum devices, as illustrated along the right side of *Figure 1.2*. For those who are members of the **IBM Q Network**, you will have access to the open devices, as well as premium quantum devices such as the 65 qubit quantum computer.

Now that you have completed the sign-up process and successfully logged in, we can start off by taking a tour of the IBM Quantum Experience application. This will be where most of the work within this book will take place, so it will benefit you in understanding where everything is so that you can easily make your way around it while developing your quantum programs.

Getting started with IBM Quantum Experience

This section provides a quick way to launch either **Circuit Composer** or the notebooks located in the Quantum Lab views, herein simply referred to as **Qiskit notebooks**, each of which we will cover in detail in *Chapter 2, Circuit Composer – Creating a Quantum Circuit*, and *Chapter 3, Creating Quantum Circuits Using Qiskit Notebooks*, respectively, so hang in there. But as with other views, know that you can kick-start either from the main dashboard view or from the left panel. Each button easily provides a quick launch for either of the two circuit generators.

Learning about your backends

This section lists the available backend quantum systems that are provisioned for your use (as shown in *Figure 1.3*). It not only provides a list of the available backends but also provides details for each, such as the *status* of each backend. The status includes whether the device is online or in maintenance mode, how many **qubits (quantum bits)** each device contains, and how many experiments are in the queue to be run on the device. It also contains a color bar graph to indicate queue wait times, as illustrated between **ibmq_16_melbourne** and **ibmq_rome** in the following screenshot. Be aware that the quantum devices listed for you may be different from those listed here:

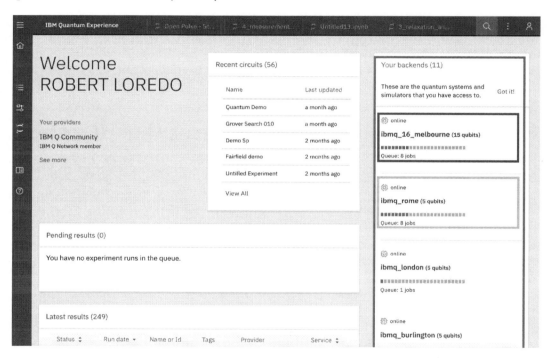

Figure 1.3 – Provisioned backend simulators and devices

From the preceding screenshot, you can see that another great feature that IQX has with respect to the backend service is the ability to see the hardware details of each real quantum device. If you hover your mouse over each device listed, you will see an expansion icon appear at the top right of the device information block. If you select a device (for example, **ibmq_16_melbourne**), you will see the device details view appear, as shown in the following screenshot:

ibmq_16_melbourne v2.3.0

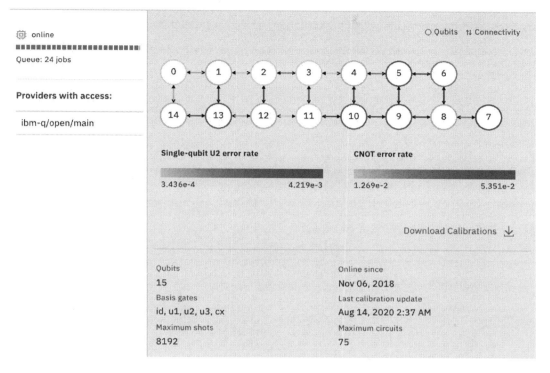

Figure 1.4 – Device details view: The status (left) and configuration and error rates (right)

From the previous screenshot, you can see that the device details view contains some very relevant information, particularly if you are working on any experiments that have intricate connectivity between qubits or analyzing error mitigation techniques. On the left of the screenshot (*Figure 1.4*), you can see the basic status information of the device. This is similar to what you see before expanding the device information. In the square on the right, we get into a little more detail with respect to the devices' configuration, connectivity, and error rates.

As described in the shaded bar area, where the error rate range is illustrated by **Single-qubit U3 error rate**, and **CNOT error rate** (single qubit and multi-qubit, respectively), qubits are identified as the circles where the number specifies the qubit number in the device. The arrows in between identify how each qubit is connected to the other qubits. The connections are specific to how the multi-qubit operations are specified.

For example, in the **15** qubit configuration in *Figure 1.4* (on the right), you can see that qubit number **4** is the source for target qubits **3** and **10** (we will get into what source and target mean later, but for now just assume that actions to the target qubit are triggered by the source qubit). You can also see that qubit **4** is the target qubit of qubit **5**. This visual representation is based on information provided by the device configuration, which you can also access programmatically using **Qiskit**.

Another piece of information you can get here is the error rates. The devices are calibrated at least once a day or so, and each time they are calibrated, they calculate the average error rates for a single gate (**u3**) and multi-gates (**CNOT**). The error rates vary per qubit, or qubits for multi-gates, and therefore, the diagram uses a color heat map to identify where the qubit sits on the error rate scale. Each qubit has a different color associated with it. This color makes it possible to visually identify where on the error rate scale that qubit falls. If you are running an experiment on a qubit that requires low error rates, then you can see from this diagram which of these qubits has the lowest error rate when last calibrated.

Below the qubit configuration, you will see a link that also allows you to download the entire configuration information in a spreadsheet. The details there are very specific to each qubit and they provide more information that isn't visible on the qubit configuration diagram.

Finally, at the bottom of the view are the specifics of the device itself, which includes the number of qubits, the date the device went online, and the basis gates available on the device.

You can now close the device configuration diagram to return to the dashboard, where we will next learn about the quantum programs and how to monitor them.

Learning about pending and latest results

The table shown in *Figure 1.5* contains the experiments that are pending completion on the backend devices. You can use this view to quickly see whether your experiments have run, and if not, where in the queue your experiment is set to run next.

Under your pending results table is the table where all your latest results are stored. These are the last few experiment results that were run on either the simulator or real devices on the backend. Each device is initially sorted by creation date but can be sorted by either backend or status, if need be.

Important Note

Details regarding job objects will be covered in *Chapter 9, Executing Circuits Using Qiskit Aer*.

As well as this, the job ID is listed so that you can call back the details from that job at a later time, as seen in the following screenshot:

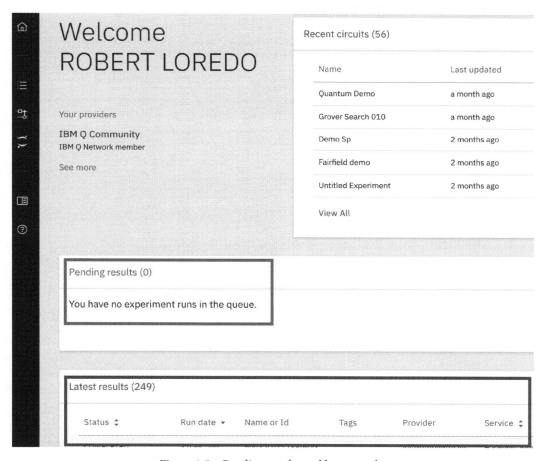

Figure 1.5 – Pending results and latest results

In this section, you have learned where to find information about your experiments, hardware details about the simulators and the real quantum devices. Next, we will explore your account profile.

Exploring My Account

In this section, you will explore your account details view, where you will find information about your account and what services are available to you. This includes services such as the ability to view the list of backend systems available to you, notification settings, and resetting your password.

To open the account view, follow these steps:

1. Click on your avatar at the top right of the dashboard (as highlighted in the following screenshot) and select **My Account**:

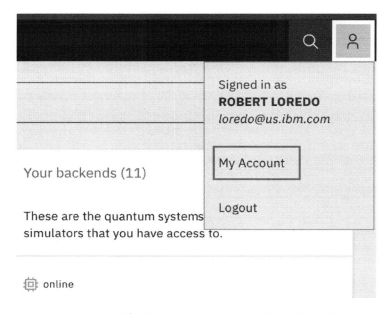

Figure 1.6 – The My Account option on the dashboard

2. Once the **My Account** view is loaded, you will see a page similar to this:

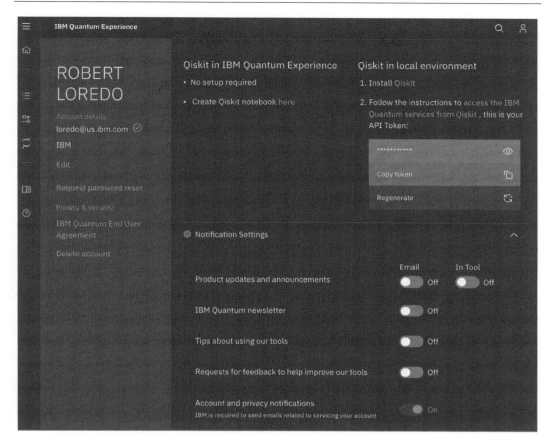

Figure 1.7 – The My Account view

From the preceding screenshot, you can see that on your account page, you will see the following information sections:

- **Account details**: This section has your account and contact information that you used to register. It also includes options such as resetting your password, privacy and security information, and the option to delete your account.

- **Qiskit in IBM Quantum Experience**: This includes a quick link to launch a Qiskit notebook to run your experiments. We will review the Qiskit notebook later in this book, but for now, just know that you can launch a Qiskit notebook from here as well.

- **Qiskit in local environment**: This section allows you to install Qiskit and run experiments from your local machine without the need to connect to IQX via the cloud. This is exceptionally helpful when you wish to run experiments but do not have access to a network. By running experiments from your local machine, this allows you to run simulators that are installed as part of the Qiskit installation. However, keep in mind that in order to run the experiments on a real quantum device, you will need network connectivity to those real devices.

  If you want to run the experiments on a real device from your local machine, then you will need to copy the token (highlighted in *Figure 1.7*) that was generated for you in the background. You should then assign it to the **Qiskit IBMQ provider** class. Details of the IBMQ provider class will be discussed in *Chapter 9*, *Executing Circuits Using Qiskit Aer*, but for now, this is where you can copy the **Application Programming Interface (API)** token.

  Also, note that there is an option to regenerate the API token. If you choose to regenerate the token, you will need to delete your old token and save the regenerated one in your local IBMQ provider class. The save account method of the IBMQ provider class will persist the value in your local machine, so you will only have to save it once and then load the account each time you wish to use a real quantum device for your experiment.

  Since this book is written primarily for use on the IBM Quantum Experience site, we will cover running and setting up on your local machine. Just in case you happen to not have network connectivity, you can still run simulated experiments locally.

- **Notification Settings**: This section simply allows you to set your notifications and how you prefer to receive information, such as when experiments have completed or other information or surveys that you wish to contribute.

- **Your accounts**: This last section toward the bottom of the **My Account** view is an overview of the accounts that you have and a list of the provisioned systems you have access to. These provisions are selected and assigned as part of the sign-up process. This includes information such as when you first signed up, the project that you are associated with (**main** is usually the default project), provider information, and the allocated backend systems that you have access to. These allocated backends that you can see are either real devices, such as **ibmq_16_melbourne**, or simulators, such as **ibmq_qasm_simulator**, which are running on the IQX cloud. We will discuss the details of the simulators and devices in later chapters.

Now that we are done with our tour of the IBM Quantum Experience layout, we're ready to get to work. In the following chapters, we will delve into each section and progress to writing quantum programs.

Summary

In this chapter, we reviewed the dashboard, which provides plenty of information to help you get a good lay of the land. You now know where to find information regarding your profile, details for each of the devices you have available, the status of each device, as well as the status and results of your experiments.

Knowing where to find this information will help you monitor your experiments and enable you to understand the state of your experiments by reviewing your backend services, monitoring queue times, and viewing your results queues.

You also have the skills to create an experiment using either Circuit Composer or the Qiskit notebooks. In the next chapter, we will learn about Circuit Composer in detail.

Questions

1. Which view contains your API token?

2. Which device in your list has the fewest qubits?

3. How many connections are there in the device with the fewest qubits?

4. What are the two tools called that are used to generate quantum circuits?

5. Which view would provide you with the list of basis gates for a selected device?

2

Circuit Composer – Creating a Quantum Circuit

In this chapter, you will learn how to use the **Circuit Composer** and what each of the composer's component functions are with respect to creating and running experiments. The composer will help you to visually create a quantum circuit via its built-in user interface, which in turn will help you to conceptualize how the basic principles of quantum mechanics are used to optimize your experiments. You will also learn how to import quantum circuits, preview the results of each experiment, and create your first quantum circuit.

The following topics will be covered in this chapter:

- Creating a quantum circuit using the Composer
- Creating our first quantum circuit
- Building a coin-flipping experiment

By the end of this chapter, you will know how to create a quantum circuit using the **Graphical Editor** to create experiments that simulate classic gates and some quantum gates. You will also learn where to examine the various results of your experiment, such as state vectors and their probabilities. This will help you understand how some quantum gate operations affect each qubit.

Technical requirements

In this chapter, some basic knowledge of computing is assumed, such as understanding the basic gates of a classic computing system; for example, **bit flip** (0 to 1), **NOT gates**, and so on. Here is the full source code used throughout the book: `https://github.com/PacktPublishing/Learn-Quantum-Computing-with-Python-and-IBM-Quantum-Experience`. Here is the link for the CiA videos: `https://bit.ly/3o5M80`

Creating a quantum circuit using the Composer

In this section, we will review the Composer layout so that you can understand the functionality and behavior of the Composer when creating or editing your quantum circuits. Here, you will also create a few circuits, leveraging the visualization features from the Composer to make it easy for you to understand how quantum circuits are created. So, let's start at the beginning: by launching the Composer editor.

Launching the Composer editor

To create a quantum circuit, let's first start by opening up the Circuit Composer. To open the Composer view, click on the Circuit Composer icon located on the left panel as shown in the following screenshot:

Figure 2.1 – Launching the Circuit Composer (left panel)

Now that you have the Composer open, let's take a tour of what each component of the Composer editor provides you with.

Familiarizing yourself with the Circuit Composer components

In this section, we will get familiar with each of the components that make up the Composer. Each of these has features specific to the various components of the Composer editor. These can provide insights by allowing you to do things such as visually inspecting the results of your experiments by displaying the results in a variety of ways. Visualizing the construction of the quantum circuit will help you conceptualize how each quantum gate affects a qubit.

Understanding the Circuit Composer

In this section, we will review the various functionalities available to ensure you have a good understanding of all the different features available to you.

In the following screenshot, you can see the landing page of the **Circuit Composer** editor view:

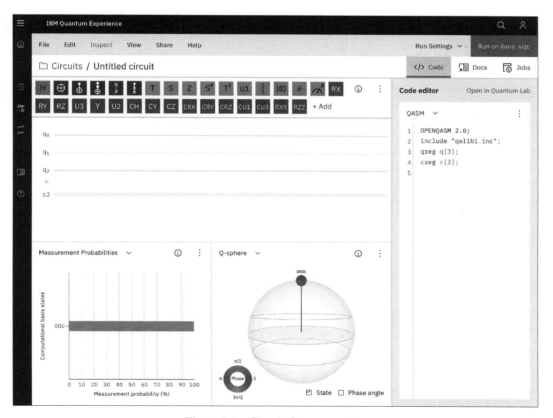

Figure 2.2 – Circuit Composer view

From the preceding screenshot, you can see at the center of the page is the **Circuit Composer** view. In the following screenshot, you can see a series of **gates** and **operations**:

Figure 2.3 – Gates and Operations

As you can see in the preceding screenshot, each of these components has a specific function or operation that acts upon the qubit(s), which we will cover in detail in *Chapter 6, Understanding Quantum Logic Gates*.

As we can see in the following screenshot, below the collection of gates and operations, we have the Circuit Composer itself:

Figure 2.4 – Circuit Composer

As you can see from the preceding screenshot, the default circuit includes three qubits, each of which is labeled with a **q**, and the index appended in order from least significant bit (in this case, q_2, q_1, q_0). Each qubit is initialized to an initial state of **0** before running the experiment.

Next to the qubit you will see a line, which looks like a wire running out from each qubit, in the circuit:

Figure 2.5 – Qubits and circuit wires

As you can from the preceding screenshot, this line is where you will be creating a circuit by placing various gates, operations, and barriers on them. The circuit has three wires, each of which pertains to one of the three qubits on the quantum computer. The reason it is called a Composer is primarily due to the fact that it looks very similar to a music staff used by musicians to compose their music. In our case, the notes on the music staff are represented by the gates and operations used to ultimately create a quantum algorithm.

In the next section, we will review the various options you have available to customize the views of the IQX. This will allow you to ensure you can only see what you need to see while creating your quantum program.

Learning how to customize your views

Continuing with our Composer tour, at the top of the Composer view is the circuit view menu option that allows you to save your circuit, clear the circuit, or share your quantum circuit. First, we will cover how to save your circuit. To do this, simply click on the default text at the top left of the circuit composer where it currently reads (Untitled circuit) and type in any title you wish. Ideally, select a name that is associated with the experiment. In this case, let's call it **My First Circuit** and save it by either hitting the *Enter* key or clicking the checkmark icon to the right of the title.

Across the top of the Composer, you will see a list of drop-down menu options. We can see these in the following screenshot:

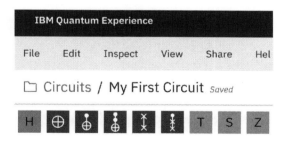

Figure 2.6 – Composer menu options

The menu items in the preceding screenshot have the following options:

- **File** provides options to create, copy, open a new circuit, or view all quantum circuits.

- **Edit** allows you to manage your circuit, clear all operators, and edit the circuit description.

- **Inspect** provides the ability to step through your circuit, similar to debug mode.

- **View** enables the various view options.

- **Share** allows you to share your quantum circuit with others.

- **Help** provides various guides, tours, and content related to quantum computing.

Let's now take a look at each of the various views in the following sections.

The Graphical Editor view

The **Graphical Editor** view contains a few components used to create quantum circuits. Which includes the following:

- **Circuit Composer**: UI components used to create quantum circuits

- **Gates and Operators**: A list of available drag and drop gates and operators available to generate a quantum circuit

- **Options**: A list of options such as the gate glossary, collapse gates, and options for downloading an image representation of your quantum circuit

The following is a screenshot illustrating each of the preceding components:

Figure 2.7 – Graphical Editor view

Now that we know where we can create a quantum circuit, let's move on to displays, which provide the results of our quantum circuit.

The Statevector view

The **Statevector** view allows you to preview the state vector results of your quantum circuit. The state vector view presents the computational basis states along the x axis, and the **Amplitude** along the y axis. In this case, since we do not have any gates or operators on our circuit, the state vector representation is that of the initial state. Where the initial state indicates that all qubits are initialized to the 0 (zero) state and with an amplitude of 1, we see that presented in the following screenshot:

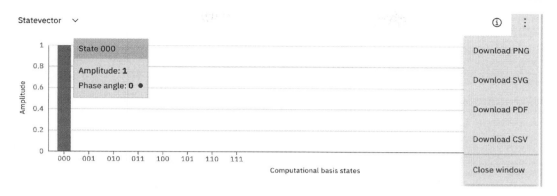

Figure 2.8 – Statevector view

Other options available to us include various ways to download the state vector information, as illustrated in the drop-down menu at the top right of the previous screenshot.

The state vector information is just one of the visual representations of your quantum circuit. There are a couple of others we want to visit before moving on.

The Measurement Probabilities view

The next view is the **Measurement Probabilities** view. This view presents the expected measurement probability result of the quantum circuit. As mentioned in the previous description, and illustrated in the following screenshot, since we do not have any operators on the circuit, the results shown are all in the initial state of 0:

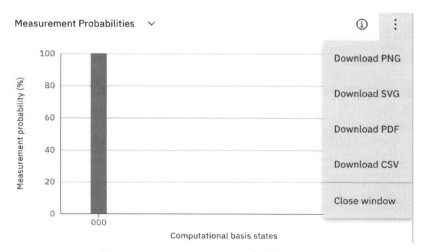

Figure 2.9 – Measurement Probabilities view

The options here also provide various formats to download the measurement probabilities.

The Q Sphere view

Finally, the last of the state visualizations we have to review is the **Q Sphere** view. The Q sphere is similar to the Bloch sphere; however, the Bloch sphere does have some limitations, particularly when working with more than one qubit. The Bloch sphere is used to represent the vector of the current state of a qubit. The Q sphere can be used to represent the state information of a single qubit or multiple qubits, including the phase information. The following screenshot shows a representation of the three qubits we have in our circuit, all of which are in the initial state:

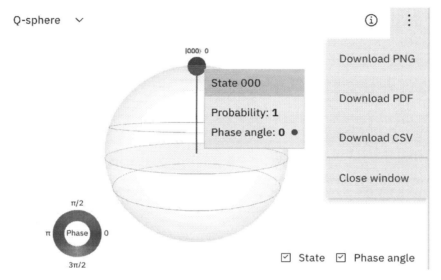

Figure 2.10 – Q Sphere view

The Q-sphere view has two components, the first is the Q-sphere itself that captures the state vector of the various qubit states represented by a vector that originates at the center of the sphere. At the end of the vector is a smaller sphere, which represents the details of the state. The states represented by these small spheres are visible when hovered over. The previous screenshot illustrates the 3 qubits in an initial state of 000, with a probability of 1, and a phase angle of 0.

The second component is located at the bottom left, which is the legend that describes the phase of the states. Since the small sphere represents the phase angle of 0, the color of the sphere is blue, which is the same that the legend indicates for the phase of 0. If the states were out of phase by a value of π, then the color of the sphere would be red.

There are various options here; to the top right you have various options to download visualizations in different image formats, and at the bottom right you can select whether to enable the state or phase angle information of the Q-sphere.

One last thing to note is at the top left, you can see a dropdown that allows you to switch between all the views we reviewed, such as the measurement probabilities and state vector.

Now that we are familiar with the various state representation views, let's look at the last view that allows us to write code and execute our quantum circuits.

The Code Editor view

The last view we will cover here is the **Code Editor** view. Here we can write code to build the circuit itself. At the top of the Code Editor view there are three tabs, namely, **Code**, **Docs**, and **Jobs**. Each tab displays details about itself.

The **Code** tab has the code editor itself, which you can use to code using **QASM** or Qiskit code, for which you make your selection with the drop-down menu at the top left of the editor. The options available in the Code Editor provide a way to copy, import, and export code. Also included is the QASM reference link, which redirects you to details of the QASM language. The following screenshot illustrates the **Code editor** view with the options expanded:

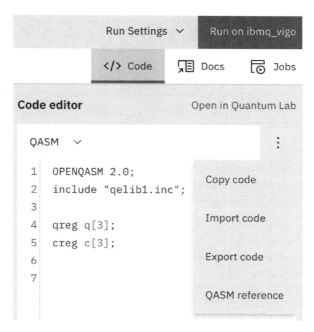

Figure 2.11 – Code Editor view

The **Docs** tab displays the documentation available and the **Jobs** tab displays your pending and completed job running on the simulators or quantum devices.

In this section, we learned about how to create a quantum circuit using the Composer. We also learned about the views and components of the Circuit Composer views.

Now that you have an understanding of the various views and components that make up the Circuit Composer views, we can start creating our first quantum circuit and leveraging a lot of these views.

Creating our first quantum circuit

Now that we know where everything is in the Circuit Composer, we will create our first quantum circuit. This will help you to get a better understanding of how all these components work together and it will show you how these components provide insights such as current state and probabilistic estimation as you build your first quantum experiment.

Building a quantum circuit with classical bit behaviors

We are all familiar with some of the basic classic bit gates such as **NOT**, **AND**, **OR**, and **XOR**. The behavior that these classic gates perform on a bit can be reproduced on a quantum circuit using quantum gates. Our first experiment will cover these basic building blocks, which will help you to understand the correlation between quantum and classic algorithms.

Our first experiment will be to simulate a NOT gate. The NOT gate is used to flip the value, in this case from $|0\rangle$ to $|1\rangle$, and vice versa. The gate we will use to do this is the **NOT gate**. We will cover details on how this gate operates on qubits in *Chapter 6, Understanding Quantum Logic Gates*.

To simulate the NOT gate on a quantum circuit, follow these steps:

1. From the open composer circuit that you previously created and titled **My First circuit**, click and drag the **NOT** gate, which is visually represented by the ⊕ symbol, from the list of gates down onto the first qubit, as shown in the following screenshot:

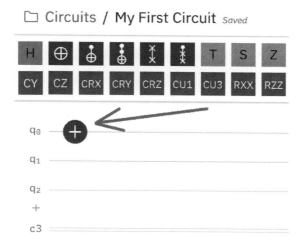

Figure 2.12 – Add an X (NOT) gate to the first qubit

2. Next, click and drag the measurement operation onto the first qubit, just after the **NOT** gate. By taking a measurement of the qubit and having its value sent out to the pertaining classic bit, we are essentially reading the state of the qubit.

   A measurement occurs when you want to observe the state of the qubit. What this means is that we will collapse the state of the qubit to either a 0 or a 1. In this example, it is pretty straightforward that when we measure the qubit after the **NOT** gate, the reading will be 1. This is because since the initial state is set to 0, applying a NOT gate will flip it from 0 to 1. Therefore, we expect the measurement to read 1.

3. Click and drag another measurement operation onto the second qubit. We'll do this just to contrast the difference between what we would see when we measure a qubit in the initial state, and after a **NOT** gate.

4.   Before we run this experiment, let's note a few things. First, note that the classic bits are all on one line (as shown in the following screenshot). This is mostly to save space. In lieu of having three additional wires where each represents a classic bit, a single wire is used to denote the classic bits. They are labeled **c3** to indicate a set of three classic bits:

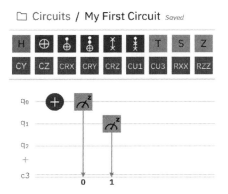

Figure 2.13 – Add a measurement operation to the first qubit

The second thing to notice is that the measurement operations match the qubit number to the classic bit number; in this case, qubit **0** will read out to bit **0**, and qubit **1** will read out to bit **1**, where bit **0** is the least significant bit.

5.   Select the **Run Settings** drop-down option located at the top right of the circuit composer view. This will display the run settings, illustrated as follows:

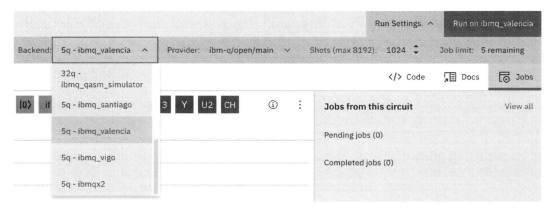

Figure 2.14 – Run settings drop-down view

6. The run dialog provides you with three options:

    First, to select which backend device you would like to run the experiment with, the choices are either on a simulator called **ibmq_qasm_simulator** or on an actual quantum device. Select any of the options you wish to run. In this example, we'll select **ibmq_valencia**.

    The second option allows you to select the **Provider**. There are different providers – the **open/main** is for the open free quantum devices, and if you are a member of the **IBM Q Network** then you'll have a provider that assigns you to the available premium quantum devices. For now, leave it at the default setting.

    The last option allows you to select how many shots of the quantum circuit you wish to run. What this means is how many times you wish the quantum circuit to run during your experiment. For now, since this is a simple experiment, let's simply set it to the default value, 1024.

7. Now that you have selected your run options, let's run the circuit. Click **Run on ibmq_valencia**. If you selected a different device, it will indicate it accordingly.

8. Once your experiment begins, you should see an entry of this experiment in the **Pending Jobs** view to the right of the Composer view. This indicates that your experiment is pending. Once completed, you will see it in the **Results view** shown as follows:

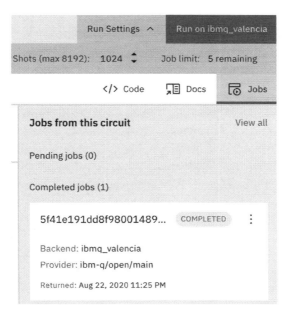

Figure 2.15 – Results view displaying pending and completed jobs for the selected circuit

While the job is in the **Pending jobs** list, it will display the status of the job. Once completed, it will automatically move from the **Pending jobs** to the **Completed jobs** list.

9. Upon completion, open your experiment from the **Completed jobs** list by clicking on the job. This opens the experiment results view; you will see details regarding your experiment at the top of the report, as illustrated in the following screenshot:

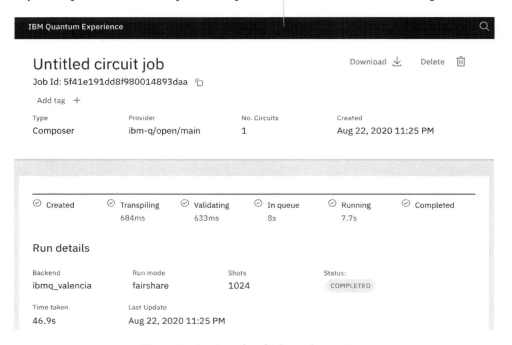

Figure 2.16 – Completed job result overview

This view provides details about the results such as the **Time taken** during each task, the **Backend** system it had run on, the number of **Shots**, the current **Status**, and the total time taken to execute. As you look further down the view you will see a histogram of the results from the circuit you just ran on the backend, as illustrated in the following screenshot:

Result

Histogram

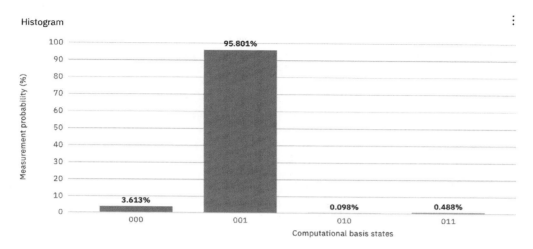

Figure 2.17 – Histogram representation of the circuit results

When you further scroll down the view/page you will see the diagram of the circuit you created, illustrated in the following screenshot:

Circuit

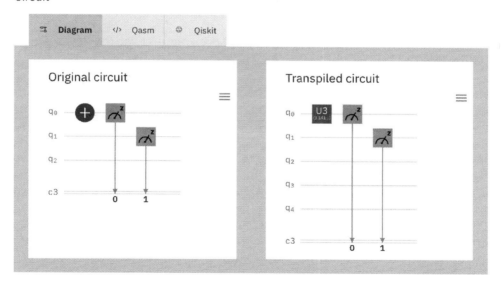

Figure 2.18 – Circuit diagram of the circuit

The diagram of the circuit is just one of the three representations of the circuit. The other two tabs will display the QASM and Qiskit representations.

Now that we have the results from running our first quantum circuit, let's take a closer look at our results and see what we got back.

Reviewing your results

The histogram result in *Figure 2.21* provides information about the outcome of your experiment. Some parts might seem straightforward, but let's review the details.

It may seem trivial now, but later on when we work on more elaborate quantum algorithms, understanding the results will prove invaluable.

There are two axes to the results. Along the x axis, we have all the possible states of our circuit. This is what the measurement operations observed when measuring the qubits. Recall that we measured the first and second qubits, so from least significant bit (on the far right), we see that the first two bits are set to 1 and 0 respectively. We know that this is correct due to the fact we placed a NOT gate on the first qubit, which changes its state from 0 to 1. For the second qubit, we simply took a measurement that equates to simply measuring the initial state, which we know to be 0.

The y axis provides the probability of the measurement. Since we ran the experiment 1024 times, the results show that we have approximately a 95% probability of the first qubit resulting in the state of **001**. The reason why the probability is 95% and not 100% is due to noise from the quantum device. We will cover the topic of noise in later chapters, but for now we can be confident to a pretty high of probability that the NOT gate worked.

So, when would the probability be different? We'll explore this in the following experiment.

In this section, we simulated a simple NOT gate operation on a qubit and ran the circuit on a quantum device. Pretty simple and straightforward. So now that you were able to create and run your first quantum program, let's start learning something a little more interesting than just changing the state of a qubit.

Building a coin-flipping experiment

If you've ever taken a course in probability and statistics, you might have seen the coin flip example. In this example, you are given an unbiased coin to flip multiple times and track the results of each flip (experiment) as either heads or tails. What this experiment illustrates is that with an unbiased coin and enough samples, you will see that the probability of either heads or tails start to converge to about 50%.

This means that, after running a sufficient number of experiments, the number of times the coin lands on heads becomes very closely equal to the number of times that it lands on tails.

Let's take a moment to make an important note regarding the previously stated analogy with respect to the reality of the preceding experiment. It has been proven that in many ways, any coin could be easily made biased so that when it is flipped, it can land on the same side each time.

That being said, I want to ensure that this is a basic example of an attempt to create a classical analogy of a quantum computing principle in order to get an understanding of the experiment we will be creating, and not to insinuate that this classical experiment equates to a quantum experiment. I will cover these differentiations as we create the next circuit that will simulate flipping a coin over 1,000 times. Let's give this a try:

1. Open the Composer Editor and create a new blank circuit.

2. Click and drag the Hadamard (H) gate onto the first qubit.

3. Click and drag the measurement operation onto the first qubit after the H gate. This will indicate that you wish the value of this qubit to be measured, and assign its resulting value of either 1 or 0 to the corresponding classic bit; in this case, the bit at position 0, as shown in the following screenshot:

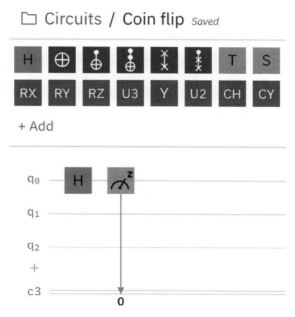

Figure 2.19 – Coin flip experiment

4. Name your circuit as Coin flip and save it.

5. Click **Run Settings** to expand the options.

6. Select the **ibmq_qasm_simulator** as the backend device and select the run count to **1024**. This will run the experiment 1,024 times.

7. Click **Run on ibmq_qasm_simulator**.

8. Once completed, click on the completed experiment in the **Completed jobs** list.

The results will now show two different states. Remember that the **Computational basis states** are represented along the x axis. The main difference you will now see is highlighted by the first classic bit of the experiment (the least significant bit on the far right of each state), which you can see is either a 0 or 1.

Another thing to note is the **Probabilities** (the y axis) of each of the two states. This will differ each time you run the experiment. For example, the results in the following screenshot will have a different result for the probability than your experiment:

Result

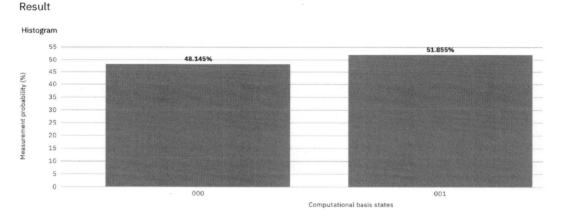

Figure 2.20 – Coin flip results

That being said, one thing you will notice from the preceding screenshot is that the results will fall fairly close to 50% each time you run the experiment. Rerun the experiment a few more times and examine the results for yourself.

The reason for this is our use of the Hadamard gate. This special gate leverages one of the two main quantum computing principles, **superposition**, that provides quantum computers with the potential to solve complex computations. We will cover what and how superposition works in *Chapter 4, Understanding Basic Quantum Computing Principles,* and how the Hadamard gate performs this gate operation on the qubit in *Chapter 6, Understanding Quantum Logic Gates.*

The use of the Hadamard gate, as you can see, allows your circuit to execute itself by leveraging a linear combination of two states, 0 and 1. As mentioned earlier, this helps to leverage superposition.

The second quantum computing principle used by quantum computers is **entanglement**. This quantum mechanical phenomenon helps us to entangle two or more qubits together. By entangling two qubits, we are in essence linking the value of one qubit and synchronizing it with another qubit. By synchronizing it, we mean that if I measure (observe) the value of one of the entangled qubits, then we can be sure that the other qubit will have the same value, whether you measure it at the same time or sometime later. The next experiment will cover this in more detail.

Entangling two coins together

Let's extend our coin-flipping example to include superposition by adding another coin and entangling them together so that when we run our experiment, we can determine the value of one coin without having to measure the other.

In the same way as our previous experiment, each qubit will represent a coin. In order to do this, we will use a multi-qubit gate called a **Control-Not (CNOT)** gate (pronounced *see-not*). The CNOT gate connects two qubits, where one is the source and the other the target. We will cover these gates in detail in *Chapter 6, Understanding Quantum Logic Gates*, but for now, here is a brief introduction so you can understand what you will expect to see.

When the source qubit (the qubit that is connected to the source of the CNOT gate) has a value equal to 1, then this enables the target of the CNOT, which as we can tell by the name is a NOT gate. This gate performs the same operation as the X gate that we ran in our previous first experiment, where we flipped the value of the qubit. Therefore, if the target qubit was set to 0, then it would flip the target qubit to 1 and vice versa. Let's try entangling our coins (qubits) to see how this works:

1. Open the Circuit Composer and create a new blank circuit.

2. Click and drag a Hadamard (H) gate onto the first qubit.

3. Click and drag the CNOT gate onto the first qubit (*round white gate with crosshairs on blue background*). This will drop the source onto the first qubit. When selecting the CNOT gate, the first qubit you drop it on will be set as the source. Visually, the source of the CNOT gate is a solid dot on the qubit to which the gate was dragged (see *Figure 2.21*).

By default, the target will set itself to the next qubit. In this case, it will drop to qubit 2. Visually, the target for a CNOT is a large dot with a cross in the middle, made to resemble a target.

4. Click and drag a measurement operator onto each of the two first qubits as shown in the following screenshot:

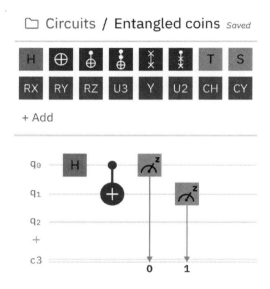

Figure 2.21 – Entangled qubit circuit representing entangled coins

5. Title and save your experiment as Entangled coins.

6. Click **Run Settings** on the circuit to launch the **Run Settings** dialog.

7. Select the **ibmq_qasm_simulator** or any other device from the backend selection as the backend device and select the run count to 1024. This will run the experiment 1,024 times.

8. Click **Run on ibmq_qasm_simulator** (or whichever device you selected in the previous step).

9. Once completed click the **Coin flip** experiment from the **Completed jobs** list.

Now let's review the results and see what happens when we entangle two qubits:

Result

Histogram

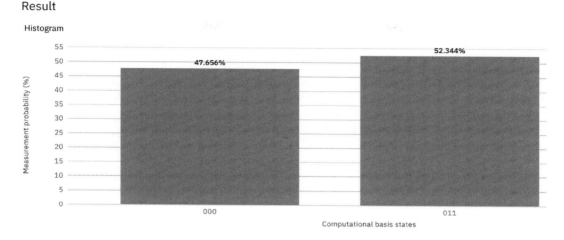

Figure 2.22 – Entangled coins results

As you can see in the preceding screenshot, the results still have two states, as they did in the previous experiment. However, one thing to observe here is the results of the two qubits. Note that the state of both qubits is either 000 or 011. Recall that the third bit (the most significant bit) was not operated on, so it remains in the initial state of 0.

What makes this experiment interesting is when we flipped one coin in the previous experiment, you saw that the results were 50% (0 or 1). However, now we are running the same experiment, but we are entangling another coin. In effect, this results in both coins becoming entangled together and thus their states will always be the same as each other. This means that if we flip both coins and we observe one of the coin values, then we know that the other entangled coin will be the same value.

Summary

In this chapter, you learned about the Circuit Composer view and its many components. You created three circuits. The first one was an experiment that simulated a classic NOT gate. The second one was an experiment in which a circuit was created using the Hadamard gate, which leveraged superposition. You then viewed the results of the experiment.

The third one was a circuit in which you expanded on the second circuit in order to include your first multi-gate, that is, a CNOT gate. From here, you demonstrated entanglement.

You were also able to review your results on a histogram, which allows you to examine how both superposition and entanglement results map from your quantum circuit to the classical bit outputs, as well as how to read the probabilities based on the results.

This has provided you with the skills to experiment with other gates and see what effect each operation has on each qubit and what information might be determined or used based on the results of the operation. This will be helpful when we look at some of the quantum algorithms and how these operations are leveraged to solve certain problems.

In the next chapter, we will move away from the click-and-drag work of the user interface and instead create experiments using Jupyter Notebooks, as well as beginning to program quantum circuits using Python.

Questions

1. Using the entangled coin-flip experiment, re-run the experiment. What is the statevector of the results?

2. What are the result states if you were to add a NOT gate before the Hadamard gate in the entangled coin-flip experiment's circuit?

3. Using the entangled coin-flip experiment from the Circuit Editor, switch the measurements so that the output of q_0 reads out to classic bit 1, and q_1 reads out to classic bit 0. What are the two states in the result and what are their probabilities?

4. What would the result states be if you were to add a Hadamard gate to the second qubit before the CNOT gate in the entangled coin-flip experiment's circuit?

3
Creating Quantum Circuits using Quantum Lab Notebooks

In this chapter, you will learn how to create circuits using the **Quantum Lab Notebooks** installed on the IBM Quantum Experience. You will learn how to save, import, and leverage existing circuits without having to install anything on your own computer. This will allow you to get a jump start on developing quantum circuits right away and ensure that you will be able to run the tutorials based on the currently installed version.

The following **Quantum Information Science Kit (Qiskit)** notebook topics will be covered in this chapter:

- Creating a quantum circuit using Quantum Lab Notebook
- Opening and importing existing Quantum Lab Notebook
- Developing a quantum circuit on Quantum Lab Notebook
- Reviewing results of your quantum circuit on the Quantum Lab Notebook

After completing this chapter, you will be able to leverage the capabilities of the Quantum Lab Notebooks, which will allow you to collaborate with others, share notebooks with others, import notebooks such as those that accompany this book, and run them directly from Quantum Lab. The Qiskit textbook is also capable of running on a Notebook, so as new features are released, you can be assured that you will be able to run them directly from your Notebook.

Technical requirements

In this chapter, some basic knowledge of programming is required, and some Python development is preferred. If you are familiar with other Notebook applications such as Jupyter Notebook then you may want to peruse this chapter, as most of the content here might be familiar to you.

We will not be using much Python-specific code here yet, but there will be some Qiskit code to help get you started in understanding and using the Qiskit Notebook. Here, I will cover the Qiskit basics as we go along, but rest assured we will have plenty of time in *Chapter 7, Introducing Qiskit and Its Elements* to review the many functions and features of Qiskit. Here is the source code used throughout this book: `https://github.com/PacktPublishing/Learn-Quantum-Computing-with-Python-and-IBM-Quantum-Experience`.

Here is the link for the CiA videos: `https://bit.ly/35o5M80`

Creating a quantum circuit using Quantum Lab Notebooks

Quantum Lab Notebooks provided to you via the IBM Quantum Experience platform will help you generate robust experiments that allow you to create quantum circuits and integrate those circuits with classical experiments or applications. Quantum Lab Notebooks generally contain a set of cells that you can use to write, test, and run your code in each cell individually.

You can also include **Markdown** language in the cells to capture any notes or non-code content, to help keep track of your learning or project. In this section, we will recreate the same quantum circuit you completed in *Chapter 2, Circuit Composer – Creating a Quantum Circuit*, only this time you will be using the Qiskit Notebook. So, let's get started!

Launching a Notebook from the Quantum Lab

To create a quantum circuit, let's start by launching the **Quantum Lab Notebook** from the **Quantum Lab** view. From the left panel under **Tools**, select **Quantum Lab** to launch the view, as illustrated in the following screenshot:

Figure 3.1 – Launching the Quantum Lab view (left panel)

Now that you have the **Quantum Lab** view open, let's take a look at what each component of the Notebook provides.

Familiarizing yourself with the Quantum Lab components

In this section, we will become familiar with each of the components that make up the **Quantum Lab** view. As you see in *Figure 3.2* (starting from the top section, where you can see there are quick links to the **Qiskit tutorials**), the quick links are grouped into three sections, as follows:

- The first one is for starters, titled **1_start_here.ipynb**. This will review the introductory functions and features of Qiskit.

- The second group contains more **advanced** level tutorials.

- The third contains tutorials specific to certain **fundamentals** such as optimization, artificial intelligence, and many other domains.

Under the quick links is the list of all previously saved notebooks. You can choose to open any of those listed, or you can create or import notebooks by selecting either the **New Notebook +** or **Import** button respectively, as illustrated in the following screenshot:

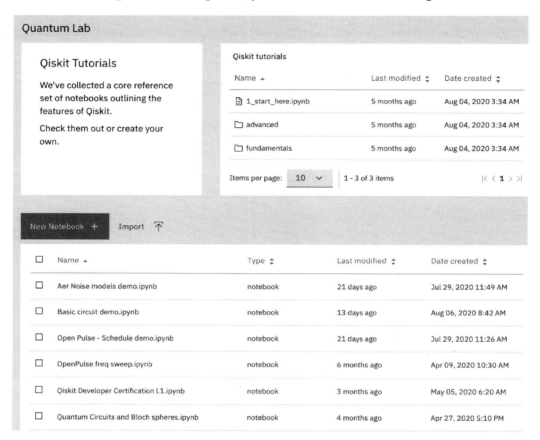

Figure 3.2 – Quantum Lab view

In the next step, we will create a new Notebook.

Creating a new Notebook

In this section, we will review the various functionalities available to ensure that you have a good understanding of all the different features available to you.

In the following screenshot, we can see the landing page of the **Circuit Composer** editor view:

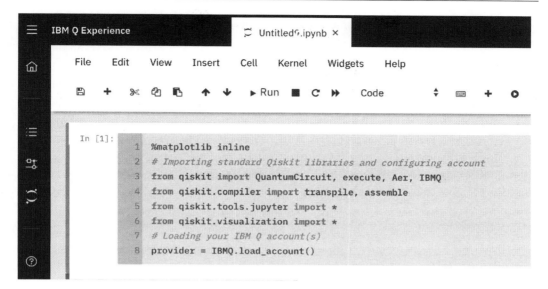

Figure 3.3 – Notebook landing page

The following points provide a description of the functions and features and what they contribute to the creation of a quantum circuit:

- When the Notebook loads up, you'll notice the first cell contains autogenerated code that includes some from Qiskit. Qiskit will be discussed in detail in *Chapter 7, Introducing Qiskit and its Elements*.

  The autogenerated code functions help to get your code up and running by adding some libraries and objects that are common when creating and running a quantum circuit. We'll review details of these objects further so that you can understand what each line pertains to and what the objects are generally used for.

  > **Important note**
  > Note that these may change as new features are added or updated to Qiskit, so the content of these lines may alter over time.

- The following lines of code, which can also be seen in the preceding screenshot, contain the most commonly used objects from the Qiskit library and the code for loading of your account details so that you can connect to the quantum systems.

  This is the first line of the autogenerated code block in your Notebook:

```
%matplotlib inline
```

The preceding code imports the **Matplotlib** plotting library, which provides the ability to embed plots and publication quality figures into applications. Details about Matplotlib can be found on their home page here: `https://matplotlib.org/`

The next line imports four Qiskit objects that are commonly used to create and run a quantum circuit. `QuantumCircuit` is used to create a new circuit, which is a list of instructions bound to some registers. `execute` is an asynchronous call to run a circuit and return a job instance handle. `Aer` and `IBMQ` are providers for backend simulators and devices and to manage account details, respectively.

In the following code snippet, you can see we import each of these from the `qiskit` package:

```
from qiskit import QuantumCircuit, execute, Aer, IBMQ
```

`transpile` and `assemble` are compiler objects used to translate and compile circuits, while `assemble` provides a list of circuit schedules, as shown in the following code snippet:

```
from qiskit.compiler import transpile, assemble
```

- The following lines in the autogenerated block of code import all tools and objects from the **Jupyter Notebook** and visualization libraries, respectively. Jupyter Notebooks is what the Qiskit Notebook is built upon, so it will leverage existing features already familiar to those of you who compose experiments on a Jupyter Notebook.

  These features include creating new files, running kernels, and triggering cells. The visualization library includes many features used to visualize results from experiments such as histograms and bar charts, and in various formats, including Matplotlib, **Latex**, and so on. The code can be seen here:

```
from qiskit.tools.jupyter import *
%from qiskit.visualization import *
```

- And finally, the `IBMQ.load_account()` function loads your account information, particularly the **application programming interface** (**API**) token that was assigned to you when you initially registered. This is done if you desire to run an experiment on an actual device; the loading of your API token and other account information needed to run an experiment is already available without any extra work on your part. The following code snippet shows this:

```
provider = IBMQ.load_account()
```

This way, the content of your experiment is not cluttered with information that is not relevant to your experiment and conclusions.

Now that we are familiar with the autogenerated code, we'll take a quick look at the Qiskit Notebook itself. You'll note that its layout is very similar to that of a Jupyter Notebook, so those who are already familiar with Jupyter Notebooks will undoubtedly recognize the layout.

Learning about the Qiskit Notebook

For those who are new to the Qiskit Notebook, there are a couple of things to note that will help you understand how coding and running your code work. Those of you who are already familiar with Jupyter Notebooks can skip this section.

The Quantum Lab Notebooks run code one cell at a time. As shown in the following screenshot, a cell is a section of the Notebook that can contain text, metadata, and source code, such that it encapsulates the autogenerated code we looked at earlier. It simplifies coding by breaking up the code into these cells. The cells can be run individually by selecting the cell with your mouse and clicking the **Run** button, as illustrated in the following screenshot:

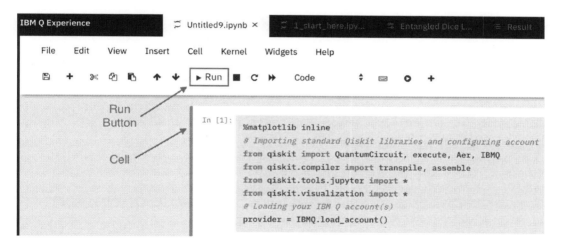

Figure 3.4 – Notebook cell and operations

From the preceding screenshot, in the top row of the Qiskit Notebook menu options you will see some usual operations you would find in a typical document editor, as follows:

- **File**: **Save**, **Checkpoint**, **Print Preview**, **Close**, and **Halt**
- **Edit**: **Modify Cells**, **Move Cells**, **Merge Cells**, and so on
- **View**: **Toggle Headers**, **Toolbars**, and other views
- **Insert**: Insert cells above or below selected cell

- **Cell**: Run cell, run all cells, and more
- **Help**: Provides support content

There is one specific operation in the Notebooks menu list to take note of, and that is the **Kernel**. For those of you with an existing version(s) of Python, do take note that Qiskit, at the time of this writing, is running on **Python version 3**.

To confirm this, you can select **Kernel** from the drop-down menu and note that there is a **Change Kernel** option. You will see **Python 3** as the only option. However, if you install Qiskit on your local machine that contains other versions of Python, you might see them listed here as well. I mention this so as to ensure you have the correct kernel selected to run Qiskit experiments. Otherwise, you may encounter some errors due to version incompatibility.

Another thing to note is related to the various different formats in which you can download a Qiskit Notebook. By selecting the **File | Download as** option you will see the various formats, as shown in the following screenshot:

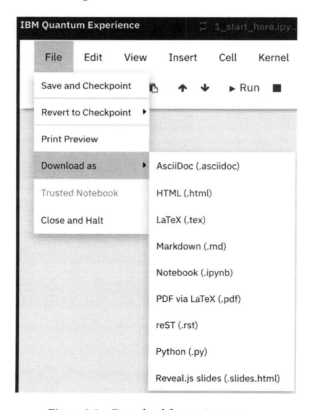

Figure 3.5 – Download formatting options

Up to now, you should be familiar with the functionality and features available on the Qiskit Notebook. These are features that make it easy to share experiments and make quick changes to them. We can now start creating and running quantum experiments on our notebooks using Qiskit.

Opening and importing existing Quantum Lab Notebook

Oftentimes, we wish to share our experiments with others and run others' experiments ourselves. Importing a Qiskit Notebook is easy in that the **Quantum Lab** home page has a link to **Import** button, next to the **New Notebook** + button, as shown in the following screenshot:

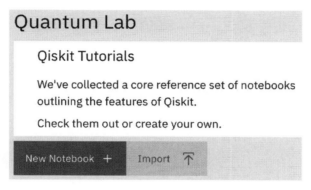

Figure 3.6 – Quantum Lab home page

This will launch your machine's file dialog to select the Qiskit Notebook you wish to import into your workspace on **IBM Quantum Experience (IQX)**. To open an existing Qiskit Notebook, or one you have just imported, simply go back to your Qiskit Notebook page and select the Notebook you wish to open from the file list at the bottom of the view, as illustrated in the following screenshot:

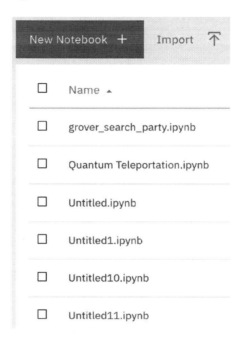

Figure 3.7 – List of previously opened notebooks

Now that you are familiar with the Notebooks and the autogenerated code, let's quickly create the same circuit we generated in the previous chapter, only this time we will create it using only the Notebook.

Developing a quantum circuit on Quantum Lab Notebooks

Let's take a quick look at the quantum circuit we created in the previous chapter. For convenience, the circuit is given as follows:

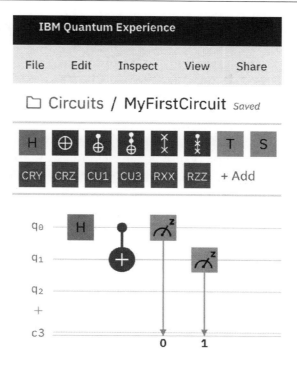

Figure 3.8 – Quantum circuit previously created using the Circuit Composer

The preceding circuit comprises of two gates—Hadamard and Controlled-Not—and two measurement operations on 2 qubits, respectively. This circuit was very easily constructed on the **Circuit Composer**; however, as we learn more about quantum circuits and begin to work on more complicated algorithms and circuits, it will be difficult to leverage a user interface such as the **Circuit Composer**. So, we will code the construction of quantum circuits and algorithms as we move forward instead.

To create the previous quantum circuit on a Notebook, follow these steps:

1. From the Quantum Lab Notebook, create a new Notebook and enter the following code in an empty cell:

```
qc = QuantumCircuit(2,2)
qc.h(0)
qc.cx(0, 1)
```

The preceding code creates QuantumCircuit. The two parameters pertain to the number of quantum bits (qubits) and classic bits we want to create, respectively. In this example, we will create two of each.

The second line adds a Hadamard gate onto the first qubit. Note that the index values of the qubits are 0 based. The third line adds a Controlled-Not gate that entangles the first qubit (q_0) as the control to the second qubit (q_1), the target. The parameters in the function pertain to the control and target, respectively.

2. Now, select **Run** to run the cell. Once the cell has completed running, you should see the output display `InstructionSet` of the results and a new cell generated below the one you just ran, as shown in the preceding code snippet. `InstructionSet` is a class of instruction collections and their contexts (classic and quantum arguments), where each context is stored separately per each instruction.

    Here is the output we are given after running the preceding code:

    ```
    <qiskit.circuit.instructionset.InstructionSet at
    0x7fc632176eb8>
    ```

3. Next, we will add the measurement operators to our circuit so that we can observe our results classically. Notice in the following code snippet that we are using the `range` method so as to simplify the mapping of each qubit to its respective classic bit:

    ```
    qc.measure(range(2), range(2))
    ```

4. Run the preceding cell to include the measurement operators to our circuit. Now that we have created the circuit and included the same gates and operations we did in *Chapter 2, Circuit Composer – Creating a Quantum Circuit*, let's draw the circuit and compare. Draw the circuit using the `draw` function, shown as follows:

    ```
    qc.draw()
    ```

    You should now see the following results, after the `draw` method is complete:

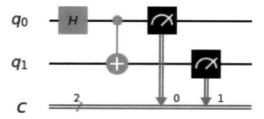

Figure 3.9 – Rendered image of the quantum circuit

Notice that the preceding circuit is identical to that which you created earlier. The only difference is the initial number of qubits. The **Circuit Composer** defaults to 5 qubits, whereas here we specified only 2. The circuit will run the same, both on the simulator and on an actual quantum device, since we are only using 2 qubits.

In this section, we have learned to navigate the Quantum Lab Notebook. We also learned how to open an existing Notebook, along with opening, creating, and importing the Notebook. We also saw how to develop a quantum circuit.

Now, we will move on to review the results of the quantum circuit.

Reviewing the results of your quantum circuit on Quantum Lab Notebooks

In this section, we'll conclude this chapter by running the circuit on a quantum simulator and a real device. We'll then review the results by following these steps:

1. From the open Notebook, enter and run the following in the next empty cell:

    ```
    backend = Aer.get_backend('qasm_simulator')
    ```

    The preceding code generates a `backend` object that will connect to the specified simulator or device. In this case, we are generating a `backend` object linked to the QASM simulator.

2. In the next empty cell, let's run the `execute` function. This function takes in three parameters—the circuit we wish to run, the backend we want to run it on, and how many `shots` we wish to execute. The returned object will be a job object with the contents of the executed circuit on the backend. The code for this can be seen here:

    ```
    job_simulator = execute(qc, backend, shots=1024)
    ```

3. We now want to extract the results from the job object. In order to do that, we will call the `result` function, illustrated as follows, and save it in a new variable:

    ```
    result_simulator = job_simulator.result()
    ```

4. Since we ran our experiment with `1024` shots, we want to get the results from the counts. In order to do that, we can call the `get_counts()` method by passing in our circuit as the argument. Once we receive the counts, let's print out the results by running the following code:

```
counts = result_simulator.get_counts(qc)
print(counts)
```

Note that the count results, shown as follows, may be different from your count results, which are based on the randomness of the qubits. But overall, the results will be similar by approximately 50%:

```
In [8]:
# get and print counts
counts = results.get_counts(qc)
print(counts)

{'00': 493, '11': 531}
```

Figure 3.10 – Count results from the quantum circuit

5. Finally, let's visualize the result counts by plotting them using a histogram. We'll first import the `plot_histogram` method from the `qiskit.visualization` library and pass our `counts` in as an argument, as follows:

```
from qiskit.visualization import plot_histogram
plot_histogram(counts)
```

As you can see in the following screenshot, the results are very similar to our results from the **Circuit Composer** in that 50% of the time our results are **00**, and the other half of the time they are **11**:

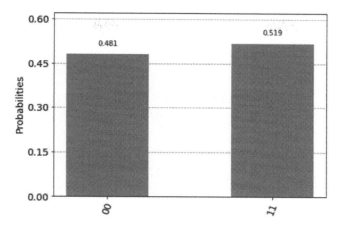

Figure 3.11 – Histogram view of the count results

Now that we have run our quantum circuit on a simulator, let's run this same quantum circuit on a real quantum computer.

Executing a quantum circuit on a quantum computer

To run this quantum circuit on a quantum device, we will continue with the following steps:

1. The only change you need to update in the steps from the preceding section is to go from running on a simulator to a real device in *Step 1* from the previous steps, which is where you specify the name of the backend. In *Step 1*, we set the backend to the qasm_simulator. In this step, we will update to an actual device. So, let's first get a list of backends from our providers by running the following code in a new cell:

```
provider.backends()
```

The preceding method will return a list of all the simulators and real devices currently available to you, shown as follows. Note that the devices listed may change over time, so the results shown may be different when you run the method:

In [10]:
```
provider.backends()
```

```
[<IBMQSimulator('ibmq_qasm_simulator') from IBMQ(hub='ibm-q', group='open', project='main')>,
 <IBMQBackend('ibmqx2') from IBMQ(hub='ibm-q', group='open', project='main')>,
 <IBMQBackend('ibmq_16_melbourne') from IBMQ(hub='ibm-q', group='open', project='main')>,
 <IBMQBackend('ibmq_vigo') from IBMQ(hub='ibm-q', group='open', project='main')>,
 <IBMQBackend('ibmq_ourense') from IBMQ(hub='ibm-q', group='open', project='main')>,
 <IBMQBackend('ibmq_london') from IBMQ(hub='ibm-q', group='open', project='main')>,
 <IBMQBackend('ibmq_burlington') from IBMQ(hub='ibm-q', group='open', project='main')>,
 <IBMQBackend('ibmq_essex') from IBMQ(hub='ibm-q', group='open', project='main')>,
 <IBMQBackend('ibmq_armonk') from IBMQ(hub='ibm-q', group='open', project='main')>]
```

Figure 3.12 – List of available quantum computers (quantum devices)

2. The only change you need to update from the steps in the previous section is to specify which quantum computer from the list of backend devices you wish to run the experiment. In the previous steps, we set the backend to the qasm_ simulator, whereas in this step we will update our backend to use a real device from the list. In this case, we'll choose ibmq_vigo. This list may appear different to you, so pick one from your list if ibmq_vigo is not listed. To do this, run the following code in a new cell:

```
backend = provider.get_backend('ibmq_vigo')
```

The preceding code assigns the ibmq_vigo quantum computer as our backend.

3. From the previous steps, repeat *Step 2* to *Step 5* to run the circuit on a real device. Your results will seem a little different. Rather than just the **00** and **11** results, you will see that there are some **01** and **10** results, shown in the screenshot that follows, albeit only a small percentage of the time.

    This is due to noise from the real device, which is why they are often referred to as **Noisy Intermediate-Scale Quantum** (**NISQ**) systems or near-term devices. The noise can come from an array of things, such as ambient noise and decoherence. Details about the different types of noise and their effects will be discussed in detail in *Chapter 11*, *Mitigating Quantum Errors Using Ignis*.

The results can be seen in the following screenshot:

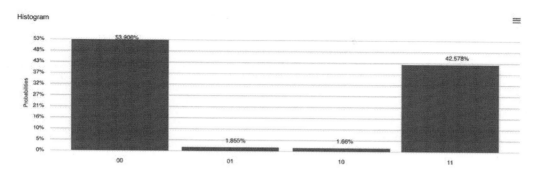

Figure 3.13 – Histogram plot of results

Congratulations! You have just completed running a quantum circuit on both a quantum simulator and a real quantum device using the Quantum Lab Notebooks. As you can see, by using the Notebook you can use many built-in Qiskit methods to create circuits and run them on various machines with a simple line of code, whereas on the **Circuit Composer** you would have to make various changes that would take a lot of time to complete.

Summary

In this chapter, you learned about the Quantum Lab Notebooks and ran a simple quantum circuit. You completed three basic functional steps: creating a quantum circuit using the Notebook and the Qiskit library, executing your circuit with a backend simulator and real device, and reviewing and visualizing your results from within the Notebook.

One thing you might have noticed is that using the Notebook with Qiskit also simplifies integrating your classical experiments with a quantum system. This has provided you with the skills and understanding to enhance your current Python experiments and run certain calculations on a quantum system, making them a hybrid classical/quantum experiment.

When the quantum calculations have completed, the results can be very easily used by your classical experiments.

Now that we are familiar with the Quantum Lab Notebooks and are able to create and execute a circuit, in the next chapter, we will start learning the basics of quantum computing and the quantum mechanical principles of superposition, entanglement, and interference.

Questions

1. Quantum Lab notebooks are built upon which application editor?

2. How would you create a 5-qubit circuit, as we did in *Chapter 2, Circuit Composer - Creating a Quantum Circuit*?

3. To run the experiment on another real device, which quantum computer would you select if your quantum circuit has more than 5 qubits?

4. When you run on a real device, can you explain why you get extra values when compared to running on a simulator?

Section 2: Basics of Quantum Computing

In this section, you will learn the basics needed to understand quantum computing, with particular focus on the mathematics and principles of quantum computing that most quantum algorithms leverage to potentially solve many intractable problems. You will also learn about the basic components, such as quantum bits, quantum gates, and quantum circuits, that we use to develop quantum algorithms.

This section comprises the following chapters:

- *Chapter 4, Understanding Basic Quantum Computing Principles*
- *Chapter 5, Understanding the Quantum Bit (Qubit)*
- *Chapter 6, Understanding Quantum Logic Gates*

4

Understanding Basic Quantum Computing Principles

Quantum computing, particularly its algorithms, leverage three quantum computing principles, namely, **superposition**, **entanglement**, and **interference**. In this chapter, we'll review each of these so that we can understand what each provides, the effect it has on each qubit, and how to represent them using the quantum gate sets provided to us. As a bonus, we will also create a quantum teleportation circuit that will leverage two of the three quantum computing principles to teleport an unknown state from one person to another.

The following topics will be covered in this chapter:

- Introducing quantum computing
- Understanding superposition
- Understanding entanglement
- Learning about the effects of interference between qubits
- Creating a quantum teleportation circuit

This chapter will focus on the three main quantum computing principles that will help you better understand how they are used in the various quantum algorithms. The quantum computers hosted on the **IBM Quantum Experience** leverage all these principles by use of the various quantum gates, some of which you used earlier in this book.

Technical requirements

In this chapter, some basic knowledge of programming is required. Some Python development knowledge is preferred as the experiments leverage Python libraries. Some general knowledge of physics is recommended; however, my goal is for the explanations to help you understand the quantum principles without the need for you to register for a physics course or read the **Feynman** lectures. Here is the full source code used throughout this book: `https://github.com/PacktPublishing/Learn-Quantum-Computing-with-Python-and-IBM-Quantum-Experience`.

Please visit the following link to check the CiA videos: `https://bit.ly/35o5M80`

Introducing quantum computing

Quantum computing isn't a subject that is as common as learning algebra or reading some of the literary classics. However, for most scientists and engineers or any other field that includes studying physics, quantum computing is part of the curriculum. For some of us who don't quite recall our studies in physics, or have never studied it, need not worry, as this section aims to provide you with information that will either refresh your recollection on the topic or at least perhaps help you understand what each of the principles used in quantum computing mean. Let's start with a general definition of quantum mechanics.

Quantum mechanics, as defined by most texts, is the study of nature at its smallest scale – in this case, the subatomic scale. The study of quantum mechanics is not new. Its growth began in the early 1900s by many physicists, whose names still chime in many of the current theories and experiments. The names of such physicists include Erwin Schrodinger, Max Plank, Werner Heisenberg, Max Born, Paul Dirac, and Albert Einstein, among others. As years passed, many other scientists expanded on the foundations of quantum mechanics and began performing experiments that would either prove, disprove, or oftentimes illustrate that there is no proof.

One of the more popular experiments is the **double slit** experiment. Although this is found in classical mechanics, it is referenced in quantum computing to describe the behavior of a quantum bit (qubit). It is in this experiment researchers were able to demonstrate that light (or photons) can be characterized as both waves and particles.

There were many distinct experiments that have been conducted over the years that illustrate this phenomenon, one of which was to fire particles through a double slit one at a time where at the other side of the double slit was a screen that captured, as a point, the location where each particle would hit. When only one slit was open, all the particles would appear as a stack of points directly in front of the slit, as shown in the following diagram:

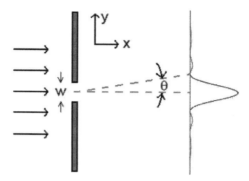

Figure 4.1 - Single-slit experiment (image source: `https://commons.wikimedia.org/wiki/File:SingleSlitDiffraction.GIF`)

From the previous diagram, you can see that all the particles are captured in an area directly across the slit.

However, when the second slit was open, it was imagined that there would be an identical stack of points on the screen. But this was not the case, as what was captured appeared to be a formation altogether different than what would be expected from a particle. In fact, it had the characteristics of a wave in that the points on the screen seemed to display a diffraction pattern, as shown in the following diagram:

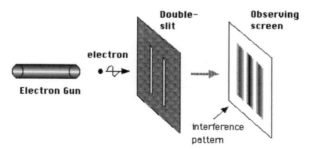

Figure 4.2 - Double-slit experiment (image source: `https://commons.wikimedia.org/wiki/File:Double-slit.PNG`)

From the previous diagram, you can see that all the particles are spread out from the center with interference gaps.

This diffraction pattern is caused by the interference of the light waves passing through the slits. Here, there are more points at the center of the screen than there are toward the outer ends of the observing screen. This wave particle phenomenon gave birth to lots of interesting research and development such as the **Copenhagen interpretation**, **many-worlds interpretation**, and the **De Broglie-Bohm** theory.

What this illustrated was that the light appeared as bands of light in certain areas of the board with some probability. By observing the preceding diagram, you can see that there is a higher probability that the electron fired from the gun will land in the center band of the screen as opposed to the outer bands. Also, note that due to interference, the spaces in between the bands that capture the electrons have less probability (blank areas between bands).

It is these effects of wave interference and probabilities that we will cover in this chapter, but first, we will start with the electron itself to understand superposition.

Understanding superposition

Superposition is something we generally can't see with the naked eye. This is typically the case when discussing the superposition of an electron. Since an electron is very small and there are so many of them, it is hard to distinguish one with even a powerful microscope. There are, however, some analogies in the classical world that we can use to illustrate what superposition is. For example, a spinning coin is what most texts use to describe superposition. While it is spinning, we can say that it is in the state of both heads and tails. It isn't until the coin collapses that we see what the final state of the coin is.

In this chapter, we're going to use this spinning coin analogy just to help you understand the general principle of superposition. However, once we start working on our quantum circuits, you will see some of the differences between superposition and its probabilistic behavior in the classical world versus its behavior in the quantum world. Let's start by reviewing the random effects in the classical world.

Learning about classical randomness

Previously, we discussed the randomness of a spinning coin as an example. However, the spinning coin and its results are not as random as we think. Just because we cannot guess the correct answer when a coin is spun on a table or flipped in the air does not make it random. What leads us to believe that it's random is the fact that we don't have all the information necessary to know or predict or, in fact, determine that the coin will land on either heads or tails.

All the relevant information, such as the weight of the coin, its shape, the amount of force required to spin the coin, the air resistance, the friction of the platform the coin is rolling on, and so on, all of this information, and the information of the environment itself, is not known to us in order for us to determine what the outcome would be after spinning a coin. It's because of this lack of information that we assume the spinning of the coin is random. If we had some function that could calculate all this information, then we would always successfully determine the outcome of the spinning coin.

The same can be said about random number generators. As an example, when we trigger a computer to generate a random number, the computer uses a variety of information to calculate and generate a random number. These parameters can include information such as the current daytime that the request was triggered, information about the user or the system itself, and so on.

These types of random number generators are often referred to as **pseudorandom number generators (PSRN)** or **deterministic random bit generators (DRBT)**. They are only as random as the calculation or seed values provided that is allowed. For example, if we knew the parameters used and how they were used to generate this random number, then we would be able to determine the generated random number each and every time.

Now, that being said, I don't want you to worry about anyone determining the calculations or cryptic keys that you may have generated. We use these pseudorandom number generators because of the precision and granularity that they encompass to generate this number, which is such that any deviation can drastically alter the results.

So, why bother reviewing the probabilistic and random nature of a spinning coin? One, it's to explain the difference between randomness, or what we believe is random, in the classical world versus the randomness in the quantum world.

In the classic world, we learned that if we had all the information available, we can more than likely determine an outcome. However, in the previous section, where we described the double-slit experiment, we saw that we couldn't determine where in the screen the electron was going to hit. We understood the probabilities of where it would land based on our experiment. But even then, we could not deterministically identify where precisely the electron was going to land on the screen. You'll see an example of this when we create our superposition circuit in the next section.

For those who wish to learn a little more about this phenomenon, I would suggest reading the book by the famous physicist Richard Feynman titled *QED: The Strange Theory of Light and Matter*.

Preparing a qubit in a superposition state

In this section, we are going to create a circuit with a single qubit and set an operator on the qubit to set it in a superposition state. But before we do that, let's quickly define what a superposition state is.

We define the qubit as having two basis energy states, one of which is the ground (0) state and the second of which is the excited (1) state, as illustrated in *Figure 4.3*. The state value name of each basis state could be anything we choose, but since the results from our circuit will be fed back to a classic system, we will use binary values to define our states – in this case, the binary values 0 and 1. To say that the superposition of two states is *being in both 0 and 1 at the same time* is incorrect. The proper way to state a qubit is in a superposition state is to say that it is *in a complex linear combination of states where in this case, the states are 0 and 1*.

The following screenshot is referred to as a **Bloch sphere**, which represents a single qubit and its two basis states, which are located on opposite poles. On the north pole, we have the basis state 0, while the south pole, we have the basis state 1. The symbols surrounding the basis state values are the commonly used notations in most quantum computing text. This is called **Dirac notation**, which was named after the English theoretical physicist Paul Dirac, who first conceived the notation, which he called the **Bra-Ket notation**. Both Bra-Ket and Dirac notation are generally used interchangeably as they refer to the same thing, as we'll see later.

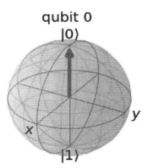

Figure 4.3 - Two basis states of a qubit on a Bloch sphere

Ok, so let's stop talking and let's start coding. We're going to create a quantum circuit with a single qubit. We will then execute the circuit so that we can obtain the same result we can see in the preceding screenshot, which is the initial state of the qubit, state $|0\rangle$.

Open a new Qiskit Notebook and enter the following code into the next empty cell:

```
from qiskit.visualization import plot_bloch_multivector
qc = QuantumCircuit(1)

# execute the quantum circuit
backend = Aer.get_backend('statevector_simulator')
result = execute(qc, backend).result()
stateVectorResult = result.get_statevector(qc)

#Display the Bloch sphere
plot_bloch_statevector(stateVectorResult)
```

The first line imports the Bloch sphere library so that we can plot our vector. The next line creates the circuit so that it includes 1 qubit, and in the next three lines, we are setting up our backend to execute the circuit to the simulator. And finally, we display the results on our Bloch sphere, which should display the same as what you can see in the preceding diagram.

So, you might be wondering what all this talk about vectors and statevector simulators is about. Good! This is what we will discuss now. The reason I wanted to run the experiment first as opposed to explaining what the vector states are and what the statevector simulator does is so that you can see it first and then hopefully the description will be a bit clearer. Let's start with the vector explanation.

Each qubit, as mentioned earlier, is made up of two basis states, which in this example reside on opposite poles of the Bloch sphere. These two basis states are what we would submit back to the classical system as our result – either one or the other. The vector representing these two points originates from the origin of the Bloch sphere, as you can see in the previous diagram, or the result from your experiment. If we were to notate this as a vector, we would write the following:

$$|0\rangle = \begin{bmatrix} 1 \\ 0 \end{bmatrix}$$

Since the opposite would apply to the opposite pole, we would notate it as follows:

$$|1\rangle = \begin{bmatrix} 0 \\ 1 \end{bmatrix}$$

From observing the vector values, you can see that flipping the values of the vector is similar to a classical bit flip. Now that we understand the vector representation of a qubit, let's continue and set the qubit in a superposition state:

1.   Insert a new cell at the bottom of the current notebook and enter the following code:

```
#Place the qubit in a superposition state by adding a
#Hadamard (H)gate
qc.h(0)
#Draw the circuit
qc.draw()
```

The previous code places a Hadamard (H) gate onto the first qubit, identified by the qubit's index value (0). It then calls the draw function, which will draw the circuit diagram.

After running the previous cell, you should see the following circuit image, which represents adding the Hadamard gate to the qubit:

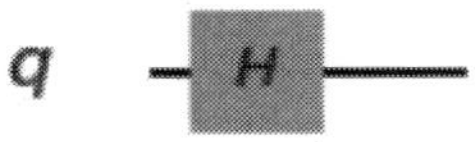

Figure 4.4 – Circuit with a Hadamard (H) gate added to a qubit

The **Hadamard gate** is an operational gate that places the qubit in a superposition state, or, more specifically, a complex linear combination of the basis states, which means that when we measure the qubit, it will have an equal probability result of measuring a 0 or 1. Or in other words, it would collapse to the basis state value $|0\rangle$ or $|1\rangle$.

Mathematically, the superposition state is represented in the following two superposition equations, which, as you can see, depends on which of the two basis states it was in prior to applying the Hadamard gate. The first superposition equation is as follows and originates from the $|0\rangle$ state:

$$|+\rangle = \frac{|0\rangle + |1\rangle}{\sqrt{2}}$$

The second superposition equation, originating from the $|1\rangle$ state, is as follows:

$$|-\rangle = \frac{|0\rangle - |1\rangle}{\sqrt{2}}$$

This is equal to a π/2 rotation about the X and Z axes of the Bloch sphere. These rotations are Cartesian rotations, which rotate counter-clockwise.

2. Now, let's execute our circuit, see what this looks like, and where the state vector lands on the Bloch sphere. In the following code, you will execute the same circuit again, the results of which will not differ in that the qubit will appear in a superposition state, which you will see in the resulting Bloch sphere's output:

```
#Execute the circuit again and plot the result in the
#Bloch sphere
result = execute(qc, backend).result()
#Get the state vector results of the circuit
stateVectorResult = result.get_statevector(qc)


#Display the Bloch sphere
plot_bloch_multivector(stateVectorResult)
```

Once the circuit has completed executing, the results will be plotted on the Bloch sphere in a superposition between |0⟩ and |1⟩, as illustrated in the following screenshot:

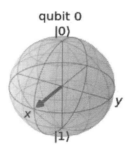

Figure 4.5 - Superposition of a qubit after 90° rotation around the X and Z axes

As you can see in the preceding screenshot, this has placed the vector on the positive X axis, as described previously when adding a H gate from the |0⟩ basis state.

3. Now, let's clear the circuit. This time, we will initialize the qubit to the |1⟩ state first and then apply a Hadamard gate to see what happens to the vector this time. Initialize qubit to the |1⟩ state and place it in a superposition. Clear the circuit and initialize qubit to 1 before applying Hadamard gate:

```
#Reset the circuit
qc = QuantumCircuit(1)
#Rotate the qubit from 0 to 1 using the X (NOT) gate
```

```
qc.x(0)
#Add a Hadamard gate
qc.h(0)
#Draw the circuit
qc.draw()
```

You should now see the following circuit:

Figure 4.6 - Applying an H gate superposition from an opposite base state |1⟩

4. Now, let's execute the circuit and plot the result on the Bloch sphere:

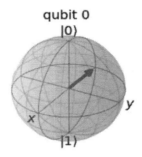

Figure 4.7 - Superposition of a qubit after 90° rotation around the X and Z axes from the |1⟩ state

Do you see the difference between adding a Hadamard gate to a qubit in the |0⟩ state (Figure 4.5) and adding it to a qubit in the |1⟩ state in the preceding screenshot?

Of course, the difference is where it lands on the X axis! Because the vector falls onto the positive X axis when applying a Hadamard gate to the |0⟩ state, this is commonly notated as |+⟩. This logically means that the vector falls onto the negative X axis when applying a Hadamard gate to the |1⟩ state. This is commonly notated as |−⟩.

Now, take a look at the superposition equations and note the initial basis state on the left-hand side of the equation, which represents the state of the qubit before it was placed in superposition, and notice the right-hand side of the equation. Pay close attention to the signs in-between.

Notice that the signs match the direction of where the vector lands after the Hadamard gate is applied. From the $|0\rangle$ state, it moves toward the positive (+) direction of the X axis, and from the $|1\rangle$ state, it moves toward the negative (-) direction of the X axis.

This difference is referred to as a phase difference between the two results. This will be very important later on in this and subsequent chapters as phase difference plays an important role in many quantum algorithms and blends itself into the topic of interference, as we will learn shortly.

One last thing that we will discuss before moving on is to now loop back to our earlier discussion on probabilities. Now that we've learned what superposition looks like in a circuit and on a Bloch sphere, let's execute and see what the probabilities are when we measure the qubit after it is in superposition. As you may recall from our first analogy of flipping or spinning a coin, we said that once the coin is spinning, it is in a superposition of heads or tails, or in this example, 0 or 1.

Once we collapse and observe, the result of the coin will be one or the other. However, classically, this is pseudorandom, as we learned. But in quantum computing, electron detection is truly random as there is no way to determine its outcome without disturbing it. This is the same as measuring a qubit; we are, in essence, measuring it, and therefore forcing it to collapse into one of two basis states.

5. Then, measure the qubit after it is in superposition and reset the circuit. Let's start from the $|0\rangle$ state and apply a Hadamard gate, as we did earlier:

```
#Reset the circuit
qc = QuantumCircuit(1,1)
#Add a Hadamard gate
qc.h(0)
```

6. Now, let's include a measurement operator so that we can measure the qubit, which should collapse it into one of two states, as follows:

```
#Create a measurement circuit with 1 qubit and 1 bit
measurement_circuit = QuantumCircuit(1,1)
#Measure function used to map the qubit and bit by their
#index value on the circuit, respectively
measurement_circuit.measure(0,0)
#Concatenate the circuits together
```

```
full_circuit = qc+measurement_circuit
#Draw the full circuit
full_circuit.draw()
```

In the previous code, we created a measurement circuit that includes a measurement operation that basically collapses the qubit from its current state to that of either 0 or 1.

You will obtain the following circuit:

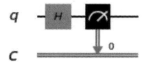

Figure 4.8 - Full circuit with rotation and measurement from qubit (q) to classic bit (c)

The previous diagram illustrates our circuit, which you can see now includes two new components, the first of which is the classic register below the quantum register. The second component is the measurement operator, which will extract the result of the qubit and pass it onto the classic bit. The result will collapse the state of the qubit to either 1 or 0.

7. Now, let's execute and run a few shots and see the results. shots refers to running through the experiment a few times and aggregating its results:

```
#Execute the circuit again and print the results
backend = Aer.get_backend('qasm_simulator')
result = execute(full_circuit, backend, shots=1000).
    result()
counts = result.get_counts(full_circuit)
print(counts)
```

The previous code will now use qasm simulator rather than the state vector simulator, which will allow us to obtain the measured results of the circuit. In this case, we will extract counts, which stores the number of times the measurement resulted in either a 0 or 1 out of 1000 shots.

The result of the previous code is as follows:

```
{'1': 491, '0': 509}
```

Notice that the results are almost 50%, which illustrates that you can have an equal probability of 0 and 1!

Important Note

Note that your actual value results might be different than what was shown previously, but the probability should be pretty close to 50%. Retry running the code a few times and play around with the number of shots to see if you get any differences. The limitation for shots at the time of writing was around 8,000.

The reason why we run so many shots of a circuit is because the near-term quantum devices used these days are not fault-tolerant yet. Fault-tolerant devices are those that exhibit very low error rates and large quantum volumes, which we will cover in *Chapter 9, Understanding Qiskit Aer*. Current near-term devices need to run multiple shots to provide your quantum algorithm with good probability results. However, once these devices reach fault-tolerant status, you can expect the probabilities to be closer to 1; that is, they are highly accurate with fewer shots.

Now that we have covered superposition, we will move onto the second quantum computing principle, which is entanglement.

Understanding entanglement

Entanglement is probably one of the most interesting of the three quantum computing principles. This is mainly because it still baffles physicists and scientists to this day, with many taking different philosophical sides on the discussion. I won't bore you with the details, but I will definitely provide you with enough information for you to understand what entanglement is, but not to have a way to prove it. Yes, it sounds confusing, but believe me, the devil is in the detail and there just isn't enough space for us to formulate a comprehensive answer to how entanglement works. But enough of that – let's get to work!

Quantum entanglement, or just entanglement, is simply defined as a quantum mechanical phenomenon that occurs when two or more particles have correlated states. What this, in essence, means is that if you have two particles or, for our purposes, qubits, that are entangled, this means that when we measure one qubit, we can determine the result of the other qubit based on the measurement of the first qubit.

As you may recall from our previous example, if we put a qubit in a superposition and we measure that qubit, we have a 50/50 split as to whether that qubit would collapse to either of two states, $|0\rangle$ or $|1\rangle$.

Now, if that same qubit were entangled with another qubit and we were to measure one of the qubits, that qubit will be either $|0\rangle$ or $|1\rangle$. However, if we were to measure the second qubit, either at the exact same time or sometime later, it too will have the same value as the first qubit we measured!

You're probably thinking, how can this be? If we take two qubits and place them in superposition and we measure them separately, we will correctly see that each qubit will collapse to a value of 1 or 0, where each time we measure the qubits individually, it may not collapse to the same value at the same time. This means that if we run the experiment one shot at a time, we would see that, sometimes, the first qubit will measure 0, while the second qubit could measure 0 or 1.

Both are separate and do not know the value of each other either before, during, or after measurement. However, if we were to entangle the two qubits and repeat the same experiment, we would see that the qubits will measure the exact same values each and every time!

Impossible, you say? Well, it's a good thing for us that we now have a quantum computer that we can run and try this out!

In the following code, we will see that when qubits are not entangled, their results are such that we cannot infer what the result of one qubit would be based on the result of the other qubit. Since we are measuring two qubits, our results will be listed as 2-bit values:

1. First, we'll create a new circuit with two qubits, place them in superposition, and measure them:

```
#Create a circuit with 2 qubits and 2 classic bits
qc = QuantumCircuit(2,2)
#Add an H gate to each
qc.h(0)
qc.h(1)
#Measure the qubits to the classical bit
qc.measure([0,1],[0,1])
#Draw the circuit
qc.draw()
```

In the preceding code, we created a quantum circuit with two qubits, added an H gate to each of the qubits so that we can place each qubit into a superposition state, and finally added a measurement from each qubit to its respective bit.

The result from the previous code should display the following circuit, where we can see that each qubit has an H gate that's measured to its respective classical bit register; that is, qubit 0 to bit 0 and qubit 1 to bit 1:

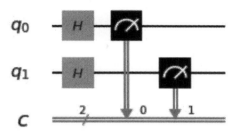

Figure 4.9 - Two qubits in superposition and measured to their respective classic bits

2. Then, we execute the circuit and display the results:

```
#Execute the circuit again and print the results
backend = Aer.get_backend('qasm_simulator')
result = execute(qc, backend, shots=1000).result()
counts = result.get_counts(qc)
plot_histogram(counts)
```

In the previous code, we created the backend to run on the simulator with 1000 shots and plot the results in a histogram to review them.

> **Important Note**
>
> Note from the following results that the outcomes are very random from each qubit, which is what we expected. One thing I would also like to mention regarding notation is the ordering of the qubits. When written, the order of the qubits are a little different than the bit order. In quantum notation, the first qubit is also listed on the left-hand side, while subsequent qubits are added toward the right-hand side. In binary notation, however, the first bit is on the right-hand side, while subsequent bits are added toward the left-hand side.

For example, if we want to represent the 3-qubit value of the number 5, we would do so using $|101\rangle$, which is the same as the bit representation of the same number. However, the qubit order here is different as the first qubit is listed in the left position (q[0]), the second qubit (q[1]) is listed in the middle position, and the last qubit (q[2]) is listed in the right position.

On the other hand, in bit notation, the first bit (b[0]) is in the right position and moves up in order to the left. When measuring, we link the results from the qubit to the bit (as shown in the preceding screenshot), which correctly maps the results of each qubit to its respective binary position so that our results are in the expected bit order.

The plotted histogram is shown in the following screenshot:

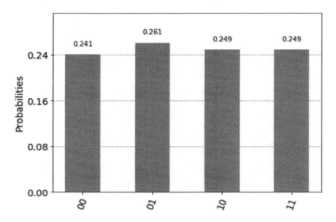

Figure 4.10 - Random results of all combinations from both qubits

In the previous screenshot, each qubit has collapsed to a state of either 0 or 1, so since there are two qubits, we should expect to see all four random results, which are **00**, **01**, **10**, and **11**. Your probability results might differ a bit, but overall, they should all be close to 25% probability.

3. This is expected, so let's entangle the two qubits and see what happens then. For this, we will entangle the two qubits and rerun the experiment.

    Let's entangle the two qubits by adding a multi-qubit gate called a **Control-NOT (CNOT)** gate. Let me explain what this gate is before we include it in our circuit.

    The CNOT gate is a multi-qubit gate that operates on one qubit based on the value of another. What this means is that the qubit gate has two connecting points – one called **Control** and another called **Target**. The T is generally some operator, such as a **NOT** (X) gate, which would flip the qubit from 0 to 1 or vice versa.

    However, the Target operator can also be almost any operation, such as an H gate, a Y gate (which flips 180° around the Y axis), and so on. It could even be another Control, but we will get into those fancy gates in *Chapter 6, Understanding Quantum Gates*.

The CNOT gate acts in such a manner that when the qubit tied to the Control is set to 0, the value of the Target qubit does not change, meaning the Target operator will not be enabled. However, if the value of the Control qubit is 1, this will trigger the Target operator. This would, therefore, in the case of a CNOT gate, enable a NOT operation on the target qubit, causing it to flip 180° around the X axis from its current position.

The following logic table represents the Control and Target value updates based on the value of the Control for a CNOT gate, as well as the states before and after the CNOT gate:

Before CNOT		After CNOT	
Control	Target	Control	Target
$|0\rangle$	$|0\rangle$	$|0\rangle$	$|0\rangle$
$|0\rangle$	$|1\rangle$	$|0\rangle$	$|1\rangle$
$|1\rangle$	$|0\rangle$	$|1\rangle$	$|1\rangle$
$|1\rangle$	$|1\rangle$	$|1\rangle$	$|0\rangle$

Table 4.1 - Two qubit CNOT logic table

Now that we can see how the CNOT gate works on two qubits, we will update our circuit so that we can entangle the qubits together. In the following code, we will create a circuit with 2 qubits where we will apply a Hadamard gate to the first qubit and then entangle the first qubit with the second qubit using a CNOT gate:

```
#Create a circuit with 2 qubits and 2 classic bits
qc = QuantumCircuit(2,2)
#Add an H gate to just the first qubit
qc.h(0)
#Add the CNOT gate to entangle the two qubits, where the
#first qubit is the Control, and the second qubit is the
#Target.
qc.cx(0,1)
#Measure the qubits to the classical bit
qc.measure([0,1],[0,1])
#Draw the circuit
qc.draw()
```

The resulting diagram of the circuit should look as follows:

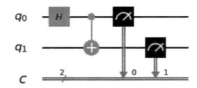

Figure 4.11 - Entanglement of two qubits

The previous screenshot shows you that, this time, we are only placing a Hadamard gate on the first qubit and leaving the second qubit to be operated on only by the CNOT gate. Since it is set as the target, it will be dependent on the Control qubit.

4. Now, we will run the experiment and plot the results. This is similar to the previous experiments we completed, where we will execute the circuit, extract the result counts, and plot them on a histogram to visualize the results:

```
#Execute the circuit again and print the results
result = execute(qc, backend, shots=1000).result()
counts = result.get_counts(qc)
plot_histogram(counts)
```

The results shown in the following screenshot show two quantum computing principles – the superposition of the qubits, 0 and 1, and the entanglement – where both qubit's (Control and Target) results are strongly correlated as either **00** or **11**:

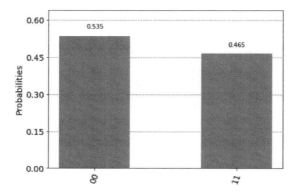

Figure 4.12 - Results of two entangled qubits

Now that you are familiar with superposition and entanglement, let's move onto the last quantum computing principle, which is interference.

Learning about the effects of interference between qubits

One of the benefits of quantum computing is its ability to interleave these principles in such a way that usually, while explaining one, you can very easily describe the other. We did this earlier in this chapter with respect to interference. Let's review and see where we have come across this phenomenon and its usage so far.

First, recall that, at the beginning of this chapter, we described the double-slit experiment. There, we discussed how an electron can act as both a wave and a particle. When acting like a wave, we saw that the experiment illustrated how the electrons traveled and landed at certain spots of the observation screen. The pattern that it displayed was generally one that we recognize from classic physics as wave interference.

The pattern had the probabilistic results along the backboard, as shown in the observing screen in *Figure 4.2*, where the center of the screen has the highest number of electrons and the blank areas along both sides had least to none. This is due to the constructive and destructive interference of the waves.

There are two types of interference, namely, **constructive** and **destructive**. Constructive interference occurs when the peaks of two waves are summed up where the resulting amplitude is equal to the total positive sum of the two individual waves.

Destructive interference occurs similar to constructive interference except that the amplitudes of the waves are opposite in that when summing them together, the two waves cancel each other out.

The following diagram illustrates the constructive and destructive wave interference of two waves when they are added together:

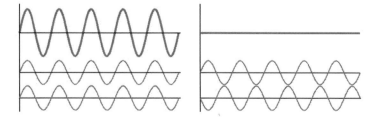

Figure 4.13 – Constructive (left) and destructive (right) wave interferences (image source: https://commons.wikimedia.org/wiki/File:Interference_of_two_waves.svg)

The preceding diagram illustrates how two waves interfere with each other constructively and destructively. The two waves toward the bottom of the diagram represent the individual amplitudes of each wave, while the top line represents the added amplitude values, which represent the result of the interference between the two waves.

Now that you understand the difference between constructive and destructive interference, *how can we apply this to what we've learned so far?* Well, if you recall, earlier, when we placed a qubit in superposition, we had two distinct results.

One was from the basis state $|0\rangle$, while the other was from the basis state $|1\rangle$. *Do you remember when we started at either of these two qubit basis states, where on the X-axis of the qubit the Hadamard landed?* From $|0\rangle$, it would land on the positive side of the X axis, but, if we placed the qubit into superposition starting from the $|1\rangle$ state, it would land on the negative X axis.

Having the ability to place the qubit state vector on either the positive or negative X-axis provides us with a way to place the qubit in either a positive or negative state. Very similar to the waves in the preceding diagram, which have positive (peaks) and negative (toughs) amplitudes, qubits can also represent similar states. Let's simplify this by re-introducing the two Dirac notation values, $|+\rangle$, and $|-\rangle$, where the $|+\rangle$ state represents the state vector on the positive X axis and the $|-\rangle$ state represents the state vector on the negative X-axis.

These new vector definitions, which represent the vector state of a qubit in superposition, will be used by some of the algorithms as a technique to identify certain values and react to them using interference – techniques such as **amplitude estimation** or search algorithms such as **Grover's** algorithm.

We can't finish this chapter without at least putting all these things together to see how these all interact in a simple example, which we will see in the next section.

Creating a quantum teleportation circuit

In this section, we will create a quantum teleportation circuit to share the state, $|\psi\rangle$, of a qubit by communicating, classically, two bits of information. Now, you may be wondering, as I did when I first learned about this scenario, why would I need to share two bits of information and not just the state of the qubit itself? Well, the answer comes down to the **no-cloning theorem**.

> **Tip**
>
> To learn more about the no-cloning theorem, I would recommend reading the *ERP Paradox* paper proposed by physicists Einstein, Podolsky, and Rosen.

Without going into the quantum mechanical proofs, the theorem states that creating a copy of a qubit from an arbitrary unknown state is not possible as there is no unitary operator that can clone all states of one qubit into another. That being said, we need to look at other means to pass the state of one qubit to another. **Quantum teleportation** helps us do that.

To properly understand this example, let's take a look at the overall process. Then, we can dig down into the specifics and see how we can make this possible. As mentioned earlier, the objective is to have a sender – let's call her Alice – who has a qubit in an arbitrary state of $|\psi\rangle = \alpha|0\rangle + \beta|1\rangle$ provide two bits of information to the recipient – let's call him Bob.

Alice will then send Bob information, classically (such as communicating by phone call or text), who will then perform operations on a qubit, which would enable Bob to generate the state that Alice had. We say *Alice had* because in order to send the bit information to Bob, she needs to perform a measurement on the arbitrary qubit state, which would therefore collapse the qubit into binary values. Therefore, we would lose all quantum information of the qubit.

The following flow diagram illustrates this from a high-level perspective. We will dig a little deeper to understand how this is done:

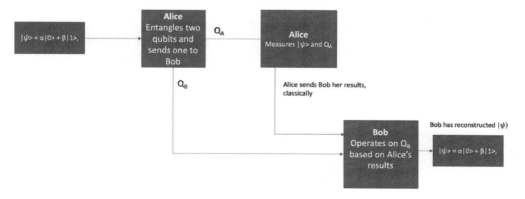

Figure 4.14 - Quantum teleportation flowchart

To understand this flow better, let's create the circuit while describing each block in the previous flowchart. This way, we can grasp each step by visualizing it as we build and execute our circuit.

Executing the quantum teleportation circuit

We need to create a new Qiskit Notebook and create a quantum circuit with three qubits and three classic bits. We will need three qubits – one to represent the state and two that we will entangle and share with Alice and Bob:

1. In a new Qiskit Notebook, enter the following code into the next empty cell to create the circuit that we need. Then, create the qubit state, which neither Alice nor Bob will know:

    ```
    q = QuantumRegister(3)
    c = ClassicalRegister(3)
    qc = QuantumCircuit(q, c)
    ```

    We now have three qubits. The first qubit q[0] will represent the unknown state, $|\psi\rangle$. The second and third qubits, q[1], and q[2], will be the entangled qubits that are shared between Alice and Bob, respectively.

2. Let's prepare the first qubit (q[0]) in an $|\psi\rangle$ unknown state of which neither Alice nor Bob will know. Of course, we will know as we are creating it. However, the idea here is to see things from the context of both Alice and Bob. To keep this example simple, we will apply two unitary operators, that is, a NOT gate and a Z gate:

    ```
    qc.x(0)
    qc.z(0)
    qc.barrier()
    ```

    Note that we added a barrier after setting up our $|\psi\rangle$ state. This is just to simplify visualizing the circuit when we draw it to know which component in our flowchart each section pertains to. In this case, it's the first block specifying $|\psi\rangle$.

3. Now that we have prepared our state, which is known to us but unknown to both Alice and Bob, we will go to the next step in our flowchart, which is for Alice to entangle the other two qubits (q[1], q[2]) together.

    Alice will keep one q[1] and send the other qubit q[2] to Bob. To entangle the two qubits, we will apply a Hadamard gate to Alice's qubit, q[1], followed by a CNOT between the two qubits, where the Control is connected to Alice's qubit and the Target is connected to Bob's qubit. We will include a barrier here, as we did previously, to segment this preparation:

    ```
    qc.h(1)
    qc.cx(1,2)
    qc.barrier()
    ```

4. Now, we'll move onto the next block, which is where Alice will entangle the qubit in the $|\psi\rangle$ state with her qubit that was entangled with Bob's, and then apply a Hadamard gate prior to measuring both the $|\psi\rangle$ qubit and her entangled qubit:

```
qc.cx(0,1)
qc.h(0)
qc.measure(0,0)
qc.measure(1,1)
qc.barrier()
qc.cx(1,2)
qc.barrier()
```

5. After measuring the two qubits, $|\psi\rangle$ and q[1], Alice calls Bob and lets him know her results. He then applies the necessary gates based on her results, as illustrated in the next block in our flowchart, where Bob will apply the corresponding gates based on the information he gathered from Alice. The unitary operation to apply is based on one of the following notions: 00 = Use I (Identity gate), 01 = Use X (NOT gate), 10 = Use Z (Z gate), 11 = Use Z, followed by X gate.

6. Since we will be running the circuit with 1,024 shots, we should expect to see all the previous results. *So, how can we determine whether the results are correct?*

    We can verify this by applying the gates that we used to prepare $|\psi\rangle$, except we need to do so in reverse. Recall from *step 1* that the unitary operators must be reversible. We will apply a Z gate first, then a NOT gate to Bob's qubit. If all goes well, we should expect the result of Bob's qubit to always be $|0\rangle$:

```
qc.z(2)
qc.x(2)
qc.measure(2,2)
```

    After this measurement, the result in the classic bit (2) should be 0 for all the results.

7. Now, let's draw the circuit to see what we have created so far. Recall that each segment separated by a barrier pertains to the previous flowchart step, where the last segment is simply to verify that we have successfully transported $|\psi\rangle$.

Note that we are not stating that we copied the state, $|\psi\rangle$, but we transported it because of the no cloning theorem. It is incorrect to state that we successfully copied the state, $|\psi\rangle$, from Alice to Bob:

```
qc.draw(output='mpl')
```

The result should look as follows:

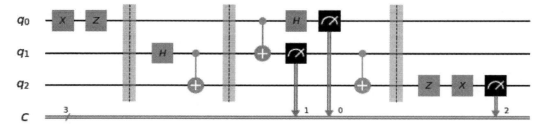

Figure 4.15 - Quantum teleportation circuit segmented into four parts

The previous screenshot shows that barriers (dotted lines) separate the circuit visually so that it is easy to segment and visualize. The first segment is where Alice prepares her qubit, while the second segment entangles two qubits where **q1** belongs to Alice and **q2** belongs to Bob. The third segment is where Alice entangles her prepared qubit **q0** with her shared qubit **q1**. She, then takes a measurement of the results of her two qubits.

The last segment that Bob reads receives the classical response from Alice, **q1**, and encodes it into his qubit, which you can see is represented here in reverse order of how Alice prepared her qubit in the first segment. This is because operations on qubits must be reversible, hence why Bob applies a Z gate first, then an X gate. Finally, when Bob measures his qubit, he should get the expected result, **0**, which is the initial state that Alice had. If this is different from **0**, then Bob can determine that the qubit was tampered with in-between transmission.

8.   We can now confirm whether the state that Bob has is the same one Alice had previously that she had collapsed and measured $|\psi\rangle$. We will run this on `qasm simulator` and run it with `1024 shots`:

```
backend = Aer.get_backend('qasm_simulator')
job = execute(qc, backend, shots=1024)
job_result = job.result()
results = job_result.get_counts(qc)
plot_histogram(results)
```

Now, we'll print out the results in a histogram to confirm we get back all the states 00 through 11, as illustrated earlier in *step 4*, just to ensure that the leading classic bit (left-most bit) is always 0. The results from the executed circuit, as illustrated in the following screenshot show that the results of the left-most classic bit are always 0 and that the two classic bits correspond to the **00** to **11** states:

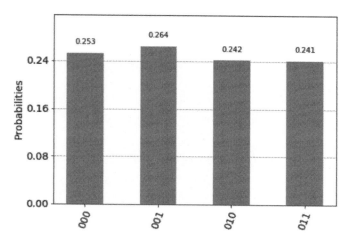

Figure 4.16 - Results of executing the quantum teleportation circuit on a simulator

In this example, we created a circuit that transports the state of a qubit from one person to the next by using a set of entangled qubits to transmit information from Alice to Bob.

Summary

In this chapter, you learned about the three quantum computing principles used in quantum computing and quantum transportation. We created a quantum circuit and placed a qubit in superposition and an entangled state between two qubits in a quantum circuit.

We also understood the two types of interference, constructive and destructive, and learned how they are notated and represented individually as qubits by placing them in superposition to create $|+\rangle$ and $|-\rangle$ simulations. We also learned how to transfer state information from one person to another using quantum transportation.

You also had a sneak peek at some Qiskit development skills by leveraging some quantum gates such as the Hadamard and Control-Not gates, as well as operations such as measurements. This will prepare you for future chapters, when you will create circuits where these gates and operations are commonly used in various algorithms. This makes sense as these gates and operations represent the core quantum computing principles that we have learned.

In the next chapter, we will learn about all the other gates, both single and multi, to understand the operations they perform on each qubit.

Questions

1. How would you create a circuit that entangles two qubits where each qubit is different (that is, 01, 10)?

2. Which simulator is used to display the Bloch sphere?

3. Execute the superposition experiment with the `shots=1` parameter, then `shots=1000`, and then `shots=8000`. What is the difference?

4. Run the quantum teleportation experiment on a real quantum device and describe the results compared to the simulator's results. What's different, if anything, and why? (Hint: noise affects near-term devices).

5
Understanding the Quantum Bit (Qubit)

We are all very familiar with the classic bit, or just bit, with respect to current computer hardware systems. It is the fundamental unit used to compute everything from simple mathematical problems, such as addition and multiplication, to more complex algorithms that involve a large collection of information.

Quantum computers have a similar fundamental unit called a **quantum bit** or **qubit**, as it is commonly referred to. In this chapter, we will describe what a qubit is, both from a mathematical (computational) and hardware perspective. We will cover the differences between qubits and bits, particularly regarding how calculations are defined. This chapter will then transition from single to multi-qubits and talk about the advantages of multi-bits.

We will also provide an overview of the various hardware implementations and how the different quantum systems implement their qubits to compute information. Finally, we will discuss how quantum systems read and control the flow of information to and from a qubit from a classical system.

The following topics will be covered in this chapter:

- Learning about quantum bits (qubits)
- Visualizing the state vector of a qubit
- Differentiating between a bit and a qubit

- Understanding single and multi-qubits
- Learning about quantum hardware systems
- Reading information and controlling single and multi-qubits

This chapter will focus on the fundamental unit of a quantum computer, the qubit, to help you understand how they are used to calculate information, as well as how various quantum systems manipulate and read information from the qubit. Since we will be using the **IBM Quantum Experience** to run our experiments, you will be using the superconducting qubit systems that are available to you. Since the descriptions and calculations are hardware independent, much of the information we will cover will apply to most of the other quantum hardware systems available.

Technical requirements

In this chapter, some basic knowledge of computer architecture and binary logic might come in handy. Knowledge of how bits are used to calculate will be useful but not a hard requirement as the focus will be primarily on the qubit. Here is the source code used throughout this book: `https://github.com/PacktPublishing/Learn-Quantum-Computing-with-Python-and-IBM-Quantum-Experience`.

Please visit the following link to check the CiA videos: `https://bit.ly/35o5M80`

Learning about quantum bits (qubits)

In this section, we will review the building blocks of a classic bit and a few of the operations that are performed on them via classic gates. We will then learn about the fundamental unit of a quantum computer, the **quantum bit (qubit)**, and how it is similar to the bit, yet due to its quantum computational principles has a larger computational space than the bit.

Reviewing the classic bit

Before we delve into what a quantum bit is and how it is used, let's take a brief moment to refresh our memories on the classic bit. Just as the quantum bit is the fundamental building block of quantum algorithms, the bit has the same role in classic computational systems.

In computational systems, the bit is used to define a logical state, often referenced as either on or off, true or false, or, the most commonly used option, 1 or 0. The transition between states can be applied physically either after it's triggered by some operation such as the result of an **AND gate**, or as a result of some input from an external entity; for example, reading from an external data source.

The following diagram illustrates that a simple process of a **NOT** operation is conducted on a bit. The bit is first initialized or set to a state, either **0** or **1**. Then, an operation is performed on the bit where, based on the result of the operation, the bit's state will either change or remain the same. The information is then available to be read and/or stored. In this example, the NOT operation would change the state from **0** to **1** or vice versa:

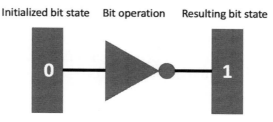

Figure 5.1 – NOT operation of a bit

The implementation of a bit can be in various forms: **flip flops, transistor-transistor logic**, and so on. The information can be stored by writing the value to a persistent data repository to be read from at a later time. Calculations using bits are usually done using a **bitstring**, which is a set of individual bits combined to represent a string of 1s and 0s, usually noted as follows:

$$x = \{0,1\}^4$$

This indicates that x is a bitstring of 4 bits, where each bit can be either 1 or 0; that is, 0010, or 1101.

Binary calculations using bits are generally done using binary logic. For example, let's say we wanted to add two numbers; say, 2 and 3. We would simply assign the values 2 and 3 to a variable, which is stored in binary. Then, we would add the two numbers using binary addition and carry the values, which will result in 5, illustrated as follows:

```
#Adding two binary numbers
two = '010'
three = '011'
answer = bin(int(two,2) + int(three,2))
print(answer)
```

Running the preceding code snippet would result in 5, but as you can see the output is written as the binary value of 5, that is, 0b101. The code reads the first two variables as a string, '010' and '011'. The string values are then cast as int prior to adding them together using modulo 2 arithmetic and return the result as a binary bitstring called answer. Modulo 2 arithmetic is the result of **XORing** two bits, that is, **(1+0) mod 2 = 1 XOR 0**, which can also be written as two binary numbers, x_1 and x_2; that is, $x_1 \oplus x_2$.

So, why did we go through such a simple example? The point was not to bore you with a simple binary calculation; the idea was to provide a refresher about the mechanics of what happens to the information on a classical system. This way, when describing the quantum system, it will help you compare and contrast the differences regarding how information is created, calculated, and stored. With that, we'll move on to the next section and describe what a qubit is.

Understanding the qubit

Similar to the bit, which we described previously, the qubit is the fundamental unit in quantum information science. The qubit is similar to the bit in that it can represent the same two states, namely 0 and 1, although a qubit is a quantum state. The value of the qubit can be read. By read, we mean we can measure the results, which we will cover soon.

They can also be manipulated to derive calculations based on operations performed on each qubit. Recall that the state of a bit can be represented by either a 0 or a 1. A qubit can also be represented by a 0 or a 1. In order to avoid confusion for ourselves and to differentiate between a bit and a qubit, we will use **Dirac notation** to describe the states of the qubit, that is, $|0\rangle$ and $|1\rangle$, to represent the qubit state of 0 and 1, respectively. Let's start by visualizing a few things to help us see the difference between the two states.

To begin, the state of a qubit is generally represented as an array or a vector, which in a **Hilbert space** is often denoted as $|\psi\rangle$. This notation is referred to as Dirac or **bra-ket notation**, named after Paul Adrien Maurice Dirac, and is commonly used in quantum mechanics and quantum computing. A Hilbert space is, in essence, a vector space of all possible real and complex numbers. The quantum state can be presented as two basis vectors that are orthogonal to each other, as follows:

$$|0\rangle = \begin{bmatrix} 1 \\ 0 \end{bmatrix}$$

The second vector is given as follows:

$$|1\rangle = \begin{bmatrix} 0 \\ 1 \end{bmatrix}$$

As we can see, bits and qubits are pretty similar in that they can represent two basis states equally of one or the other. Where the qubits differ from classical bits is that a qubit is always in a linear combination of basis states, which is to say that they are always in a superposition of $|0\rangle$ and $|1\rangle$. More formally, this is represented in the following format:

$$|\psi\rangle = \alpha|0\rangle + \beta|1\rangle$$

From the previous equation, we can say that α and β are complex in that the sum of their magnitudes is equal to 1 and each squared coefficient represents the probability amplitude of the corresponding basis state:

$$|\alpha|^2 + |\beta|^2 = 1$$

Another thing to know about quantum mechanics is that we cannot obtain the value of α and β, even when measuring the qubit. Measuring a qubit requires a qubit to collapse into one of the basis states of 0 or 1.

α and β merely provide some probabilistic information as to whether the results would be one or the other, but this is not a certainty. This is one of the mysteries of quantum mechanics. For now, you can think of measuring a qubit similar to observing or collapsing a spinning coin to reveal whether it is heads or tails. Once measured, or collapsed, you are not able to have the coin *continue* spinning without restarting the experiment, so all information is lost. You would have to repeat the full operation of spinning the coin again. We will talk about what exactly a measurement is in *Chapter 6, Understanding Quantum Gates*, on quantum gates.

Visualizing the qubit states can be done using a complex plane where the x-axis is used to denote the real component and the y-axis is used to denote the imaginary component. We should be familiar with this from our studies of linear algebra, so I will leave it up to you as an exercise to plot these using **Matplotlib**, or your favorite plotter, to plot the $|0\rangle$ and $|1\rangle$ states.

In this section, we covered the differences between bits and qubits. In the next section, we will learn how to visualize the qubits and their states using state vectors.

Visualizing the state vector of a qubit

Another visual representation of a qubit and its states is the **Bloch sphere,** named after Felix Bloch. The Bloch sphere is a three-dimensional ordinary sphere that's generally used as a geometrical representation of the qubit. By this, we mean the sphere can represent the qubit states as a point anywhere on the surface of the Bloch sphere.

Conventionally, the north pole of the Bloch sphere represents the $|0\rangle$ state, while the south pole represents the $|1\rangle$ state. Any point on the surface of the Bloch sphere can represent the linear combination of states as a unit vector from the center (origin), as we described previously, to the surface of the Bloch sphere.

Since we have the quantum mechanical constraint that the total probability of the vector must equal to 1, we get the following formula:

$$|||\psi\rangle||2 = 1$$

The vector can then only rotate along the Bloch sphere by using the following representation:

$$|\psi\rangle = \cos(\theta/2)\,|0\rangle + (\cos\phi + i\,\sin\phi)\,\sin(\theta/2)\,|1\rangle$$

Here, θ and φ have the values (limits) $0 \le \theta \le \pi$ and $0 \le \phi < 2\pi$. What this illustrates is that any point on the sphere is unique as long as the values of θ and φ themselves are unique, where θ represents the colatitude to the z-axis and φ represents the longitude from the x-axis, as illustrated in the following diagram:

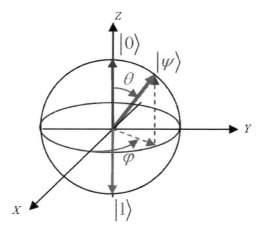

Figure 5.2 – Qubit Bloch sphere (image source: `https://commons.wikimedia.org/wiki/`
`File:Sphere_bloch.jpg`)

To continue describing a qubit, we will use our Qiskit Notebook to illustrate some key concepts that can be visualized on the Bloch sphere. This will also help provide further hands-on exercises for you.

Creating the Bloch sphere representation of a qubit

Follow these steps to create the Bloch sphere of a qubit in the initial state of $|0\rangle$ so that we can visualize the state vector and phase of a qubit:

1. Open a new Qiskit Notebook and enter the following into a cell. We will be using a few visualization tools that are included with Qiskit to help visualize the qubit states. In future chapters, we'll look at how operators such as qubit gates affect the vector states:

    ```
    from qiskit.visualization import plot_state_qsphere
    from qiskit.visualization import plot_bloch_multivector
    ```

    The preceding code imports two functions that allow you to see the state of a qubit. These are ideal for when you want to find out some information about the state while creating your circuit. There are many other visualization tools that you can leverage that are included with Qiskit, but for the purposes of this chapter, we will focus on these two as they provide enough detail to cover the information we need.

2. Next, we will create a simple circuit with just a single qubit and use the visualization tools we imported to visualize the qubit state. We'll import the first one in its initial state of $|0\rangle$.

    The following snippet will create the quantum circuit with a single qubit, and then we will get the state vector simulator from our backend. We will be using the state vector simulator to obtain the state information about the circuit once it has completed, whereas the qasm simulator only returns count information. Finally, we will execute our circuit and get the state vector results:

    ```
    #Create a simple circuit with just one qubit
    qc = QuantumCircuit(1)
    #Get the state vector simulator backend
    statevector_simulator = Aer.get_backend('statevector_
        simulator')
    #Run the circuit and get the state vector of the qubit
    result = execute(qc, statevector_simulator).result()
    statevector_results = result.get_statevector(qc)
    ```

After the preceding cell has finished executing, you should have the state vector results, which means you can now visualize them. In the next step, we will display the state vectors using both visualization functions. Note that we should expect to see our state vector in the initial state of |0⟩ since we have not performed any operations on the qubit.

3. We will start by displaying the state vector results on the Bloch sphere by passing the statevector_results object into the argument of the plot_bloch_multivector function:

```
plot_bloch_multivector(statevector_results)
```

The output that you will see from the preceding function is the Bloch sphere with the qubit state pointed to the north pole or to the |0⟩ state, illustrated as follows:

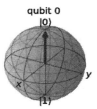

Figure 5.3 – Qubit Bloch sphere state vector initialized to |0⟩

4. Next, we will display the state vector results on the quantum sphere. In this visualization, you will see the state vector in the same state as the Bloch sphere shown in the preceding diagram:

```
plot_state_qsphere(statevector_results)
```

You will also see that it includes the phase of the state vector represented by the color-shaded sphere at the bottom-left, as shown in the following output:

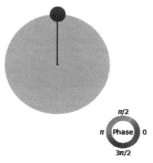

Figure 5.4 – Qubit state vector initialized to |0⟩ with phase = 0

From the preceding diagram, note that the color of the state vector at the surface of the Bloch sphere is not only pointed toward the north pole, indicating it is in the state |0⟩, but that it is also shaded red. This is to indicate the phase of the state vector. The color chart at the bottom-right of the preceding diagram is a reference to the phase of the state vector, which is currently highlighted as 0.

5.   Now that we are familiar with the state vector of a qubit, let's take it out for a spin. We'll start by flipping the vector from the initial state of |0⟩ to the state of |1⟩ using the NOT gate:

```
qc = QuantumCircuit(1)
qc.x(0)
#Execute the circuit
result = execute(qc, statevector_simulator).result()
statevector_results = result.get_statevector(qc)
plot_state_qsphere(statevector_results)
```

As you can see, we are now at the |1⟩ state with the phase still at **0**, as illustrated in the following diagram:

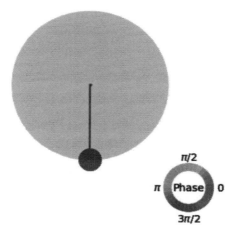

Figure 5.5 – Qubit state vector set to |1⟩ with phase = 0

6. Next, we will place the qubit into superposition by adding a Hadamard gate and executing the circuit again. We'll create a new circuit and include a Hadamard gate, as shown in the following code snippet, followed by executing the circuit and plotting the Bloch sphere of the state vector results, which indicates the position of the state vector. In this case, it is on the equator:

```
qc = QuantumCircuit(1)
qc.h(0)
#Execute the circuit
result = execute(qc, statevector_simulator).result()
statevector_results = result.get_statevector(qc)
plot_bloch_multivector(statevector_results)
```

Note that the state vector is a precise linear combination of $|0\rangle$ and $|1\rangle$:

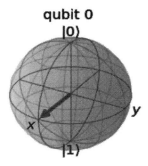

Figure 5.6 – Bloch sphere superposition representation, a linear combination of $|0\rangle$ and $|1\rangle$

Let's see what this looks like on the Qiskit sphere by plotting the state vector results.

7. Plot the state vector results on the Qiskit sphere:

```
plot_state_qsphere(statevector_results)
```

The results might seem a little confusing. You may be asking yourself why there are two vectors when we only have one qubit and why they are based on the Bloch sphere result. *Shouldn't we only see one?* You can see the output of the previous code snippet in the following diagram:

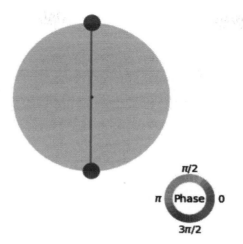

Figure 5.7 – Qubit state vector set to a linear combination of |0⟩ and |1⟩, superposition

Well, the difference is that the Qiskit sphere visualizes something that the Bloch sphere does not; that is, the visual representation of the amplitude of each possible state. If you look at the size of the ball on the surface of the previous outcome of the *q-sphere* when we executed either the |0⟩ or |1⟩ state, the diameter of the ball was much larger than the two on the surface of the preceding diagram. This is because the amplitude is equal for both |0⟩ and |1⟩, so the size is split between the two, whereas in the previous examples, the amplitude was purely in one of the two states.

In this section, we learned that the qubit can represent itself as a bit by using the two basis states of 0 and 1. We also saw that it can be represented as a linear combination of the two basis states; that is, 0 and 1 (longitudinal) and phase shifts (latitudinal).

It is by leveraging these features that quantum algorithms can provide potential in optimizing computational solutions much more than using classical bits. We also saw how to visualize the state of a qubit using two Qiskit visualization functions, the Bloch sphere and the Qiskit sphere, which provided information such as amplitude and phase.

In the next section, we will look at how multi-qubits are presented and how to visualize and plot both their real and imaginary components.

Understanding multi-qubits

So far, we've learned the various ways to represent a qubit, both as a vector $|\psi\rangle$ and visually as a Bloch sphere. We did something similar with the Qiskit sphere. In this section, we will learn how to represent multiple qubits and how to represent them in their general state. We will start by making a slight update to the notation. A single qubit is presented as the following vector:

$$|\psi\rangle = \alpha_0|0\rangle + \alpha_1|1\rangle = \begin{pmatrix} \alpha_0 \\ \alpha_1 \end{pmatrix}$$

We can therefore represent two qubits similarly in the following form:

$$|\Psi\rangle = \alpha_{00}|00\rangle + \alpha_{01}|01\rangle + \alpha_{10}|10\rangle + \alpha_{11}|11\rangle = \begin{pmatrix} \alpha_{00} \\ \alpha_{01} \\ \alpha_{10} \\ \alpha_{11} \end{pmatrix}$$

From the preceding equation, you can see that the state $|\Psi\rangle$ is used to represent multiple qubits, versus $|\psi\rangle$ in the single qubit. The probabilistic amplitudes, along with the constraint by the normalization of 1, can therefore be represented as follows:

$$|\alpha_{00}|^2 + |\alpha_{01}|^2 + |\alpha_{10}|^2 + |\alpha_{11}|^2 = 1$$

Let's look at an example that comprises two qubits, the first one in the state, shown as follows:

$$|\psi\rangle = \alpha_0|0\rangle + \alpha_1|1\rangle$$

The other qubit in the state is as follows:

$$|\varphi\rangle = \beta_0|0\rangle + \beta_1|1\rangle$$

Combining the two entails taking the **tensor product** of the two qubit states, as follows:

$$|\Psi\rangle = |\psi\rangle \otimes |\varphi\rangle = (\alpha_0|0\rangle + \alpha_1|1\rangle) \otimes (\beta_0|0\rangle + \beta_1|1\rangle)$$

Multiplying across, we will get the following:

$$= \alpha_0\beta_0|00\rangle + \alpha_0\beta_1|01\rangle + \alpha_1\beta_0|10\rangle + \alpha_1\beta_1|11\rangle$$

This results in the amplitude vectors, as follows:

$$= \begin{pmatrix} \alpha_0 \beta_0 \\ \alpha_0 \beta_1 \\ \alpha_1 \beta_0 \\ \alpha_1 \beta_1 \end{pmatrix}$$

Finally, another way to state multi-qubits by their tensor product is by representing them by their product state. Here, the product state of n qubits is 2^n. We'll use the same two-vector example described previously. The first is the 00 state:

$$|00\rangle = \begin{pmatrix} 1 \\ 0 \end{pmatrix} \otimes \begin{pmatrix} 1 \\ 0 \end{pmatrix} = \begin{pmatrix} 1 \\ 0 \\ 0 \\ 0 \end{pmatrix}$$

The 01 state is shown as follows:

$$|01\rangle = \begin{pmatrix} 1 \\ 0 \end{pmatrix} \otimes \begin{pmatrix} 0 \\ 1 \end{pmatrix} = \begin{pmatrix} 0 \\ 1 \\ 0 \\ 0 \end{pmatrix}$$

The 10 state is shown as follows, along with its tensor product:

$$|10\rangle = \begin{pmatrix} 0 \\ 1 \end{pmatrix} \otimes \begin{pmatrix} 1 \\ 0 \end{pmatrix} = \begin{pmatrix} 0 \\ 0 \\ 1 \\ 0 \end{pmatrix}$$

Lastly, the 11 state is given as follows:

$$|11\rangle = \begin{pmatrix} 0 \\ 1 \end{pmatrix} \otimes \begin{pmatrix} 0 \\ 1 \end{pmatrix} = \begin{pmatrix} 0 \\ 0 \\ 0 \\ 1 \end{pmatrix}$$

The main takeaway from the previous equations is that we can describe two qubits individually as a *2 x 1* column vector. However, when we want to represent the joint state of the full system, we represent them as a tensor product, which produces the *4 x 1* column vector illustrated previously. This is the mathematical representation of the quantum circuit, also referred to as the computational basis state of a two-qubit system.

In the next section, we'll briefly discuss the implementation of qubits on the IBM Quantum Experience systems and also discuss other technologies that are used for implementing qubits.

Learning about superconducting qubits

At the beginning of this chapter, we learned that classical bits can be implemented by various platforms that detect differences between voltages or the phase of a current, or by the state of a flip flop. Just as a bit has different platforms that are used for their implementation, so do qubits.

Some of the more common qubit platforms are **neutral atoms**, **Quantum dots**, **Nitrogen-vacancy** (**NV**) centers in diamond, **trapped ions**, and **superconducting qubits**. Out of these platforms, it is the superconducting qubits that are used on the quantum devices hosted on the IBM Quantum Experience. So, in this section, we will cover this platform. If you want to learn more about the other platforms, you can review *Appendix A*, which you can find at the end of this book.

Superconductors that are made up of a combination of **niobium** and **aluminum** are at the base of the qubit. There, they are used as the basic charge carriers that comprise a pair of electrons, more commonly referred to as **Cooper pairs**. This is different from other conductors that generally use single electrons. Talking about the specifics of the quantum mechanics or superconducting behavior of the Cooper pairs is beyond the scope of this book. However, you can find various references in *Appendix A* to these if you are interested. For now, we can think of the superconductors as one of the components of the superconducting circuit that makes up the qubit.

Let's see what the other components are in the superconducting circuit. As the following diagram illustrates, at the core of the qubit, we have a capacitor and **Josephson Junction** (to those of you familiar with electronic circuits, this may look very similar to an **Inductance Capacitance (LC)** circuit):

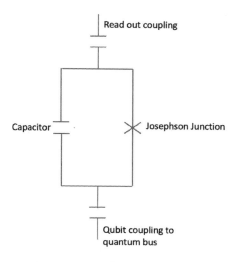

Figure 5.8 – Schematic of a qubit

From the preceding diagram, you can see that the difference is that rather than there being a linear inductor, there's a Josephson Junction, which is an **anharmonic oscillator**. This allows us to easily differentiate between the different energy levels, which we map as the states of the qubit.

On the ends of the qubit, there are two external coupling points, the top of which is the read out (or read-in) resonator. This resonator is used to perform operations on the qubit from your quantum circuit and read out the measured result of the qubit when you wish to obtain the collapsed result (0 or 1). At the other end of the qubit is the coupling to a neighboring qubit, which is used to connect qubits together to create connectivity between them.

The following diagram shows that, at the core of the superconducting qubit, there are capacitors made up of superconducting material – in this case, **niobium** – which is separated by an **aluminum** inductor – the **Josephson Junction**:

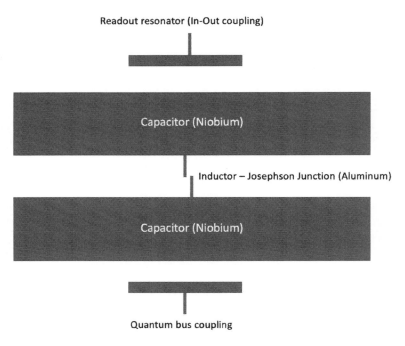

Figure 5.9 – Physical components of a qubit

The components shown in the preceding diagram are constructed and placed on top of a **silicon wafer**, where each qubit is then connected to each other via microwave resonators (**Quantum bus coupling**) and each qubit has its own readout resonator (**In-Out coupling**).

The layout of the qubits can be set up in a configuration that can vary from one device to another. For example, in the following diagram, you can see a qubit configuration from one of the many five qubit devices, often referred to as a Bowtie configuration because it resembles a bowtie:

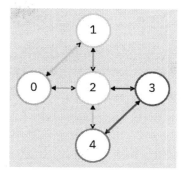

Figure 5.10 – Bowtie configuration of a qubit

The following diagram shows another qubit configuration using the five different qubit devices. This one has a T-shaped configuration:

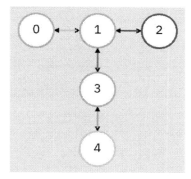

Figure 5.11 – T-shaped configuration of a qubit

As you can see by comparing the layouts from *Figure 5.10* and *Figure 5.11*, the qubits in the preceding diagram are connected in various ways – some to just one qubit, and others to as many as three.

> **Important Note**
>
> Note that each qubit has its own read out coupling so that we can perform operations on individual qubits. They also have their own read out couplings because they include bus couplings to complete the full connection space of the qubits.

The connection space here refers to the ability to entangle qubits, even though they may not be directly connected, by performing multi-gate operations such as **Swap** gates, **Controlled NOT (CNOT)** gates, and so on. We will go into details of single and multi-qubit gates and operations in the next chapter, but for now, we will cover how operations are sent to the qubit from a hardware perspective.

Each qubit is tuned to a certain frequency, usually limited to under 1 THz due to the constraint that the Cooper pairs would break them apart at that frequency. But given the fact that the qubits are in a dilution chamber that cools the qubit down to almost 0, which is approximately 15 millikelvin (*which is many times colder than outer space!*), this allows the energy level separation to reach about 5 GHz.

If you download the calibration file from one of the real devices and look at the *Frequency (GHz)* column values, you will see that they are all in that range, with a few MHz separating them. To download the configuration, simply go to the IBM Quantum Experience **Dashboard** and select a backend from the list of devices.

The following table shows the frequency values of a five-qubit device:

Qubit	Frequency (GHz)
0	5.253959147430724
1	5.04860346965249
2	5.230134730378009
3	5.200779259727545
4	5.065775710053278

Table 5.1 – Frequency of each qubit

By having each qubit set to a different frequency, operations can then be addressed to the specific qubit via its frequency. For example, if an operation, such as a rotation, is to be performed on a qubit, then microwave pulses are sent via microwave transmission lines onto the microwave resonators at a frequency resonating for the specific qubit.

Here, the axis of the pulse is set by the amplitude modulation of the microwave pulse and the angle of rotation requested is set by the pulse's length. Don't worry if this seems a little strange right now; we will cover this in more detail and actually run an experiment directly on a qubit in this way in *Chapter 8, Programming with Qiskit Terra*, with **OpenPulse**.

Now that we know how operations are sent to the qubit, let's look at how we can couple two qubits together. First and foremost, when we couple two qubits together, we want to make sure that there is enough of a gap between their resonant frequencies or that they're out of resonance from each other. This is to ensure we don't introduce the effect of undesirable neighboring signals, known as crosstalk, to the system.

Coupling the qubits together

This is where the quantum bus comes in handy as it adds a microwave cavity in-between the qubits. Once the energy states between the coupled qubits are separated, we can then send cross-resonant gate operations, such as a CNOT gate, which is a two-qubit operation gate that flips the target qubit if the source qubit is set to 1; otherwise, it will not flip the target qubit.

Cross-resonant gate operations are fairly simple to understand if you think of them using the following analogy of the game *Simon says*. In the game, someone screams out commands and you are only allowed to perform the command if the command is prefaced with the phrase "*Simon says...*". If the command starts with *Simon says*, then whatever that command is, you listen and then perform it. If the command does not start with *Simon says*, you ignore it.

Now, let's relate the preceding example to how cross-resonant gates work. First, a pulse command is sent to the source qubit, which relates to the command in the *Simon says* example. The source qubit will then determine whether it is set, which relates to checking if "*Simon says*" is prefixed to the command.

If so, it will then allow the pulse to continue to the target qubit. The target qubit then performs the operation, which in the case of the CNOT gate is to flip the qubit around the x-axis. This relates to performing the given action because the command included *Simon says*.

Now that we have covered how to visualize the state of a qubit using the state vector simulator and display it on both a Bloch Sphere and a Q-sphere, as well as what a qubit is made of and how single and multi-qubit operations are sent to the qubits, we can move on to the next chapter, which describes all the qubit gate operators and what effects they have on each other.

Summary

In this chapter, you learned the difference between bits and qubits and how they are represented, both mathematically and visually. You also saw the difference between how single and multi-qubit systems are represented, including their mathematical representations, as well as how they are constructed and operated on. We also covered how to visualize the qubit as a Bloch sphere and a Qiskit sphere.

We now have the skills to represent the vector states of single and multi-qubits. We also understand the difference between representing multiple qubits as separate entities and as part of a complete system by using the tensor products of the qubits. This will help you to implement and operate the qubits on IBM Quantum devices.

In the next chapter, we will learn how to perform operations on single and multi-qubits and how those operations are triggered on the qubits of the real devices.

Questions

1. What is the transpose of the single qubit $|0\rangle$ state, stated as a column vector?

2. Which would provide visual information about the phase of a qubit – the Bloch sphere or the Qiskit sphere?

3. Can you visualize multi-qubits on the Bloch sphere? If yes, then why? If no, then why?

4. Write out the tensor product of three qubit states in all their forms.

5. What is the probability amplitude of a three-qubit system?

6. What material is used to create the capacitors of a qubit?

7. What are Josephson Junctions made of?

8. What approximate temperature do the qubits have to be at in order to operate properly?

6
Understanding Quantum Logic Gates

Quantum logic gates are very similar to their classical counterparts in that they are used to perform operations by manipulating the qubits in such a way that the results serve to provide a solution. Of course, that's about as far as the comparison can go. Classical gates transition the state of a bit from one to the other by a single operation, in this case, flipping the bit value from 0 to 1, or vice versa. **Quantum gates**, sometimes referred to as **qubit gates**, are different in part because they perform linear transformations on the qubit in a complex vector space to transition the qubit(s) from one state to another.

The following topics will be covered in this chapter:

- Reviewing classical logic gates
- Understanding unitary operators
- Understanding single-qubit gates
- Understanding multi-qubit gates
- Understanding non-reversible operators

After reading this chapter, you will have gained knowledge about the fundamental operations that can be performed on both single and multiple qubits. But before we dive right in, let's discuss the format with which I'll try to explain each qubit gate. First, from a learning perspective, some of you tend to learn quicker when content is presented purely with mathematics; others are more visual and prefer visual aids such as graphs; others still prefer a more intuitive approach with analogies and examples.

With that in mind, I shall do my best to ensure that each gate is presented by combining as many of these learning styles as possible. This will be done by providing not only the mathematical representation of each qubit gate, but also a visual representation, and of course the source code to run the qubit gate operation and its result.

Technical requirements

In this chapter, we will discuss linear transformations of matrices in the **Hilbert space**, so it is highly recommended that you should know the basics of linear algebra. Some basic knowledge of Python or another programming language is required due to the experiments leveraging Python libraries and the **Qiskit Notebook** on the **IBM Quantum Experience**.

Knowledge of the qubit and how its states are represented on a Bloch sphere, **QSphere**, or mathematically, is recommended as this chapter will perform complex linear transitions of those qubit states. Knowledge of basic classical single-bit and multi-bit gates is also recommended, but not required, as there is a refresher if needed.

Here is the full source code used throughout this book: `https://github.com/PacktPublishing/Learn-Quantum-Computing-with-Python-and-IBM-Quantum-Experience`

Please visit the following link to check the CiA videos: `https://bit.ly/3o5M80`

Reviewing classical logic gates

This section will serve as a refresher for classical logic gates such as **AND, OR, NOR**, and so on. If you are familiar with this subject, you can either skim through this chapter to refresh your memory or skip it entirely and jump to the next section. *Otherwise, let's get logical!*

Logic gates are defined as a device, electronic or otherwise, that implements a logical (usually Boolean) operation. Single-bit and two-bit gates generally have one or two inputs, respectively. Each input bit value is a state value of either 0 or 1. The operation carried out on the input varies by the type of gate. Each gate operation is usually described using logic truth tables, as illustrated in the following table:

Gate	Operation	Input A B	Output Y	Graphical Representation
Buffer	Outputs the same value as the input	0 1	0 1	
NOT	Reverses the input state	0 1	1 0	
AND	Outputs a 1 if and only if both inputs are 1, otherwise output is 0	0 0 0 1 1 0 1 1	0 0 0 1	
OR	Outputs a 0 if and only if none of the inputs is 1, otherwise output is 1	0 0 0 1 1 0 1 1	0 1 1 1	
XOR	Outputs a 1 if and only if both inputs are different, otherwise output is 0	0 0 0 1 1 0 1 1	0 1 1 0	
NAND	Outputs a 0 if and only if both inputs are 1, otherwise output is 1	0 0 0 1 1 0 1 1	1 1 1 0	

NOR	Outputs a 1 if and only if both inputs are 0, otherwise outputs a 0	0 0 0 1 1 0 1 1	1 0 0 0	
XNOR	Outputs a 1 if and only if inputs are both either 0 or 1, otherwise outputs 0	0 0 0 1 1 0 1 1	1 0 0 1	

Table 6.1 – Classical logic gates

The preceding table lists some of the common classical gates, descriptions of the operation that each gate performs on the input state, the result (output) of the gate operation, and their graphical representations.

Let's consider some things of note regarding classical bits that will help you later understand the differences they have compared to **quantum bits (qubits)**. First is that there are only two single-bit gates, the buffer and the NOT gate. Among these two, only the NOT gate performs a Boolean operation on the classical bit by flipping the bit value of the input, so if the input to the NOT gate was a 0, then the output would be a 1. On the other hand, the buffer gate simply outputs the same value as the input. All the other gates operate on two input bit values that output a single value, which is determined by the gate's Boolean operation. For example, if both input values to an AND gate are 1, it will output a 1. Otherwise, the output will be 0.

One problem, however, particularly with regard to the two-bit gates, is that if you only have access to the output then the information about the input is lost. For example, if you obtain the result from an AND bit and the value is 0, *could you tell what the input values were for A and B(inputs)?* Unfortunately, the answer to this question is no.

The input information is lost because the output does not include any information about the input value, which renders the gates irreversible. Likewise, with other two-bit gates, if I gave you just the output value of the gate, you could not tell me with 100% certainty about all the possible output values which the input values would be able to produce. **Reversibility** is a unique property that qubit gates have, in that you can reverse the operation of the qubit gate to obtain the previous state.

Another point to keep in mind about classical-bit gates is that their output is deterministic. By this, I mean that if you know the input values and the gate type that you are going to use, then you can determine the output of the gate without running them through the gate.

And finally, to close our discussion on classical gates, we'll discuss **universal logic gates**. These gates are the type of gates used to create other logic gates. **NOR** and **NAND** gates are good examples of universal gates in that they can be used to create NOT and AND gates. Let's take a look at the following diagram that illustrates creating a NOT gate (inverter) by using a NAND gate:

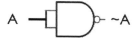

Figure 6.1 – Using a NAND gate to create a NOT gate

As you can see, by wiring both inputs of the NAND gate together, forming a single input (**A**), this logically creates a NOT gate that flips the value of the input. Computational systems having universal gates is an important feature as it provides the ability to create logical circuits to solve problems. This of course led to the creation of integrated circuits, which are specialized circuits used to compute problems or to perform specific operations such as an adder or a counter, respectively.

Now that we have reviewed the functionality of classical gates, we can continue to the next section where we will cover the basics of quantum logic gates. There we will also see some similarities and some unique properties that they display with regard to the classical bit.

Understanding unitary operators

Unitary operators are defined as a unitary transformation of a rigid body rotation of the Hilbert space, which results in a transformation of the state vector that doesn't change its length. Let's see what this means for a qubit. The basis states of a qubit are mapped on the Hilbert space $\mathbb{C}$ as orthonormal states; $|v_0\rangle = \alpha|0\rangle + \beta|1\rangle$, and $|v_1\rangle = \gamma|0\rangle + \delta|1\rangle$, where α, β, γ, and $\delta \in \mathbb{C}$ are linear transformations that preserve orthogonality are unitary transformations. We'll wrap our heads around this definition a bit by looking at this mathematically first.

A linear transformation on a complex vector space can be described by a matrix, **U**:

$$U = \begin{pmatrix} \alpha & \gamma \\ \beta & \delta \end{pmatrix}$$

Furthermore, if we obtain the complex transpose of the matrix U as $U^\dagger$, by transposing the matrix U and applying the complex conjugate, as illustrated:

$$U^\dagger = \begin{pmatrix} \alpha^\dagger & \beta^\dagger \\ \gamma^\dagger & \delta^\dagger \end{pmatrix}$$

Then we can say that the matrix U is unitary if $UU^\dagger = I$, where I represents the Identity matrix $\begin{pmatrix} 1 & 0 \\ 0 & 1 \end{pmatrix}$ as shown here:

$$UU^\dagger = U^\dagger U$$

$$= \begin{pmatrix} \alpha & \gamma \\ \beta & \delta \end{pmatrix}\begin{pmatrix} \alpha^\dagger & \beta^\dagger \\ \gamma^\dagger & \delta^\dagger \end{pmatrix}$$

$$= \begin{pmatrix} 1 & 0 \\ 0 & 1 \end{pmatrix} = I$$

An intuitive way to think of this is to just imagine unitary transformation simply as rotations of the complex vector space that preserve the module of the original vector. The rotation of the complex vector space further ensures that quantum transformations are not just unitary operations but are also **reversible operations**.

Reversibility of quantum gates is realized by unitary transformations. As seen in the previous unitary equation, if you have a unitary operator **U** applied to a qubit via a gate, then by applying the complex conjugate $U^\dagger$ of the unitary operator, the result would be equivalent to applying an Identity matrix to the original vector.

An example of this would be if you were to trigger an operation that would rotate the vector space around the x axis by an angle π, and you then apply the complex conjugate of that operation, then you'll return to the original position from which you started. This reversible functionality is something that is not possible with some classical-bit gates we mentioned earlier, such as an AND gate.

With unitary transformations, there is no loss of information. Should you need to return to the previous state, you would merely have to repeat all unitary operations, in reverse order, and you'd get back to where you originally started. We will see some interesting examples of reversibility in all gates. There is a special case operator that is not reversible, the **measurement** operator, which we will learn about in the *Understanding non-reversible operators* section.

Now that we understand unitary and reversible operators, we can get down to learning about quantum gates.

Understanding single-qubit gates

Before we get into the specifics of quantum gates, let's take a quick moment to review the quantum state representation of a qubit. The state of a qubit is generally represented in the following format:

$$|\psi\rangle = \alpha|0\rangle + \beta|1\rangle = \begin{pmatrix} \alpha \\ \beta \end{pmatrix}$$

In the preceding equation, α and β are complex numbers representing the amplitudes of the $|0\rangle$ and $|1\rangle$ basis states, respectively.

Furthermore, the orthogonal basis states can be represented as column vectors, where the basis vector for $|0\rangle$ is as follows:

$$|0\rangle = \begin{bmatrix} 1 \\ 0 \end{bmatrix}$$

And the basis vector for $|1\rangle$ is the following:

$$|1\rangle = \begin{bmatrix} 0 \\ 1 \end{bmatrix}$$

This will help you understand how qubit gates operate uniquely depending on which state the qubit is in prior to applying the unitary operator.

The first group of single-qubit gates we will discuss are commonly referred to as **Pauli matrix** gates, named after the physicist Wolfgang Pauli. The complex matrix representation of the four gates, **I**, **X**, **Y**, and **Z**, are defined as a *2 x 2* complex matrix, which are both Hermitian and unitary and are represented by the Greek letter sigma $(\sigma_0, \sigma_x, \sigma_y, \sigma_z)$, respectively. Note that the Identity matrix is subscripted with a 0, and the x, y, and z subscripts can also be represented as $\sigma_1, \sigma_2, \sigma_3$.

Before we start digging into the description of quantum gates, let's simplify the format so it's easy to both understand and reference. Intuitively, the easiest way to imagine the operation of each gate is by rotating the Bloch sphere, or QSphere, around a specified axis. Recall as well that the Bloch sphere always starts with the unit vector set to the initial state. The initial state is set when the quantum circuit is first created, in this case, it is initialized to the basis state $|0\rangle$ (the north pole of the QSphere) as illustrated in the following diagram:

Figure 6.2 – QSphere representation of the basis state $|0\rangle$

One thing that will help us understand some of the labels we will see in the gate's truth table is to define the values of each axis, where each axis is referred to as **basis elements**. For example, we can see from the previous figure that the z axis has the north pole labeled as $|0\rangle$ and the south pole as $|1\rangle$. These two points form the computational basis elements for the basis state vectors $|0\rangle$ and $|1\rangle$. However, we do not yet have labels for the x or y axes. Let's define those now.

Each basis element (axis) has a positive and negative side that originate at the center of the Bloch sphere. Each basis has a name associated with each axis: **Computational** for the z axis, **Hadamard** for the x axis, and **Circular** for the y axis.

The x basis has a label defined as follows:

$$x = |+\rangle$$
$$= 1/\sqrt{2} \ (|0\rangle + |1\rangle)$$

The -x basis has a label defined as follows:

$$-x = |-\rangle$$
$$= 1/\sqrt{2} \ (|0\rangle - |1\rangle)$$

The y basis has a label defined as follows:

$$y = |i\rangle$$
$$= 1/\sqrt{2} \; (|0\rangle + i|1\rangle)$$

The -y basis has a label defined as follows:

$$-y = |-i\rangle$$
$$= 1/\sqrt{2} \; (|0\rangle - i|1\rangle)$$

The labels are also illustrated at the ends of each axis in the following diagram, where the dotted line indicates the negative direction of the axis:

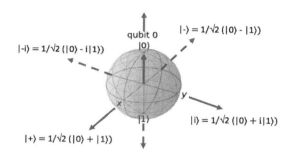

Figure 6.3 – Basis state labels of each axis of a Bloch sphere

Each gate we apply in the code snippets will operate on the qubit starting from this initial state. There are some gates you will see that we will have to prepare int a superposition state in order to see the effects. For example, if I wanted to see what a rotation about the z axis is on the Bloch sphere, it would be difficult to see the effect if the vector was in the initial state $|0\rangle$ as it would just spin without any effect to the position of the basis vector.

In this case, by transitioning the vector down onto the x axis, and then applying a Z gate rotation, you can then more clearly see the rotation take effect. Details on how this is done will be in the description of—yes, you guessed it—the Z gate. But for now, let's create a helper function that will help us visualize the gates without having to write so much code.

Helper function, used to reduce repeating code, let's us create a function that will handle some of the repetitive functions such as executing and visualizing the circuits. This way we will just create the quantum circuits, add the gates, and execute the circuits using a function that will return the results and the images to visualize the results and the circuit diagrams. To start, let's define the following function that will handle this:

```
# Will execute the circuit on the state vector (sv) simulator
# Returns state vector results, circuit diagram, and QSphere
```

```
def execute_circuit_sv(quantum_circuit):
    #Create a state vector simulator
    statevector_simulator = Aer.get_backend('statevector_
        simulator')
    #Execute the circuit on the simulator
    result = execute(quantum_circuit, statevector_simulator).
        result()
    #Assign state vector results
    statevector_results  = result.get_statevector(quantum_
        circuit)
    #Draw the circuit diagram
    circuit_diagram = quantum_circuit.draw()
    #Draw the QSphere
    q_sphere = plot_state_qsphere(statevector_results)
    #Return the results, circuit diagram, and QSphere
    return statevector_results, circuit_diagram, q_sphere
```

The preceding code will return the three components we will use to illustrate each gate and the visual representation.

Now we can focus on the quantum gates and their effect on the qubits, and not so much on executing the circuits or displaying the results. We'll start with the easiest of the gates, the Identity gate.

Working with Identity (I) Pauli gate

The **I gate**, also known as the **Identity gate** is a gate that does not perform any operation on the qubit. It does not change the state of the qubit. Mathematically, this is represented as an Identity matrix, hence the name of the gate. This equation is given as follows:

$$I = \sigma_0 = \begin{pmatrix} 1 & 0 \\ 0 & 1 \end{pmatrix}$$

The truth table for this gate results in the same state of the input:

Input	Output
$|0\rangle$	$|0\rangle$
$|1\rangle$	$|1\rangle$

Table 6.2 – Truth table of Identity gate

Not too surprisingly, there is no Identity gate in Qiskit. The idea of an Identity gate is generally used mathematically to illustrate certain properties of operations, as we did earlier in this chapter to prove that unitary operators are reversible. In that example, the Identity matrix was used to illustrate that by multiplying a unitary operator with its complex conjugate would produce the same output as applying no operation, or an Identity matrix, to the qubit.

Let's move on to the next gate section.

Applying the NOT (X) Pauli gate

The **X gate** is also called the NOT gate because of the similar effect it has on the basis states as its classical-bit gate counterpart. One notable difference is that the X gate moves the state vector from one basis state to the other, as illustrated in *Table 6.3*. Visualizing this operation can be seen via the Bloch sphere result as a rotation of the vector from the initial state, $|0\rangle$. Because of its spherical presentation, we refer to operations as rotations around some axis, in this case, the X gate is a π (180^0) rotation about the x axis, which is represented by the Pauli X-gate operator as follows:

$$X = \sigma_1 = \begin{pmatrix} 0 & 1 \\ 1 & 0 \end{pmatrix}$$

The following truth table illustrates here that the operation rotates the input around the x axis by π (180^0), hence if the input is the $|0\rangle$, then the output is $|1\rangle$ and vice versa:

Input	Output
$|0\rangle$	$|1\rangle$
$|1\rangle$	$|0\rangle$

Table 6.3 – Truth table of X (NOT) gate

Let's now create a circuit by following the next steps:

1. First, add an X gate to it, and execute it using our helper function to do the heavy lifting for us:

```
#X-gate
#Create the single qubit circuit
qc = QuantumCircuit(1)
#Add an X gate to the qubit
qc.x(0)
#Execute the circuit and capture all the results
result, img, qsphere = execute_circuit_sv(qc)
```

2. Let's first examine the state vector results by running the following cell:

```
result
```

This prints out the state vector values of the qubit:

```
array([0.+0.j, 1.+0.j])
```

3. Then, to draw the circuit diagram for the X gate, run the following in a cell:

```
img
```

This displays the circuit diagram with the **X** gate added to the qubit, as shown in the following diagram:

Figure 6.4 – X gate

4. Now to view the QSphere representation, run the following in a cell:

```
qsphere
```

The QSphere, as you can see, has rotated the state of the qubit from $|0\rangle$ to $|1\rangle$:

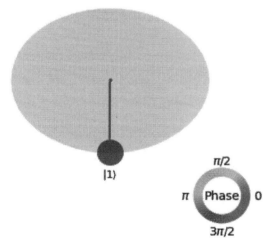

Figure 6.5 – X gate QSphere

As we have seen the X gate serves as a good example that quantum gates can also be used to perform the same operations as classical gates. One another thing you will notice from the QSphere result is color wheel that represents the phase of the state vector, which is in this case is red to indicate it's in phase (0^0).

Working with the Y Pauli gate

The **Y gate** is a rotation around the y axis by π (180^0), shown as follows:

$$Y = \sigma_2 = \begin{pmatrix} 0 & i \\ i & 0 \end{pmatrix}$$

Here, the following truth table illustrates that the operation rotates the input around the y axis by π (180^0), hence if the input is the $|0\rangle$, then the output is $|1\rangle$ and vice versa:

Input	Output
$|0\rangle$	$i\,|1\rangle$
$|1\rangle$	$-i\,|0\rangle$

Table 6.4 – Truth table representing phase rotation of y axis

Let's now create a circuit by using the following steps:

1. First add a Y gate to it, and execute it using our helper function that provides the quantum circuit and the visual representations of each circuit we execute:

```
#Y-gate operation on a qubit
#Create the single qubit circuit
qc = QuantumCircuit(1)
#Add a Y gate to the qubit
qc.y(0)
#Execute the circuit and capture all the results returned
result, img, qsphere = execute_circuit_sv(qc)
```

2. Let's first examine the state vector results by running the following cell:

```
result
```

This prints out the state vector values of the qubit:

```
array([0.-0.j, 0.+1.j])
```

3. To draw the circuit diagram for the X gate, run the following in a cell:

```
img
```

The preceding code displays the circuit diagram with the Y gate added to the qubit, as shown in the following diagram:

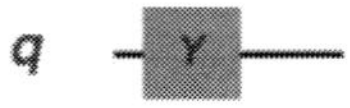

q — Y —

Figure 6.6 – Y gate

4. To view the QSphere representation, run the following in a cell:

```
qsphere
```

The QSphere, as you can see, has rotated the state of the qubit from $|0\rangle$ to $|1\rangle$:

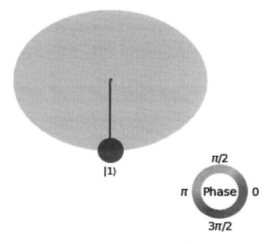

Figure 6.7 – Y gate QSphere

The Y gate, as we can see from the results, operates very similar to the X gate, at least when the origin of the state vector is the same.

Before proceeding the third and final Pauli gate, let's look at the **Hadamard (H)** gate. The reason I want to review the H gate before the last Pauli gate, the Z gate, is because we will need to include the H gate in order to see the effects of the Z gate when applied. This is not to say that you need to include an H gate prior to using a Z gate; it's merely because it helps to visualize the circuit.

Using the Hadamard (H) gate

The **H gate**, is one of the most commonly used quantum gates. It's not surprising as this is the gate that places the quantum state of the qubit into a complex linear superposition of the two basis states. This is what establishes the superposition of all qubits that are leveraged by most quantum algorithms. It is denoted as follows:

$$H = \frac{1}{\sqrt{2}} \begin{pmatrix} 1 & 1 \\ 1 & -1 \end{pmatrix}$$

The following truth table illustrates that the operation rotates the state vector of the qubit along the x axis and z axis by $\pi/2$ (180^0), causing the state vector to be in a complex linear position of $|0\rangle$ and $|1\rangle$:

Input	Output
$|0\rangle$	$\dfrac{|0\rangle + |1\rangle}{\sqrt{2}}$
$|1\rangle$	$\dfrac{|0\rangle - |1\rangle}{\sqrt{2}}$

Table 6.5 – Truth table of a Hadamard operation

Let's continue and create a circuit using these steps:

1. First, we add an H gate to the qubit, and execute it on the backend, the same as we did in the previous example:

```
#H-gate
#Create the single qubit circuit
qc = QuantumCircuit(1)
#Add an H gate to the qubit
qc.h(0)
#Execute the circuit and capture all the results
result, img, qsphere = execute_circuit_sv(qc)
```

2. Let's first examine the state vector results by running the following cell:

```
result
```

This prints out the following state vector values of the qubit:

```
array([0.70710678+0.j, 0.70710678+0.j])
```

3. To draw the circuit diagram for the H gate, run the following in a cell:

```
img
```

This displays the circuit diagram with the **H** gate added to the qubit, as shown in the following diagram:

$$q \quad -\boxed{H}-$$

Figure 6.8 – Circuit diagram with an H gate

4. To view the QSphere representation, run the following in a cell:

```
qsphere
```

The QSphere, as you can see, has an equal probability of being either $|0\rangle$ or $|1\rangle$. The ends of the vectors, as you'll notice, have the same diameter, indicating visually that both have equal probability:

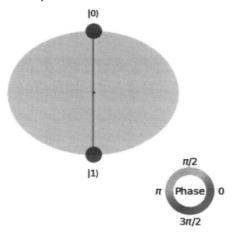

Figure 6.9 – H gate QSphere representation

The Hadamard (H) gate is a unique gate. We will see this gate many more times in this chapter and future chapters. Let's go back to our last Pauli gate, the Z gate, and continue.

Working with the phase (Z) Pauli gate

The **Z gate** is commonly referred to as a **phase gate**, mostly because rather than rotating along the vertical axis as the X and Y gates do, the Z gate rotates along the longitude of the Hilbert space, hence the phase of the Hilbert space. This is denoted as follows:

$$Z = \sigma_3 = \begin{pmatrix} 1 & 0 \\ 0 & -1 \end{pmatrix}$$

The following truth table illustrates that the operation rotates the input around the z axis by π (180^0). If the rotation initializes from the $|0\rangle$ basis state, then phase does not change, however, if the input initializes from the $|1\rangle$ state, then the output is a phase shift of π to -$|1\rangle$. This negation is a very important feature that you will see in many quantum algorithms:

Input	Output
$|0\rangle$	$|0\rangle$
$|1\rangle$	-$|1\rangle$

Table 6.6 – Truth table of a phase shift around the x axis

Let's now create a circuit for the Z gate:

1. First, we place the qubit into a superposition state using the H gate, and then add a Z gate operator to it:

```
#Z-gate
#Create the single qubit circuit
qc = QuantumCircuit(1)
#Add an H gate to the qubit to set the qubit in
#superposition
qc.h(0)
#Add a Z gate to the qubit to rotate out of phase by п/2
qc.z(0)
#Execute the circuit and capture all the results
result, img, qsphere = execute_circuit_sv(qc)
```

2. Let's first examine the state vector results by running the following cell:

```
result
```

This prints out the state vector values of the qubit:

```
array([ 0.70710678+0.j, -0.70710678+0.j])
```

3. To draw the circuit diagram for the Z gate, run the following in a cell:

```
img
```

This displays the circuit diagram with the H gate removed, so don't think you have to include the H gate in order to use the Z gate – as mentioned earlier, the H gate was just added to illustrate the operational effect of the gate:

Figure 6.10 – Circuit diagram with a Z gate

4. To view the QSphere representation, run the following in a cell:

```
qsphere
```

The QSphere, as you can see, has an equal probability of being $|0\rangle$ and $|1\rangle$, however, the $|1\rangle$ state you see is out of phase by π, as illustrated in the following output:

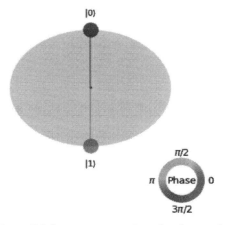

Figure 6.11 – Z gate QSphere representation after first applying an H gate

As you can see in the preceding diagram, the Z gate provides a way to perform a phase shift on a qubit, causing the state of the qubit to change its sign from positive to negative. If you want to see this for yourself, then try the following.

Recall the code you ran earlier to execute an X gate in the *Applying the Not (X) Pauli gate* section. In that example, we started with the qubit initially at the basis state $|0\rangle$, and we then applied an X gate that resulted in the state $|1\rangle$. Now, add another line after adding the X gate and include the Z gate. You'll notice that the result is the same $|1\rangle$, only now you'll notice that the state result is negative. I'll leave it to you to try it out for yourself and observe the difference.

Having the ability to negate a state vector is also very useful in many quantum algorithms. This is often referred to as a phase kick, which we will cover in *Chapter 13, Understanding Quantum Algorithms*.

Let's move on to the next section where we will discuss **phase gates**. Phase gates are what we use to map $|1\rangle$ to $e^{i\phi}|1\rangle$. This does not have an effect on the probability of measuring a $|0\rangle$ or a $|1\rangle$, however it does affect the phase of the quantum state. This may not make sense just yet, but once you start learning about phase kickback and other algorithms that leverage phase shifts, it will be very clear. For now, let's learn about the gates that operate the various phase shifts on a qubit.

Applying the S gate

The **S gate** is like that of a Z gate, where the only difference is the amount by which the state vector is rotating. For the S gate, that rotation is $\pi/2$. The matrix representation of the S gate is described here:

$$S = \begin{pmatrix} 1 & 0 \\ 0 & e^{i\frac{\pi}{\sqrt{2}}} \end{pmatrix}$$

The following truth table illustrates that the operation rotates the input around the z-axis by $\pi/2$ (180^0), hence if the input is $|0\rangle$, then the output is a phase shift of $e^{i\frac{\pi}{\sqrt{2}}}|1\rangle$:

Input	Output
$|0\rangle$	$|0\rangle$
$|1\rangle$	$e^{i\frac{\pi}{\sqrt{2}}}|1\rangle$

Table 6.7 – Truth table representing phase rotation S

We will follow these steps to create a circuit with an S gate:

1. The truth table is best illustrated by placing the vector onto the x axis first, we will add an H gate first before appending the S gate. Also, as before, the circuit diagram will only contain the S gate and not the added H gate:

```
#S-gate
#Create the single qubit circuit
qc = QuantumCircuit(1)
#Add an H gate to the qubit to drop the vector onto the
#X-axis
qc.h(0)
#Add an S gate to the qubit
qc.s(0)
#Execute the circuit and capture all the results
result, img, qsphere = execute_circuit_sv(qc)
```

2. Let's first examine the state vector results by running the following cell:

```
result
```

This prints out the state vector values of the qubit:

```
array([ 0.70710678+0.j        , -0.        +0.70710678j])
```

3. To draw the circuit diagram for the S gate, run the following in a cell:

```
img
```

This displays the circuit diagram with the **S** gate added to the qubit, as shown in the following diagram:

Figure 6.12 – Circuit with a S gate

4. To view the QSphere representation, run the following in a cell:

```
qsphere
```

The QSphere, as you can see, has an equal probability of being $|0\rangle$ and $|1\rangle$ with a phase shift of **π/2**:

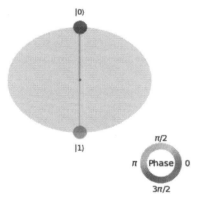

Figure 6.13 – S gate, π/2 phase rotation on the QSphere

As the S gate is a set rotation around the positive Z axis by π/2, we will now see how to rotate in the opposite direction by π/2.

Applying the S† (dagger) gate

The S† **gate** is the exact same as the S gate, only it rotates in the opposite, or negative, direction. Hence the results are the same, only negated. The matrix representation illustrates this by including the negative in the phase shift:

$$S^\dagger = \begin{pmatrix} 1 & 0 \\ 0 & e^{-i\frac{\pi}{\sqrt{2}}} \end{pmatrix}$$

The following truth table illustrates that the operation rotates the input around the z axis by $-\pi/2$ (-180°). As with the S gate, if the input is the $|0\rangle$ state, then the output is $|0\rangle$, but if the input is the $|1\rangle$ state, the output is a phase rotation in the negative direction:

Input	Output
$|0\rangle$	$|0\rangle$
$|1\rangle$	$e^{-i\frac{\pi}{\sqrt{2}}}|1\rangle$

Table 6.8 – Truth table representation of phase gate $S^\dagger$

This is best illustrated by placing the qubit into a superposition first with an H gate. We then create a circuit diagram for S† gate by using these steps:

1. We will add an H gate first before appending the S† (sdg) gate. Also, as before, the circuit diagram will only contain the S† gate and not the added H gate:

```
#Sdg-gate
#Create the single qubit circuit
qc = QuantumCircuit(1)
#Add an H gate to the qubit to drop the vector onto the
#X-axis
qc.h(0)
#Add an S† gate to the qubit
qc.sdg(0)
#Execute the circuit and capture all the results
result, img, qsphere = execute_circuit_sv(qc)
```

2. Let's first examine the state vector results by running the following cell:

```
result
```

This prints out the state vector values of the qubit:

```
array([0.70710678+0.j        , 0.        , -0.70710678j])
```

3. To draw the circuit diagram for the $S^\dagger$ gate, run the following in a cell:

```
img
```

This displays the circuit diagram with the $S^\dagger$ gate added to the qubit, as shown in the following diagram:

q —[H]—[S†]—

Figure 6.14 – Circuit with a $S^\dagger$ gate

4. To view the QSphere representation, run the following in a cell:

```
qsphere
```

The QSphere, as you can see, has an equal probability of being $|0\rangle$ and $|1\rangle$ with a phase shift of $3\pi/2$ or $-\pi/2$:

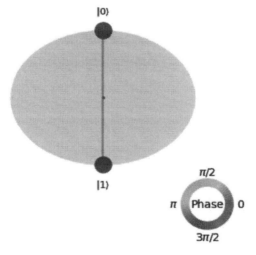

Figure 6.15 – $S^\dagger$ gate, $-\pi/2$ phase rotation on the QSphere

Now that we have created the circuit with an $S^\dagger$ gate, we will move on to the next section that will help us understand how to create a circuit with a T gate.

Using the T gate in a circuit

The **T gate** is the same as the S gate, only the rotation is $\pi/4$. The matrix representation of the gate is as follows:

$$T = \begin{pmatrix} 1 & 0 \\ 0 & e^{i\frac{\pi}{\sqrt{4}}} \end{pmatrix}$$

The following truth table illustrates that the operation rotates the input around the z axis by $\pi/4$ (45^0), hence if the input is the $|0\rangle$ state, then the output will be the same. If the input is $|1\rangle$, however, then the output would be a phase rotation of $\pi/4$:

Input	Output
$|0\rangle$	$|0\rangle$
$|1\rangle$	$e^{i\frac{\pi}{\sqrt{4}}}|1\rangle$

Table 6.9 – Truth table representation of phase gate T

As with all phase gates, it's best to begin in a superposition state so we will start by including a Hadamard gate, then we will create a circuit using the T gate, as illustrated in the following steps:

1. First, we add an H gate first before appending the T gate. Also, as before, the circuit diagram will only contain the T gate and not the added H gate:

```
#T-gate
#Create the single qubit circuit
qc = QuantumCircuit(1)
#Add an H gate to the qubit to drop the vector onto the
#X-axis
qc.h(0)
#Add a T gate to the qubit
qc.t(0)
#Execute the circuit and capture all the results
result, img, qsphere = execute_circuit_sv(qc)
```

2. We then examine the state vector results by running the following cell:

```
result
```

This prints out the state vector values of the qubit:

```
array([0.70710678+0.j , 0.5        +0.5j])
```

3. To draw the circuit diagram for the X gate, run the following in a cell:

```
img
```

This displays the circuit diagram with the **T** gate added to the qubit, as shown in the following diagram:

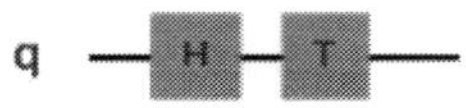

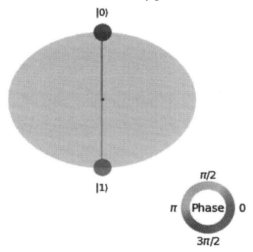

Figure 6.16 – Circuit representation of the T gate

4. To view the QSphere representation, run the following in a cell:

```
qsphere
```

The QSphere, as you can see, has rotated by phase $\pi/4$:

Figure 6.17 – T gate, $\pi/4$ phase rotation on the QSphere

Similar to the S gate, we will want to rotate in all directions, so let's take a look at rotating this gate in the opposite direction.

Working with T† (dagger) gate

The T† gate has the same phase rotation as the T gate, that is, $\pi/4$, only in the opposite direction. Its matrix representation is given as follows:

$$T^\dagger = \begin{pmatrix} 1 & 0 \\ 0 & e^{-i\frac{\pi}{\sqrt{4}}} \end{pmatrix}$$

The following truth table illustrates that the operation rotates the input around the z axis by $-\pi/4$ (-45^0), so if the input is $|0\rangle$, then the output is $|0\rangle$. If the input is $|1\rangle$, then the output is a negative rotation of $-\pi/4$:

Input	Output
$|0\rangle$	$|0\rangle$
$|1\rangle$	$e^{-i\frac{\pi}{\sqrt{4}}}|1\rangle$

Table 6.10 – Truth table representation of phase gate $T^\dagger$

This too is best illustrated by placing the vector onto the x axis first, so we will create a circuit using the $T^\dagger$ gate by following these steps:

1. First, we add an H gate before then appending the $T^\dagger$ (tdg) gate. Also, as before, the circuit diagram will only contain the $T^\dagger$ gate and not the added H gate:

```
#Tdg-gate
#Create the single qubit circuit
qc = QuantumCircuit(1)
#Add an H gate to the qubit to drop the vector onto the
#X-axis
qc.h(0)
#Add a Tdg gate to the qubit
qc.tdg(0)
#Execute the circuit and capture all the results
result, img, qsphere = execute_circuit_sv(qc)
```

2. Next, we examine the state vector results by running the following cell:

```
result
```

This prints out the state vector values of the qubit, where you will notice that the imaginary number is now negative:

```
array([0.70710678+0.j , 0.5        -0.5j])
```

3. To draw the circuit diagram for the $T^\dagger$ gate, run the following in a cell:

```
img
```

This displays the circuit diagram with the $T^\dagger$ gate added to the qubit, as shown in the following diagram:

$$q \quad \boxed{T^\dagger}$$

Figure 6.18 – Circuit representation using $T^\dagger$ gate

4. To view the QSphere representation, run the following in a cell:

```
qsphere
```

The QSphere, as you can see, has rotated the state of the qubit $-\pi/4$:

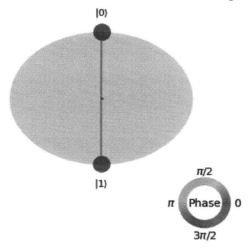

Figure 6.19 – $T^\dagger$ gate, $-\pi/4$ phase rotation on the QSphere

The preceding gates, as you might have noticed, have predetermined rotation angles from the horizontal (θ) or vertical (ϕ) axis. If you wish to specify the angle of rotation yourself by leveraging the rotation gates. The following rotation gates allow you to specify the angle by which to rotate around a given axis. Like the other gates, these rotation gates are also reversible and unitary.

Using the R_ϕ gate in a circuit

You can think of **R_ϕ gates** as your custom rotation gates. The R_ϕ gate is named after its classical-bit gate counterpart because it performs a similar operation in that if the current state is 0 or 1, then the gate will rotate from 0 to 1, and vice versa. Note that I used the term *rotate* and not *flip*. This is because visualizing the operation of the quantum gates is usually done via the QSphere.

Because of its spherical presentation, we refer to operations as rotations around the axis by $-\pi < \theta < \pi$ (we will see this clearly in the following code examples):

$$R_X(\theta) = \begin{pmatrix} \cos(\theta) & -i \cdot \sin(\theta) \\ -i \cdot \sin(\theta) & \cos(\theta) \end{pmatrix}$$

By applying a Y rotation, we get the following formula:

$$R_Y(\theta) = \begin{pmatrix} \cos(\theta) & -\sin(\theta) \\ \sin(\theta) & \cos(\theta) \end{pmatrix}$$

Finally, a Z rotation will yield the following formula:

$$R_Z(\theta) = \begin{pmatrix} e^{-i\theta} & 0 \\ 0 & e^{i\theta} \end{pmatrix}$$

We'll create a circuit using one of the rotation gates – let's go with the R_z gate:

1. First, we will rotate along the z axis by $\pi/6$. We'll be using the `math` library to `import pi`, and our friendly H gate will be applied to help illustrate the phase shift:

```
#Rz-gate
#Create the single qubit circuit
qc = QuantumCircuit(1)
#Import pi from the math library
from math import pi
#Add an H gate to help visualize phase rotation
qc.h(0)
#Add an RZ gate with an arbitrary angle theta of pi/6
qc.rz(pi/6, 0)
#Execute the circuit and capture all the results
result, img, qsphere = execute_circuit_sv(qc)
```

2. Next, we examine the state vector results by running the following cell:

```
result
```

This prints out the state vector values of the qubit:

```
array([0.70710678+0.j        , 0.61237244+0.35355339j])
```

3. To draw the circuit diagram for the R$_z$ gate, run the following in a cell:

This displays the circuit diagram with the **R$_z$** gate added to the qubit, as shown in the following diagram:

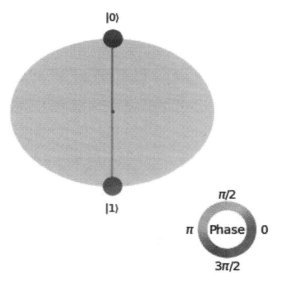

Figure 6.20 – Circuit representation using R$_z$ gate

4. To view the QSphere representation, run the following in a cell:

```
qsphere
```

The QSphere, as you can see, has rotated the state $\pi/6$:

Figure 6.21 – R$_z$ gate QSphere rotated $\pi/6$

These rotation gates help us provide specific gate rotations around each axis. There are more universal gates that allow us to create these other gates using only one of these universal gates, so let's review those next.

Applying the universal U_x gates

U_x **gates**, as mentioned earlier, are used in order to define a universal quantum system where you would need to ensure that the quantum system adheres to a certain criterion, he most popular of which is the **DiVincenzo criteria**, which as part of its list states that it should have a universal set of quantum gates.

We discussed how, in a classical system, both NOR and NAND gates are considered classical universal gates. In a quantum system, the U_1, U_2, and U_3 gates are defined as universal gates, due to their ability to provide up to 2 degrees of freedom to rotate about the Hilbert space of a qubit. Each gate has parameter fields that determine by how much the state vector should move along the given axis. Let's look at them individually first and then we'll apply each gate to a qubit to examine the results. Let's start with the U_3 gate.

The U_3 **gate** has three parameters that are applied as rotations on all axes, that is, the x axis, y axis, and z axis, respectively. The matrix representation of the U_3 gate is defined as follows:

$$U_{3\,(\theta,\phi,\lambda)} = \begin{pmatrix} \cos(\theta/2) & -e^{i\lambda}\sin(\theta/2) \\ e^{i\phi}\sin(\theta/2) & e^{i(\phi+\lambda)}\cos(\theta/2) \end{pmatrix}$$

In the preceding equation, θ, ϕ, and λ are the angles of rotation in radians around the x axis, y axis, and z axis, respectively. Note that for the U gate to remain a unitary operation, that is, $U^\dagger U = I$, the angles must be confined to the range $0 \le \theta \le \pi$, and $0 \le \phi \le 2\pi$. We can also see these ranges in the U_3 matrix, where these values lay in the arguments of the matrix, which leaves the phase λ to also have a range of $0 \le \lambda \le 2\pi$.

Let's create a circuit that implements the U_3 gate:

1. First, we will create a single-qubit circuit and apply the U_3 gate to it with each angle set to $\pi/2$. We'll reuse our state vector helper function, `execute_circuit_sv`, so we can extract the state vector results, and the QSphere to visualize the state vector:

```python
#U3-gate
from math import pi
#Create a single qubit circuit
qc = QuantumCircuit(1)
#Add a U3 gate and rotate all parameters by pi/2, and
#apply it to the qubit
qc.u3(pi/2, pi/2, pi/2, 0)
#Execute the circuit and capture all the results
result, img, qsphere = execute_circuit_sv(qc)
```

The result value we shall see is set to the following:

```
array([7.07106781e-01+0.j    , 4.32978028e-17+0.70710678j])
```

Note that for convenience, I replaced the value `4.32978028e-17` from the results with a `0`, because the number is too small and insignificant.

2. The expected circuit diagram for U_3 is as follows, with the parameters listed at the bottom:

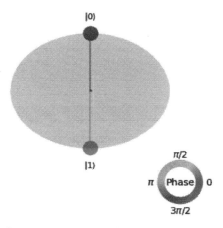

Figure 6.22 – The U_3 gate set with the rotation parameters set at $\pi/2$

The QSphere representation is shown as follows:

Figure 6.23 – The QSphere representation of the U_3 gate set with all parameters to $\pi/2$

The U_3 gate is a superset gate to both the U_2 and U_1 gates, in that the parameters passed into the U_2 and U_1 gates would populate the respective parameters in the U_3 gate. The U_3 gate is then used by the transpiler to execute the circuit. As we describe the gates, we will decompose the circuit to see how this is done.

The next gate is the U_2 gate, which has two parameters that are applied as a rotation to the ϕ and λ values of the U_3 gate, respectively. The matrix representation of the U_2 gate is defined as follows:

$$U_{2(\phi,\lambda)}$$
$$= 1/\sqrt{2}\begin{pmatrix} 1 & e^{-i\lambda} \\ e^{i\phi} & e^{i(\phi+\lambda)} \end{pmatrix}$$

In the preceding equation, ϕ and λ are the angles of rotation in radians, respectively.

One very important thing to note here is that the U_2 gate defaults the U_3 parameter θ to $\pi/2$ as described in the U_3 gate description.

Let's update the code we used to implement the U_3 gate earlier with a U_2 gate:

1. We'll begin by importing NumPy to provide some math variables and create a quantum circuit that implements the U_2 gate with rotation parameters of `pi/2`:

```
#U2-gate
from math import pi
#Create a single qubit circuit
qc = QuantumCircuit(1)
#Add a U2 gate and rotate all parameters by pi/2, and
#apply it to the qubit
qc.u2(pi/2, pi/2, 0)
#Execute the circuit and capture all the results
result, img, qsphere = execute_circuit_sv(qc)
```

The resulting value we shall see is the same as the U_3 gate, as expected, since we applied the same angles for ϕ and λ. Try running the circuit with different angles for each:

```
array([7.07106781e-01+0.j, 0+0.70710678j])
```

2. The expected circuit diagram for the circuit we executed for U_2 should include the parameters, just like the U_3 gate. If you changed the parameters, those changes would reflect in the resulting `img` variable:

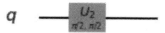

Figure 6.24 – The U_2 gate set with the rotation parameters at $\pi/2$

3. As mentioned earlier, we can decompose the circuit to the core gates that it uses to create the circuit. Let's do that now to see how the U_2 gate is decomposed. In a new cell, enter the following, which will decompose the quantum circuit we created, and then draw the circuit representation for us:

```
qc_decomposed = qc.decompose()
qc_decomposed.draw()
```

This results in the following circuit:

Figure 6.25 – The circuit decomposition of the U_2 gate down to the base gate, U_3

As you can see from the result of decomposing the circuit, the U_2 gate is actually a U_3 gate with the θ value default to $\pi/2$, and the ϕ and λ values are set to what you had defined in the code.

As we have used the U_2 gate in the circuit, we will now learn about the U_1 gate.

The **U_1 gate** has one parameter applied as a rotation to the z axis, or λ. Because of this, it is similar to the R_Z gate and the matrix representation is also the same as the Z gate:

$$U_{1\,(\lambda)} = \begin{pmatrix} 1 & 0 \\ 0 & e^{\lambda} \end{pmatrix}$$

In the preceding equation, λ is the angle of rotation in radians around the z axis, also referred to as a **phase rotation**.

Let's create a circuit for the U_1 gate. The code that we will use to implement the U_1 gate will be a little different this time:

1. As this is a phase rotation as the Z gate, we will, as before, include a Hadamard gate to help visualize the effect of the U_1 gate, and apply a rotation parameter of $\pi/2$:

```
#U1-gate
from math import pi
#Create a two qubit circuit
qc = QuantumCircuit(1)
qc.h(0)
#Add an U1 gate and rotate by pi/2
qc.u1(pi/2, 0)
#Execute the circuit and capture all the results
result, img, qsphere = execute_circuit_sv(qc)
```

If we examine the result, we should see the same array output as we did in the Z gate, if we look at the circuit diagram (img), we will see the Hadamard and U_1 gates. Notice that the U_1 gate also provides the angle that was passed in as $\pi/2$:

Figure 6.26 – The U_1 gate set with the rotation parameter $\pi/2$

2. If you examine the QSphere result, you should also see that it is the same as a Z gate rotation of $\pi/2$ after the Hadamard gate had been applied:

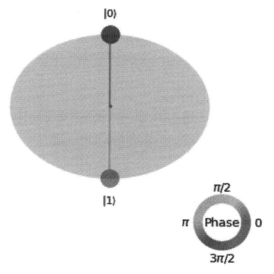

Figure 6.27 – QSphere representation of a U_1 rotation of $\pi/2$

3. Since the U_1 gate is a single rotation around the z axis, this gate can also be used to create the Z, S, S†, T, and T† gates by simply setting the parameter to their respective angles of π, $\pi/2$, $-\pi/2$, $\pi/4$, and $-\pi/4$.

Now, let's repeat the decompose code we ran earlier for the U_2 gate to this circuit to see how the U_3 gate implements the U_1 gate:

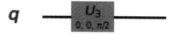

Figure 6.28 – The circuit decomposition of the U_1 gate down to the base gate, U_3

Notice here that the θ value of the U_3 gate is set to 0, rather than $\pi/2$, as was the default on the U_2 gate.

In this section, we learned about single-qubit gates, along with the Pauli matrix and its four gates (I, X, Y, and Z). We also reviewed the Hadamard gate. We also learned about phase gates such as the S, T, and R_ϕ gates and their dagger forms.

Now you know that single-qubit gates provide many ways to create a complex linear combination of their basis states, but manipulation of a single qubit alone is not enough to carry out the functionality that most quantum algorithms require. One such example is **quantum entanglement**. This is where multi-qubit gates come into play. Let's learn about those in the next section.

Understanding multi-qubit gates

Two or more qubits can combine their states by their **tensor product**, or sometimes referred to as the **Kronecker product**. For convenience, I have provided the vector representation here:

$$|a\rangle \otimes |b\rangle = |ab\rangle$$

For two qubits, namely, $|0\rangle = \begin{pmatrix} 1 \\ 0 \end{pmatrix}$, and $|1\rangle = \begin{pmatrix} 0 \\ 1 \end{pmatrix}$, and their complex amplitudes v_0 and v_1 respectively, their tensor product would equate as follows:

$$v_{00}|00\rangle + v_{01}|01\rangle$$
$$+ v_{10}|10\rangle + v_{11}|11\rangle$$
$$= \begin{pmatrix} v_{00} \\ v_{01} \\ v_{10} \\ v_{11} \end{pmatrix} = |\psi\rangle$$

The vector that results by applying the tensor product is the basis state of the two qubits, $|\psi\rangle$.

In this section, we will discuss the multi-qubit gates and how they operate on the qubits similarly to how single-qubit gates do, which includes them being unitary and reversible. In the following equation, a multi-qubit gate, represented by a matrix U, is multiplied by a quantum state vector $|\psi_1\rangle$ to produce the resulting quantum state vector $|\psi_2\rangle$:

$$U|\psi_0\rangle = |\psi_2\rangle$$

To keep the descriptions and examples uniform, the following descriptions of the multi-qubit gates will be presented the same way as the single-qubit gates. We will create a new helper function that is similar to what we used earlier for single-qubit circuits. The helper function will have a few differences, the first of which will be the `simulator` that we will be using to execute the circuits:

```
# Will execute the circuit on the qasm simulator
# Returns results, circuit diagram, and histogram
def execute_circuit(quantum_circuit):
    #Create a qasm simulator
    simulator = Aer.get_backend('qasm_simulator')
    #Execute the circuit on the simulator
    result = execute(quantum_circuit, simulator,
    shots=1024).result()
    #Get the result counts
    results = result.get_counts(quantum_circuit)
    #Draw the circuit diagram
    circuit_diagram = quantum_circuit.draw()
    #Create a histogram of the results
    histogram = plot_histogram(results)
    #Return the results, circuit diagram, and histogram
    return results, circuit_diagram, histogram
```

We will switch from using the state vector simulator to using the qasm simulator. **Qasm**, short for **Quantum Assembly language** and pronounced *kazm*, is a programming language used to describe the functions that make up quantum circuits and operations. It is the programming language that Qiskit is built upon as a **Python** library.

The purpose as to why we are switching over to the Qasm simulator is not that we can't use the state vector simulator, it's primarily so we can observe some of the interesting characteristics of our circuit and the gates. For those who wish to use the state vector simulator, not to worry. There will be some challenges in the *Questions* section, at the end of this chapter, that will allow you to use it.

Another difference you will see is that we are no longer using the QSphere to visualize the quantum states. Rather, we will replace the QSphere output with a `histogram` plot of the result counts. For each circuit we will be creating, we will include more than one qubit, as these multi-qubit gates all operate on two or more qubits.

Now that we have our helper function, go ahead and run it, and let's move on to the next set of gates, the **multi-qubit gates**. These include the following:

- The **CNOT** gate
- The **Toffoli** gate
- The **Swap** gate

We will learn about these gates in the following sections.

Learning about the CNOT multi-qubit gate

The **CNOT gate**, often referred to as a **Control-NOT** gate, is similar to the **XOR** classical-bit gate. The CNOT gate is composed of two parts.

The first part is the **Control** , which is connected to one of the qubits, and is what triggers the CNOT gate to perform an operation on the other qubit connected to the other end of the CNOT gate, the **Target**.

The Target is an operation that will be performed on the other qubit; in this case, it's a **NOT** operation. Recall from the previous section on single-qubit gates that the NOT gate rotates the qubit about the x axis by $\pi/2$. The CNOT gate is one of the more commonly used multi-qubit gates as it is how qubits get entangled.

The CNOT gate is also described as a **Control-X (CX)** gate since the target is often coded as an X operation. You will see this CX gate convention when running the following example.

The matrix representation of a CNOT gate is a *4 x 4* matrix due to the tensor product of two qubits as illustrated here:

$$CNOT = \begin{bmatrix} 1 & 0 & 0 & 0 \\ 0 & 1 & 0 & 0 \\ 0 & 0 & 0 & 1 \\ 0 & 0 & 1 & 0 \end{bmatrix}$$

Notice that the top left *2 x 2* quadrant of the CNOT matrix represents an Identity matrix, I, and the bottom right *2 x 2* quadrant represents the **X** matrix.

The following truth table illustrates that when the Control qubit (the left side of the input vector) is 0, there is no change to the target qubit (the right side of the input vector). When the Control qubit is set to 1, then the Target qubit operation is enabled and therefore rotates the target qubit around the x axis by π (that is, 180^0):

Input	Output
$|00\rangle$	$|00\rangle$
$|01\rangle$	$|01\rangle$
$|10\rangle$	$|11\rangle$
$|11\rangle$	$|10\rangle$

Table 6.11 – Truth table representation of CNOT gate

Let's now create a circuit, add a CNOT gate, and execute it:

1. We'll begin by creating a two-qubit quantum circuit and applying a Hadamard gate on the first qubit, and a CNOT gate on the two qubits, where the Control is set to the first qubit and the Target is set to the second qubit:

```
#CNOT-gate
#Create a two qubit circuit
qc = QuantumCircuit(2)
#Add an H gate to the qubit
qc.h(0)
#Add an CNOT gate where, control = first, target = second
#qubit
qc.cx(0,1)
#Measure all qubits and send results to classical bits
qc.measure_all()
#Execute the circuit and capture all the results
result, img, histogram = execute_circuit_sv(qc)
```

2. Then we examine the state vector results by running the following cell:

```
result
```

This prints out the state vector values of the qubit:

```
array([1.+0.j, 0.+0.j, 0.+0.j, 0.+0.j, 0.+0.j, 0.+0.j,
0.+0.j, 0.+0.j])
```

3. To draw the circuit diagram for the CNOT gate, run the following in a cell:

    img

    This following circuit diagram illustrates the CNOT gate. Note we added an H gate and measurements for the sake of the results, but the CNOT gate in the following illustration is for convenience:

    Figure 6.29 – Circuit representation using a CNOT gate

4. To view the histogram results with the counts after executing the previous circuit, enter the following into a cell:

    histogram

    The following illustrates the results including an H gate. The following graph shows the probabilities of the results being either 00 or 11:

    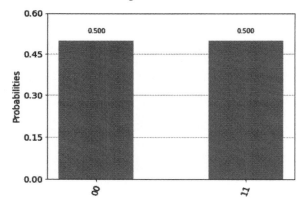

    Figure 6.30 – Histogram representation of CNOT results from circuit

The results from the previous gates are just a handful, as you can see from some of the custom qubits, such as the R_x gate, or CNOT, which allow you to rotate into any state on the QSphere for each qubit.

Let's now look at operators that are not reversible, yet still quantum. Not to worry, I am not contradicting myself from an earlier statement that requires quantum operators to be unitary and therefore reversible.

In the following section, I will clarify what this means. There are other Control gates which implement other operations, such as, **Control-Y (CY)**, **Control-Z (CZ)**, **Control-H (CH)**, and more. These gates all share the same characteristics of the CNOT (**CX, Control-X**) gate, in that, they have a Source and Target. The main difference, as you can imagine, is the operation that the Target would follow. For the CNOT gate, the Target would operate with a X gate, and naturally a Control-Y gate would operate a Y gate on the Target qubit. Try out a few for yourself and see how the results differ. Notice that the operations will be the same as if you ran the single gate to the Target gate.

The last multi-qubit gate we will focus on, which is also used in a variety of quantum algorithms, is the **Toffoli** gate.

Applying the Toffoli multi-qubit gate

The **Toffoli** gate is named after Tommaso Toffoli, an Italian American professor in computer and electrical engineering at Boston University. This gate is very similar to that of the multi-qubit Control gates mentioned earlier, only this gate has multiple Controls and a single Target. To simplify the description of multi control gates, they are written out in the following format, **CCX**. This is to indicate it is a dual controlled Control-Not gate, and a **CCCX** is a triple controlled Control-Not gate.

The general matrix representation of a Toffoli gate is an 8×8 matrix because of the tensor product of three qubits, as illustrated in the following matrix. Notice that the first three diagonal 2×2 matrix blocks are the Identity matrix and the last 2×2 matrix (bottom right) is a NOT gate representation that flips the qubit. Note that the matrix for the Toffoli gate in Qiskit is slightly different but still produces the same results:

$$\text{Toffoli} = \begin{bmatrix} 1 & 0 & 0 & 0 & 0 & 0 & 0 & 0 \\ 0 & 1 & 0 & 0 & 0 & 0 & 0 & 0 \\ 0 & 0 & 1 & 0 & 0 & 0 & 0 & 0 \\ 0 & 0 & 0 & 1 & 0 & 0 & 0 & 0 \\ 0 & 0 & 0 & 0 & 1 & 0 & 0 & 0 \\ 0 & 0 & 0 & 0 & 0 & 1 & 0 & 0 \\ 0 & 0 & 0 & 0 & 0 & 0 & 0 & 1 \\ 0 & 0 & 0 & 0 & 0 & 0 & 1 & 0 \end{bmatrix}$$

Let's run this gate to see the results of it on our quantum circuit:

1. We'll begin by creating a three-qubit quantum circuit and applying a CCX (Toffoli) gate where the first two qubits are the control qubits, and the third qubit is the target qubit:

```
#Toffoli (CCX)-gate
from math import pi
```

```
#Create a three qubit circuit
qc = QuantumCircuit(3)
#Add the Toffoli gate (CCX)
qc.ccx(0,1,2)
#Execute the circuit and capture all the results
result, img, qsphere = execute_circuit_sv(qc)
```

The result of executing this circuit will be no surprise, and consists of 8 possible states since we are running everything on three-qubit circuit, which means 2^3 basis states:

```
array([1.+0.j, 0.+0.j, 0.+0.j, 0.+0.j, 0.+0.j, 0.+0.j,
       0.+0.j, 0.+0.j])
```

2. As the QSphere only represents single-qubit information, it does not present multi-qubits, particularly when they are entangled. So, in this case, the results from the QSphere visualizations will not be proper presentations, so we will ignore them.

    The circuit diagram for the Toffoli gate is as follows:

Figure 6.31 – Circuit representation of a Toffoli (CCX) gate

3. Let's see how the base gates are used to create this three-qubit gate. In a new cell, run the decompose function of the quantum circuit:

```
qc_decomposed = qc.decompose()
qc_decomposed.draw()
```

This will result in the following illustration of all the gates needed to create a single Toffoli gate:

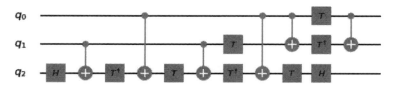

Figure 6.32 – Gates necessary to create a Toffoli (CCX) gate

Needless to say, this looks very complicated. You can see that the use of the various single-qubit and multi-qubit gates used to represent this one gate are quite complex. If this is run on a near-term device on qubits with low coherence times, you are most certainly going to have some effects related to noise. In this example, you can see the use of H, CNOT, and $T^\dagger$ gates. There are other multi-qubit gates that leverage gates in order to operate.

Let's look at a gate we would use to swap information between one qubit and another.

Using the Swap gate in a circuit

The **swap gate** is used to swap two qubit values. The matrix representation of the swap gate is defined as follows:

$$\text{SWAP} = \begin{bmatrix} 1 & 0 & 0 & 0 \\ 0 & 0 & 1 & 0 \\ 0 & 1 & 0 & 0 \\ 0 & 0 & 0 & 1 \end{bmatrix}$$

Let's create a circuit and implement this by swapping two qubits:

1. We will set the first qubit to the $|0\rangle$ state, and the second qubit to the $|1\rangle$ state, then we will invoke a swap between the two using the swap gate and verify the results of each qubit:

```
#Swap-gate
from math import pi
#Create a two qubit circuit
qc = QuantumCircuit(2)
#Qubit 0 is initialized to |0> state
#Prepare qubit 1 to the |1> state
qc.x(1)
#Now swap gates
qc.swap(0,1)
#Execute the circuit and capture all the results
result, img, qsphere = execute_circuit_sv(qc)
```

By viewing the resulting diagram of the circuit (img) you will see a circuit diagram of the swap gate as shown here, just after the X gate we included for comparison:

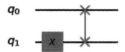

Figure 6.33 – Circuit diagram of an X gate followed by a Swap gate

2. Before viewing the QSphere result for each qubit, let's take a moment to review what we expect to see. Our two qubits are first initialized to the $|0\rangle$ state, and we then applied an X gate to the second qubit (q_1) to change its state to $|1\rangle$. Finally, we added a Swap gate to swap the value of q_0 and q_1, which would result in $q_0 = |1\rangle$ and $q_1 = |0\rangle$. Let's see the results:

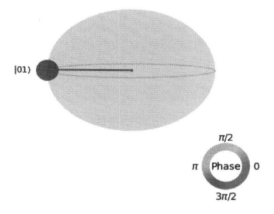

Figure 6.34 – State vector results after applying the Swap gate

Excellent! The results, as we can see in the previous diagram, show that the state vectors for both qubits are set as expected with $q_0 = |1\rangle$ and $q_1 = |0\rangle$.

In this section, we have learned about multi-qubit gates, namely, CNOT and Toffoli gates. We also learned about an extra gate, that is, the Swap gate.

Now that we are familiar with single-qubit and multi-qubit gates, let's review the non-reversible operators.

Understanding non-reversible operators

What is meant by a **non-reversible operator** is that if we apply these operators on a qubit(s), and apply the operator again on the same qubits, then the results will not return the qubits to the same state that they had prior to applying the operator.

This section will cover the non-reversible operators and the reasons why they are just as important as the other operators discussed previously.

Measurement is an operator that instructs the quantum system to measure the quantum state of the system. Before we dive into how we include the measurement instruction to our quantum circuits, let's first define what is meant by measuring the quantum state of the system.

We know from quantum mechanics that the information about a quantum system is impossible to access, specifically the measurement of the qubit's complex amplitudes. For example, let's say that we have a qubit in a superposition state $|\psi\rangle$, where the complex amplitudes sum up to 1:

$$\sum_{j=0}^{k-1} \alpha_j \, |j\rangle = 1$$

A measurement of the preceding cannot provide the complex amplitude information in α, due to the aforementioned constraint upon the system from the principles of quantum mechanics. Instead, what the measurement of a qubit returns is the basis $|j\rangle$ with a probability $|\alpha_j|^2$ of the state $|\psi\rangle$ in the standard basis.

We viewed an example of this earlier when describing the Hadamard gate. When we set the qubit in a complex linear combination of $\alpha|0\rangle$ and $\beta|1\rangle$, where α and β are the complex amplitudes of the basis states, the measurement result was based on the probability $|\alpha|^2$ of measuring $|0\rangle$ and $|\beta|^2$ of measuring a $|1\rangle$, which for a Hadamard gate results in 50%, or $|1/\sqrt{2}|^2$.

An important thing to note about measuring the state of a system is that once you measure it, the information of the system is then lost. What this means is that by measuring the qubit(s) the state will collapse into one of the two basis states, $|0\rangle$ or $|1\rangle$, based on the amplitude of the qubit. After the measurement, you no longer have the information contained in α and β to do anything else.

If you were to try to measure again, the result will be the same as the first measurement. Therefore, measurement is a non-reversible operator in that if you apply it again, it will not produce the quantum state that the qubit was in prior to the measurement.

Once the measurement is completed, the result is then sent over to the classical bit that will return the information back to the classical system. Now that we understand how the measurement works and what the results of the measurements are, let's run some code to see it at work!

In this example, we will create a simple two-qubit circuit that include a both a Hadamard and a CNOT gate:

1. First, we will add the measurement function `measure_all()` at the end of the circuit, which will automatically map the results of measuring the qubits to their respective classical bits. We will also add Hadamard and CNOT gates:

```
#CNOT-gate
#Create a two qubit circuit
qc = QuantumCircuit(2)
#Add an H gate to the qubit
qc.h(0)
#Add an CNOT gate where, control = first, target = second
#qubit
qc.cx(0,1)
#Measure qubits and map to classical bits
qc.measure_all()
#Execute the circuit and capture all the results
result, img, histogram = execute_circuit(qc)
```

2. Let's now view our results by entering the following in a new cell:

```
result
```

This will output the result counts for each measurement, recall that we set the number of shots to be executed in our helper function, so the total counts should equal the number of shots we declared. The following results, of course, will vary as they are random each time you execute the circuit. Therefore, your results may differ from those listed here:

```
{'11': 484, '00': 540}
```

3. Our helper function also included the `histogram` plot, which helps visualize the preceding results. To view the histogram plot, enter the following into the next cell:

```
histogram
```

The output is the following histogram plot:

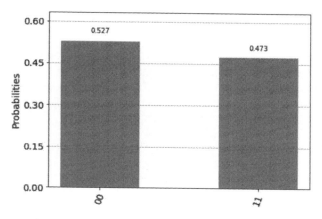

Figure 6.35 – Histogram chart of measured results

4. Now let's see what the circuit looks like with the measurement operators added. Run the following in another cell:

```
img
```

At the end of the circuit illustrated in the following diagram, you will see that the measurement operators were added to all qubits. You'll see that the labels for the classical bits are titled **measure**, and the qubits are mapped to their respective bits labeled by the index numbers where the measurement terminates onto the classical bit:

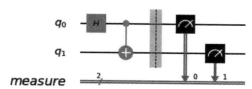

Figure 6.36 – Measurement operators added to a quantum circuit

The barrier is added there just for convenience to visualize where the circuit operations end and where the measurement will commence.

5. The `measure_all()` function is a nice and convenient way to apply measurement operators to your quantum circuit. You can also apply a `measurement` operator to each qubit separately and at separate times, or you can arrange the mapping using a list if you wish to interchange the assignment of a qubit to a classical bit. Let's rewrite our function again, only this time we'll add the measurement operators individually for the first circuit (`qc1`) and then do the same with the second circuit (`qc2`) using a list:

```
#Measurement operator
#Create two separate two-qubit, and two-classical bit
#circuits
qc1 = QuantumCircuit(2,2)
qc2 = QuantumCircuit(2,2)
#In the first circuit (qc1), measure qubits individually
qc1.measure(0,0)
qc1.measure(1,1)
#In the second circuit (qc2) measure using a list
qc2.measure([0,1],[0,1])
#Execute the circuit and capture all the results
result, img, histogram = execute_circuit(qc1)
result2, img2, histogram2 = execute_circuit(qc2)
```

After executing the code, display the two images (`img` and `img2`) in separate cells and notice that both results are equal.

In this section, you learned about non-reversible operators. We also created a simple two-qubit circuit using a measurement operator.

Summary

In this chapter, you learned all the various ways you can operate on both single and multiple qubits. The operations provide various vector states that each qubit can rotate into. You also learned how to visualize the gates on a circuit and learned to decompose them down to universal gates so you can realize the information that is passed onto the quantum system.

You have now understood how these gates operate on qubits. You now have skills that will greatly help you understand how gates are used in many quantum algorithms to position the vectors in the Hilbert space of each qubit to help resolve various problems.

In the next chapter, we will learn about the **Quantum Information Science Kit** (**Qiskit**, pronounced *kiss-kit* (depending on who you ask, it may also be pronounced *kwis-kit*). Qiskit provides, besides many of the objects and functions we have been using so far to manipulate qubits, other functionality that helps to create quantum algorithms, to mitigate against noise found in near-term devices, and to produce quantum algorithms for users to leverage without having to learn about them at the gate level.

Questions

1. For the multi-qubit gates, try flipping the Source and Target. Do you see a difference when you decompose the circuit?

2. Decompose all the gates for both single and multi-qubit circuits. What do you notice about how the universal gates are constructed?

3. Implement the Toffoli gate where the target is the center qubit of a three-qubit circuit.

4. Decompose the Toffoli gate. How many gates in total are used to construct it?

5. Apply the Toffoli gate along with a Hadamard gate to a state vector simulator and compare the results to that from the Qasm simulator. What differences do you see and why?

6. If you wanted to sort three qubits in the opposite direction, which gates would you use and in which order?

7. Given a three-qubit circuit, how would you go about swapping the first and third qubits?

8. Given a three-qubit circuit, how would you set the second qubit as the Target of a Toffoli gate?

Section 3: Algorithms, Noise, and Other Strange Things in Quantum World

In this final section, we will describe the various quantum algorithms and their types, including things that appear strange to us in classical systems but are typical of quantum systems. This includes things such as noise, decoherence, affinity, and quantum volume, all of which can drastically affect the outcomes of your experiment.

You will also learn about Qiskit here, which has a library of tools that can be used to address, and at times avoid, many of these problems.

This section comprises the following chapters:

- *Chapter 7, Introducing Qiskit and its Elements*
- *Chapter 8, Programming with Qiskit Terra*
- *Chapter 9, Monitoring and Optimizing Quantum Circuits*
- *Chapter 10, Executing Circuits Using Qiskit Aer*

7
Introducing Qiskit and its Elements

In this chapter, you will learn about the **Quantum Information Science Kit (Qiskit)** and all its elements in order to develop and implement various quantum computing programs. Qiskit (pronounced kiss-kit) is comprised of four elements, each of which has a specific functionality and role that can be leveraged based on the areas that you wish to experiment with. These elements are **Terra (Earth)**, **Aer (Air)**, **Ignis (Fire)**, and **Aqua (Water)**. This chapter will also discuss how to contribute to the open source community and the development of each of the elements, as well as how to connect to other like-minded developers via the **Qiskit community**.

The following topics will be covered in this chapter:

- Understanding quantum and classical system interconnections
- Understanding Qiskit basics and its elements
- Installing and configuring Qiskit on your local machine
- Getting support from the Qiskit community

First, we'll introduce the Qiskit package, which is used for developing quantum algorithms, creating noise models, running experiments on real devices, and visualizing results. Each of these elements has a certain purpose or domain for the various needs of developing quantum algorithms. We'll also discuss ways in which you can contribute to the Qiskit community and its open source development. You will also learn how to benefit from Qiskit's community support and educational community.

Finally, you'll learn how each element provides you with the resources you need to create optimal algorithms. Details of each element will be discussed in future chapters, but for now, let's understand how each are linked together and their area of focus.

Technical requirements

Since **Qiskit** is a **Python** package, you need to be familiar with Python programming. Knowledge of GitHub is also recommended as we will review how to contribute to the Qiskit open source project, which is hosted on GitHub. Having **Agile** and **open source development** practice is also recommended, but not required. Here is the source code used throughout this book: `https://github.com/PacktPublishing/Learn-Quantum-Computing-with-Python-and-IBM-Quantum-Experience`.

Please visit the following link to check the CiA videos: `https://bit.ly/3o5M80`

Understanding quantum and classical system interconnections

In this section, we'll review how the most quantum computational systems are integrated with classical systems. Since quantum computers do not have ways to store qubit information or any sort of quantum storage, there is a dependency on classical systems to provide persistent storage for information that is sent to or received from a quantum computer.

Since most data sources, whether they are from data repositories or remote sensors, originate from classical sources, there is a need to prepare the data to be used in a quantum system. Likewise, the results from the quantum systems need to be returned, not in a quantum state but in binary form, so that they can be read back to a classical system for any post-processing that's required.

This hybrid or interconnectivity between classic systems and quantum systems is what we will be reviewing in this section so that you understand how both systems work together to provide you with the most optimal results.

Reviewing the quantum programming process

If you have worked on some of the previous chapters, then you would have noticed that we used Qiskit to create some sample circuits that we used to describe some quantum concepts. As Python developers, you would have also noticed that Qiskit is functionally no different than using any other Python package, such as **NumPy**, **scikit-learn**, and so on. How we use it within our Python notebooks is also the same as we would use any other package, where we can import the complete package or just a subset of classes and functions. By having the Qiskit modules available through Python, this allows us to integrate our classical algorithms and applications into a quantum system. Leveraging the libraries available in Qiskit to create quantum circuits that execute on quantum devices from a classical development environment such as Python makes integration very seamless and straightforward.

Qiskit, much like most other open source projects, is easy to set up, both as a package with Python or as a branch or a fork if you're just acting as a contributor. It's very compact and does not require much with respect to resources on local machines in order to run. Since most of the devices and heavy lifting is offloaded onto the **IBM Cloud** infrastructure, which is connected to all the quantum devices, resources such as the electronic components necessary to send *microwave pulses* to the qubits, the large **dilution refrigerators** that are used to cool the qubits to **15 millikelvin**, and many other components and tasks are taken care of by quantum systems such as **IBM Q System One**.

This is a good thing because those dilution refrigerators, which look like chandeliers, are quite large. The infrastructure takes care of many things, including the queuing process, to ensure the projects that you, and hundreds of thousands of other users from around the world, can execute on the devices in a timely and non-chaotic manner. In fact, during the fourth anniversary of the IBM Quantum systems going live, they had successfully run over 1 billion circuits in a day!

Another advantage of creating it as a package for an existing platform such as Python is that there is no need to install a separate integrated development environment, nor set up complex build systems with confusing dependencies. For those of you who already have Python installed with the current supported version, you can install Qiskit with a simple `pip` command:

```
>pip install qiskit
```

But let's not get too ahead of ourselves. First, we will review how Qiskit is organized and then we'll cover how it interacts with your classic systems such as your laptop, server, or cloud application.

> **Important Note**
> Again, installing Qiskit is not a requirement for this book, so as we mentioned earlier, please skip the installation section, should you not want to install Qiskit locally.

Now that we understand the organization of Qiskit and its functionality, we will work our way to installing Qiskit locally.

Understanding how to organize and interact with Qiskit

If you use Python for most of your development, which I assume you do, based on the title of this book, then you understand that most packages are created in some form of hierarchy. At the top level, there's the modules, while the lower levels refer to the components within each module.

Qiskit has components such as classes or objects, and under each of those components, you have functions and members. Qiskit is no different regarding how everything is organized compared to most other packages, which makes it very easy to find certain features. Qiskit is composed of four main modules called **Terra**, **Aer**, **Ignis**, and **Aqua**, as illustrated in the following diagram:

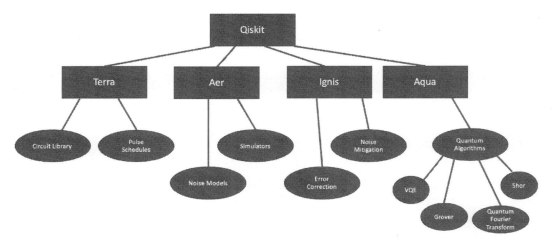

Figure 7.1 – Qiskit module hierarchy

As shown in the preceding diagram, each of the components provides a different set of functions and features so that it's easy to manage and locate certain functionalities. One thing to note is that there are some objects in **Terra** that are bundled under **Qiskit**, which simplifies managing components and creating circuits.

As illustrated in the preceding diagram, you will notice that both **Terra** and **Aer** are separate modules under **Qiskit**. However, if you look at the following code, you will see that only `Aer` is imported. This is because Terra components such as `execute`, `QuantumCircuit`, and more are all just listed under the root Qiskit module:

```
from qiskit import QuantumCircuit, QuantumRegister
from qiskit import Aer, execute
from qiskit.providers.aer import QasmSimulator,
StatevectorSimulator
```

Looking at the first and second line, it seems like the `QuantumCircuit`, `QuantumRegister`, `Aer`, and `execute` functions are all under **Qiskit**, even though the graph shows them under **Terra**. This is primarily due to the evolution of Qiskit over time, where there were some classes that were originally under one module but were then moved to the other modules. To keep yourself sane, rather than importing as `qiskit.terra`, simply import the `terra` modules directly from `qiskit`, as shown in *line 1* and *2* in the preceding code. You will notice the same with *lines 2* and *3* regarding the Aer providers.

Of course, the preceding information is based on the current version of Qiskit. In the future, like many projects, this may change. I highly recommend keeping up to date with the current **Application Programming Interface (API)** documentation to ensure that you are using the proper calls when writing your code. The API for this can be found on the Qiskit documentation page at `https://www.qiskit.org/documentation/`.

The documentation page provides the latest information on the four available modules, often referred to as elements due to their names, as explained at the beginning of this chapter.

So far, we have covered how Qiskit integrates into a classical application via Python, as well as how the four modules are configured under the main Qiskit library.

The following section will describe what each element provides so that you have an understanding of how to leverage them in your code. Development specifics will be covered in future chapters, where we will talk about the functionality and operations that each can provide.

Understanding Qiskit basics and its elements

Qiskit was built for anyone who wants to work with quantum computers at every level and domain. By this, we mean that if a quantum researcher wanted to work on how the pulses are scheduled on a quantum device, they can do so very easily. The same can be said about users who simply want to extend their applications to leverage a quantum computer to compute information.

In this section, we will learn about the four elements of Qiskit, along with its basics.

Let's take, for example, chemistry researchers, who wish to compute the energy state of two molecules but don't want to go through the hassle of learning about quantum gates and pulses. They just want to load their dataset, classically, to a quantum algorithm and obtain the results transparently. Qiskit was built as a full stack open source software package to facilitate those and many more user type scenarios.

Quantum physicists can experiment at the hardware level by researching ways to schedule pulses to single and multi-qubits. Quantum researchers can work on developing quantum circuits that could minimize noise, which would optimize the results of your quantum circuits.

Algorithm researchers and developers usually work on creating quantum algorithms that could be used by various domains and industries to solve problems either faster or to provide more accurate results with less data. Finally, domain researchers such as chemists, data scientists, economists, and many others can integrate their classic applications into a quantum system in order to compute complex problems more optimally or accurately.

As we already know, the elements in Qiskit are as follows:

- **Terra**
- **Aer**
- **Ignis**
- **Aqua**

Each element in Qiskit provides the tools needed for each of the aforementioned user types. We will learn about each element in the upcoming sections. We'll start with the foundational element – Terra – in the next section.

Terra

Terra, as defined in the Qiskit documentation, is used for composing quantum programs at the level of circuits and pulses within the code foundation.

What this means is that Terra is at the foundation of all the other elements, hence its translated name, Earth. It contains all the necessary components needed to not only create quantum circuits, but to generate and schedule the pulses that are sent to operate on the qubits.

Other features contained in Terra include the ability to execute quantum circuits, specify which device or simulator will execute the circuit, and allow others to configure the parameters as to how those circuits will be executed on the devices. It also facilitates the ability to communicate with the quantum systems and ensure that every user can run their experiments easily and without having to wait for too long.

This makes Terra the perfect module for our hardware engineers, quantum algorithm researchers, and developers.

Aer

Aer is, just as it is pronounced, the air element of Qiskit. It provides a framework that can be used to develop optimal simulators, debugging tools, and emulators. These tools help replicate a lot of the characteristics of a quantum system by simulating the noise that affects not just the qubit, but also the environment and computations. There are generally four highly efficient C++ compiled simulators available in Aer, as follows:

- **Qasm simulator**
- **Statevector simulator**
- **Unitary simulator**
- **Pulse simulator**

We will look at each of the simulators in the upcoming sections.

Qasm simulator

The **Qasm** simulator allows us to run our circuits in both clean and noisy simulated environments. The difference between the two is the amount of noise that you wish to apply to the simulator.

On one hand, it could run as an error-free ideal system that you can use to confirm the computational results of your circuit. On the other hand, you could run your circuit through a simulator that includes noise models so that you can replicate the noise and understand how it affects your computations. The results of this can be used to obtain the total count each time the circuit was executed and measured for analysis. I suggest referring to the official documentation for a complete breakdown of this. For instance, shot noise default behavior for different algorithms and backends is likely to change according to the new Qiskit release.

The Qasm simulator also has multi-functional capabilities and methods to simulate circuits, such as **Statevector, density matrix, stabilizer, matrix product state**, and many more. By allowing you the flexibility to configure the Qasm simulator using any of these methods, you can expect an ideal outcome from the measured circuits, along with any models that you wish to incorporate.

The Qasm simulator also provides a list of backend options you can use to execute your quantum circuit. These options include setting threshold values to truncate results or setting floating-point precision values and maximum value constraints for executing circuits. These features make Aer the ideal component for those who wish to develop an ideal or replicated noisy system. Typically, Aer is used by researchers who wish to develop noise mitigation or error correction techniques.

Statevector simulator

The **Statevector** simulator is, as its name suggests, a state vector simulator that provides the final state vector of the circuit after just one shot. Similar to the Qasm simulator, the Statevector simulator also provides you with backend options so that you can set thresholds and set maximum values each time you execute a circuit.

Results from the Statevector simulator can be visualized by leveraging the various visualization tools of quantum states, such as **histograms** and **cityscape**. The cityscape option provides a nice 3D view of both the real and imaginary components of the Density matrix (ρ). Other visualization plots include **Hinton**, **Pauli vector** plots, and **Bloch sphere**, to name a few. We will cover these and other visualization tools in future chapters as they will help you visualize some of the effects that gates have on qubits.

Unitary simulator

The **Unitary** simulator is quite simply just that – it provides the unitary matrix of your circuit. It does this by applying your circuit to an identity matrix based on the size of your circuit. This is very helpful if you want to confirm that the operations you applied to the qubits match your expected calculations. Let's look at an example to see how this works. We will create as simple one-qubit circuit that we will apply a Hadamard (H) gate to in order place the qubit in a superposition state.

Let's open up a new Qiskit notebook and create a circuit with a single qubit. After that, we'll add a Hadamard gate to the qubit, set up the backend so that it uses `unitary simulator`, and then execute our circuit, as follows:

```
# Create a quantum circuit with 1 qubit, add an H gate
qc = QuantumCircuit(1)
qc.h(0)
# Set backend to unitary simulator
simulator = Aer.get_backend('unitary_simulator')
# Execute on unitary simulator
result = execute(qc, simulator).result()
# Obtain results and print it out on console
unitaryState = result.get_unitary(qc)
print(unitaryState)
```

This results in the following output:

```
[[0.70710678+0.00000000e+00j  0.70710678-8.65956056e-17j]
 [0.70710678+0.00000000e+00j -0.70710678-8.65956056e-17j]]
```

This is expected since we know that the unitary operator for the Hadamard gate is as follows:

$$H = \frac{1}{\sqrt{2}}\begin{bmatrix} 1 & 1 \\ 1 & -1 \end{bmatrix}$$

The preceding simple example illustrates how we can determine the overall unitary matrix of the circuit. You can imagine how helpful this will be when you start to work on multiple qubits with many operators. The unitary simulator helps provide state information so that you can ensure that the results are what you expected.

Pulse simulator

The **Pulse** simulator is used to schedule pulse-level control and execute them on a pulse simulator and quantum computer. What the Pulse simulator offers is the ability to simulate the **Hamiltonian dynamics** of a quantum system. This is done by the Pulse simulators' ability to generate pulse schedules, which are similar to executions of circuits, in that they provide a schedule of when to trigger certain operations on the qubits via microwave pulses.

The simulator also allows us to reproduce the physical system by using its built-in pulse system model objects. These objects provide information for the simulator, such as the Hamiltonian representation of the system and local oscillator frequencies of each qubit. The results that are returned after executing on the simulator should very closely resemble those returned by an actual device with similar settings. We will learn how to run schedules in *Chapter 10, Executing Circuits Using Qiskit Aer*.

Ignis

Ignis is the element that represents fire, which might seem appropriate as it is used primarily to focus on errors, typically noise models that affect qubits. The effect that noise has on qubits can greatly reduce the ability to effectively compute operations on a qubit before the noise introduces issues such as *decoherence*, *crosstalk*, or a series of other problems.

Ignis has many tools that can help mitigate the effects of noise and errors, such as providing error correction. It also allows us to measure the capabilities of devices by offering randomized benchmarking and forms to measure **Quantum Volume**.

Quantum Volume is a way to measure the performance of a quantum computer, which, in turn, may help determine the quantum volume necessary for your quantum algorithm or application if you can correlate the two. Ignis is the ideal tool for researchers interested in mitigating errors and characterizing a quantum system.

Aqua

Aqua is the last of the elements and probably the most ideal for researchers who simply want to leverage a quantum system without having to dig deep into the details of the qubits, pulses, error mitigation, and everything else that goes into creating an optimal quantum algorithm.

Aqua is built for those who wish to simply use the quantum algorithms by integrating Aqua into their classical applications as simply as possible. Aqua, an acronym for **Algorithms for Quantum Applications**, was built for just that purpose. It provides various utilities, components, and algorithms that can be leveraged to create a quantum application by combining a set of components. This, along with the associated simulators, error mitigation, and any other Qiskit features are included to simplify the construction and modification at the user level. In this case, the user level is a researcher who is interested in leveraging what is available rather than having to construct everything from the circuit level up.

From the perspective of the researcher, they merely have to import the Aqua modules needed into their Python application, prepare their input data, specify the parameters (as described by the algorithm), and run the application. The results are then returned so that the application can leverage the results in whatever way it needs to complete the experiment. Each algorithm is flexible and includes general information so that any researcher knows how to connect their application. Aqua continues to churn out various components so that users from multiple domains such as chemistry, finance, data science, and others can leverage common components and algorithms that are specific to their domains.

> **Important Note**
> I highly suggest going to the Qiskit GitHub page, `https://www.github.com/Qiskit/qiskit`, to verify the latest instructions as they may they have changed since this book's publication.

Now that we have a basic understanding of what each of the four Qiskit elements provide and the purpose of each with respect to various research areas, you can move on and install these elements on your local machine. The next section will cover the installation steps for Qiskit at the time of writing. Please check the latest release information from Qiskit for any changes or updates: `https://qiskit.org`.

If you don't wish to install Qiskit on your local system, feel free to skip the next section.

Installing and configuring Qiskit on your local machine

In this section, we will walk you through the installation process of Qiskit. The installation will include installing Anaconda, which is a distribution of Python, and many other data science packages. It also serves as a simple way to manage packages and how they are installed on your local machine. In our case, it will help by installing the prepackaged dependencies we will need, such as Python, **Jupyter Notebooks**, PIP, and many others. Once installed, you can create an environment specific to quantum development with all the dependencies and features already installed.

Preparing the installation

Qiskit is an open source project that is available for free to everyone. It is licensed under the **Apache 2.0** license (`https://apache.org/licenses/LICENSE-2.0`). A copy has also been included in each Qiskit module (for example, `https://www.github.com/Qiskit/qiskit/blob/master/LICENSE.txt`). This allows you to use the source code, along with all its rights and privileges, as defined in the license.

Having Qiskit as open source helps in contributing to the open source community, which is a fantastic way to help evolve the technology compared to the times when classical computers were being developed decades ago. *Could you imagine how much slower the evolution of the technology would be if we did not have full stack access to the devices?* We'd have to submit requests to schedule time to use the devices, and even before that, find some way to understand it enough before even approaching the devices. Having the ability to run experiments on the devices directly from your machine, through the cloud, is definitely a game-changer. Alas! I digressed from the main topic. Let's get back to installing Qiskit.

The installation of Qiskit is quite simple, particularly if you are already familiar with the package management application known as **pip**. To review the Qiskit metadata package information, such as its current stable version, build status, and other details, go to `https://pypi.org/project/qiskit`.

Now that we are up to speed on the licensing and package management system that we will be using to install Qiskit, we'll get started by installing the *full version* of Anaconda. We have highlighted that you should install the full version as there have been issues with the mini version. You can, of course, try either, but if you get issues with the mini version, it is recommended that you install the full version.

Installing Anaconda

Before you begin the installation process, it is recommended that you install Qiskit via **Anaconda** (`https://www.anaconda.com/distribution`). Anaconda is an open source cross-platform distribution of Python. It allows the user to create separate environments so that they can install multiple versions of Python. This is very useful, particularly for those of you who are Python developers, who already have a version of Python installed on your machine.

By creating a separate environment using Anaconda, you can eliminate issues that may come up from installing a different version of Python that may affect your existing Python projects or applications. *It is recommended to follow the installation instructions on the Anaconda site.* Having separate environments also provides you with the ability to have multiple versions of Qiskit. You need to have a working version of Qiskit up and running, while you install an update on a separate environment, so that you can test if your quantum applications currently support the latest releases without worrying about dependency issues.

The installation steps of Anaconda also include versions of Jupyter Notebook, which comes in handy as the Qiskit notebooks will not be available locally. However, since the Qiskit notebooks are built on Jupyter Notebooks, you shouldn't expect to see much of a difference between the two.

After installing Anaconda with the supported version of Python, be sure to create an environment in your installation and switch to that environment before proceeding and installing Qiskit. Otherwise, it will install it on your base environment. After successfully completing the installation and created your Anaconda environment, you are now ready to install Qiskit!

Installing Qiskit

The following steps will lead you through the installation process:

1. We'll begin by ensuring that you are in the environment you created. The best way to determine this is to launch your Terminal and enter the following on the command line:

    ```
    >conda info --envs
    ```

The preceding code will list all the environments on your system. You will see one titled `base` and another with the name of the environment that you created. The current environment is identified by an asterisk, as illustrated in the following screenshot:

```
# conda environments:
#
base                     /anaconda3
QiskitEnv            *   /anaconda3/envs/QiskitEnv

(QiskitEnv) Roberts-MacBook-Pro-2:~ loredo@us.ibm.com$
```

Figure 7.2 – Output of the current environment command

As shown in the preceding screenshot, another way to identify the environment is to look at the far left of the command line before the machine name. There, in parenthesis, is the current environment. In the preceding screenshot, I created an environment called **QiskitEnv**.

2. Once you are in the Qiskit environment, you can run the `pip` command to install Qiskit:

```
>pip install qiskit
```

Based on your machine and network speed, this may take a few moments. Once completed, you can verify the installation by entering the following on the command line:

```
>pip list | grep qiskit
```

This will list the installed Qiskit packages and their respective versions, which you should see includes all four elements. There are other optional dependencies, such as the **IBMQ Provider**, which allows you to run your quantum circuits on the real devices from your local machine. To see the most current list of optional packages, just visit the Qiskit metadata package information page at `https://pypi.org/project/qiskit`.

With that, you have installed and verified that Qiskit is installed on your local device. Now, you can launch a Jupyter Notebook and start using Qiskit!

Wait! Not so fast. There are just a couple of steps we should cover before we start coding and running circuits. We want to make sure your local machine is configured. The first thing you need to ensure is that you have your **token ID** saved on your local device. This way, when you are ready to run an experiment on a real device or on the simulator on the cloud, you can do so very easily.

Configuring your local Qiskit environment

One of the benefits of learning and programming using the **IBM Quantum Experience** (**IQX**) is that it has taken care of the setup and configuration steps for you. This means you don't need to install Qiskit or any of the underlying dependencies, such as Python and its various package libraries needed by Qiskit, in order to execute circuits.

However, this is not the case when installing it locally. Lucky for us, with very special thanks to the Qiskit open source contributors and community, these steps are very easy.

You'll install the optional visualization package so that you can visualize the results from your circuit. Then, you will save your account information onto your machine, which will be used to connect to the IBM Quantum Experience.

The steps needed to get yourselves up and running are as follows:

1. Open your Terminal and enter the following:

    ```
    >pip install qiskit-terra[visualization]
    ```

    Once the installation completes, you can move on to the next step, which is to set up your account information on your local machine by copying your account API token.

2. To obtain your API token, go to the IBM Quantum Experience page at https://quantum-computing.ibm.com.

3. Next, to get to your account page, just click on your avatar at the top-right of the page and select **My Account** from the drop-down list, as illustrated in the following screenshot:

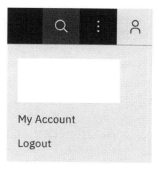

Figure 7.3 – Account page

4. After the account page opens, click **Copy token**, as highlighted in the following screenshot:

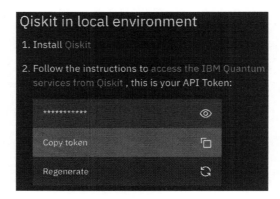

Figure 7.4 – Copy your account API token

Now that you have copied your **API Token**, save it on your local machine.

5. Launch **Jupyter Notebook** from within any folder in your directory by entering the following on the command line:

```
>jupyter notebook
```

6. Once it has launched, enter the following into the first cell:

```
from qiskit import IBMQ
IBMQ.save_account('PASTE-API-TOKEN-HERE')
```

Now that we have saved our API token locally, we won't have to save it to our local system again, unless we delete or change the API token value. Remember to copy your token, as indicated in the preceding command.

Important Note

Be sure to include the single quotes (' ') around your API token in the argument; otherwise, you will get an error.

Congratulations! You have successfully configured your local version of Qiskit! Let's take it out for a test run to verify that everything has been done correctly.

Important Note

Note that you only have to run this command once. If, by chance, you forget and rerun the IBMQ.save_account() function again, you will get a warning.

---

7. Next, enter the following code into a new cell in the notebook that you have opened:

```
from qiskit import QuantumCircuit, QuantumRegister,
ClassicalRegister, execute
from qiskit.tools.monitor import job_monitor

#You only need to load your account ONCE for each
#notebook.
IBMQ.load_account()

q = QuantumRegister(1)
c = ClassicalRegister(1)
qc = QuantumCircuit(q,c)
qc.h(0)
qc.measure([0],[0])
# Specify a backend from the list available to you,
# In this example we will use ibmq_'valencia'
backend = provider.get_backend('ibmq_valencia')
job_object = execute(qc, backend)
job_monitor(job_object)
```

The preceding code will execute the circuit on the `ibmq_valencia` backend, and `job_monitor` will display status information regarding the circuit that you have submitted. If you see that the job status is currently placing your job on the queue, then it is safe to assume that you have successfully configured your local machine.

For completeness, let's finish this execution. Depending on the queue, the job should complete fairly quickly. Once complete, continue to the next step to output your results.

8. In the next cell, run the following code to output your results (keep in mind that the specific result values might be different, but the probabilities should be fairly close to 50%):

```
from qiskit.visualization import import plot_histogram
result = job_object.result()
counts = result.get_counts(qc)
plot_histogram(counts)
```

The preceding code will extract the results after executing. From the results, we will extract the counts, which represent the number of times (each time) we ran the circuit when the result was either 0 or 1. We'll then plot the count results using a histogram, as follows:

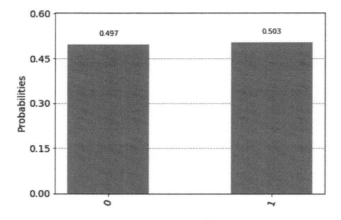

Figure 7.5 – Output histogram of total counts

You are now ready to run circuits both locally and on the IBM Quantum Experience. Creating and executing circuits can now be done locally on a simulator for those times when you are unable to obtain network access. Of course, once you are back online, you can use your local version to execute circuits on real devices. This also allows you the freedom to integrate with your own applications or systems with ease.

In this section, you learned how to install Anaconda, which includes a lot of the dependencies necessary to install Qiskit; how to create a quantum circuit; how to execute the circuit on a simulator; and how to execute the circuit a quantum computer. Now, we'll learn how to contribute, collaborate, and get support from the Qiskit global community.

Getting support from the Qiskit community

The Qiskit community is a global group of developers, researchers, and pretty much anyone who is curious about quantum computing who come together, collaborate, and support each other to help build knowledge across all community members. It is also used keep everyone up to speed on the latest in quantum research, education, events, and updates.

In this section, you will learn about the community, its many programs, and how you can contribute and become a **Qiskit Advocate**. Qiskit Advocates are members of the Qiskit community who have passed a rigorous exam, have made many contributions to the Qiskit community, and who have helped many others along the way. Let's start by introducing you to the community itself.

Introducing the Qiskit community

Ever since Qiskit was first deployed as an open source project, the open source community has contributed so many features and enhancements that it has only improved over time. The development ecosystem itself has flourished so much that it is being used in universities, industry, and governments around the world, even in Antarctica!

Members of the Qiskit community, often referred to as **Qiskitters**, often work together as a solid diverse group to ensure everyone is supported. Whether they are newbies to quantum computing or veteran quantum researchers, they all share a passion for collaborating and connecting on various projects. The link to the Qiskit community is https://www.qiskit.org/education.

One of the early projects was to create resources for those new to quantum computing. These resources vary from generating enablement materials to **YouTube** video series. The topics included both hardware and software, which describes what happens on the backend, to software that describes new research that others are working on. Along with the resources, there are also events that are planned all over the world at any given time. This includes events such as workshops, where communities join either in person or virtually in order to learn the latest in quantum computing.

Other events also include **hackathons** and code camps, of which the largest is the **Qiskit Camp**, which the IBM Quantum team hosts quarterly in different continents around the world. The 3-to-4-day camp usually includes accommodations in very exotic locations, meals, transportation to and from airports, and so on. Researchers from **IBM Research** also participate as lecturers, coaches, and judges. Teams are created and brainstorm ideas for projects that they work together on during the weekend, where they then have the opportunity to compete and win prizes. This is very similar to hackathons.

Recently, the Qiskit community initiated the **Qiskit Advocate program**. This program was created to provide support to individuals who have actively been involved with the Qiskit community and have contributed over time. To become a Qiskit Advocate, you would need to apply online (https://qiskit.org/advocates), where you will be given an exam to test your knowledge of Qiskit and specify at least three community contributions. These qualifications, of course, can change over time, so it is recommended that you check the site for any updates and application deadlines.

The test covers all four elements and some quantum computing knowledge. Besides knowledge and a passing score, the Qiskit Advocate candidate must also have contributed to the Qiskit community. This can be done in a variety of ways, such as contributing to the Qiskit open source code and supporting other community members by either providing assistance or creating educational material that helps others learn about quantum computing and Qiskit.

Once accepted into the Qiskit Advocate program, you will have the opportunity to network with other experts and access core members of the Qiskit development team. You will also gain support and recognition from IBM through the Qiskit community, as well as receive invitations to special events such as Qiskit Camp, hackathons, and other major events where you can not only collaborate with others but lead or coach as well.

Contributing to the Qiskit community

Support across members is key, not just for Qiskit Advocates but for all members. The Qiskit community has set up various channels to offer support to all the members of the community. They have a **Slack workspace** (http://ibm.co/joinqiskitslack) that is very active and has various channels so that members can ask questions, post event updates, or just chat about the latest quantum research that had been recently published. There are also other collaborative sources that Qiskit connects through. The current list of collaboration tools can be found at the bottom of the main Qiskit page: https://www.qiskit.org/.

Specializing your skill set in the Qiskit community

One of the most common questions asked about contributing to the Qiskit community, particularly those who are interested in becoming Qiskit Advocates, is, *what are the various ways you can contribute?* There are many ways in which you can contribute to the Qiskit community. Ideally, you want to become familiar with the different forms of contributions, such as the following:

- **Code contributions**: Adding a new feature, optimizing the performance of a function, and bug fixes are some of the good ways to start if you are a developer. If you are new to coding, there is a label that the Qiskit development team has created for this called **good first issue**. This is an umbrella term for the issues that are ideal for those who are new to the code base.

- **Host a Qiskit event in your area or virtually**: You can host an event and invite a Qiskit Advocate to run a workshop or talk to a group about the latest updates in Qiskit.

- **Help others**: You can help others by answering questions asked by other community members, reporting bugs, identifying features that may enhance the development of circuits, and so on.

Specializing in an area such as noise mitigation, error correction, or algorithm design is an advantage to the community. The **Qiskit Slack community** has a number of channels that focus on specific areas of quantum computing, including each of the four elements, quantum systems, quantum experience, Qiskit Pulse, Qiskit on Raspberry Pi, and many more. If you specialize in any of these areas, you can join the Slack group and collaborate on the many technologies and topics.

In this section, you learned about the open source contribution process and how to find tasks for starters and experts so that everyone can contribute.

Summary

In this chapter, you learned about the general features and capabilities provided by each of the four Qiskit elements so that you can create highly efficient quantum algorithms. You then learned how to install Qiskit locally, as well as how to contribute and find support from the Qiskit community.

Out of the four Qiskit elements available, we learned about Terra first. This provided you with the skills and functionality to create circuits, and you then applied these operations to the qubits via gates and operators.

Then, we learned about Aer, which allows us to create better simulators, and Ignis, which helps us mitigate errors and calculate the quantum volume of a system.

After that, we learned about Aqua. We understood that it is generally a high-level view of quantum computing that eliminates a lot of the underlying details of building a circuit and mitigating noise and errors. This helps simplify integrating your classical applications into a quantum system by leveraging the many quantum and classical algorithms available. Then, we learned about Qiskit community support and its advantages to all, particularly those who are new to quantum computing and need a little support to understand some of the challenging content.

With that, you now have the skills to install and configure Qiskit on your local machine in order to create and execute quantum circuits in offline mode.

In the next chapter, we will start delving into the first of the four Qiskit elements – Terra – to explore many of the functions and features available to create and execute quantum circuits.

Questions

1. Which of the four elements would financial analysts use to integrate their risk analysis applications into a quantum computer?

2. In your own words, describe what each element would provide to a quantum algorithm researcher.

3. If you wanted to run schedules on a quantum computer, which simulator would you need to use?

4. If you wanted to obtain the unitary of a circuit, which element would provide the necessary simulator?

5. If you wanted to analyze the computational power of a quantum system, which element would your application need?

6. Can you name and describe each of the simulators that are provided by Aer?

7. Which module would I need to import to plot a histogram?

8
Programming with Qiskit Terra

Terra is one of the four natural classical elements. It represents earth. **Qiskit** is packaged to contain all four elements: **Terra**, **Aer**, **Ignis**, and **Aqua** (*earth, air, fire*, and *water*, respectively), which together make up the universe of quantum programming.

Terra represents the link between the core hardware of a quantum system and the other elements, which transcend upward through the application stack. It is, therefore, the foundation used for creating quantum circuits, as well as generating and scheduling pulses from the circuits onto the hardware devices. Other features, such as optimizers and transpilers, are used to ensure the circuits are optimal to reduce coherence and improve performance. In this chapter, we will explore all the key features available in Terra to help you create your own circuits, optimizers, and pulse schedules.

The following topics will be covered in this chapter:

- Understanding quantum circuits
- Generating pulse schedules on hardware
- Leveraging provider information

Qiskit Terra has so many features and enhancements that it would take an entire book to write about them all. To cover as much of them as possible, we will create a quantum circuit and walk you through the various features. After reading this chapter, you will be able to modify the circuit as needed, but generally, the idea is to help you understand how each feature can improve the circuit functionally, both logically and visually.

We'll even delve into the hardware to schedule a pulse operation on a qubit to better understand how the circuit is translated from digital to analog signals to perform an operation on a qubit(s), followed by reading the information from the qubit and converting the signal back from analog to digital.

Sound exciting? Great! Let's get to it!

Technical requirements

In this chapter, it is expected that you are familiar with the basics of quantum circuits described in previous chapters, such as creating and executing quantum circuits, visualizing circuit diagrams, and knowledge of qubit logic gates. Here is the source code used throughout this book: `https://github.com/PacktPublishing/Learn-Quantum-Computing-with-Python-and-IBM-Quantum-Experience`

Please visit the following link to check the CiA videos: `https://bit.ly/35o5M80`

Understanding quantum circuits

In previous chapters, you had some exposure to quantum circuit operations in order to understand some of the basic quantum components. These basic operations included creating a quantum circuit, applying quantum gates to the circuit, and executing the circuit on a simulator.

We will now take a deeper look into quantum circuits to better understand what properties and functionalities are available to us to not just execute these circuits on a real device but to do so as optimally as possible. In this section, we will learn how to extract circuit properties, such as circuit depth, width, size, and obtaining the number of actual operators. Let's first start by reviewing the various forms of creating a quantum circuit.

Creating a quantum circuit

There are various ways to create a quantum circuit, each depending on how much information you need throughout your circuit. For example, *would you access either the quantum or classical registers*? Up to this point, we have been creating circuits using a single constructor that automatically creates the circuit registers needed. In this section, we will describe other ways to create a circuit and discuss the advantage of using one form or the other.

Terra provides various forms to create a quantum circuit. The form we have used throughout this book is the **single-line constructor**. In this form, the arguments indicate the number of qubits and bits of both the quantum and classical registers, respectively:

```
qc = QuantumCircuit(2,2)
```

Another way to construct a QuantumCircuit class is to create the quantum and classical registers independently of the quantum circuit constructor. Here, we will first create the quantum and classical registers, each with two qubits and two bits, respectively, and then draw the circuit. The constructor allows us to customize the label of our registers, which we were not able to do in the previous form:

```
qr = QuantumRegister(2, 'my_Q')
cr = ClassicalRegister(2, 'my_C')
qc = QuantumCircuit(qr,cr)
qc.draw()
```

From the preceding code, note that the underscore used in the second argument – that is, the name attribute – of the register constructors allows us to subscript our labels as in the following screenshot:

Figure 8.1 – Customized quantum and classical register labels

Customizing the labels of our registers simplifies reading our circuits, particularly as the circuits become more complex when having multiple registers performing different processes. You may want to have one register created with a fixed number of qubits and another dynamic register where defining the number of qubits would vary based on some preprocessed step. You'll see the value of this when we create composites later in this chapter.

Of course, you can also combine creating the registers and the circuit constructor all in one line if needed:

```
qc = QuantumCircuit(QuantumRegister(2,'my_Q'), ClassicalRegister(2,'my_C'))
```

Figure 8.2 – Combining creating registers and circuit constructors in one line

Let's assume now that you have two quantum circuits and you want to concatenate them together. The following example will illustrate how to concatenate two circuits into one without having to explicitly recreate one based on the two existing quantum circuits:

1. In the following code, we will create the first circuit and include labels on both the quantum and classical registers so that we can monitor that they are, in fact, combined:

```
#Import the register classes
from qiskit import QuantumRegister, ClassicalRegister
#Create the quantum and classical registers, each with
#labels
qr1 = QuantumRegister(2, name='qr1')
cr1 = ClassicalRegister(2, name='cr1')
#Create the quantum circuit using the registers
qc1 = QuantumCircuit(qr1, cr1)
#Draw the circuit
qc1.draw()
```

The following screenshot shows what should be displayed after running the previous code:

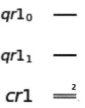

Figure 8.3 – The first of the two quantum circuits we will join

2. Next, we will create a second circuit, which is very similar to the first one, only we will update the labels to identify it as the second:

```
#Create two Quantum and Classical registers
qr2 = QuantumRegister(2, name='qr2')
cr2 = ClassicalRegister(2, name='cr2')
#Create a second circuit using the registers created
#above
qc2 = QuantumCircuit(qr2, cr2)
#Draw the second quantum circuit
qc2.draw()
```

The results of the code should be no surprise – that it is the same as the first one only with the labels updated as expected:

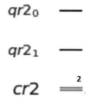

$qr2_0$ ——

$qr2_1$ ——

$cr2$ $\overset{2}{=\!=}$

Figure 8.4 – The second of the two quantum circuits we will join

3. Now, let's finish up by creating a circuit that concatenates the two previously created circuits together in one line:

```
#Concatenate the two previous circuits to create a new
#circuit
qc_combined = qc1 + qc2
#Draw the concatenated circuit
qc_combined.draw()
```

As you can see in the following screenshot, the results are now a concatenation of the two previous quantum circuits:

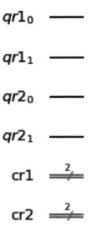

Figure 8.5 – Concatenation of two quantum circuits

We originally created two individual quantum circuits, each with two quantum registers and two classical registers. We then concatenated them to create a quantum circuit with four quantum and classical circuits. The order of the quantum circuits is based on the order in which they were concatenated. As an extra exercise, repeat the previous concatenation code and switch the order to confirm or create more quantum circuits and add more circuits together.

One last circuit creation object I would like to share is the **random circuit generator**, which, as the name suggests, will generate a random circuit for you. As the following code block indicates, the random circuit object requires two parameters. They are the number of qubits you want the random circuit to contain and the depth of the circuit, respectively – where depth indicates the number of standard gates, selected from the Qiskit circuit extensions listed in the API documentation, to add randomly per qubit. You can also indicate whether you want the circuit to include measurement operators:

```
#Import the random_circuit class
from qiskit.circuit.random import random_circuit
#Construct the random circuit with the number of qubits = 3
#with a depth = 2, and include the measurement operator for
#each qubit
qc = random_circuit(3, 2, measure=True)
#Draw the circuit
qc.draw()
```

The results from the random circuit will vary, of course, each time you execute it, as it should. What will not vary are the parameter options, particularly the number of qubits and the depth count. Your results should have a circuit that contains three qubits and a depth of two operators. The following random circuit is the result of running the preceding code. Note that the measurement operator is not included in the depth count:

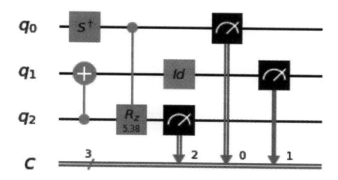

Figure 8.6 – Random circuit generated with number of qubits = 3 and depth = 2

Now that you are familiar with the various ways to generate quantum circuits, we will continue and see what properties we can extract from the circuits created. These properties could be used to analyze the generated circuit and ensure it is optimized by leveraging some optimization features available to us in Terra.

Obtaining circuit properties and analysis

Constructing circuits could get very complex once you start building them out, particularly if you create composites of gates and combine them to form larger gates. You're going to want to get some information about your circuit along the way should you need to analyze your results.

The good thing for us is that Terra has taken care of some of this by making a lot of these properties available to us. Let's start with some basic properties. Let's say we want to know how many qubits we have in our circuit. As we learned in the previous section, we know that we can concatenate two or more circuits together. As we add more circuits together, it becomes difficult, or tedious, to determine the number of qubits and gates that our concatenated circuit will have. It's here that the width, depth, and operator count functions come in handy.

In the following code, we will create two two-qubit random circuits, each with different gate counts. We will then concatenate them and use our circuit property functions to help us get the total width, depth, and operator count:

```
#Import the random circuit class
from qiskit.circuit.random import random_circuit
#Create two random circuits, each with 2 qubit registers and
#random #gate operator counts.
qc1 = random_circuit(2,2)
qc2 = random_circuit(2,4)
#Concatenate the two random circuits
qc = qc1 + qc2
#Draw the circuit
qc.draw()
```

The result should be a two-qubit circuit with a random set of gate operators with a total depth of 6. We know this because we created them and can see the values from the `random_circuit` constructor:

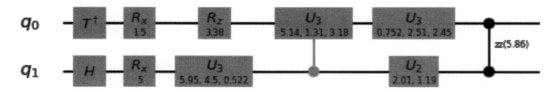

Figure 8.7 – Randomly generated two-qubit circuits with a depth of 6

Now, let's use our circuit property functions to get the width, depth, size, and operator count of our circuit. To simplify this, we will create a helper function that will print out the circuit properties of the quantum circuit we will pass in as an argument:

```
#Define function to print circuit properties:
def print_circuit_props(qc):
    width = qc.width()
    depth = qc.depth()
    num_operators = qc.count_ops()
    circuit_size = qc.size()
```

```
print('Width = ',width)
print('Depth = ', depth)
print('Circuit size = ',circuit_size)
print('Number of operators = ', num_operators)
```

Now, we can run our circuit through our helper function, which will print out all the properties we need:

```
#Pass our quantum circuit to print out the circuit properties
print_circuit_props(qc)
```

Our results should have the same value for `width` and `depth`. However, since we are using random circuits, our circuit size and the number of operators will be different as it is based on the random choice of gates selected. However, observing the circuit, you will see that the result values of `size()` and `count_ops()` are the same. The difference between the two is that the circuit size returns the total number of gates in the circuit, while the operator count lists the total number of each gate type in the circuit:

```
Width = 2
Depth = 6
Circuit size = 10
Number of operators = OrderedDict([('rx', 2), ('u3', 2), ('h',
1), ('tdg', 1), ('rz', 1), ('cu3', 1), ('u2', 1), ('rzz', 1)])
```

Now, let's try adding some classic registers, measurements, and barriers to see what we get back. We can use a shortcut to include all of these by using `measure_all()`, which will append a barrier, a measurement for each qubit, and the classical registers to match the number of qubits in the quantum register of our circuit:

```
#Use measure_all() to automatically add the barrier,
#measurement, and #classical register to our existing circuit.
qc.measure_all()
#Draw the circuit
qc.draw()
```

The result now includes the classical components needed to measure and read out our qubits. These include the two-bit classical registers labeled as **measure**, a barrier separating the quantum gates from the measurement operators, and the measurement operators, as illustrated in the following screenshot:

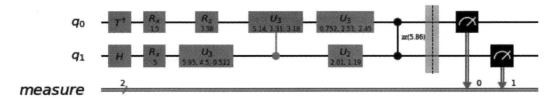

Figure 8.8 – Random circuit with classical components added

Let's now print our circuit property functions to see an updated count:

```
#Print out the circuit properties
print_circuit_props(qc)
```

The results show what we generally would expect. The width count increased by 2, due to the addition of the two-bit classical register. The depth increased by 1 to add the barrier. Note that the measurement operator is not included in the size or operator count, as follows:

```
Width = 4
Depth = 7
Circuit size = 12
Number of operators = OrderedDict([('rx', 2), ('u3', 2),
('measure', 2), ('h', 1), ('tdg', 1), ('rz', 1), ('cu3', 1),
('u2', 1), ('rzz', 1), ('barrier', 1)])
```

Before moving on to the next section, let's look at an interesting caveat to our circuit property functions. Most gates are created from basis gates that are specific to the quantum computers used. For most of the quantum systems, there are a set of basis gates used to create other gates.

For example, a Hadamard gate is really just a U_2 gate with parameters 0 and π. However, some gates, such as the **Toffoli** and **Swap** gates, not only require more than a single qubit but are also composed of several basis gates. Let's look at the Toffoli gate as an example:

1. We will create a quantum circuit with 3 qubits and add only a Toffoli gate to it, as shown here:

```
qc = QuantumCircuit(3)
qc.ccx(0,1,2)
qc.draw()
```

Here, we see the Toffoli gate as expected with the 0 and 1 Source qubits entangled, with qubit 2 as the Target:

Figure 8.9 – The Toffoli gate on a quantum circuit

2. We print out our circuit properties of the quantum circuit with the Toffoli gate:

```
#Print out the circuit properties
print_circuit_props(qc)
```

As we can see, the results are not surprising in that the values are not surprising either – a three-qubit gate with a width of 3 and a depth of 1:

```
Width = 3
Depth = 1
Circuit size = 1
Number of operators = OrderedDict([('ccx', 1)])
```

3. Now, let's print our circuit property, only this time, let's decompose our quantum circuit to see the results. As you will recall, when we invoke the `decompose()` function on our quantum circuit, we are requesting the circuit to be decomposed down to its basis gates used to create the gates in our circuit. In this case, the basis gates that are used to create a Toffoli gate:

```
#Print out the circuit properties
print_circuit_props(qc.decompose())
```

Notice the difference? Quite surprising indeed! By observing the results, we see that the Toffoli gate requires 15 operators, which are made up of various basis gates, such as T, T†, H, and CNOT:

```
Width = 3
Depth = 11
Circuit size = 15
Number of operators = OrderedDict([('cx', 6), ('t', 4),
('tdg', 3), ('h', 2)])
```

The reason why I wanted to mention this was to make you aware that some of the gates used are not basis gates but are rather composites of basis gates used to generate the functionality of the desired gate. This is good to know when analyzing your circuit with respect to qubit noise or decoherence.

Try the same exercise, only this time try creating a two-qubit circuit with a Swap gate, and see what results you get back.

Now that you are familiar with the various forms of creating quantum circuits, let's now look at how we can reuse these circuits in a modular way that is easy to combine and comprehend them.

Customizing and parameterizing circuit libraries

There are times when you are going to want to reuse a circuit on multiple occasions. To simplify this, you can create a composite of operators and reuse them throughout your circuit. This not only simplifies creating the circuit from modules, but it also makes it very easy for others to understand what your circuit is doing in those composites.

In the following steps, we are going to create a composite gate that is made up of multiple qubits and gates:

1. First, we create a two-qubit quantum circuit, give it a name, and convert it into a generic quantum instruction:

```
#Create a custom two-qubit composite gate
#Create the quantum register
qr = QuantumRegister(2, name='qr_c')
#Generate quantum circuit which will make up the
#composite gate
comp_qc = QuantumCircuit(qr, name='My-composite')
#Add any gates you wish to your composite gate
comp_qc.h(0)
comp_qc.cx(0, 1)
#Create the composite instructions by converting
#the QuantumCircuit to a list of Instructions
composite_inst = comp_qc.to_instruction()
#Draw the circuit which will represent the composite gate
comp_qc.draw()
```

The preceding code will create the following two-qubit circuit, which we will use as our composite gate:

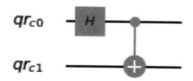

Figure 8.10 – The quantum circuit that will represent the composite gate

2. Now, let's create a quantum circuit that will append the composite gate we created:

```
#Create your 2-qubit circuit to generate your composite
#gate
qr2 = QuantumRegister(3, 'qr')
#Create a quantum circuit using the quantum register
qc = QuantumCircuit(qr2)
#Add any arbitrary gates that would represent the
#function
```

```
#of the composite gate
qc.h(0)
qc.cx(0,1)
qc.cx(0,2)
#Draw the composite circuit
qc.draw()
```

The preceding code will create the circuit, which we prepopulated with some gates before including our composite gate:

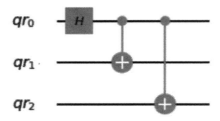

Figure 8.11 – The quantum circuit that we will append to the composite gate

3. Since our composite gate is made up of two qubits, we will need to append the composite gate and indicate which of the three qubits to use to append our two-qubit composite gate. For this example, we will append it to the first two qubits:

```
#Append your composite gate to the specified qubits.
qc.append(composite_inst, [qr2[0], qr2[1]])
#Draw the complete circuit
qc.draw()
```

As we can see from the results, our composite gate was successfully appended to the first and second qubits. It also includes the name of the composite gate, which makes it simple for anyone, including yourself, to read the circuit and understand what the composite gate is doing within the circuit:

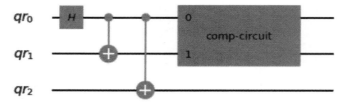

Figure 8.12 – The quantum circuit with a composite gate representation of a predefined circuit

This makes reading your circuit much easier compared to how it would be if you were to just concatenate the two quantum circuits together.

Of course, this is ideal if you have a circuit that would run as is. However, there may be times where you wish to perhaps control the amount of rotation of some of the gates in the composite gate you generated. This is where the parameterization of composite gates comes in handy. We will now create another composite gate, only this one will include the ability to add parameters to your composite gate so that it is more dynamic.

4. To parameterize a gate, we will need to create a `Parameter` class and set it to a rotation gate; in this example, we will apply the parameter to an R_z gate:

```
#Import the Parameter object
from qiskit.circuit import Parameter
#Construct the Parameter set to Theta
param_theta = Parameter('θ')
#Create a two-qubit quantum circuit and add some gates
qc = QuantumCircuit(2)
qc.h(0)
qc.cx(0, 1)
#Include a rotation gate which we wish to apply
#the Parameter value
qc.rz(param_theta,0)
qc.rz(param_theta,1)
#Draw the circuit
qc.draw()
```

Note that the parameter value is defined as θ, but is not set as an explicit value. It just reserves the `Parameter` value to later include a rotation value of θ:

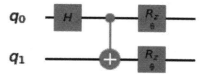

Figure 8.13 – Set the parameter of the R_z gate to θ

5. Let's bind the `Parameter` value of our gates to 2π and draw the circuit:

```
import numpy as np
#Bind the parameters with a value, in this case 2π
qc = qc.bind_parameters({param_theta: 2*np.pi})
#Draw the circuit with the set parameter values
qc.draw()
```

Note that our rotation gate has its theta value set to 2 as expected:

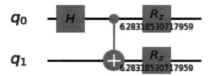

Figure 8.14 – Rotation gates R_z now have the Parameter value θ set to 2π

Our circuit is now ready to run with the bound parameter values. By having this feature, we can iterate it over a loop and bind multiple values if need be so that we can iterate over all of them without having to manually update the bound values. This greatly optimizes our ability to run and analyze the results of our circuit for each iteration.

In this section, we learned about various forms and ways to create quantum circuits. We also learned how to reuse the created circuits.

In the next section, we will dig even deeper into manipulating qubits, only this time not from basis gates, but to directly manipulate the qubits using the hardware itself!

Generating pulse schedules on hardware

So far, you have learned how to create quantum circuits, add gates that manipulate the qubits of the circuit, and execute the circuits. In this section, we'll go a little deeper to see how a quantum circuit is converted from digital instructions into pulse instructions that physically manipulate the qubits as instructed by the quantum circuit. We'll begin by illustrating how the hardware components are connected to the various pulse channels.

IBM Quantum Experience provides you with access to the machines in a way that is unique from most other quantum systems available on the cloud. Terra includes a **Pulse** library that allows you to control the pulses sent to the hardware that controls the device. Based on the **OpenPulse** documentation (https://arxiv.org/abs/1809.03452), it is tailored to provide the functionality to generate pulse signals used to control the qubits.

In order to understand how the pulse functionality works, we'll start by describing the four main components you will be using:

- **Instructions**
- **Channels**
- **Schedules**
- **Pulse libraries**

In the following sections, we will learn about the preceding components.

Before we proceed to the next section, we will use the following code that will import everything we need to create, schedule, and trigger a pulse on a quantum device directly:

```
#Import pulse classes
from qiskit.pulse import SamplePulse, DriveChannel, Play,
Schedule
#Import some helpful utils
from qiskit.scheduler.utils import measure_all
```

Now that we have imported the files needed, we will move on to the next section about instructions.

Learning about instructions

Pulse programs, or, as described in the Qiskit API documentation, **Schedules**, are a set of instructions used to describe the control of the electronic components of the quantum system. There are various instruction objects included within Qiskit Pulse that have capabilities such as modulation of the frequency and phase of the pulse signal.

You can also delay an instruction from triggering, similar to a `sleep()` function in most programming languages. Finally, it gives you the ability to trigger and acquire the pulse by playing and acquiring, respectively.

Now, let's describe each instruction and its parameters:

- `SetFrequency(frequency, channel, name)`, where `frequency` is in Hz, `channel` indicates which channel the frequency will be applied to, and `name` is the name you can set for the instruction. The default *duration* of the `SetFrequency` instruction is 0. This very simply sets the frequency of the channel so that the pulses applied to the channel are tuned accordingly. If you do not specify a frequency when creating a pulse for a specific qubit, the default frequency for the qubit on the drive channel will be used.

- `ShiftPhase(phase, channel, name)`, where `phase` is the rotation angle in radians, `channel` indicates the channel that the frequency will be applied to, and the `name` parameter is the name you can set for the instruction. This instruction shifts the phase of the pulse by increasing its rotation angle by the provided amount in radians.

- `Delay(duration, channel, name)`, where `duration` is the length of time in the delay (in the documentation, this is also referred to as *time step*, or **dt**), `channel` indicates which channel the delay will be applied to, and `name` indicates the name that you can set for the instruction. The `Delay` instruction is generally used to align pulses with respect to other pulse instructions. For example, if you wish to send two pulses and include a time gap in between the pulses, you can specify the time gap by adding a `Delay` instruction with the desired time gap amount.

- `Play(pulse, channel, name)`, where `pulse` is the pulse waveform you wish to apply, `channel` indicates which channel the pulse will be applied to, and `name` is the name you can set for the instruction. The `Play` instruction will apply the pulse output onto the channel specified, where the pulse output was previously modulated using both the `SetFrequency` and `SetPhase` instructions.

- `Acquire(duration, channel, mem_slot, reg_slot, kernel, discriminator, name)`, where `duration` is the number of **time steps (dt)** to acquire the data information, `channel` indicates which channel to acquire the data from `mem_slot`, which is the classical memory slot in which to store each of the returned results, and `reg_slot` is the register slot used to store the classified and readout results. The `kernel` parameter is used to integrate the raw data for each slot, `discriminator` is used to classify kernelled IQ data into 0 or 1 results, and `name` indicates the name you can set for the instruction.

Each instruction includes an operator that will be applied to the specified channels stated. The operators include pulse modulators, delays, and readouts from channels. Before we get into discussing channels, let's create some pulses using the Qiskit Pulse library.

Understanding pulses and Pulse libraries

Pulses are what actually manipulate the qubits on the quantum devices. A signal is generated and tuned to a specific qubit so that the signal only affects the qubit that the pulse is tuned to. The pulse is created by an **arbitrary waveform generator** (**AWG**), which specifies the frequency and phase of the pulse signal output. The frequency and phase are set by the `SetFrequency` and `ShiftPhase` instructions we learned about earlier, respectively.

Important Note

Qiskit Pulse provides a nice library of waveforms, which can simplify creating the pulses we need to operate on a qubit. The following are the types of available waveforms, at the time of writing this chapter: **Constant**, **Drag**, **discrete**, **Gaussian**, **GaussianSquare**, and **Waveform**.

`SamplePulse` allows you to define your own pulse by providing an array of complex value samples as an argument. These samples each have a predefined time step, dt, which is the time period played for each and varies based on the specified backend. The following code is an example of a sample pulse for a simple sine waveform of 128 samples:

```python
#Import numpy and generate the sin sample values
import numpy as np
x = np.linspace(0,2*np.pi,64)
data = np.sin(x)
#Generate our SamplePulse
sample_pulse = SamplePulse(data, name="sin_64_pulse")
#Draw the generated sample pulse
sample_pulse.draw()
```

This following screenshot is the result of creating our sample pulse of a sine waveform:

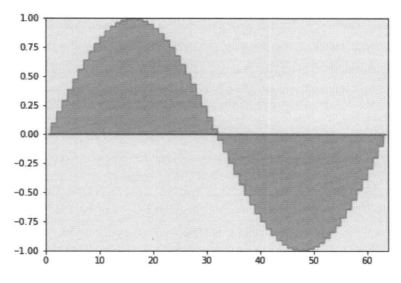

Figure 8.15 – Sample pulse of a sine waveform

Let's now try generating one of the waveforms from the Pulse library.

The **Pulse library** has an array of various different waveforms, such as **Gaussian**, **GaussianSquare**, **Constant**, and **Drag** (just to name a few). Each has its own distinct shape that we can leverage in order to fine-tune any pulse we wish.

Let's create a `GaussianSquare` pulse, which is simply a square pulse with Gaussian edges on both ends, rather than squared-off edges:

```
#Import the Gaussian Square pulse from Pulse Library
from qiskit.pulse.pulse_lib import GaussianSquare
#Create a Gaussian Square pulse:
#Args: duration, amp, sigma, width, name
gaussian_square_pulse = GaussianSquare(128,1,2,112,
"gaussian square")
gaussian_square_pulse.draw()
```

The preceding code will result in the following pulse, where the duration (dt) is `128`, the amplification max is at `1`, sigma is set to `2`, and the width of the pulse peak is `112` (dt):

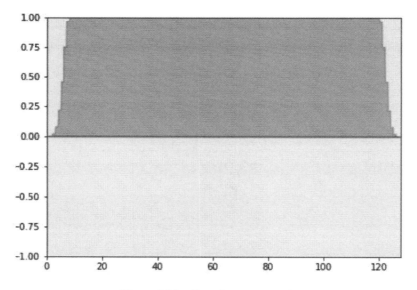

Figure 8.16 – Gaussian square pulse

Now that we can create pulses, let's learn about the channels that we will transmit these pulses through.

Leveraging channels to transmit and receive instructions

There are two types of channels in Qiskit Pulse:

- The first type is the **Pulse channel**, which transmits the generated pulses. These include the **Drive channel**, **Control channel**, and the **Measure channel**.

- The other type of channel is the **Acquisition channel**. Currently this type only includes the **Acquire channel**, which is the channel that receives pulses from the quantum device.

All channels only have one parameter, the index, which is used to assign the channel. The following list describes all the channels:

- The **Drive channel** is the channel used to transmit the pulse signal down to the qubit to execute the gate operation.

- The **Control channel** is commonly used on multi-qubit gate operations such as **Control-Not, Control-Phase**, and more. They generally provide auxiliary control over the qubit over the drive channel.

- The **Measure channel** transmits a measurement stimulus pulse to the qubit for a readout from the qubit.

- The **Acquire channel** is the only channel that is used to receive information from the device. It is used to collect data from the quantum device.

So far, we have learned that pulse programs are instructions that are made up of waveform pulses that are constructed to perform gate operations on the quantum devices. We also covered the different channels available to transmit and receive information to and from the quantum devices. With this information, we can now look at how to schedule these instructions to be executed on a real device.

Generating and executing schedules

Pulse schedules are a set of instructions sent through specified channels to be executed on a quantum device. The `Schedule` class can be made up of instructions or other schedules. That means you can create a schedule with one of the instructions we learned about earlier, or you can create or append schedules to existing schedules. We will do all this in this section.

We will use what we have learned so far in this chapter to build a schedule. First, we will construct a schedule and insert a pulse from the Pulse library to it that will be triggered at time = 0. Then, we will create another schedule and insert a different pulse from the Pulse library into it. Only the second one will be appended to the first schedule and then shift it, so it is triggered at some time after the first pulse has completed. We'll then execute the schedule on a quantum device and get back its result:

1.   Let's continue using the notebook we have been using so far to create our first schedule, and name it schedule_1. We'll also use the Play instruction to insert the Gaussian square pulse we generated earlier and assign the schedule to drive channel 0:

```
#Create the first schedule with our Gaussian Square pulse
schedule_1 = Schedule(name='Schedule 1')
schedule_1 = schedule_1.insert(0, Play(gaussian_square_
pulse, DriveChannel(0)))
#Draw the schedule
schedule_1.draw()
```

The result we see is that our Gaussian square pulse was added to the schedule starting at time = 0, as follows:

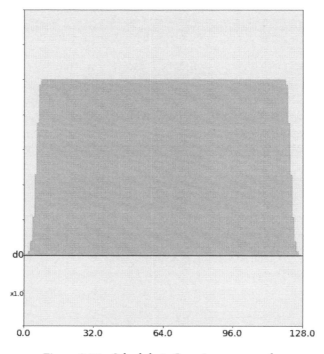

Figure 8.17 – Schedule 1: Gaussian square pulse

2. Now, let's continue and create the second schedule, `schedule_2`, with the sample pulse we generated earlier:

```
#Create a second schedule with our sample pulse
schedule_2 = Schedule(name='Schedule 2')
schedule_2 = schedule_2.insert(0, Play(sample_pulse,
DriveChannel(0)))
#Draw the schedule
schedule_2.draw()
```

This results in the following schedule; note the duration of our sample pulse is 64, whereas the Gaussian square pulse has a duration of 128:

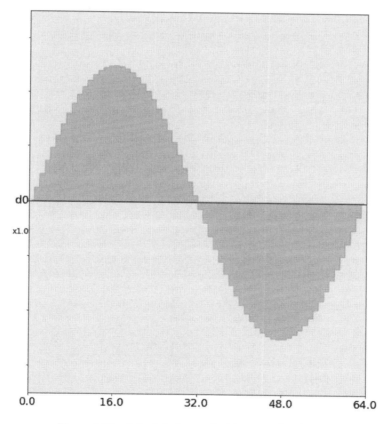

Figure 8.18 – Schedule 2: sample (sine waveform) pulse

3. Next, we will create a third schedule, schedule_3, and we will construct it by inserting both schedule_1 and schedule_2 together with a gap of 5 time steps (dt) in between the two:

```
#Let's create a third schedule
#Where we add the first schedule and second schedules
#And shift the second to the right by a time of 5 after
#the first
schedule_3 = schedule_1.insert(schedule_1.duration+5,
schedule_2)
schedule_3.draw()
```

The result is a combination of schedule_1 starting at time = 0 and then we insert schedule_2 starting at 5 time units after the first schedule. Note the use of the duration variable to ensure that the pulse does not overlap with the first. Schedule 3, therefore, has a total time of the two pulses plus the 5 time units, totaling 197, as the following figure illustrates:

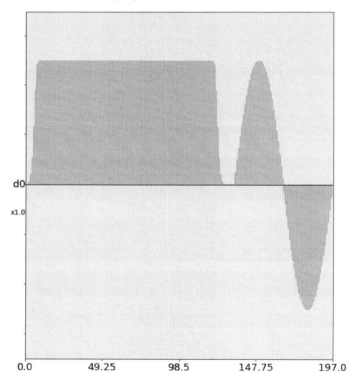

Figure 8.19 – Schedule 3, combining schedule 1 and 2 with a 5 time-unit difference in between

4. Of course, there are other ways to combine pulses. If you want to combine the two schedules without a gap in between, then you can simply use the append function to combine them:

```
#We could have also combined the two using the append
#operator
#The two schedules are appended immediately after one
#another
schedule_3_append = schedule_1.append(schedule_2)
schedule_3_append.draw()
```

The preceding code results in the following output. Note how the total time units are equal to the total time units of both pulses, with no additional time in between:

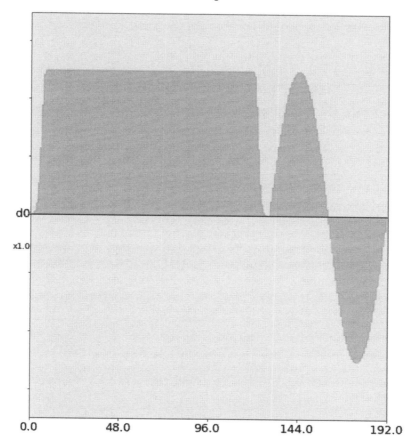

Figure 8.20 – Schedule 3, appending two schedules without a time gap in between

Up to this point, we were able to generate a pulse, apply it to an instruction, and schedule it to run on a specified channel to manipulate the qubit. Now, let's see how the quantum circuits generate the schedules by creating our own quantum circuit and running it on a quantum device.

Scheduling existing quantum circuits

We will use the following steps to create a schedule from an existing quantum circuit:

1. Since the backend that we are currently using only has a single qubit, let's create a single qubit circuit with a Hadamard gate to run it on:

```
qc = QuantumCircuit(1, 1)
qc.h(0)
qc.measure(0,0)
#Draw the circuit
qc.draw()
```

This circuit places the qubit in superposition using the Hadamard gate, as illustrated here:

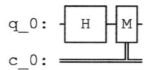

Figure 8.21 – Single qubit circuit in superposition

2. Now, let's prepare the rest of the code to send this circuit to the quantum device. We'll first import the transpiler and the `schedule` class. The transpiler is what will translate and compile the circuit into the basis gates available to the specified backend. In this case, we will be using the `ibmq_armonk` backend as it is both enabled to run Qiskit Pulse and is available in the open group of devices. Don't be too concerned about what the transpiler is for now; we will go into the details later on in this chapter:

```
#Import transpile and schedule
from qiskit import transpile, schedule
#Set the backend to ibmq_armonk
```

```
backend = provider.get_backend('ibmq_armonk')
#Transpile the circuit using basis gates from the
#specified backend
transpiled_qc = transpile(qc, backend)
#Draw the transpiled circuit
transpiled_qc.draw()
```

The results of the quantum circuit we created have been transpiled into a circuit that is represented by the basis gates supported by the given backend – in this case, ibmq_armonk. Note that the only change was that the Hadamard gate is now using the U_2 gate. Details about the Hadamard and the U_1 gates can be found in *Chapter 6, Understanding Quantum Logic Gates*:

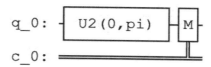

Figure 8.22 – Transpiled quantum circuit with a U_2 gate representing the Hadamard gate

3. Then, create the circuit schedule using the transpiled circuit and draw the schedule:

```
#Create the circuit schedule using the transpiled circuit
circuit_schedule = schedule(transpiled_qc, backend)
#Draw the circuit
circuit_schedule.draw()
```

Figure 8.23 represents the entire schedule created by the transpiled circuit.

4. Let's review the graph to get a better understanding of what we are seeing here. First, along the bottom, we see the time steps of the schedule, starting at `time` = 0 up to `time` = 16640. These are the time units taken up by the circuit. Along the left, we see the channels used in this circuit, where **a0** represents the acquisition channel, **d0** represents the drive channel, and **m0** represents the measurement channel. Across the top, we see the information on the drive channel where the pulse begins at `time` = 0:

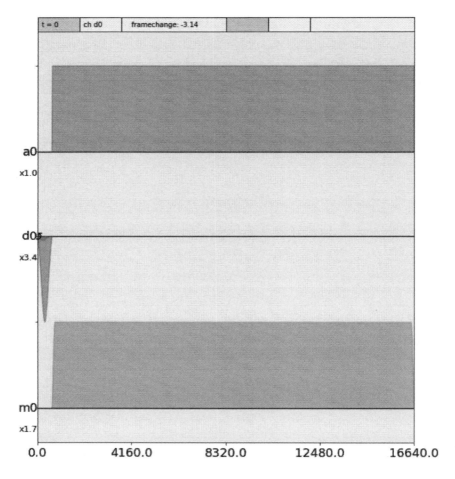

Figure 8.23 – The schedule of the quantum circuit, with a0, d0, and m0

As you can see from the previous figure, both the acquisition and measurement channels take a large number of time steps. To simplify reading the pulse and not the acquisition or measurement channels, you can specify how much of the schedule to display when drawing.

5. Let's adjust that now to a point just after the acquisition and measurement channels started, which would be approximately 1,500 time steps (dt), and redraw:

```
#Draw the circuit with a shorter time range to ease
#visibility
circuit_schedule.draw(plot_range=[0, 1500])
```

Much better! We can now get a better view of the generated pulse and other details:

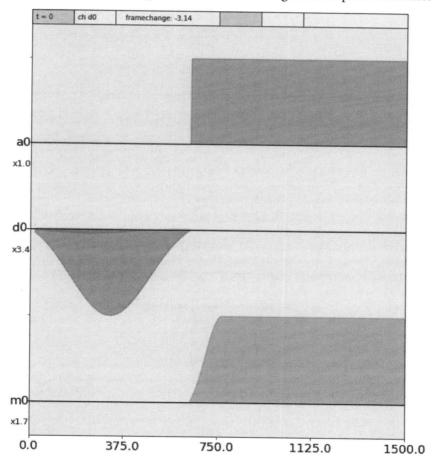

Figure 8.24 – The schedule redrawn at a more readable scale of 1,500 time steps (dt)

Scheduling a single qubit circuit is interesting, but let's now look at multi-qubit schedules. For this one, we will create a two-qubit quantum circuit where we will have a Hadamard gate on the first qubit, similar to the previous circuit we just ran. Only this time, we will also include a CNOT gate that entangles the first and second qubit as the Source and Target, respectively:

1.   First, let's create the circuit as we have done previously, where we apply a Hadamard gate to the first qubit, apply a CNOT gate, and add measurement gates:

```
#Create a 2-qubit circuit
qc2 = QuantumCircuit(2, 2)
#Apply a Hadamard to the first qubit
qc2.h(0)
#Apply a CNOT gate where the Source is qubit 0, and
#Target qubit 1
qc2.cx(0, 1)
#Add measurement gates to all qubits
qc2.measure([0, 1], [0, 1])
#Draw the circuit
qc2.draw()
```

The result should be as follows:

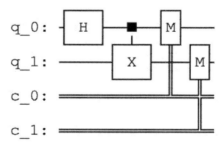

Figure 8.25 – The two-qubit quantum circuit with a Hadamard gate, CNOT gate, and measurement operators

2. Now, just as in the previous example, we will transpile this to a backend so that
    we have this circuit generated using the basis gates from the specified backend.
    However, as you will recall from our previous example, when we were using `ibmq_`
    `armonk`, this was a single qubit quantum device. Therefore, we cannot run this
    example on this device because we would be short one qubit. So instead, let's use
    one of test backend systems – in this case, there is one titled `FakeAlmaden`. This is
    a multi-qubit test backend that has preconfigured data such as calibrations and basis
    states that mimic many of the real devices:

```
#Import the test backend
from qiskit.test.mock import FakeAlmaden
#Construct the backend
backend = FakeAlmaden()
#Transpile the circuit to the test backend and its basis
#states
transpiled_qc2 = transpile(qc2, backend)
#Draw the transpiled circuit
transpiled_qc2.draw()
```

Note that the result has the expected gates of the U_2 (replacing the H gate; see the previous example for details), as well as the CNOT gate and measurement operators:

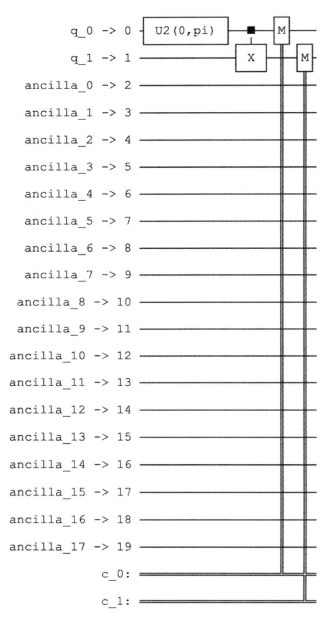

Figure 8.26 – The transpiled quantum circuit with a U_2 gate representing the Hadamard gate and a CNOT gate

3. Now, let's create the circuit from the transpiled circuit and draw the results, as well as limit the time steps displayed to 2000:

```
#Create the circuit from the transpiled circuit results
circuit_schedule2 = schedule(transpiled_qc2, backend)
#Draw the 2-qubit circuit schedule with range of 2000
#time steps
circuit_schedule2.draw(plot_range=[0, 2000])
```

The results are as we expected. We now have two drive channels, **d0** and **d1**, two acquisition channels, **a0**, and **a1**, and two measurement channels, **m0** and **m1**, which correspond to qubits 0 and 1, respectively:

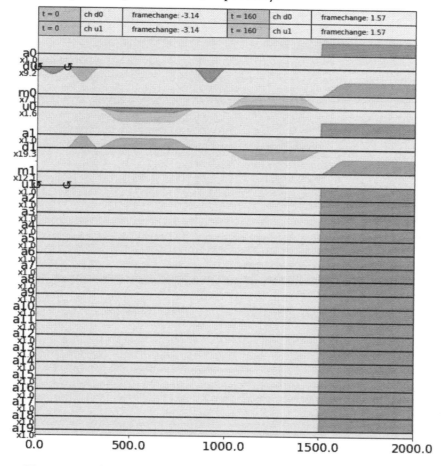

Figure 8.27 – The schedule of the two-qubit quantum circuit using two drive, acquisition, and measurement channels

Congratulations! You have completed quite a bit in this section. In all, you're capable of generating any waveform you wish, within the constraints of the device, of course, either as defined by your own specifications, such as frequency or phase shift, or by leveraging those waveforms provided to you in the Pulse library. You created instructions on which channels those pulses would be applied to. Finally, you created schedules that specify how and when those instructions would be applied and executed onto the device.

Let's move away from the hardware for a moment and look at the backends themselves, particularly how we can leverage some of the information they provide to optimize executing our quantum circuits.

Leveraging provider information

So far in this book, we have been specifying which backends to use; however, as you may recall, we have quite a few options to choose from. *How can we determine which backend would be optimal to run our circuits? Take, for example, the queue time, how can we determine which backend has the least amount of jobs in the queue? How can we get the status of a job we have running in the background and get regular updates to a specific job?* All these questions will be answered in this section, and thankfully for us, there are built-in features that we can use to obtain information about the backend system and the jobs running on them.

Learning about the IBM Quantum Experience components

Each time you open a new Qiskit Notebook on IBM Quantum Experience, you may have noticed that a cell is auto-generated with some standard Qiskit libraries and configuration for your account. The reason it does this is so that you can start coding right away without having to always import and set them each time. This is thanks to one of the IBM Quantum Experience interfaces that handle the accounts related to the system executing the circuits.

In this section, we will discuss the IBM Quantum Experience interface, which is the primary interface to the Account, Providers, Backends, and Jobs being executed. It is because of this that the IBM Quantum Experience interface has four components – namely, **Account**, **Providers**, **Backends**, and **Jobs**. Each of these provides various features that can be used to simplify the use of the systems and their processes. Let's start with Account.

Learning about the Account component

The **Account** object is generally used to handle account information on the local machine where Qiskit is installed, whether that machine is a laptop, mainframe, server, or even a mobile device. The Account object manages the credentials of the system by using any of the following functions:

- `enable_account(TOKEN)` enables the account associated with the TOKEN to the current running notebook or session.

- `save_account(TOKEN)` saves the provided TOKEN to the local filesystem.

- `load_account()` loads the account associated with the saved TOKEN on the system.

- `disable_account()` disables the account associated with the currently running notebook or session.

- `stored_account()` lists all the accounts stored on the currently running session.

- `active_account()` lists the account currently running on the session.

- `delete_account()` deletes the account saved on the local filesystem.

The following code snippet illustrates how to save your TOKEN onto the local filesystem. If you are running a Qiskit notebook on IBM Quantum Experience, you don't need to do this as it is done while the notebook is being loaded. Afterward, the `load_account()` function is called.

This too is taken care of when the Qiskit notebook is first loaded in the first cell and is run. If you run either of these on **IBM Quantum Experience (IQX)**, you will see a warning along with information should you want to override the currently saved account information:

```
#Import the IBMQ interface
from qiskit import IBMQ


#Save account ONLY needed if running on a local system for
#first time
#Uncomment below if running for the first time on a local
#machine.
#IBMQ.save_account('API_TOKEN')
```

```
#Load the account which was saved on local system using
#save_account.
#Note: this is handled each time a Qiskit Notebook is loaded on
#IQX.
IBMQ.load_account()
```

The preceding code will successfully load your account onto your local machine. But since we are running things on IQX, we will likely see warning messages and instructions. We can ignore these and move on.

Understanding the Provider object

The **Provider** object is accessed via the Account object we described previously. Its role is to provide the list of backends available to us based on our account settings. For example, if you are a member of a particular **IBM Q Network** hub, then you could specify that information as an argument to the provider so that the proper access to premium machines is available to you. By default, if no hub information is provided, the provider will fall back to the freely open available devices. The following code example illustrates a few sample settings:

```
#Indicate a hub to link account to:
IBMQ.get_provider(hub='ibm-q')
#Indicate a project which your account is associated with
IBMQ.get_provider(project='my_project')
```

If you run the preceding code. you will certainly get an error for the last line unless you actually have a project associated with your account titled my_project. If so, then it should work just fine.

As you can see in preceding example, the provider is accessed via the IBM Quantum Experience interface and linked through the account. Once the link is successful, you can then query the provider to provide you with a list of the backends available to you. In the following code, we will list out the backends associated with the open group, as shown here:

```
#Create the Provider object using the IBMQ interface
provider = IBMQ.get_provider(group='open')
#Query the list of backends available to your account
provider.backends()
```

The preceding code will output an array of the backends available, as follows:

```
[<IBMQSimulator('ibmq_qasm_simulator') from IBMQ(hub='ibm-q',
group='open', project='main')>,
 <IBMQBackend('ibmqx2') from IBMQ(hub='ibm-q', group='open',
project='main')>,
 <IBMQBackend('ibmq_16_melbourne') from IBMQ(hub='ibm-q',
group='open', project='main')>,
 <IBMQBackend('ibmq_vigo') from IBMQ(hub='ibm-q', group='open',
project='main')>,
 <IBMQBackend('ibmq_ourense') from IBMQ(hub='ibm-q',
group='open', project='main')>,
 <IBMQBackend('ibmq_valencia') from IBMQ(hub='ibm-q',
group='open', project='main')>,
 <IBMQBackend('ibmq_london') from IBMQ(hub='ibm-q',
group='open', project='main')>,
 <IBMQBackend('ibmq_burlington') from IBMQ(hub='ibm-q',
group='open', project='main')>,
 <IBMQBackend('ibmq_essex') from IBMQ(hub='ibm-q',
group='open', project='main')>,
 <IBMQBackend('ibmq_armonk') from IBMQ(hub='ibm-q',
group='open', project='main')>,
 <IBMQBackend('ibmq_santiago') from IBMQ(hub='ibm-q',
group='open', project='main')>]
```

Some of these systems may seem familiar to you as we have used some of them in our code so far. Along with their name, you can also see the hub, group, and main parameters that they pertain to. Should you need to get a subset of the list of all the backends, you can do so by filtering only those you wish to see by including the value in the argument of the `get_provider` function.

We can, of course, filter this list down even more by providing specifics about the type of backend we want to obtain. The following code shows an example of how you can filter and view the specifics:

```
#Filter the list of backends to include only non-simulator,
#and operational (meaning, not offline or under maintenance)
provider.backends(simulator=False, operational=True)
```

The results, as follows, don't include `ibmq_qasm_simulator` and any devices currently in maintenance when you run the cell:

```
[<IBMQBackend('ibmqx2') from IBMQ(hub='ibm-q', group='open',
project='main')>,
 <IBMQBackend('ibmq_16_melbourne') from IBMQ(hub='ibm-q',
 group='open', project='main')>,
 <IBMQBackend('ibmq_vigo') from IBMQ(hub='ibm-q', group='open',
 project='main')>,
 <IBMQBackend('ibmq_ourense') from IBMQ(hub='ibm-q',
 group='open', project='main')>,
 <IBMQBackend('ibmq_valencia') from IBMQ(hub='ibm-q',
 group='open', project='main')>,
 <IBMQBackend('ibmq_london') from IBMQ(hub='ibm-q',
 group='open', project='main')>,
 <IBMQBackend('ibmq_burlington') from IBMQ(hub='ibm-q',
 group='open', project='main')>,
 <IBMQBackend('ibmq_essex') from IBMQ(hub='ibm-q',
 group='open', project='main')>,
 <IBMQBackend('ibmq_armonk') from IBMQ(hub='ibm-q',
 group='open', project='main')>,
 <IBMQBackend('ibmq_santiago') from IBMQ(hub='ibm-q',
 group='open', project='main')>]
```

You can also specify to the provider a specific device to return, as shown here:

```
#Select a specific device from the provider
backend = provider.get_backend('ibmq_santiago')
```

Another `provider` feature is the ability to query the least busy backend. Rather than going back and forth to your list of backends on the IQX dashboard each time you want to execute a circuit, you can ask the provider to search for the least busy backend.

You can also provide further details about the type of device you need to successfully run your circuit. These details include the minimum number of qubits, whether or not you want to include simulators, and so on. The following is an example that queries both the least busy backend devices that have less than 6 qubits and are not a simulator, and those with more than 6 qubits and are not a simulator:

```
#Import the least_busy function
from qiskit.providers.ibmq import least_busy
```

```
#Identify the least busy devices
#smaller than 6 qubits and not a simulator
small_devices = provider.backends(filters=lambda x:
x.configuration().n_qubits < 6 and not x.configuration().
simulator)

#Identify the least busy devices
#larger than 6 qubits and not a simulator
large_devices = provider.backends(filters=lambda x:
x.configuration().n_qubits > 6 and not x.configuration().
simulator)

#Print the least busy devices
print('The least busy small devices: {}'.format(least_
busy(small_devices)))
print('The least busy large devices: {}'.format(least_
busy(large_devices)))
```

The preceding code will print out the least busy devices that are not a simulator and with less than 6 qubits and more than 6 qubits, respectively. The results, of course, will vary based on which devices are least busy when you execute the code.

Now that we know how to query a backend device, let's dig into what information we can pull from each backend.

Learning about the Backend component

The **Backend**, as we have seen so far, is a representation of either real devices or simulators hosted on the IQX cloud platform. It has a variety of functions, which we have used to execute circuits or pulse schedules on various devices. In this section, we will look at some of the other functionality provided by the backend to us.

We'll begin by looking at some of the functionalities that we will commonly use:

- status() provides the current state of the backend.
- configuration() provides the configuration of the backend.
- properties() provides the properties of the backend.
- jobs() provides a list of jobs executed on the backend at a specific instance.
- name() provides the name of the backend.
- retrieve_job(JOB_ID) provides the Job object by using the specified job ID.

We'll run the following code to sample the output of a typical backend; we'll choose one at random for now. At the time of writing, we have chosen ibmq_valencia as an option from the list of available backends. If it is not listed as a backend for you, then just pick any other backend:

```
#Set ibmq_valencia as the backend, or whichever backend you
#wish
backend = provider.get_backend('ibmq_valencia')
#Confirm this is the backend selected by querying for its name,
backend.name()
```

The following code should output the name of the backend you queried – in this case, ibmq_valencia.

The following code will get the status information of the backend and provide information such as whether it is operational. It will also list the number of pending jobs:

```
#View the status of the backend
status = backend.status() is_operational = status.operational
jobs_in_queue = status.pending_jobs
print('Number of pending jobs in the queue: ', jobs_in_queue)
```

The following code will display the status of the backend, which includes the version, whether it's operational, the name, and other information, in a nice UI:

```
#View the configuration of the backend
backend.configuration()
backend
```

The preceding code will output a rather verbose amount of information, in an easy-to-read UI, from the backend configuration, such as coupling maps, basis gates, the number of qubits, gate parameters, and more.

In the following code, we can extract specific property values, such as the number of qubits:

```
# Display the number of qubits from the backend properties
backend.properties().qubits
```

Depending on the backend you selected, you should see the number of qubits of the backend displayed.

The following code will output the properties of the backend system. Similar to the configuration output, this too is a bit verbose but does contain a good amount of information about the system's properties. These properties include gate errors, gate length, qubit T_1 and T_2 coherence times, qubit frequencies, and more. To access them specifically, you can simply append the function to pull the specific property information. For example, to obtain the frequency and readout error of the first qubit, simply run the following:

```
#Print out the frequency of qubit (0)
print('Frequency of first qubit is: '+ str(backend.
properties().frequency(0)))
#Print out the readout error of qubit (0)
print('Readout error of first qubit is: '+ str(backend.
properties().readout_error(0)))
```

The frequency and readout errors are just a few of the various fields available in the backend properties. Refer to the API documentation for others.

Finally, to check the last jobs executed on the backend, we may need to execute a few circuits so that we can have a healthy stock of jobs in the job history for the backend. Otherwise, when you query the backend for the last jobs executed, it will return an empty list, and that's not very amusing. We'll execute a few simple circuits on the backend to help us out:

```
#Run a few jobs on this backend to generate jobs on the backend
qc = QuantumCircuit(1,1)
qc.h(0)
qc.measure_all()
for i in range(0,3):
    result = execute(qc, backend, shots=1024).result()
```

Now that we have four quantum circuit jobs executed and loaded, we can run the following to get some information about each of the jobs we executed on the backend:

```
#List out the last 3 jobs we ran on the device
for executed_job in backend.jobs(limit=3):
    print('Job id: '
            + str(executed_job.job_id()) + ', '
            + str(executed_job.end_date) + ', '
            + str(executed_job.status()))
```

This will loop through all the backend jobs – in this case, we limited this to the last three. However, you can remove the limit from the argument and list out all jobs if you wish. What you will see displayed are the details of the last three jobs, such as the job ID, the date and time the execution was completed, and the status of the job.

Understanding the Job component

The last component we will cover is the **Job** component. The **Job** component is basically an instance of the circuit that has been executed on the backend. What that means is that once you send the circuit to the backend to get executed, the backend will generate the **Job** instance and append information about the job – information such as status, result, job identifier, and so on. The following is a list of the available **Job** functions:

- `backend()` provides the backend that the job is running on.
- `status()` provides the status of the job.
- `result()` provides the job result after execution is completed on the backend.
- `cancel()` provides the ability to cancel the job.
- `job_id()` provides the alphanumeric job identifier.

We'll reuse one of the jobs we ran in the previous section, *Learning about the backend component*, to get some details:

```
#From the previous output of executed jobs, enter its job id.
job = backend.retrieve_job(executed_job.job_id())
```

The preceding code will retrieve the job object by the job ID. Now that we have one of the last job instances, we can extract some information:

```
#Print the job instance status
job.status()
```

We will obtain the status, which in this case should result in the following:

```
<JobStatus.DONE: 'job has successfully run'>
```

If the job has completed successfully, we can review the results returned after executing the job instance on the backend:

```
job.result()
```

The returned result will include quite a bit of information about how the job was executed, such as the measurement level, memory slots, backend details, status, and so on.

Finally, we can get a nice display of the backend itself:

```
job.backend()
```

This will result in a visual representation of the backend, obviously much easier to read and visualize than the raw data output that the `backend.properties` and `backend.configuration` output provides. It has a few tabs across the top to separate the various sets of information besides the properties and configuration. It also includes details about the **Multi-Qubit Gates**, **Error Map** that indicates qubit gate and readout error values, and **Job History**, as shown in the following screenshot:

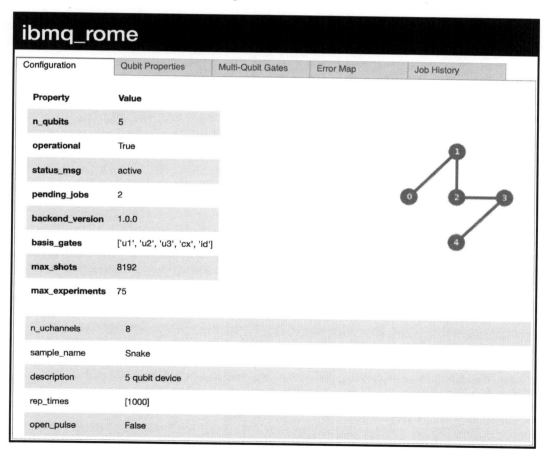

Figure 8.28 – Visual backend device information

In this section, we learned about provider components and what each one does. We also learned about what information they contain. In the next chapter, we will continue on and learn how to monitor multiple jobs without having to query each one individually.

Summary

In this chapter, we covered just some of the many features included in the Terra library. We reviewed creating quantum circuits, as well as executing them on the simulator and real quantum devices. We also reviewed how to concatenate circuits so as to enable you to combine and create composite circuits, which included binding parameters to enable adjustments to various gates. Learning how to extract provider information allows you to obtain information about the various backend devices available to you.

We covered how the circuits are converted into pulses using Terra's open Pulse library and created schedules, which are programs that send pulse information via various channels down to the hardware.

In the next chapter, we will cover techniques to optimize your quantum circuits by reviewing the features available via Pass Managers and Optimizers. We'll also learn various ways to visualize your quantum circuits and monitor your jobs as they are executed on the quantum backend systems.

Questions

1.   What are the four elements of Qiskit?

2.   Construct a random quantum circuit with a width of 4 and a depth of 9.

3.   Create a quantum circuit with the same width as the circuit you created in *question 2* and concatenate it so that it is added before the random quantum circuit you created.

4.   Print the circuit properties of the concatenated quantum circuit from *question 3* and specify the total number of operators, not including any measurement operators.

5.   Create a circuit with a parameterized R_Y gate that would rotate by an angle of $\pi/2$.

6.   Create and draw a schedule with any of the available waveforms from the Pulse library.

7.   Using the `Provider` object, how many quantum systems do you have access to that have 5 or more qubits?

9
Monitoring and Optimizing Quantum Circuits

In the previous chapter, you learned how to program **Qiskit Terra**, using both circuits and pulse schedules.

We'll continue with the topic of circuits in this chapter, specifically monitoring and optimizing circuits. When running a quantum circuit on a quantum device, it helps to be able to monitor and track the status of your circuit, particularly when running multiple circuits on multiple devices at once.

Luckily, **IBM Quantum Experience (IQX)** provides plenty of features to allow us to do this with ease. Additionally, IQX provides a set of classes and features, available to optimize and enhance the visualizations of your circuits. Learning about these features will not only help optimize your circuit results but will also allow you to render the circuits in various styles and representations, such as a directed cyclical graph.

We will cover the following topics in this chapter:

- Monitoring and tracking jobs
- Capturing quantum information and metrics
- Optimizing circuits using the transpiler
- Visualizing and enhancing circuit graphs

After reading this chapter, you will be able to monitor and track your circuits by using a visual and programmatic representation of the backend systems and custom widgets. You'll also get some insights into the various transpiler features available that help optimize the transpilation of your circuit for a given quantum backend system. You'll learn about pass managers and how they can be leveraged to ensure you customize the passes to transform your circuits before executing them on a quantum device.

Technical requirements

In this chapter, it is expected that you are familiar with creating and executing quantum circuits on both a simulator and a quantum computer. Knowledge of quantum hardware, such as qubits and connectivity between qubits, is also recommended.

Here is the full source code used throughout this book: `https://github.com/PacktPublishing/Learn-Quantum-Computing-with-Python-and-IBM-Quantum-Experience`.

Please visit the following link to check the CiA videos: `https://bit.ly/35o5M80`

Monitoring and tracking jobs

The **Qiskit Notebooks** hosted on IQX are built on **Jupyter Notebooks**. This allows us to use some of the features that are available to us to enhance our experience and optimize our time when programming quantum circuits. One of these features is the ability to track jobs in real time while they are executing. We'll try this out here with a test circuit using the following steps:

1. First, we'll create a new Qiskit notebook and enter the following in a new cell:

```
# Import the Qiskit Jupyter tools
from qiskit.tools import jupyter
```

2. Now that we have imported the Qiskit Jupyter tools and have created our provider, we can launch the job tracking widget:

```
# Initialize the job tracker to automatically track all
# jobs
%qiskit_job_watcher
```

The preceding code will launch the Job Watcher widget to the top left of your Qiskit notebook to track your jobs.

3. We'll then create and execute a circuit to test the job watcher:

```
# Let's run a simple circuit on the least busy quantum
# device and check the job watcher widget.
from qiskit.providers.ibmq import least_busy

backend = least_busy(provider.backends(filters=lambda
    x: x.configuration().n_qubits >= (2) and
    not x.configuration().simulator and
    x.status().operational==True))

#Create a simple circuit
qc = QuantumCircuit(1)
qc.h(0)
qc.measure_all()
#Execute the circuit on the backend
job = execute(qc, backend)
```

Once you execute this circuit, expand the IBMQ job watcher, located at the top left of your Qiskit notebook, to see the active status of the circuit. There you will see a queue that indicates how many other users are waiting to execute their circuits on the backend. Once your circuit starts running, you will see the status update accordingly, finally completing in a successful execution.

4. To disable the job watcher, just enter the following:

```
#Disable the job watcher
%qiskit_disable_job_watcher
```

Once disabled, you won't see the IBMQ Jobs widget at the top left of your Qiskit notebook.

5. One last thing to review is the overview of the backend available to you. As you will recall from *Chapter 8, Programming with Qiskit Terra*, we were able to visualize the backend details by running the `job.backend()` function. You can get the same results if you just enter the backend in a cell. The Qiskit Jupyter tool offers another helpful visualization tool to get an overview of all the available backends by entering the following:

```
#Display the list of all available backends and provide
#a brief overview of each
%qiskit_backend_overview
```

The preceding code will result in the following screen, which provides information such as the number of qubits for each backend, whether it supports OpenPulse, the qubit configuration and whether it's least busy, and pending jobs in the queue:

	ibmq_santiago	ibmq_armonk	ibmq_valencia
Num. Qubits	5	1	5
Quantum Vol.	32	-	16
Pending Jobs	50	50	
Operational	True	True	True
Least Busy	False	True	False
Avg. T1 / T2	127.5 / 112.0 us	183.7 / 121.3 us	78.0 / 77.8 us
Avg. CX Err.	0.0076	NA	0.0107
Avg. Meas. Er	0.0223	0.0567	0.035

Figure 9.1 – Visual overview of all the available backends

Now, we are familiar with creating quantum circuits, obtaining information from the various backends available to us, and decomposing the circuits down to the basis gates available on the backend systems. In the next section, we can look at how to optimize the circuit so that we can ensure that we are taking advantage of the configuration and properties of the backend.

Optimizing circuits using the Transpiler

In order to accomplish this, we will learn about the **Transpiler**, it's usage, and the various features it makes available for us to create and execute optimal circuits. By optimizing the execution of the circuit to match the circuit topology of the quantum device, we reduce the noise and its effect on our results.

In this section, we will learn about transforming a quantum circuit so that it is best matched to the quantum device. We will also learn how to optimize the circuit by using the layout optimizer. We will then learn about the backend configuration and its optimization, along with the pass manager and passes.

Transformation of a quantum circuit

When you create a circuit and run it on a quantum device, there are many things occurring between the time you send the circuit to be executed on the quantum device and the time the results are returned. We looked at a few of those steps when we discussed OpenPulse in *Chapter 8, Programming with Qiskit Terra*, and when we decomposed a circuit to its basis states.

The following flowchart illustrates the general process in which the circuit is rewritten so that it can run on the specified backend and be optimized as per the provided settings:

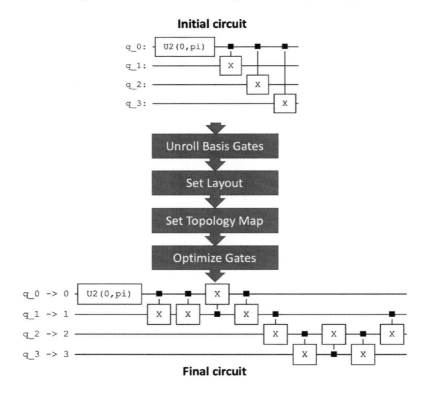

Figure 9.2 – The transpiler process of a circuit from the initial circuit, with passes

One feature we want to cover is the transformation of the quantum circuit and how we can specify its optimization.

> **Important Note**
> Passes are a set of optimization components used in the Transpiler process of a circuit.

We'll begin by introducing the general steps taken, as shown in the preceding flowchart, during the execution process:

1. First, when executing a circuit on a backend, the transpiler identifies any constraints that the backend may have with respect to your circuit and optimizes the circuit accordingly. An example could be the number of qubits available, or how those qubits are connected on the backend.

2. Next, once the constraints are identified and an optimization level is set, the transpiler will package up the circuit in such a way that the transpiler ensures that the circuit to be executed on the quantum device adheres to the constraints of the backend and is optimized accordingly, as described in *step 1*.

3. Finally, the circuit will be sent off to the specified backend for execution.

> **Important Note**
>
> *Step 1* is what we will concentrate on in this section as it deals with the transpiling process.

The **Transpiler** is made up of two primary components – that is, the **pass** and the **pass manager**:

- The transpiler **pass** is the component that transforms the circuit from its current state into a new state that adheres to the task that the pass is configured to perform. For example, some are focused on layout selection, routing, optimizations, circuit analysis, and many others. To see the exhaustive list of available passes, you can run the following:

```
# Import the transpiler passes object
from qiskit.transpiler import passes
# List out all the passes available
print(dir(passes))
```

The preceding code will list all the passes available. For a detailed description of each pass, I would recommend reviewing the API documentation under `qiskit.transpiler.passes`. To ensure you have the latest code information, check the main API documentation page found here: `https://qiskit.org/documentation`

- The **pass manager** is the component that is available to you to specify which passes you wish to use. The pass manager also allows the passes themselves to communicate with other passes. This is ideal for scenarios where one pass would provide or obtain information from other passes in order to ensure the final circuit adheres to any configuration or optimization settings.

  The pass manager also has some preset passes that it makes available to simplify the optimization of a circuit.

In the following section, we will create a simple circuit and pass it through a series of passes where we will leverage existing preset pass managers that optimize the circuit. We'll also run the same circuit on two different backend devices to see how the optimizer differentiates between the two. Finally, we will create a custom topology to transpile the circuit and compare the results of that to a circuit created via the preset optimizer. This will illustrate the consequences of selecting a layout that has not been optimized.

Optimizing the circuit by leveraging the layout optimizer

When creating a circuit, you often don't think about the configurations of the backend – configurations such as whether the qubits you wish to entangle are directly connected with each other or have multiple qubits in between. You might also not think about whether the qubits are aligned in an optimal way to minimize the number of gate operations, usually gate swaps or other multi-qubit gates, such as the **Control Not (CNOT)** or **Toffoli gates**.

We'll start with a fairly simple circuit that contains a few single and multi-qubit gates. As you will recall from the previous chapter, *Chapter 8, Programming with Qiskit Terra*, when we decomposed the Toffoli gate down a level, it expanded from a circuit depth of 1 to a depth of 11, all of which was a collection of various gates in order to create the Toffoli gate.

An analogy of this is to think of the Toffoli gate as a car. When you decompose a car down a level, you are now looking at the components that make up the car, such as the engine, hood, wheels, seats, doors, rearview mirror, and so on. The following steps will provide a refresher of what this looks like:

1. We will create a quantum circuit with a Toffoli gate. Recall that a Toffoli gate has two control qubits and a single target qubit (ccx):

    ```
    #Basic Toffoli gate,
    qc = QuantumCircuit(3)
    qc.ccx(0,1,2)
    qc.draw()
    ```

    The preceding code draws the quantum circuit with the Toffoli gate added. Following our analogy, this represents a car:

Figure 9.3 – Toffoli gate representation

2. We'll decompose the Toffoli gate down a level to its representative gates:

```
qc_decomposed = qc.decompose()
qc_decomposed.draw()
```

The preceding code draws the component gates of the Toffoli gate. Following the car analogy, this represents the components of our car:

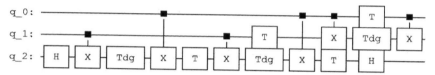

Figure 9.4 – Toffoli gate, down to lower-level representative gates

3. Now, in order to run a proper comparison between backends and layout passes, we will create the following four-qubit quantum circuit:

```
#Basic circuit with a single and multi-qubit gates
qc = QuantumCircuit(4)
qc.h(0)
qc.cx(0,1)
qc.cx(0,2)
qc.cx(0,3)
qc.draw()
```

The resulting circuit is represented by a collection of Hadamard and CNOT gates, as follows:

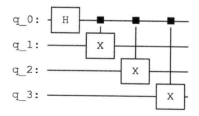

Figure 9.5 – A simple four-qubit quantum circuit comprising H and CNOT gates

4. Next, we will decompose the circuit down a level, which, in this case, will decompose it to its basis gate, U_2, and CNOT gates:

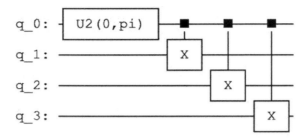

Figure 9.6 – Decomposed four-qubit quantum circuit to its basis gate representation

5. Next, we will view the circuit depth and the operator count of both the initial circuit and the decomposed circuit:

```
#Print the depth of both inital and decomposed circuit
print('Initial circuit depth: ', qc.depth())
print('Decomposed circuit depth: ',
qc_decomposed.depth()
#Get the number of operators in initial circuit
print('Initial circuit operation count: ',
qc.count_ops()
#Get the number of operators in decomposed circuit
print('Decomposed circuit operation count: ',
qc_decomposed.count_ops()
```

The preceding code should print out roughly the same numbers for both circuits. The only difference between the two is the replacement of the **H** gate with the U_2 basis gate, as shown in the following operation count output:

```
Initial circuit depth:  4
Decomposed circuit depth:  4
Initial circuit operation count:  OrderedDict([('cx', 3),
('h', 1)])
Decomposed circuit operation count:  OrderedDict([('cx',
3), ('u2', 1)])
```

So far, nothing looks too surprising regarding our quantum circuits. The operations are fairly straightforward and simple enough.

In the next section, we will run the circuit on two different backends to illustrate the difference and importance of the backend layouts and optimizers, particularly how the optimizers select the proper qubit mapping from the circuit to the backend device. The backends we will use for this example will be using `ibmq_santiago` and `ibmq_16_melbourne`. You can, of course, choose whichever backend you wish; just note that there may be some differences based on the configuration of the backend selected.

Leaning about backend configuration and optimization

To visualize information on the backend, we learned earlier that we can call the configuration and properties functions to output all the information. That can be handy if we want to extract specific data from the results; however, it is quite difficult to read. This is where the visualization tool comes in very handy. Let's first pull the backend information from one of our devices by running the following cell. In this example, I'll choose `ibmq_santiago`, but you can select whichever quantum device you have available:

```
# Get the backend device: ibmq_santiago
backend_santiago = provider.get_backend('ibmq_santiago')
# Launch backend viewer of ibmq_santiago
backend_santiago
```

The preceding code should launch the following viewer that lists the backend properties and configuration information, along with a lot of other content related to **ibmq_santiago**. In this view, you will see several tabs across the top that group information pertaining to the backend device:

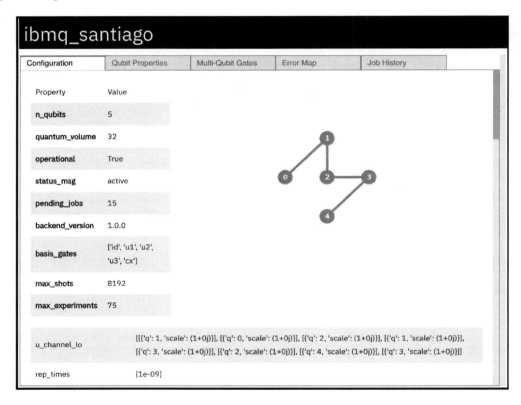

Figure 9.7 – Backend properties and configuration viewer for ibmq_santiago

As you can see in the preceding screenshot, the tabs are listed as follows:

- **Configuration** lists out the configuration information of the quantum device, such as the number of qubits, the operational status, how many pending jobs are in the queue, its basis gates and coupling map, and much more.

- **Qubit Properties** lists out the details about each qubit, such as its frequency, decoherence (T1 and T2), the gate error for each basis gate, and its readout errors.

- The **Multi-Qubit Gates** properties contain the multi-qubit gate type (for example, cx) and its respective multi-gate error for each direction. For example, cx0_1 means a **CNOT (CX)** gate with the 0th index qubit as the source and the 1st indexed qubit as the target.

- **Error Map** is a visual representation of the error rates for each qubit. The error rates are indicated by the gates tested – in this case, **H** and **CNOT**. The color coding is used to visually represent the difference between the qubits with lower error rates and those with higher error rates. Readout errors are listed as well and compared against other qubits.

- **Job History** breaks down the number of jobs you executed on this device by date, where each color represents the different dates.

Now, we will view the `ibmq_16_melbourne` device similarly to how we did for the previous device, as follows:

```
# Get the backend device: ibmq_16_melbourne
backend_melbourne = provider.get_backend('ibmq_16_melbourne')
# Launch backend viewer of ibmq_16_melbourne
backend_melbourne
```

This will launch the same viewer with the same views pertaining to **ibmq_16_melbourne** (we'll refer to this device simply as **Melbourne** for simplicity):

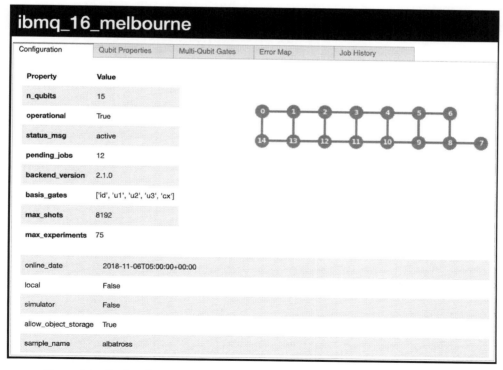

Figure 9.8 – Backend properties and configuration viewer for ibmq_16_melbourne

Now that we have both backend views open in our notebook, let's take a look at the visual representation of the gates and how they are physically connected.

In *Figure 9.7*, ibmq_santiago (we'll refer to this backend device as **Santiago** moving forward for simplicity), we can see that not only is it a five-qubit device, but also that the qubits are connected linearly. This means that qubit **0** is only connected to qubit **1**, qubit **1** is connected to qubit **2**, and so forth. However, this does not necessarily mean that the qubit information flows in only one direction. If you scroll down on the **Configuration** view, you will see the **coupling_map** field.

In the **coupling_map** field, you will see how the direction of the qubits is configured. The first two entries are related to the first two qubits. Note that the coupling map between qubit **0** and qubit **1** is defined and illustrated bidirectionally – that is, qubits can be entangled in either direction, [0,1] and [1,0]. What that means is that you can place a CX gate where the source is either the first or second qubit and the target is the opposite qubit, second or first, respectively. To visualize the coupling directional map, just run the following cell:

```
# Visualize the coupling directional map between the qubits
plot_gate_map(backend_santiago, plot_directed=True)
```

Now, we can see the gate map with the coupling directional mapping between each qubit, as illustrated here:

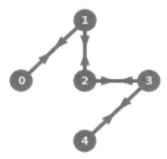

Figure 9.9 – Qubit plot view with the coupling directional map enabled (ibmq_santiago)

Let's see the same for **Melbourne**, as illustrated in *Figure 9.8*, by entering the following into a cell:

```
# Visualize the coupling directional map between the qubits
plot_gate_map(backend_melbourne, plot_directed=True)
```

The preceding code displays a similar mapping to what we saw earlier with a clear difference in the configuration:

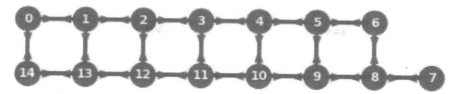

Figure 9.10 – Qubit plot view with the coupling directional map enabled (ibmq_16_melbourne)

You may notice that the coupling maps have some similarities between the two systems. Take note of the first five qubits of **Santiago** compared to that of **Melbourne**; you will see that the connections are linear. However, this is where the similarities stop because unlike **Santiago**, **Melbourne** has the first five qubits connected to other qubits. **Santiago**, as you will recall, has all the qubits, except the first and last, connected to two adjoining qubits. **Melbourne** has three qubits connected to any qubit, except, of course, qubit **7**, which is connected to only one qubit; all the others have between two and three qubits connected.

Because of the different configuration of the qubits, the layout of the qubits from our quantum circuit might not be defined in the most optimal way when mapping them to the hardware configuration. Lucky for us, we have the execute and transpile functions, which include a parameter setting that allows us to set the level of optimization of the circuit layout. This optimization level comprises four different levels, where each is associated with one of various mapping layout strategies, called **Transpiler Passes**. The next section will cover the various passes available and also the pass manager used to manage their usage.

Understanding passes and pass managers

Passes are generally used to transform circuits so that they are set up to perform as optimally as desired. There are five general types of passes that transform circuits:

- **Layout Selection** determines how the qubit layout mapping will align with the selected backend configuration.

- **Routing** maps the placement of swap gates onto the circuit based on the selected swap mapping type, which can be set by providing a coupling map or backend topology, or by using stochastic methods.

- **Basis Change** offers various ways to decompose or unroll the gates down to the basis gates of the backend or using the circuit's decomposition rules.

- **Optimizations** optimizes the gates themselves by either removing redundant gates, such as having two of the same gates back to back, which reverts the gate to the original state. It can also combine basis gates, such as the U_1, U_2, or U_3 gates, into a single gate.

- **Circuit Analysis** provides circuit information, such as the depth, width, number of operations, and other details about the circuit.

- **Additional passes** are those that offer some other form of optimization, such as the various **check maps**, which check whether the layout of the CNOT gates are in the direction stated in the coupling maps and rearrange the directions if needed.

We covered most of the **Circuit Analysis** information in *Chapter 8, Programming with Qiskit Terra*, to detect the size, width, and number of operations in a circuit. Let's look at **Layout Selection** to see how we can leverage the provided layouts and learn the difference between the various optimization levels.

Learning about the Layout Selection type

There are various layout passes to choose from. Let's look at a few of the basics:

- **TrivialLayout**: This layout assigns n qubits to the device qubits in the same order as stated in the original quantum circuit.

- **DenseLayout**: This layout selects a layout that has the most connected subset of qubits. If there is a need for a large number of entangled qubits, this layout will find a subset of which qubits are closely connected to each other so as to avoid long distances and swaps.

- **NoiseAdaptiveLayout**: This layout leverages a qubit mapping technique that leverages the calibration information from the backend device and evaluates several optimal and heuristic mappings, as described in this paper: `https://arxiv.org/abs/1901.11054`.

For each of the aforementioned passes, there is a different default setting for the optimization level. **TrivialLayout** is the default layout when `optimization level = 0`, **DenseLayout** is the default when `optimization = 1`, and **NoiseAdaptiveLayout** is the default when the optimization level is set to either 2 or 3, depending on the device.

We'll set the various optimization levels in the transpiler function parameter and apply it to the two backend devices, **Santiago** and **Melbourne**, in the following steps:

1. We'll reuse the same four-qubit quantum circuit we created earlier. I'll include it again here for your convenience:

```
# Quantum circuit with a single and multi-qubit gates
qc = QuantumCircuit(4)
qc.h(0)
qc.cx(0,1)
qc.cx(0,2)
qc.cx(0,3)
qc.draw()
```

We'll start with **Santiago** and set the optimization level to 0, which is to say we will use TrivialLayout and map the circuit qubit index to the respective qubit index of the backend. What this will result in is the qubit on our quantum circuit [0,1,2,3,4], which will map to the same qubit index values on the backend device, **Santiago** [0,1,2,3,4].

2. In the following code, we will leverage the same quantum circuit we had set up earlier (qc) and use it as our quantum circuit to test the various optimization levels. We'll then print out the transpiled circuit depth and visualize the layout with the mapped qubits drawn as an overlay over the backend device:

```
# Transpile the circuit with an optimization level = 0
qc_santiago_0 = transpile(qc, backend_santiago,
seed_transpiler=10258, optimization_level=0)
# Print out the depth of the circuit
print('Depth:', qc_santiago_0.depth())
# Plot the resulting layout of the quantum circuit after
# Layout
plot_circuit_layout(qc_santiago_0, backend_santiago)
```

The result, as follows, is as expected, where the qubits are mapped with no layout optimization at all, and there is the direct mapping of qubits from the quantum circuit to the hardware device:

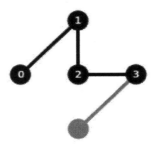

Figure 9.11 – Transpiled quantum circuit on Santiago with optimization = 0, direct qubit mapping with no changes

3. Now, let's draw the transpiled circuit on **Santiago**:

```
# Draw the transpiled circuit pertaining to Santiago
qc_santiago_0.draw()
```

This will render the transpiled circuit using the basis gates available on **Santiago**:

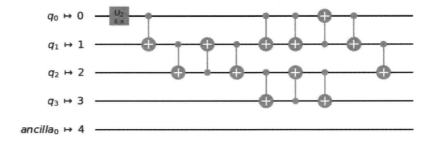

Figure 9.12 – Transpiled circuit of basis gates on Santiago

Please note that the unused qubits are prefixed as `ancilla_n` to indicate unmapped qubits.

4. Now, let's run the same thing on **Melbourne** with the same level of optimization set to 0. We should see the same results, in that the transpiled circuit is mapped to the same qubits as our quantum circuit:

```
# View the transpiled circuit with an optimization
# Level = 0
qc_melbourne_0 = transpile(qc, backend_melbourne,
    seed_transpiler=10258, optimization_level=0)
```

```
print('Depth:', qc_melbourne_0.depth())
plot_circuit_layout(qc_melbourne_0, backend_melbourne)
```

The preceding code will result in the following depth information:

```
Depth: 10
```

The resulting layout mapping, as follows, is also displayed:

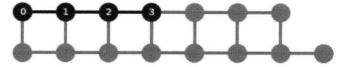

Figure 9.13 – Transpiled circuit on Melbourne

Let's now look at the transpiled circuit for the **Melbourne** quantum device.

5.   We'll now draw the transpiled circuit using the following code:

```
# Draw the transpiled circuit pertaining to Melbourne
qc_melbourne_0.draw()
```

The preceding code will display the following circuit:

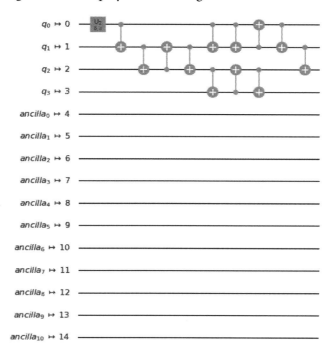

Figure 9.14 – Transpiled circuit on Melbourne

Please note, as you can see in *Figure 9.12*, that the unused qubits are prefixed as `ancilla_n` to indicate unmapped qubits.

As we can see in the preceding circuit diagram, there is no difference between the layout when the transpiler does not try to optimize the circuit.

6. Let's now maximize the optimization level to 3 and see whether there is a difference:

```
# Transpile the circuit with the optimization level = 3
qc_transpiled_santiago = transpile(qc, backend_santiago,
optimization_level=3)
# Print the depth of the transpiled circuit
print('Depth:', qc_transpiled_santiago.depth())
# Print the number of operations of the transpiled
# circuit
print('Ops count: ', qc_transpiled_santiago.count_ops())
# Plot the layout mapping of the transpiled circuit
plot_circuit_layout(qc_transpiled_santiago,
backend_santiago)
```

The preceding code will print out the total circuit depth and the total number of operators (`Ops count`) in the transpiled circuit, along with the rendering of the transpiled mapping of the qubits onto **Santiago**:

```
Depth: 10
Ops count:  OrderedDict([('u2', 10), ('cx', 5), ('u3',
1)])
```

The following diagram shows the rendering of the transpiled mapping of the qubits, as mentioned earlier:

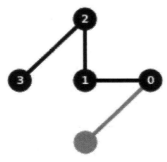

Figure 9.15 – Transpiled circuit with the optimization level set to 3

As you can see in the preceding diagram, in an effort to reduce noise, the qubit order is reversed from the previous example on **Santiago**.

7. Then, draw out the circuit to review the transpiled circuit using the `matplotlib` palette:

```
# Redraw the transpiled circuit at new level
qc_transpiled_santiago.draw()
```

The result, as follows, is the same circuit that is now mapped to different qubits compared to the circuit in *Figure 9.12*. The difference between this circuit and the previous one is simply that the transpiler has the maximum optimization level set, so it will map the qubit operators to the most optimal qubits, as follows:

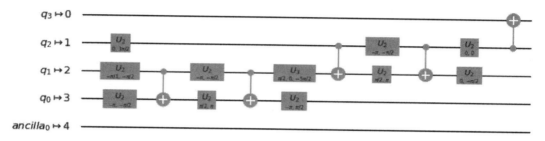

Figure 9.16 – Transpiled circuit with the optimization level set to 3

8. We'll set the same optimization level on **Melbourne** to 3 and transpile the circuit then:

```
# Transpile the quantum circuit with the optimization
# level = 3
qc_transpiled_melbourne = transpile(qc,
backend_melbourne, optimization_level=3)
# Get the depth and operation count of the transpiled
# circuit.
print('Depth:', qc_transpiled_melbourne.depth())
print('Ops count: ', qc_transpiled_melbourne.count_ops())
# Print the circuit layout
plot_circuit_layout(qc_transpiled_melbourne,
backend_melbourne)
```

Here, the total depth is the same, as is the number and type of operators:

```
Depth: 10
Ops count:  OrderedDict([('u2', 10), ('cx', 5), ('u3',
1)])
```

However, note that the layout is not necessarily linear; it seems *T-shaped*, where qubit 0 is connected with 3 qubits rather than 2, as it was in **Santiago**:

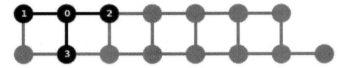

Figure 9.17 – Transpiled circuit with the optimization level set to 3

As you can see, in an effort to reduce noise, the qubit order is reversed from the previous example run on **Melbourne**.

9. Let's draw the circuit and see how this mapping looks compared to the previous circuit mapping:

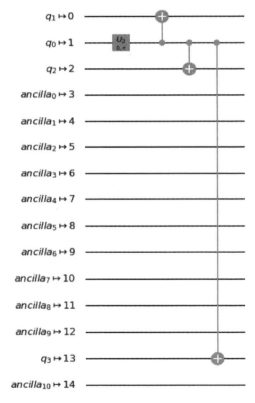

Figure 9.18 – Transpiled circuit with the optimization level set to 3

Note the use of qubit **13**, which is closer to grouped qubits **0–2**. This is a good example where the optimizer mapped qubit **3** to qubit **13** on the device so as to avoid extra swap gates.

10. Finally, let's now create our own custom mapping, or **topology**, as it is often referred to. Let's begin by reviewing the coupling map of an existing device; in this case, let's try another device, ibmqx2, one of the original five-qubit devices that has a bowtie configuration of qubits. We'll review the configuration of the backend first:

```
# View the ibmqx2 backend device configuration and
# properties
backend = provider.get_backend('ibmqx2')
backend
```

The preceding code launches a visualization widget that contains all the configuration and property values of the quantum device, **ibmqx2**, nicknamed *the bowtie*. The reason for the nickname – the bowtie – is that it is based on the qubit topology, which seems to represent a tilted bowtie, shown in the following screenshot:

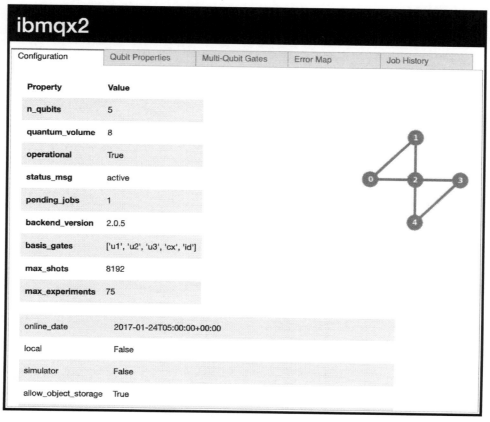

Figure 9.19 – Visualization of ibmqx2 configuration and properties

11. Let's examine the coupling map for `ibmqx2` by calling the configuration's `coupling_map` field:

```
# View the backend coupling map, displayed as CNOTs
# (Control-Target)
backend = provider.get_backend('ibmqx2')
# Extract the coupling map from the backend
ibmqx2_coupling_map = backend.configuration().coupling_
    map
# List out the extracted coupling map
ibmqx2_coupling_map
```

The preceding code will result in the following coupling layout of `ibmqx2`. You can verify this by comparing it to the backend view:

```
[[0, 1],
 [0, 2],
 [1, 0],
 [1, 2],
 [2, 0],
 [2, 1],
 [2, 3],
 [2, 4],
 [3, 2],
 [3, 4],
 [4, 2],
 [4, 3]]
```

12. Next, we will draw the coupling map to see how efficient our circuit is with the default map:

```
# Transpile a custom circuit using only the coupling map.
# Set the backend to 'None' so it will force using the
# coupling map provided.
qc_custom = transpile(qc, backend=None,
coupling_map=ibmqx2_coupling_map)
# Draw the resulting custom topology circuit.
qc_custom.draw()
```

Our circuit, using this topology, is now different from what we saw in **Santiago** in *Figure 9.16*. Here, we see that the same circuit is now transpiled based on the **ibmqx2** topology, as follows:

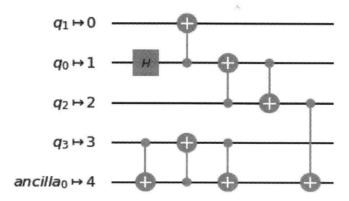

Figure 9.20 – The circuit using the topology provided by the ibmqx coupling map

13. Now, let's create our own custom topology. For simplicity, we will create a simple linear topology, where the qubits are joined together in a line, as follows:

```
# Create our own coupling map (custom topology)
custom_linear_topology = [[0,1],[1,2],[2,3],[3,4]]
# Set the coupling map to our custom linear topology
qc_custom = transpile(qc, backend=None,
coupling_map=custom_linear_topology)
# Draw the resulting circuit.
qc_custom.draw()
```

The result from the preceding circuit code is clearly not ideal. The circuit required many gates and is quite deep, which increases the risk of having noisy results. This is a good illustration of the importance of optimizers, which handle many of these potential issues. It's no surprise why there is a lot of research in identifying better ways to optimize circuits to avoid inefficient and noisy circuits:

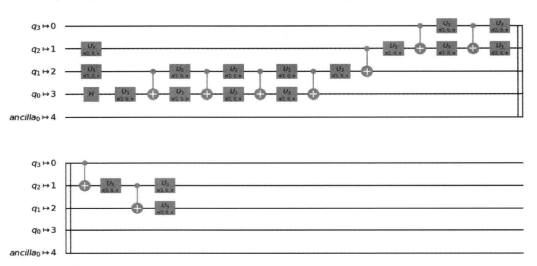

Figure 9.21 – Custom linear topology of our circuit

Now that we have a better understanding of passes and how some of them help the transpiler generate optimal circuits, we just need to conclude with the pass manager. The pass manager is what allows the passes to communicate with each other, and also schedules which passes should execute first.

This is not as simple as it sounds as there may be a significant difference if one pass is used before another, or perhaps is unable to communicate with another pass. We'll conclude this section with a simple example of the pass manager, using the following steps to create it:

1. We'll first append `TrivialLayout` to `PassManager` and execute the circuit:

```
# Import the PassManager and a few Passes
from qiskit.transpiler import PassManager, CouplingMap
from qiskit.transpiler.passes import TrivialLayout,
BasicSwap
# Create a TrivialLayout based on the ibmqx2 coupling map
trivial = TrivialLayout(CouplingMap(ibmqx2_coupling_map))
```

```
# Append the TrivialLayout to the PassManager
pm.append(trivial)
# Run the PassManager and draw the resulting circuit
tv_qc = pm.run(qc)
tv_qc.draw()
```

The resulting circuit is as follows. Note the specifics of this circuit as we will be comparing the differences between the layouts of this circuit and the upcoming circuit (in *Figure 9.23*):

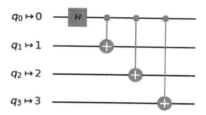

Figure 9.22 – PassManager with the appended TrivialLayout Pass circuit

2. In the following code, we will create a `BasicSwap` pass, rerun `PassManager` on the circuit, and compare the results to the previous circuit:

```
# Create a BasicSwap based on the ibmqx2 coupling map we
# used earlier
basic_swap = BasicSwap(CouplingMap(ibmqx2_coupling_map))
#Add the BasicSwap to the PassManager
pm = PassManager(basic_swap)
# Run the PassManager and draw the results
new_qc = pm.run(qc)
new_qc.draw()
```

The previous code will create a `BasicSwap` router and add it to `PassManager` upon construction. The executed circuit result is as follows:

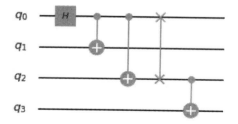

Figure 9.23 – PassManager with a BasicSwap router pass circuit

As you can see, the circuit will adapt to each of the passes called from PassManager – in this case, BasicSwap was called and rendered in one format, and the TrivialLayout pass rendered in a different format.

Now that you are familiar with pass managers, you can see that they can be very helpful if you want to use a combination of passes in a way that when leveraged one after the other, the optimization of the circuit improves as the circuit is modified along the way.

In this section, we also learned about the Transpiler and how to optimize circuits using it. We also learned about transforming and optimizing the circuit using the layout optimizer. We also learned about backend optimization and configuration.

The next section of this chapter is a bit more visual, using **Directed Acyclic Graphs (DAGs)** to view the circuits and their functionality.

Visualizing and enhancing circuit graphs

This section will focus on the various visualizations available in Terra. The graphs we have been using were from the default drawer library in Qiskit. However, we can specify other drawing tools that may be better suited for your documentation purposes. Say, for example, that you are authoring a research paper with **Latex** and you want to use the latex content.

By simply adding style parameters from the Qiskit drawer library, you can then leverage the many features included with the visualization library. We'll cover a few of those now to get you started.

Learning about customized visual circuits

When rendering a circuit, it is often necessary or convenient to have the results in a format that suits the format of your document. It's here where the Qiskit drawer comes in handy with various features. Let's begin with a simple quantum circuit to illustrate the various visual rendering examples:

1. First, let's create a quantum circuit with various operators to get a good representation of all the visual components in the various formats:

```
# Sample quantum circuit
qc = QuantumCircuit(4)
qc.h(0)
qc.cx(0,1)
qc.barrier()
```

```
qc.cx(0,2)
qc.cx(0,3)
qc.barrier()
qc.cz(3,0)
qc.h(0)
qc.measure_all()
# Draw the circuit using the default renderer
qc.draw()
```

This will render the following circuit drawing, which is just a random representation of gates. This circuit does not do anything special, it's just used to represent various components. As an option, you can use the `random_circuit` method to create a random circuit:

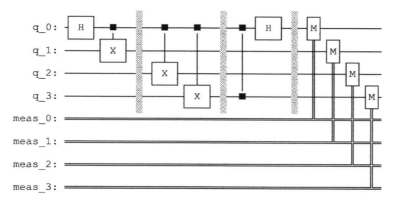

Figure 9.24 – Circuit rendering using the default library

2. Now, let's redraw the circuit using the `matplotlib` library using the same `draw()` method we have been using throughout this book:

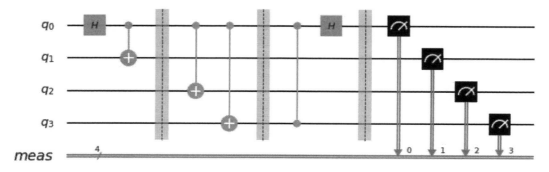

Figure 9.25 – Circuit rendering using the matplotlib library

3. Next, we will render the preceding circuit using `latex`:

```
draw('latex')
```

This will render the `latex` version. If you're running this on your local machine and not on IQX, you may have some warnings or errors indicating you need to install some file dependencies, such as installing `pylatexenc`. In that case, simply install any missing dependencies and you will be able to render the circuit using the latex drawers, as illustrated in the following circuit diagram:

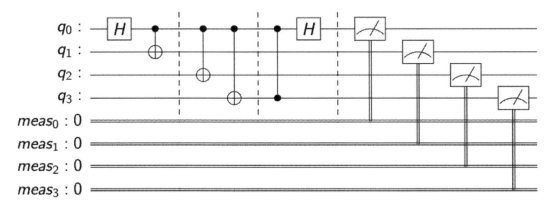

Figure 9.26 – Circuit rendering using the Latex library

4. If you are planning to post your circuit onto a website, blog, or social media and would like to include some styles on the image, you have the ability to do that as well by passing in the style contents as a parameter, such as `backgroundcolor`, `gatetextcolor`, and `fontsize`, just to name a few:

```
# Define the style to render the circuit and components
style = {'backgroundcolor': 'lightblue','gatefacecolor':
    'white', 'gatetextcolor': 'black', 'fontsize': 9}
# Draw the mpl with the specified style
qc.draw(style=style)
```

The preceding code results in adjusting the background, gate color schemes, and the font size, as illustrated here:

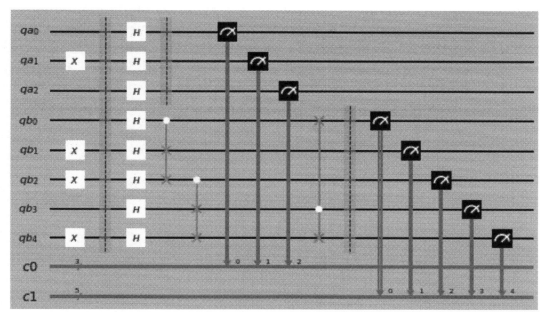

Figure 9.27 – Rendered circuit with the custom style dictionary on matplotlib

To use the style setting, you must use the output `matplotlib` as this is the only support for the styles. Details on the available list of styles can be found in the *Style Dict Details* section of the Qiskit API documentation (`https://qiskit.org/documentation`).

Finally, we will cover a full view of the circuit as a **Directed Acyclic Graph (DAG)**, which will be helpful to see the circuit as a graph in order to understand the flow of the circuit.

Drawing the DAG of a circuit

As circuits get larger, they will naturally get more complex, and even visualizing a circuit can get complicated. Imagine a circuit with a million qubits and with a depth of over 1,000. This would be difficult to render and almost impossible to read. This is where DAGs may help. If you break down a circuit into composites, you can then render each composite as a DAG. Let's create one based on the circuit that we previously created to illustrate rendering and see how the DAG of that circuit looks.

In the following code, you will need two components; the first is the circuit-to-DAG converter. This will convert the circuit into a DAG. The second component is the DAG drawer, which will draw out the DAG where the nodes are represented as quantum registers, classical registers, quantum gates, barriers, and measurement operators. The edges are directional, which illustrates the flow of the circuit:

```
# Import the Circuit to DAG converter
from qiskit.converters import circuit_to_dag
# Import the DAG drawer
from qiskit.tools.visualization import dag_drawer
# Convert the circuit into a DAG
dag = circuit_to_dag(qc)
# Draw the DAG of the circuit
dag_drawer(dag)
```

This results in the following rendering of the DAG:

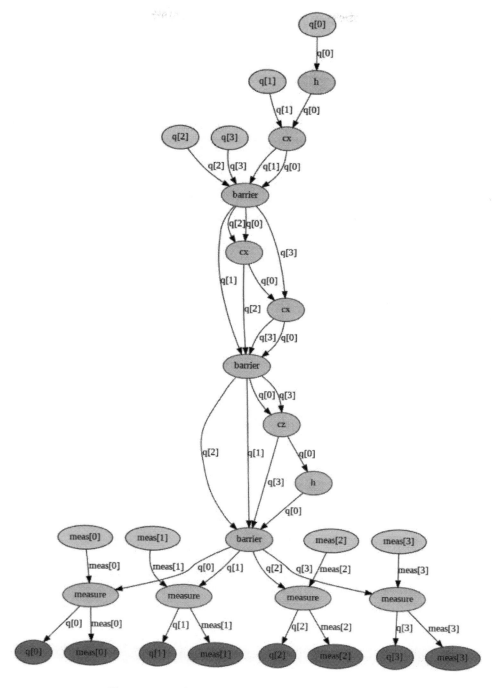

Figure 9.28 – The DAG rendering of a quantum circuit

The DAG can help illustrate the flow and expected paths of the circuit. For example, the preceding graph starts at the top with the qubits in green, then following the graph, we see that each qubit is operated upon by the specified operation represented by the nodes and the applied qubits by the edge label between nodes. The graph terminates at the end in red, where the measurement applied on the qubit is mapped to the specified classical bit, represented by the parameter values.

In this section, we learned about visualizing the circuit graphs with the help of customized visual circuits. We also learned how to use DAGs to enhance our circuit graphs.

Summary

In this chapter, we learned various ways to monitor your circuits when they are running on one of the many quantum computers. You also learned about the different passes available to optimize the execution of your circuit on a specified quantum device. This includes the pass manager, which allows you to customize which passes to leverage and also allows you to choose their order.

We then covered topology and coupling maps, which helped you understand the importance of knowing the device configurations, should you want to create your own passes. By visualizing the circuits in various formats, you now have the skills to customize the rendering of images, particularly if you are documenting your work and would like to keep a certain look and feel.

In the next chapter, we will learn about noise models and the advantages between the simulators and how they can help us understand the noise models so that we can mitigate and run more efficient algorithms.

Questions

1. Create a filter that will return the least busy backend to run a quantum circuit that includes any constraint other than those covered in this book (*Hint: use the* `backend.configuration()` *function to view other backend configuration variables*).

2. Can you name two components of the Transpiler?

3. Which component allows you to specify the passes to use?

4. What is the depth of a Toffoli gate when decomposed?

5. Is there a difference between when decomposing a Toffoli gate using `decompose()` versus the Transpiler?

6. What are the basis gates on the `ibmq_santiago` device?

7. What are the five pass types?

8. What is the default `optimization_level` value when running the `execute()` function?

9. What are the default `optimization_level` values set for `TrivialLayout` and `DenseLayout`?

10
Executing Circuits Using Qiskit Aer

Aer is a provider of high-performance backends that can be used to execute quantum circuits. The various backend simulators available can be used in unique ways where each can provide various information pertaining to your circuit. Aer also provides a variety of tools that can be leveraged to construct noise models to simulate various errors that occur on real quantum devices. These tools are very helpful should you need to compare the difference between your results from an ideal simulator and that which replicates the effects of noise from a quantum device.

Both the simulators, and tools such as the **noise model**, will help you understand the reasons for some of the effects on your results as well as provide insights should you later want to mitigate those errors yourself.

The following topics will be covered in this chapter:

- Understanding the differences between the Aer simulators
- Generating noise models
- Building your own noise model
- Executing quantum circuits with custom noise models

In this chapter, we will review all four Aer simulators, and understand the differences between each of them and what unique functionality each one provides. We will also delve into the Aer noise models that we can generate based on the specified backend devices to allow us to simulate noise on our ideal Aer simulators.

After reading this chapter, you will be able to reproduce similar noise effects on the simulator. This will allow you to observe how the noise affects our results, which would allow us to simulate a real quantum device. Finally, we will cover how you can create your own noise models and apply them to your circuits.

Technical requirements

In this chapter, it is expected that you are familiar with the basics of quantum circuits described in previous chapters, such as creating and executing quantum circuits, obtaining backend properties and configurations, and customizing and visualizing circuit diagrams, and you should have knowledge of qubit logic gate operators and states. Also, some familiarity of noise effects such as decoherence time would be ideal, however we will cover some of the basics in this chapter as a refresher.

Here is the source code used throughout this book: `https://github.com/PacktPublishing/Learn-Quantum-Computing-with-Python-and-IBM-Quantum-Experience`

Please visit the following link to check the CiA videos: `https://bit.ly/35o5M80`

Understanding the differences between the Aer simulators

The **IBM Quantum Experience** (**IQX**) has an array of not only real backend quantum devices, but also a multitude of simulators as well, many of which we have used so far in this book. IQX always has the latest Qiskit packages installed. This makes it easy for anyone new to quantum computing to simply log on and start learning and coding right away.

In this section, you will learn about the various Aer simulators, including the differences between them and their distinct features. These features include generating noise models and configuring the simulator backends that allow you to take advantage of modifying their behavior and characteristics to suit your needs.

Of course, you can always install **Qiskit** locally on your own machine, servers, or any supported device. However, one advantage to using the simulators on IQX is the fact that the server it is installed onto is a pretty large, high-performance system with plenty of resources. As shown in the following screenshot, **ibmq_qasm_simulator** can run wider circuits than most local machines and has a larger variety of basis gates:

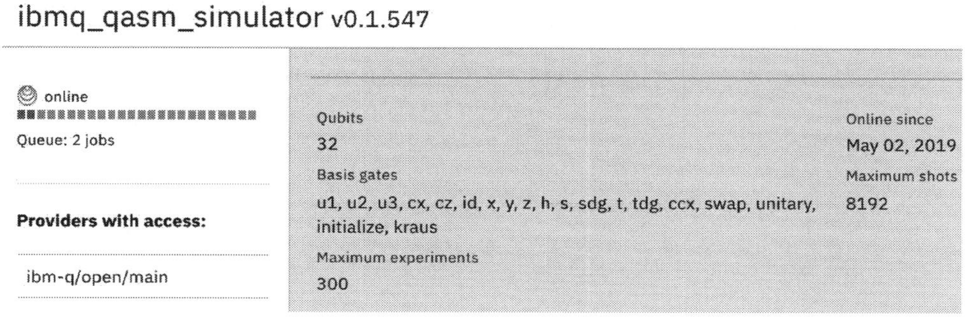

ibmq_qasm_simulator v0.1.547

⊚ online ■■□■■■■■■■■■■■■■■■■■■■ Queue: 2 jobs	Qubits 32	Online since May 02, 2019
	Basis gates	Maximum shots
Providers with access:	u1, u2, u3, cx, cz, id, x, y, z, h, s, sdg, t, tdg, ccx, swap, unitary, initialize, kraus	8192
ibm-q/open/main	Maximum experiments 300	

Figure 10.1 – ibmq_qasm_simulator on the IQX

As you can see from the preceding screenshot, at the time of writing, the **ibmq_qasm_ simulator** has the maximum number of experiments allowed set to **300**, the **Maximum shots** per circuit set to **8192**, and has a timeout of 10,000 seconds, which approximates to just under 3 hours.

In the following sections, we will learn about the following simulators and their key features:

- The Qasm simulator, which executes a quantum circuit with multiple shots to simulate a noisy backend quantum system

- The statevector simulator, which provides the state vector of the quantum circuit

- The unitary simulator, which provides the unitary matrix of the quantum circuit being executed

- The pulse simulator, which simulates pulse schedules to execute directly to the various channels on the hardware

Let's move on to the next section, looking at the backends.

Viewing all available backends

If you have read the previous chapters of this book, then you are aware of some of the simulators we have used. But they are just a small subset of what is available on IQX. Let's start off by displaying every simulator available from the various sources.

We will create a new **Qiskit Notebook** on IQX and run the autogenerated cell to ensure you have loaded some base classes and methods, and loaded your account information so we can access IQX:

1. We'll begin by displaying all of the available simulators in the Aer library by using the following code:

    ```
    # View all available Aer backends
    Aer.backends()
    ```

    This will display a list of all the available simulators, which are part of the AerProvider class:

    ```
    [<QasmSimulator('qasm_simulator') from AerProvider()>,
    <StatevectorSimulator('statevector_simulator') from
    AerProvider()>,
    <UnitarySimulator('unitary_simulator') from
    AerProvider()>,
    <PulseSimulator('pulse_simulator') from AerProvider()>]
    ```

2. The following code will list out the simulators that are part of the BasicAer class. These are also available as Python built simulators, should you not want to install Aer and just use Terra:

    ```
    from qiskit import BasicAer
    BasicAer.backends()
    ```

    This will list the same simulators as Aer with the exception of the pulse simulator:

    ```
    [<QasmSimulatorPy('qasm_simulator') from BasicAer()>,
    <StatevectorSimulatorPy('statevector_simulator') from
    BasicAer()>,
    <UnitarySimulatorPy('unitary_simulator') from
    BasicAer()>]
    ```

3. And finally, we can list out all the simulators and devices available from the IBM Quantum Provider:

```
# View all available IBMQ backends
provider.backends()
```

This will not only list the simulator, but also list the real quantum devices available to you based on your account:

```
[<IBMQSimulator('ibmq_qasm_simulator') from
IBMQ(hub='ibm-q', group='open', project='main')>,
<IBMQBackend('ibmqx2') from IBMQ(hub='ibm-q',
group='open', project='main')>,
<IBMQBackend('ibmq_16_melbourne') from IBMQ(hub='ibm-q',
group='open', project='main')>,
<IBMQBackend('ibmq_vigo') from IBMQ(hub='ibm-q',
group='open', project='main')>,
<IBMQBackend('ibmq_ourense') from IBMQ(hub='ibm-q',
group='open', project='main')>,
<IBMQBackend('ibmq_london') from IBMQ(hub='ibm-q',
group='open', project='main')>,
<IBMQBackend('ibmq_burlington') from IBMQ(hub='ibm-q',
group='open', project='main')>,
<IBMQBackend('ibmq_essex') from IBMQ(hub='ibm-q',
group='open', project='main')>,
<IBMQBackend('ibmq_armonk') from IBMQ(hub='ibm-q',
group='open', project='main')>,
<IBMQBackend('ibmq_athens') from IBMQ(hub='ibm-q',
group='open', project='main')>,
<IBMQBackend('ibmq_valencia') from IBMQ(hub='ibm-q',
group='open', project='main')>]
```

Equally, if you wanted to list out only the available simulators or only the real devices, you can set the `simulator` parameter to `True` or `False`, respectively. Setting the parameter as `simulator=False` will list only the real quantum devices, and setting `simulator=True` will list only the simulators in the results, illustrated as follows:

```
# View all IBMQ provider simulators only
provider.backends(simulator=True)
```

This correctly lists out the simulator we see in the IQX backend dashboard:

```
[<IBMQSimulator('ibmq_qasm_simulator') from
IBMQ(hub='ibm-q', group='open', project='main')>]
```

As this chapter is focused on Aer, we will learn about the Aer simulators going forward. We'll start with the Qasm simulator, which is one of the most commonly used simulators for executing circuits.

Running circuits on the Qasm simulator

The **Qasm simulator** is used mostly to not only execute quantum circuits but is also very versatile because of its ability to apply various simulation methods and configuration options. **Qasm**, incidentally, is short for **Quantum Assembly**.

A few of the available simulation methods are described as follows:

- `statevector`: This is a statevector simulation that allows ideal circuit measurements at the end of the quantum circuit. In addition, each shot that executes the circuit can sample random noise from noise models to provide noisy simulations. There are also `statevector_gpu` simulators that run on systems equipped with a **Graphical Processing Unit (GPU)**.

- `density_matrix`: This method provides a density matrix simulation which, similar to the statevector, samples the quantum circuits with measurements given at the end of each circuit.

- `matrix_product_state`: This is a tensor-network statevector simulator that leverages a Matrix Product State as the representation of the state.

- `automatic`: If no method is set, then this method will select one automatically based on the number of qubits, the quantum circuit, and the noise model.

The available backend options that are used with the `backend_options` kwargs are as follows:

- `method`: This sets the simulation method to run on the simulator. If no method is specified, it will be set to `automatic` by default.

- `precision`: This sets the floating point to either single or double precision, where the default is `double`.

- `zero_threshold`: This truncates values to zero.

- `validation_threshold`: This threshold is used to verify if the initial states of the quantum circuit are valid, with the default value set to $1x10^{-8}$.

- `max_parallel_threads`: This is used to set the maximum number of parallel CPU cores, where the default value is set to 0, which means the maximum number of CPU cores.

  The minimum number of cores in any processor is 1. Since we do not know the maximum number of cores a system could have, we set the value to 0 (to indicate an infinite number of cores).

- `max_parallel_experiments`: The maximum number of **Qobj** circuits in parallel, not to exceed the `max_parallel_threads` value, where the default value is set to 1 (disabled). If 0, it will be maximally set.

- `max_parallel_shots`: This sets the maximum number of shots of the circuit in parallel up to the value of `max_parallel_threads`. The default value is set to 0, which means it will set to `max_parallel_threads`. If set to 1, it will be disabled.

- `max_memory_mb`: This sets the maximum size of memory to be used to store the state of the vector, where the default value is set to 0. The maximum value is locked at half the size of the system memory.

Now that you have knowledge of the simulation methods and backend options, we'll create a simple circuit and execute it using Aer's `QasmSimulator` class. For this example, we will create the same circuit example we have been using so far, consisting of Hadamard and CX gates, that places the quantum circuit in a superposition and entangles both qubits together:

```
# Create a quantum circuit
qc = QuantumCircuit(2, 2)
qc.h(0)
qc.cx(0, 1)
qc.measure([0, 1], [0, 1])
```

Now, let's create the Qasm simulator using the `QasmSimulator` class:

```
# Import the QasmSimulator from Aer provider
from qiskit.providers.aer import QasmSimulator
backend_simulator = QasmSimulator()
# Set the backend options, method set to statevector
options = {'method': 'statevector'}
# Execute circuit using the backend options created
job = execute(qc, backend_simulator, backend_options=options)
# Print out the result counts
result = job.result()
counts = result.get_counts(qc)
print(counts)
```

This will print out the results from executing the quantum circuit on the Qasm simulator, with the method set to a state vector, obtaining the result counts.

As you can see, this runs the same results as if you ran `qasm_simulator` as follows:

```
# Get the Qasm simulator and set the backend options
aer_qasm_simulator = Aer.get_backend('qasm_simulator')
options = {'method': 'statevector'}
# Execute the circuit with the Aer Qasm simulator
job = execute(qc, aer_qasm_simulator, backend_options=options)
```

Both forms execute the circuit in the same manner, with varying values in the results, of course.

We'll continue by extending the backend options to include other parameters that we might find useful, such as shots and memory in the next section.

Adding parameters to the backend options

We may already be familiar with the `shots` parameter, which specifies how many times to execute the circuit on the backend. However, as illustrated in the previous example, the counts returned are the total values of all the shots, but not in the order in which each result was returned. There may be situations when you would like to examine the results of each shot in chronological order.

In order to examine the measured results that are stored in the individual memory slots, you will need to set the memory parameter in the backend options. Let's rerun the previous circuit again, however, this time we will set the memory flag to True and display the results. We'll run just 10 shots this time to avoid a very large output string:

```
# Set the backend options, method set to statevector
options = {'method': 'statevector', 'memory':True, 'shots':10}
# Execute circuit using the backend options created
job = execute(qc, backend_simulator, backend_options=options)
result = job.result()
# Pull the memory slots for the circuit
memory = result.get_memory(qc)
# Print the results from the memory slots
print('Memory results: ', memory)
```

This will output the 10 memory slot entry results from the execution of the circuit. Notice that the results are varying combinations of 00 and 11, as expected for the circuit:

```
Memory results: ['00', '11', '11', '00', '11', '11', '00',
    '11', '11', '00']
```

Just as before, the same parameters can be set using the Aer backend call directly, as follows. Note however that we will be setting the memory value as a kwarg in the execute method rather than in the options object as before:

```
# View each measurement individually by enabling the memory
# parameter
aer_backend = Aer.get_backend('qasm_simulator')
# Set backend, shots, and memory parameters and retrieve
# results
result = execute(qc, backend=aer_backend, shots=5,
    memory=True).result()

# Pull the memory slots results
memory = result.get_memory(qc)

# Print the memory slots
print('Memory results: ', memory)
```

The expected results can be seen as follows:

```
Memory results: ['00', '00', '00', '11', '00']
```

Having the memory feature built into the Qasm simulator gives you the ability to initialize the qubits of your circuit. The next section will illustrate how to initialize and set up all, or just a subset, of the qubits.

Initializing the qubits on a circuit

As we learned early on, each qubit is initialized to the ground state, or the $|0\rangle$ state. However, there may be times when we would like to set a different initial state. Luckily for us, the Qasm simulator allows us to initialize the state of the circuit to some other state $|\psi\rangle$ in lieu of all $|0\rangle$ states.

We will follow the next steps to initialize the qubits:

1. In the previous example, we created a circuit that contained a Hadamard and Control-Not gate in order to obtain the entangled state results of $|00\rangle$ or $|11\rangle$. In this example, we will initialize our circuit so that the results are the same without the need to add any gates:

```python
# Construct a 2 qubit quantum circuit
qc_init = QuantumCircuit(2, 2)
# Import numpy to simplify some math for us
# import numpy as np
# Select the qubits by their index which you wish to
initialize
init_qubits = [0, 1]
# Inititialize qubit states
qc_init.initialize([1, 0, 0, 1] / np.sqrt(2),
init_qubits)
# Add measurements and draw the initialized circuit
qc_init.measure(range(2), range(2))
qc_init.decompose()
qc_init.draw()
```

This results in the following circuit diagram. Notice that the first two qubits have been initialized in the state of $[1/\sqrt{2}, 0, 0, 1/\sqrt{2}]^T$. This circuit now has an initialized state that can be applied to any circuit should you wish a circuit to begin in a state other than the ground/zero state:

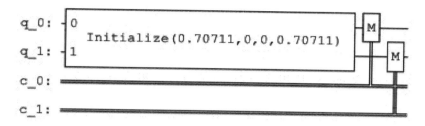

Figure 10.2 – Initialized qubits to an initial state other than the zero state

2. Now let's execute this circuit and observe each result:

```
# Set the memory to True so we can observe each result
result = execute(qc_init, aer_backend, shots=10,
    memory=True).result()
# Retrieve the individual results from the memory slots
memory = result.get_memory(qc_init)
# Print the memory slots
print(memory)
```

As you can observe from the results, we get only the two initialized state results of $|00\rangle$ or $|11\rangle$, as expected.

3. Now, you don't have to initialize all qubits in a circuit, you can also specify a specific group of qubits to initialize, as illustrated in the following code:

```
# Create a 4 qubit circuit
qc_init2 = QuantumCircuit(4, 4)


# Import numpy to help with some arithmetic
import numpy as np
# Initialize only the last 3 qubits
initialized_qubits = [1, 2, 3]


# Set the initial state, remember that the sum of
# amplitudes-squared
```

```
# must equal 1
qc_init2.initialize([0, 1, 0, 1, 0, 1, 0, 1] /
np.sqrt(4), initialized_qubits)

# Add a barrier so it is easier to read
qc_init2.barrier(range(4))

# Measure qubits, decompose and draw circuit
qc_init2.measure(range(4), range(4))
qc_init2.decompose()
qc_init2.draw()
```

This results in the following circuit, which initializes the state of the **q_1** to **q_3** qubits, while all the other qubits that are initialized remain in the ground/zero state:

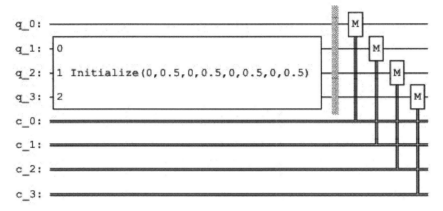

Figure 10.3 – Initialization of the last three qubits

Here our 3-qubit initialized state is set to $|001\rangle$, $|011\rangle$, $|101\rangle$, $|111\rangle$. However, since we are executing a 4-qubit circuit, and we have initialized the last 3 qubits, our results should include the fourth qubit (q0), which would append a 0 to the least significant bit.

4. Let's run the experiment and see whether the initial state of the partial qubits is successful:

```
# Execute the circuit and print results and histogram
result = execute(qc_init2, backend_simulator).result()
counts = result.get_counts(qc_init2)
```

```
print(counts)
plot_histogram(counts)
```

As expected, our results are as follows:

```
{'0010': 252, '1010': 270, '0110': 249, '1110': 253}
```

We also get the following output graph:

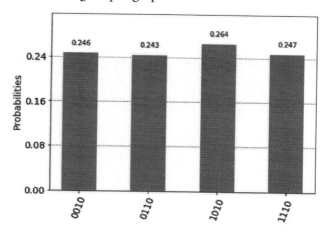

Figure 10.4 – Results of initialized quantum circuit

As we can see, the results are exactly as we expected them to be. Notice that the least significant bit (the bit on the far right) is always set to 0 as it was not one of the initialized qubits. The other thing to take note of is that the other bits are exactly as we expected, $|0010\rangle$, $|0110\rangle$, $|1010\rangle$, $|1110\rangle$, where the bold indicates the initialized bits and if you combine them all together, they will provide the results displayed.

5. Now that we have initialized a circuit, we can apply any gates as needed. The only difference is that the gates applied to the circuit after initialization will then be applied to the initialized state of each qubit, rather than the initialized state $|0\rangle$. Let's test this out by adding a NOT (X) gate to all the qubits. This should result in all the values being flipped:

```
# Create a 4-qubit circuit
qc_init_x = QuantumCircuit(4, 4)
# Import numpy
import numpy as np
# Initialize the last 3 qubits, same as before
```

```
initialized_qubits = [1, 2, 3]
qc_init_x.initialize([0, 1, 0, 1, 0, 1, 0, 1] /
np.sqrt(4), initialized_qubits)

# Add a barrier so it is easier to read
qc_init_x.barrier(range(4))
# Include an X gate on all qubits
for idx in range(4):
    qc_init_x.x(idx)
# Measure and draw the circuit
qc_init_x.measure(range(4), range(4))
# Decompose the circuit down a level
qc_init_x.decompose()
# Draw the completed circuit
qc_init_x.draw()
```

This results in the following circuit. Notice the initialized qubits are as before, only after the **X** gates on all qubits that we have added just before measuring. This should result in all bits flipping from 0 to 1, and vice versa:

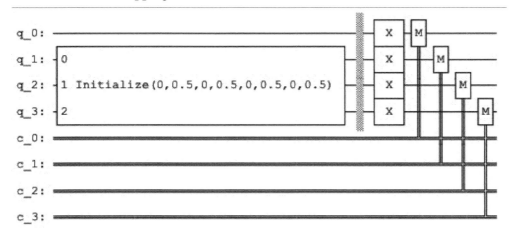

Figure 10.5 – Initialized quantum circuit with X gates applied to all qubits before measuring

6. Let's execute the circuit and display the results using the following code:

```
# Execute and get counts
result = execute(qc_init_x, backend_simulator).result()
counts = result.get_counts(qc_init_x)
print(counts)
plot_histogram(counts)
```

This results exactly as expected: the results are based on the initialized state, followed by the NOT gates being applied on all qubits:

```
{'1001': 246, '1101': 254, '0001': 262, '0101': 262}
```

We also get to see the following graph:

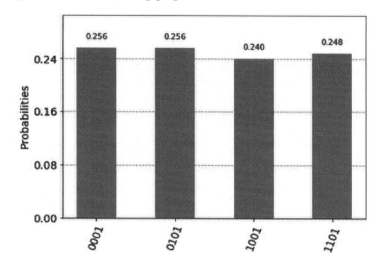

Figure 10.6 – Results of initialized circuit with X gate applied to all qubits

The Qasm simulator's ability to be very flexible and configurable means that creating custom circuits with the ability to initialize qubit states is quite an advantage. We will see this in more detail later in *Chapter 13, Understanding Quantum Algorithms*.

Now that we are familiar with the Qasm simulator, let's move on to the statevector simulator and see what unique features we have available.

Running circuits on the statevector simulator

The **statevector simulator**, similar to the Qasm simulator, allows you to initialize and execute a quantum circuit. There are of course some distinct differences, one of which is that it returns the state vector of the quantum circuit by executing a single shot. This allows you to capture a snapshot of the state vector so you can, in some sense, calculate or observe the expected results on the qubits. We will also leverage some of the Qiskit visualization tools to help display the state information of the qubits and the quantum circuit. We will follow the next steps to do so:

1. To begin, let's create a simple one-qubit circuit and add a Hadamard gate to it so we have a qubit in a superposition:

```
# Construct quantum circuit
qc = QuantumCircuit(1)
# Place qubit in superposition
qc.h(0)
qc.draw()
```

The result of this is as follows, where we have a single qubit in a superposition, that is, a complex linear combination of $|0\rangle$ and $|1\rangle$:

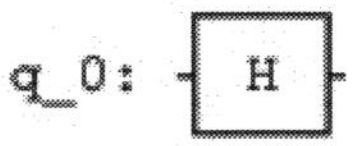

Figure 10.7 – Single qubit circuit with a Hadamard gate

2. Next, we want to see the state vector representation of the circuit. Before coding it, let's review the mathematics around it. We know that each basis state is represented by state vectors, such as the following for the $|0\rangle$ state:

$$|0\rangle = \begin{bmatrix} 1 \\ 0 \end{bmatrix}$$

Similarly, the $|1\rangle$ state can be represented by a state vector as follows:

$$|1\rangle = \begin{bmatrix} 0 \\ 1 \end{bmatrix}$$

3. The initial state of a qubit is $|0\rangle$. The Hadamard gate generally applies the Hadamard matrix to the current state of the qubit. Therefore, if a Hadamard gate is applied to a qubit in the state $|0\rangle$, the operation would be as follows:

$$H|0\rangle$$

$$= \frac{1}{\sqrt{2}}\begin{bmatrix} 1 & 1 \\ 1 & -1 \end{bmatrix}\begin{bmatrix} 1 \\ 0 \end{bmatrix}$$

$$= \begin{bmatrix} \frac{1}{\sqrt{2}} & \frac{1}{\sqrt{2}} \\ \frac{1}{\sqrt{2}} & -\frac{1}{\sqrt{2}} \end{bmatrix}\begin{bmatrix} 1 \\ 0 \end{bmatrix}$$

Multiplying the matrix by the vector results in the following:

$$H|0\rangle = \begin{bmatrix} \frac{1}{\sqrt{2}} \\ \frac{1}{\sqrt{2}} \end{bmatrix}$$

$$= \begin{bmatrix} 0.707 \\ 0.707 \end{bmatrix}$$

4. Now, let's execute our circuit using the state vector simulator and output the state vector values:

```
# Select the Statevector simulator from the Aer provider
simulator = Aer.get_backend('statevector_simulator')
# Execute the circuit
result = execute(qc, simulator).result()
# Get the state vector and display the results
statevector = result.get_statevector(qc)
statevector
```

From the results we can obtain the state vector of the quantum circuit by simply extracting it from the Job object, in this case, result.get_statevector().

This should result in the following output which correctly matches our expected results where the amplitudes are exactly $\frac{1}{\sqrt{2}}$. Furthermore, if we square the amplitudes, the results will provide us with the probability of obtaining a 0 or a 1, as indexed in the values of the array, respectively:

```
array([0.70710678+0.j, 0.70710678+0.j])
```

5. Let's extend this by adding another qubit in superposition:

```
# Construct quantum circuit
qc = QuantumCircuit(2)
# Place both in superposition
qc.h(0)
qc.h(1)
qc.draw()
```

The result of this circuit is similar to the previous, just an addition of an added qubit:

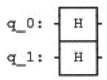

Figure 10.8 – Two qubits in superposition

6. Let's execute this circuit using the state vector simulator and print out the results of our state vector:

```
# Execute the circuit using the state vector simulator
result = execute(qc, simulator).result()
# Extract the state vector of the circuit from the
# results
statevector = result.get_statevector(qc)
# Output the state vector values
statevector
```

This results in the following output, which represents equal amplitudes for all 4 possible outcomes, $|00\rangle$, $|01\rangle$, $|10\rangle$, and $|11\rangle$:

```
array([0.5+0.j, 0.5+0.j, 0.5+0.j, 0.5+0.j])
```

Here, if we square each of the values to obtain the probability measurements, we will see that each has a 25% probability of being correct. Recall that all probabilities must equal 1.

7. Finally, let's entangle the qubits and see what the state vector results would be when applying a Hadamard gate to the first qubit:

```python
# Construct quantum circuit
qc = QuantumCircuit(2)
# Place the first qubit in superposition
qc.h(0)
# Entangle the two qubits together using a CNOT gate,
# where the first is the control and the second qubit is
# the target
qc.cx(0, 1)
# Execute the circuit on the state vector simulator
result = execute(qc, simulator).result()
# Obtain the state vector of the circuit
statevector = result.get_statevector(qc)
# Output the state vector values
statevector
```

The state vector results are as expected, with equal amplitude values for 00 and 11, and no values for the states 01 and 10:

```python
array([0.70710678+0.j, 0.+0.j, 0.+0.j, 0.70710678+0.j])
```

8. We can also seek the aid of the visualization tools to help illustrate the state vector results as follows for the circuit we just executed. We will add the plot state vector library:

```python
# Display state vector
plot_state_city(statevector)
```

The results are the same values we have seen earlier, only here we can see the amplitudes of both the real (left) and imaginary (right) components. When we square the amplitudes of our result, we will get a 50% probability for the 00 and 11 states, which is what we see in the following state vector plot:

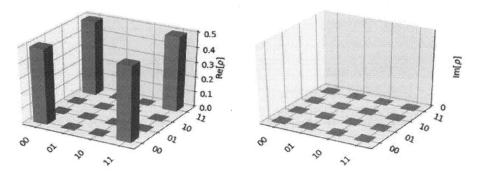

Figure 10.9 – State vector plot with real (left) and imaginary (right) components

The state vector plot isn't the only visualization tool we have available. Another great tool available is the **Qiskit QSphere**. This plots the state vector onto a two-dimensional graph and includes unique visualization features that allow you to identify the state vector information of your circuit.

9. Let's plot the same state vector results and compare it with the earlier state vector plot:

```
# Import the qsphere class
from qiskit.visualization import plot_state_qsphere
%matplotlib inline
# Create quantum circuit
qc = QuantumCircuit(1)
# Place the qubit in a superposition state
qc.h(0)
# Execute the circuit on the statevector simulator
backend = Aer.get_backend('statevector_simulator')
job = execute(qc, simulator).result()
# Display the QSphere with results from the previous cell
plot_state_qsphere(statevector)
```

Let's review the state vector results and how they are displayed in the QSphere:

First, notice the vectors point to $|0\rangle$ and $|1\rangle$ with the spheres at the end of each vector having equal diameters. This is to illustrate that there is an equal probability that the result will either be a 0 or 1, hence they are in superposition as expected.

Next, the color of each sphere matches the color of the phase wheel located at the bottom right of the QSphere. This indicates that each vector is in phase (0°). The results here match the expected equation we derived earlier, where

$$H|0\rangle = \frac{1}{\sqrt{2}}(|0\rangle + |1\rangle):$$

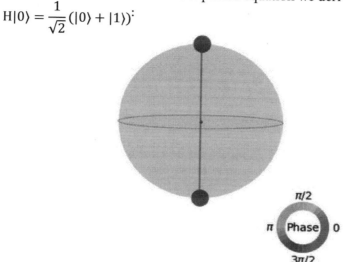

Figure 10.10 – QSphere representation of the state vector in phase

10. Let's do something interesting by introducing a phase shift. As we have seen in the preceding screenshot, the vector moves from $|0\rangle$ to $|+\rangle$ in phase (0°) when we apply the Hadamard gate. We'll now include a Z gate, also known as a phase gate, which rotates the vector by an angle of π around the z axis. As before, we'll review the mathematics first to confirm what we should expect to see. Recall earlier how we described the effects of applying the Hadamard gate when the state vector originates from $|0\rangle$. The following applies the Hadamard gate to the $|1\rangle$ state:

$$H|1\rangle$$

$$= \frac{1}{\sqrt{2}}\begin{bmatrix} 1 & 1 \\ 1 & -1 \end{bmatrix}\begin{bmatrix} 0 \\ 1 \end{bmatrix}$$

$$= \begin{bmatrix} \frac{1}{\sqrt{2}} & \frac{1}{\sqrt{2}} \\ \frac{1}{\sqrt{2}} & -\frac{1}{\sqrt{2}} \end{bmatrix}\begin{bmatrix} 0 \\ 1 \end{bmatrix}$$

Multiplying the matrix with the vector results produces the following:

$$H|1\rangle = \begin{bmatrix} \dfrac{1}{\sqrt{2}} \\ -\dfrac{1}{\sqrt{2}} \end{bmatrix}$$
$$= \begin{bmatrix} 0.707 \\ -0.707 \end{bmatrix}$$

11. We will create a circuit originating from the $|1\rangle$ state and apply the H gate on it to confirm the preceding vector results:

```
# Create a quantum circuit
qc = QuantumCircuit(1)
# Rotate the state from |0⟩ to |1⟩ by applying an X gate
qc.x(0)
# Place qubit in a superposition from the |1⟩ state
qc.h(0)
# Execute the circuit on the state vector simulator
job = execute(qc, simulator).result()
# Extract the state vector results and plot them onto the
# QSphere
plot_state_qsphere(job.get_statevector(qc))
```

The resulting QSphere now has the same probability, however, since the rotation originated from the $|1\rangle$ state, it is now at the $|-\rangle$ side, therefore out of phase by π, which we can confirm by observing the following phase color chart:

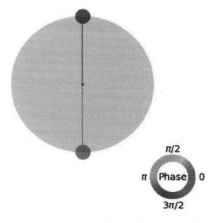

Figure 10.11 – A superposition state that is also out of phase by an angle of π

12. Now, let's try the same thing, this time originating from the $|0\rangle$ state:

```
# Create a quantum circuit
qc = QuantumCircuit(1)
# Place qubit in a superposition from the |0> state
qc.h(0)
# Apply a Z (phase) gate, to rotate it by an angle π
# around the Z axis
qc.z(0)
# Execute the circuit on the state vector simulator
job = execute(qc, simulator).result()
# Plot the results onto the QSphere
plot_state_qsphere(job.get_statevector(qc))
```

The results, as we can see, are the same – our vector is out of phase by an angle of π:

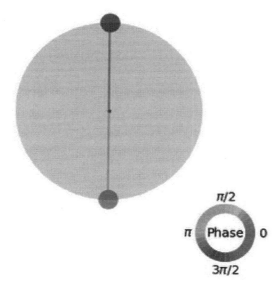

Figure 10.12 – A state vector in superposition and out of phase by π

We can see that the state vector representation illustrates what we see mathematically, which is the following in this case:

$$H|1\rangle = \frac{1}{\sqrt{2}}(|0\rangle - |1\rangle)$$

From the preceding equation, the negative value represents the out-of-phase component. We will see later on how various quantum algorithms leverage this in order to take advantage of the effects of interference in *Chapter 13, Understanding Quantum Algorithms*.

Now that we know how to obtain and visualize the final state vector of our circuit, next we will look at how we can obtain the unitary matrix of our circuit by leveraging the unitary simulator.

Running circuits on the unitary simulator

The **unitary simulator** provides the construction of the unitary matrix, **U**, of the circuit. The unitary simulator builds out the unitary matrix by stepping through the circuit and applying each gate to the initial state of the circuit. As described in the API documentation, the semantic validations will verify the constraints of the **Qobj** and backend options, which are as described as follows:

- The number of shots is set to 1, so only a single shot will be run to calculate the unitary matrix.
- The circuit cannot contain any resets or measurements.
- The number of qubits must fit into the local memory allocated for this purpose.
- No noise models can be applied.
- If the circuit contains any the preceding constraints, it will raise an `AerError`.

We will leverage the same circuit we created earlier for the state vector example to run through our unitary simulator so we can compare and contrast the results:

1. First, let's validate what we should expect to see mathematically. As we will be applying a single Hadamard gate, it should be fairly simple to determine the unitary matrix. Starting from the initial state, we will apply an H gate to the circuit:

$$H = \frac{1}{\sqrt{2}} \begin{bmatrix} 1 & 1 \\ 1 & -1 \end{bmatrix}$$

$$= \begin{bmatrix} \dfrac{1}{\sqrt{2}} & \dfrac{1}{\sqrt{2}} \\ \dfrac{1}{\sqrt{2}} & -\dfrac{1}{\sqrt{2}} \end{bmatrix}$$

2. Now, we will run our circuit on the unitary matrix, where we will create a quantum circuit and add a Hadamard gate, then set the simulator to the unitary simulator provided by Aer. We should expect to see the same result:

```
# Create a quantum circuit and add a Hadamard gate
qc = QuantumCircuit(1)
qc.h(0)


# Set the simulator to the UnitarySimulator from the Aer
# provider
simulator = Aer.get_backend('unitary_simulator')


# Execute the circuit on the unitary simulator
result = execute(qc, simulator).result()
# Extract the unitary matrix from the results
unitary = result.get_unitary(qc)
# Print out the unitary matrix representation of the
# circuit
print("Unitary of the circuit:\n", unitary)
```

Your unitary results should match the results we calculated earlier; you can ignore the significantly small numbers in the imaginary component:

```
Unitary of the circuit:
 [[ 0.70710678+0.00000000e+00j 0.70710678-8.65956056e-
17j]
 [ 0.70710678+0.00000000e+00j -0.70710678+8.65956056e-
17j]]
```

3. Now, let's add a Z gate after the H gate:

```
# Create a new circuit, adding an H gate followed by a Z
gate
qc = QuantumCircuit(1)
qc.h(0)
qc.z(0)


# Execute the circuit on the unitary simulator
result = execute(qc, simulator).result()
# Retrieve the unitary matrix from the results
```

```
unitary = result.get_unitary(qc)
# Print the unitary matrix representation of the circuit
print("Unitary of the circuit:\n", unitary)
qc.draw()
```

This will produce the following unitary matrix representation of the quantum circuit we created:

```
Unitary of the circuit:
 [[ 0.70710678+0.00000000e+00j 0.70710678-8.65956056e-
17j]
 [-0.70710678+0.00000000e+00j 0.70710678-8.65956056e-
17j]]
```

This will also give us the following circuit diagram:

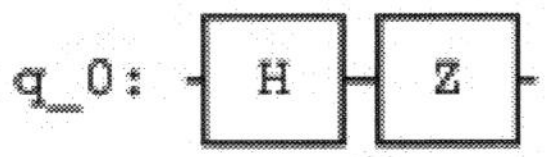

Figure 10.13 – 2-gate circuit applying an H gate followed by a Z gate

We can confirm this using a bit of linear algebra. One thing to note is that when we apply gates on a circuit and visualize them, we generally apply them from left to right, as illustrated in the preceding circuit diagram where we see the **H** gate first, followed by the **Z** gate.

4. However, when calculating the unitary matrix, we place the unitary matrices of each gate we add from right to left. For example, for this circuit, we will calculate the unitary matrix in the **ZH = U** manner, where **U** is the unitary matrix solution. Let's calculate this vector now:

$$ZH$$

$$= \frac{1}{\sqrt{2}} \begin{bmatrix} 1 & 0 \\ 0 & -1 \end{bmatrix} \begin{bmatrix} 1 & 1 \\ 1 & -1 \end{bmatrix}$$

$$= \frac{1}{\sqrt{2}} \begin{bmatrix} 1 & 1 \\ -1 & 1 \end{bmatrix}$$

As you can see from the preceding equation, we have now confirmed that it is the same result we received from the unitary simulator for this circuit.

As with the previous simulators, we can also initialize the unitary simulator with a given unitary matrix. Let's use the results from the previous example as our initial unitary matrix:

```
# Create a quantum circuit
qc_init = QuantumCircuit(1)
# Set the initial unitary using the result from the
# previous
# example.
opts = {"initial_unitary": np.array([[ 1,   1],
                                     [-1, 1]]/
    np.sqrt(2))}


# Execute and obtain Unitary matrix of the circuit
result = execute(qc_init, simulator, backend_
options=opts).result()
# Retrieve the unitary matrix from the result
unitary = result.get_unitary(qc_init)
# Print the unitary matrix results representing the
# circuit
print("Unitary of the circuit:\n", unitary)
```

The results from the initialized circuit are now the same as the previous circuit, without the need to add any of the gates used to generate this unitary matrix:

```
Unitary of the circuit:
 [[ 0.70710678+0.j   0.70710678+0.j]
 [-0.70710678+0.j   0.70710678+0.j]]
```

We've seen how the unitary simulator is an exceptional component to use should you wish to experiment using a predefined unitary matrix.

We will now move on to the next section about running circuits on the last simulator.

Running circuits on the pulse simulator

The **pulse simulator** can be used to simulate many parts of a quantum system such as the dynamics of the controls, or the circuit used to generate the controls, specified by pulse **Schedule** objects. Furthermore, by using `PulseSystemModel` the physical system itself can be simulated when executing pulse schedules.

In this section, we will create a pulse schedule, which is a set of instructions to run on a quantum computer. We will create a simple *sin* wave made up of 64 time slots and use this to generate a sample pulse that we will insert into our schedule to run on drive channel 0, which applies it to qubit 0. Once the pulse schedule is created, we will assemble the schedule using the pulse simulator as the backend.

Finally, we will generate `PulseSystemModel` from the actual quantum system backend, `ibmq_armonk`, to run the pulse model object on the pulse simulator. This will simulate running the schedule on the `ibmq_armonk` system and returning the results to print out:

```python
# Import the PulseSystemModel
from qiskit.providers.aer.pulse import PulseSystemModel
# Import Pulse classes needed to generate a schedule
from qiskit.pulse import Play, DriveChannel
from qiskit.pulse import Schedule, Waveform


# Import numpy and generate the sin sample values
import numpy as np
x = np.linspace(0,2*np.pi,64)
data = np.sin(x)
# Generate a SamplePulse
sample_pulse = Waveform(data, name="sin_64_pulse")
# Create a schedule
schedules = Schedule(name='pulse_sample_schedule')
# Operate on the first qubit
qubit_idx = 0
# Insert the sample pulse
schedules = schedules.insert(0, Play(sample_pulse,
DriveChannel(qubit_idx)))


# Instantiate the PulseSimulator
```

```
from qiskit.providers.aer import PulseSimulator
backend_sim = PulseSimulator()


# Assemble schedules using PulseSimulator as the backend
pulse_qobj = assemble(schedules, backend=backend_sim)
# Set the system model by replicating the ibmq_armonk backend
armonk_backend = provider.get_backend('ibmq_armonk')
system_model = PulseSystemModel.from_backend(armonk_backend)

# Run simulation on a PulseSystemModel object and print results
results = backend_sim.run(pulse_qobj, system_model)
print(results.qobj())
```

The results are the same as if you were to run the scheduled pulses on the modeled backend. In the following example, we modeled the ibmq_armonk system:

```
Pulse Qobj: 306d72c5-ebd5-4923-96a8-f1359f03b12f:
Config: {'init_qubits': True,
 'meas_level': 2,
 'meas_lo_freq': [inf],
 'meas_return': 'avg',
 'memory': False,
 'memory_slot_size': 100,
 'memory_slots': 1,
 'parametric_pulses': [],
 'pulse_library': [{'name':
'2f613389417215751c42c82118155cdf2abc
                  51325c3c997a5c836d970b0ddd64',
                'samples': array([ 0.00000000e+00+0.j,
   9.95678466e-02+0.j,   1.98146143e-01+0.j,
   2.94755174e-01+0.j,   3.88434796e-01+0.j,
   4.78253979e-01+0.j,
   5.63320058e-01+0.j,   6.42787610e-01+0.j,
   7.15866849e-01+0.j,
   7.81831482e-01+0.j,   8.40025923e-01+0.j,
   8.89871809e-01+0.j,
   9.30873749e-01+0.j,   9.62624247e-01+0.j,
```

      9.84807753e-01+0.j,
      9.97203797e-01+0.j,   9.99689182e-01+0.j,
      9.92239207e-01+0.j,
      9.74927912e-01+0.j,   9.47927346e-01+0.j,
      9.11505852e-01+0.j,
      8.66025404e-01+0.j,   8.11938006e-01+0.j,
      7.49781203e-01+0.j,
      6.80172738e-01+0.j,   6.03804410e-01+0.j,
      5.21435203e-01+0.j,
      4.33883739e-01+0.j,   3.42020143e-01+0.j,
      2.46757398e-01+0.j,
      1.49042266e-01+0.j,   4.98458857e-02+0.j,
      -4.98458857e-02+0.j,
      -1.49042266e-01+0.j,   -2.46757398e-01+0.j,
      -3.42020143e-01+0.j,
      -4.33883739e-01+0.j,   -5.21435203e-01+0.j,
      -6.03804410e-01+0.j,
      -6.80172738e-01+0.j,   -7.49781203e-01+0.j,
      -8.11938006e-01+0.j,
      -8.66025404e-01+0.j,   -9.11505852e-01+0.j,
      -9.47927346e-01+0.j,
      -9.74927912e-01+0.j,   -9.92239207e-01+0.j,
      -9.99689182e-01+0.j,
      -9.97203797e-01+0.j,   -9.84807753e-01+0.j,
      -9.62624247e-01+0.j,
      -9.30873749e-01+0.j,   -8.89871809e-01+0.j,
      -8.40025923e-01+0.j,
      -7.81831482e-01+0.j,   -7.15866849e-01+0.j,
      -6.42787610e-01+0.j,
      -5.63320058e-01+0.j,   -4.78253979e-01+0.j,
      -3.88434796e-01+0.j,
      -2.94755174e-01+0.j,   -1.98146143e-01+0.j,
      -9.95678466e-02+0.j,
         -2.44929360e-16+0.j])}],
  'qubit_lo_freq': [inf],
  'shots': 1024}
Header: {'backend_name': 'pulse_simulator', 'backend_version':
 '0.6.1'}

```
Experiments:

Pulse Experiment:
Header:
{'memory_slots': 1, 'name': 'pulse_sample_schedule'}
Config:
{}
        Instruction: 2f613389417215751c42c82118155cdf2abc51325c3
                     c997a5c836d970b0ddd64
            t0: 0
            ch: d0
```

Try running a few samples from the pulse library, which can be found in `qiskit.pulse.pulse_lib` and in *Chapter 8, Programming with Qiskit Terra*.

Now that we have a better understanding of the various simulators and the differences between them, we'll use them to simulate some of the noise we get when running a circuit on a real quantum device. You've also learned the various options and parameters each simulator has available to you so you can leverage each one in multiple ways to obtain various results, such as count and state vector information, from the provided quantum circuit. This will help simulate the results from circuits where noise models affect the outcome, as opposed to the results from running on an ideal, noiseless simulator. So, let's generate the noise models in the next section.

Generating noise models

Noise models are used to represent various noise effects that cause errors in quantum circuits. The origin of the noise stems from many sources within the quantum system. As the current devices are for near term future, the amount of errors on a device could be significant based on the quantum circuit executed on them.

In this section, we will review the various types of errors that can affect a qubit, gates, and readouts. We will also learn how to generate noise models either based on the configuration information from the real devices, or noise models created by ourselves, with which we can simulate the real devices using the simulator. We'll begin by understanding the various types of noise that can be found on a quantum system:

1. We'll create a simple circuit, add some arbitrary gates and measurement operators, and execute it on an ideal simulator, with no errors:

```
from qiskit.tools.visualization import plot_histogram
# Create a 2-qubit circuit
qc = QuantumCircuit(2, 2)
# Add some arbitrary gates and measurement operators
qc.h(0)
qc.cx(0, 1)
qc.measure([0, 1], [0, 1])


# Execute the circuit on the qasm simulator
result = execute(qc, Aer.get_backend('qasm_simulator')).
result()
# Obtain and print results
counts = result.get_counts()
# Plot the count results on a histogram
plot_histogram(counts)
```

The results from this circuit on an ideal simulator are as follows. Notice we only obtain two values; **00** and **11**:

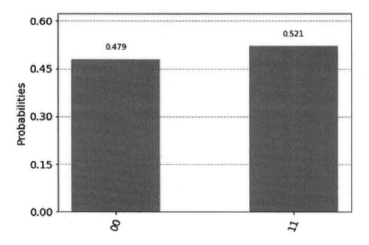

Figure 10.14 – Results from an ideal simulator with no effects of noise

2. Now we will execute the same circuit on an actual device instead of a simulator:

```
# Execute the same circuit on a real quantum computer
result = execute(qc, provider.get_backend('ibmq_
valencia')).result()
# Obtain and print results
counts = result.get_counts()
plot_histogram(counts)
```

The results are very similar to that of the earlier execution on the simulator, only this time, notice there are some errors in the results. Rather than only obtaining results of **00** and **11**, we see a few instances of **01** and **10**. These are the effects of backend noise on the results of the circuit:

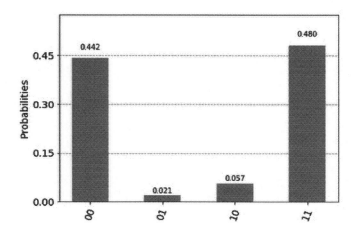

Figure 10.15 – Results from a quantum computer with slight noise effects

3. Now let's do something interesting. Let's create a noise model based on the properties of a specific backend device. Aer's `NoiseModel` provides the ability to do this with a simple method call.

In this following code snippet, we will generate a noise model based on `ibmq_valencia` and its properties, `coupling_map`, and the available basis gates. When executing the quantum circuit, we will provide the noise model, `coupling_map`, and basis gates. This way, when executing the quantum circuit on the simulator, it will simulate the results as experiencing the same effects that would occur when running on the circuit on a real device, noise and all:

```python
# Import the NoiseModel
from qiskit.providers.aer.noise import NoiseModel
# Obtain the backend to simulate
backend = provider.get_backend('ibmq_valencia')
# Create the noise model based on the backend properties
noise_model = NoiseModel.from_backend(backend)


# Get coupling map from backend
coupling_map = backend.configuration().coupling_map


# Get basis gates from noise model
basis_gates = noise_model.basis_gates


# Execute the circuit on the simulator with the backend
# properties,
# and generated noise model
result = execute(qc, Aer.get_backend('qasm_simulator'),
                 coupling_map=coupling_map,
                 basis_gates=basis_gates,
                 noise_model=noise_model).result()
# Obtain and print results
counts = result.get_counts()
plot_histogram(counts)
```

The following plot of the results of the preceding code, as you can see, are not as ideal as before. We can observe a few errors here:

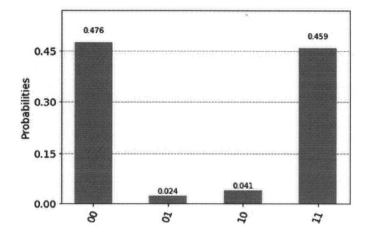

Figure 10.16 – Results from a simulator with noise effects based on a specified backend

Now that we are able to simulate the effects of noise from a backend system onto a simulator, let's develop an understanding of what the cause is of some of these noise effects.

Understanding decoherence (T$_1$ and T$_2$)

When executing quantum circuits on a real device, there are various effects that can cause errors in our computations. In this section, we will review some of those effects, so that when you're generating or building your noise models, you will have a better understanding as to how they affect each qubit.

Decoherence is defined as the loss of quantum coherence due to a quantum system's physical interaction with its environment. Decoherence effects each qubit in many varying ways, one of which is when each qubit starts in a $|0\rangle$ ground state, and we operate on the qubit to move it from the $|0\rangle$ state to the $|1\rangle$ state. For example, we say the qubit has transitioned from the ground state, $|0\rangle$, to the excited state, $|1\rangle$. An analogy of this is to think of yourself sitting peacefully and perfectly at rest. This peaceful relaxed moment is you in the ground state.

Then, imagine someone jumping out of nowhere and screaming at you. You're immediately startled as your heart rate jumps up and your adrenaline kicks in. This is you now in the excited state. Now, after telling the person who startled you to never do that again, you manage to catch your breath and get your heart rate down. You begin to relax and get your body back down to the grounded state it was in before. The time required to change from the excited state to the grounded state is, coincidentally, called the energy **relaxation time**.

The relaxation time, denoted as T_1, is the time constant of the longitudinal loss (oriented along the z axis) of the signal intensity. Another decoherence effect is that of **dephasing**, denoted as T_2, where the phase information spreads out across widely so that the phase information is lost. An example of this is if we set the qubit to the $|+\rangle$ state, the dephasing time is a decay constant time where the initial state decays down to a mixed state of $|+\rangle$ and $|-\rangle$, where it is difficult to predict the state of the system.

There are two ways to measure T_1 and T_2 decoherence times. To measure T_1, you would apply a series of pulses separated by a fixed time delay and capture the statistical results of the state as it moves from $|0\rangle$ to $|1\rangle$. **Rabi oscillations** are generally used to provide the pulses that are then measured over time.

To measure T_2, you would set the state of the qubit to $|+\rangle$ or $|-\rangle$, and then apply π pulses at particular sequences to apply a phase rotation. After applying a particular sequence of pulses over time, the state should return to its original position, that is, $|+\rangle$ or $|-\rangle$. If dephasing occurs, then the result will have a lower probability of returning to its original starting position. This technique of measuring T_2 is called a **spin echo**.

Now that we are a bit more familiar with the sources of noise, let's shift our discussion to the contributors to decoherence and how they vary based on their sources. There are generally two source types; **intrinsic** and **extrinsic**. Intrinsic noise, often regarded as generic in nature, originates from sources within the system such as temperature, or defects within the system, so essentially, materials or defects. Extrinsic noise originates from environmentally coupled systems such as wave interference, vibrations, electromagnetic fields, and others.

Let's run a quick example of thermal relaxation on a pair of qubits. In the following example, we will define our T_1 and T_2 values and apply them to a set of basis gates for all qubits. We'll then run a sample circuit with these thermal relaxation errors to see the difference. The circuit that we will create and execute will be the same one we created earlier and ran on a simulator, so we can compare and contrast the results:

```python
# Initialize your T1 and T2 values
t1 = 0.0125
t2 = 0.0025


# Apply the T1 and T2 to create the thermal relaxation error
from qiskit.providers.aer.noise import thermal_relaxation_error
t_error = thermal_relaxation_error(t1, t2, 0.01)


# Add the errors to a noise model
# and apply to all basis gates on all qubits
noise_model = NoiseModel()
noise_model.add_all_qubit_quantum_error(t_error, ['id', 'u1',
'u2', 'u3'])
# Print out the noise model
print(noise_model)


#Create the same 2-qubit quantum circuit as before
qc_error = QuantumCircuit(2,2)
qc_error.h(0)
qc_error.cx(0,1)
qc_error.measure(range(2), range(2))


# Set the simulator
simulator = Aer.get_backend('qasm_simulator')
# Apply the noise model we created to the execution method
result = execute(qc_error, simulator, shots=1024, basis_
gates=noise_model.basis_gates, noise_model=noise_model).
result()


# Obtain results and print
```

```
counts = result.get_counts(qc_error)
# Plot the result counts on a histogram
plot_histogram(counts)
```

The `NoiseModel` output provides a description of the noise model by indicating which basis gates are available, which gate instructions would be affected by the noise, and which basis gates errors are applied to the qubits:

```
NoiseModel:
   Basis gates: ['cx', 'id', 'u1', 'u2', 'u3']
   Instructions with noise: ['id', 'u1', 'u3', 'u2']
   All-qubits errors: ['id', 'u1', 'u2', 'u3']
```

As you can see, the results after executing this circuit on the simulator with the generated noise are not quite the same as before. In the earlier case, without errors, we had a very close 50/50 split between **00** and **11**. However, as you can see in the following screenshot, the result is more of a 75/25 split between **00** and **11** respectively. This of course is due to the thermal relaxation error we added to the simulator, thus causing much of the results to encounter a relaxation from the excited state to the ground state, as illustrated in the following plot:

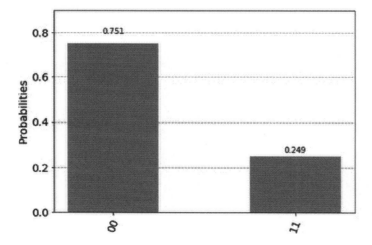

Figure 10.17 – Results on a simulator with thermal relaxation errors

Both T_1 and T_2 are environmental effects that act upon the qubits and their ability to maintain their states. Other effects that contribute to the overall noise of a system are those contributed by the gates that manipulate the qubits. Let's take a look at a few of those now.

Understanding single-gate, multi-gate, and readout errors

Single-gate errors and **multi-gate errors** are generally those introduced when a qubit is operated upon by the various gates on the system. These errors are based on probabilities that the gate applied to the qubit may not operate exactly as expected. For example, if we apply a 5% gate error probability to a single-qubit gate such as a NOT gate, then the result of the operation has a 5% probability of not resulting in the expected value. The Aer library has a list of noise model methods to choose from, including **Pauli error**, **depolarizing error**, **amplitude damping error**, and many more for us to use.

Single-gate and multi-gate errors can be applied to all qubits at once using the `add_all_qubit_quantum_error()` method contained in the `NoiseModel` class. This method applies a quantum error object to the noise model for the specified basis gates, which is then applied to all qubits. The first argument is the quantum error, and the second is the list of basis gates to apply the error to.

Readout errors are those that occur when a measurement and acquisition is triggered to read out the value of the qubit. During the operations of measuring and acquiring the signal from the qubit, errors can exist that may interfere with the results of the qubit measurement. The `NoiseModel` class also has methods available to add readout errors to the noise model.

Let's build our own noise model with single-qubit, multi-qubit, and readout errors on a circuit to observe the effects of these errors on our quantum circuit.

Building your own noise model

There may be times where you wish to build your own custom noise models. Whether it's to generate specific errors to test your error-mitigation methods or to create something resembling a specific device, having the ability to customize your own noise model is a handy feature to have available.

In the following steps, we will create single- and multi-qubit errors, along with readout errors. The single-qubit error will have an amplitude dampening error, the multi-qubit error will have a depolarizing error, and the readout error will be applied to one of the two qubits in the circuit:

1. We'll begin by defining the single- and multi-qubit probability error values, followed by initializing and setting the depolarizing errors. First to the single qubit, and then to the multi-qubit error:

```
# Import the error classes and methods
from qiskit.providers.aer.noise import depolarizing_error
from qiskit.providers.aer.noise import ReadoutError

# Single and multi-qubit probability error
single_qubit_gate_p = 0.25
multi_qubit_gate_p = 0.1

# Apply the depolarizing quantum errors
single_error = depolarizing_error(single_qubit_gate_p, 1)
multi_error = depolarizing_error(multi_qubit_gate_p, 2)
```

2. Next, we will create our `NoiseModel` object and add both the single- and multi-qubit errors. The single qubit error will be assigned to the basis gate u2, and the multi-qubit error will be assigned to the CNOT (cx) gate:

```
# Add the single and multi-qubit errors to the noise
# model
noise_model = NoiseModel()
noise_model.add_all_qubit_quantum_error(single_error,
['u2'])
noise_model.add_all_qubit_quantum_error(multi_error,
['cx'])

# Print out the noise model
print(noise_model)
```

3. We'll now print out the `NoiseModel` to confirm. As we can see from the output of the noise model, we have a list of all basis gates available, a list of instructions that have been assigned noise, and a list of all the basis states that will affect all of the qubits in our circuit:

```
NoiseModel:
  Basis gates: ['cx', 'id', 'u2', 'u3']
  Instructions with noise: ['u2', 'cx']
  All-qubits errors: ['u2', 'cx']
```

4. Next, let's include some readout errors. Readout errors are defined in the Qiskit API documentation as follows:

Classical readout errors are specified by a list of assignment probabilities vectors P(A|B), where A is the recorded classical bit value, and B is the true bit value returned from the measurement.

This means that the probabilities of the expected values will be recorded and used to apply readout errors based on the probability values we pass in as arguments to the noise model.

The equation for a single-qubit readout probability vector is defined as follows:

$$P(A|B)$$
$$= [P(A|0), P(A|1)]$$

When constructing the `ReadoutError` class, $P(A|B)$ is provided as the argument. For our example, we will provide the probability of 0 given 1 as 0.7, and the probability of 1 given 0 as 0.2. We will also add our readout error to the noise model and print out the results, as illustrated in the following code:

```
# Set the readout error probabilities for 0 given 1, & 1
# given 0,
p0_1 = 0.7
p1_0 = 0.2
p0 = 1 - p0_1
p1 = 1 - p1_0


# Construct the ReadoutError with the probabilities
readout_error = ReadoutError([[p0, p0_1], [p1_0, p1]])
# Apply the readout error to qubit 0.
noise_model.add_readout_error(readout_error, [0])
# Print the noise model
print(noise_model)
```

We will see the addition of some instructions and listings of qubits in the result. The first line specifies `Basis gates`, and the following line is the list of `Instructions with noise` added to them. Notice that it now includes the `measure` instruction. Next, we see the `Qubits` that have been specified for a particular noise – in this case, we added the readout error to qubit 0. Next, we see which basis gates have all errors applied. This is the same since we still have the depolarized errors applied in this noise model. Finally, we have `Specific qubit errors`, which now also includes the `measure` readout error applied to qubit 0:

```
NoiseModel:
  Basis gates: ['cx', 'id', 'u2', 'u3']
  Instructions with noise: ['u2', 'cx', 'measure']
  Qubits with noise: [0]
  All-qubits errors: ['u2', 'cx']
  Specific qubit errors: [('measure', [0])]
```

Now that we have our noise model complete and are able to customize the types and amounts of impact the specified errors will contribute, we'll continue by creating a quantum circuit. We'll add our custom noise model and execute it on the Qasm simulator to see the results.

Executing quantum circuits with custom noise models

We'll create our standard circuit out of a Hadamard and **CNOT** circuit, which, as we know from earlier, will result in equal probabilities of 00 and 11. Let's now run it with our noise model and see what results we get and compare them:

```
# Create a simple 2 qubit circuit
qc_error = QuantumCircuit(2,2)
# Place in superposition and entangle
qc_error.h(0)
qc_error.cx(0,1)
# Measure the qubits to the classical bits.
qc_error.measure(range(2), range(2))
```

Now that we have our circuit created, we'll add our custom noise model.

Adding custom noise models to our circuits

We'll begin by obtaining the Qasm simulator, calling the execute method and including the usual arguments, namely, circuit, backend, and the number of shots. We'll also include the noise model information. Similar to how we included a thermal relaxation noise model earlier, we will provide the noise model `basis_gates`, and `noise_model`. This will bind the errors that we customized to the basis gates and qubits, causing the results to include noise, as shown in the following code:

```
# Get the Qasm Simulator
simulator = Aer.get_backend('qasm_simulator')
# Set the backend parameters, including our noise model, and
# execute
result = execute(qc_error, simulator, shots=1024, basis_
gates=noise_model.basis_gates, noise_model=noise_model).
result()
# Obtain the result counts and print
counts = result.get_counts(qc_error)
plot_histogram(counts)
```

The results as you can see in the following plot are now not as ideal as before. We can observe various errors here, caused by noise. First and foremost, our expected results of **00** and **11** are no longer visible. In this sense, we see that qubit 0 has a higher probability of 1, which therefore causes the probability results to be higher for the values **01** and **11**. This is caused by both the depolarization and readout errors that are both applied to qubit 0. We also see that the results affected qubit 1 because of the depolarization error, as we have an output of **10**:

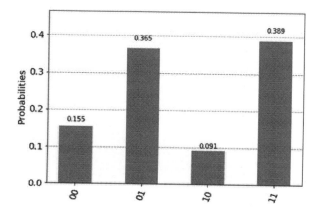

Figure 10.18 – Result with effects from our custom noise model on a quantum circuit

The advantage to all this noise is that you have an insight as to the cause of this noise based on the type of noise we included, and the amount of noise applied to a specified qubit(s). This allows you to simulate certain noise effects should you wish to work on some noise-mitigating techniques.

By applying noise and understanding its effects, you can create noise-mitigating techniques and verify the results on a simulator. By doing this you can test various combinations of noise effects, which can help minimize the error rate on some algorithms, and therefore increase the performance of the quantum computer. We will look at noise-mitigating techniques in the next chapter.

Summary

In this chapter, we covered various simulators. You now have the skills to leverage various simulators to simulate running circuits on a quantum computer and obtain specific content from the circuits, such as state vectors, a unitary matrix, and any scheduled pulses.

We also covered various visualization techniques. The skills that you have gained will help you visualize the various pieces of information from the simulator, such as visualizing the state and phase information of a qubit using the QSphere and plotting state vector graphs. And finally, we looked into the noise models that Aer provides by either extracting the noise from an existing quantum computer, or creating our own noise models and applying them to the simulators.

In the next chapter, we will learn how to characterize and mitigate noise using Ignis. This will allow us to optimize the performance of the quantum computer and increase its computational power. We will also learn how to measure a quantum computer's computational power and performance by understanding what Quantum Volume is and how to measure it.

Questions

1. Can you list all the simulators found in the Aer library?

2. How many total simulators are there altogether in Qiskit? (*Hint*: This includes Basic Aer, Aer, and IBM Quantum Provider.)

3. Create a QSphere representation of a qubit on the negative y axis, creating the state $\frac{|0\rangle - i|1\rangle}{\sqrt{2}}$, using only a single Hadamard gate along with the phase gates.

4. What must the initialized probability value of a circuit be in order to be valid?

5. Can you use the QSphere to visualize both the phase and probability information of a qubit?

6. How would you apply a noise function to qubits 2, 3, and 4 of a 5-qubit system?

7. What would happen if you set the depolarization error values close to 1?

8. If you applied a readout error equally to all qubits, what results would you expect, and why?

11
Mitigating Quantum Errors Using Ignis

Ignis, as described in the Qiskit library, is a framework that contains various functionalities, such as **characterization**, **verification**, and **mitigation**. What this means is that it provides the ability to characterize the effects of noise on the system, verify the performance capabilities of the various gates and circuits, and calibrate circuits to generate routines that lessen the errors in your results.

This chapter will cover these topics by taking you through the process of characterizing and estimating the decoherence of the qubits from noise models. This will help you visualize and mitigate errors after measuring your results. We'll also work on mitigating quantum errors from the results we get back from the quantum devices using some of the features from the Ignis library.

In quantum systems, this noise originates from various sources: thermal heat from electronics, decoherence, dephasing, connectivity, or signal loss. Here, we will see how to measure the effects of noise on a **qubit**, and how to mitigate readout error noise to optimize our results. In the end, we will compare and contrast the differences to better understand the effects and ways to mitigate them.

The following topics will be covered in this chapter:

- Generating the noise effects of relaxation
- Estimating T_1 decoherence time
- Generating the noise effects of dephasing
- Estimating T_2 decoherence time
- Estimating T_2^* (T_2 star) decoherence time
- Visualizing the T_1, T_2, and T_2^* characterization
- Mitigating readout errors using measurement calibrations

In this chapter, we will cover one of the challenges faced by most systems: noise. By the end of the chapter, you will know how to generate test circuits used to estimate the characteristics of each qubit, measure varying noise effects, such as relaxation and dephasing, and visualize the characteristics of each qubit. Finally, you'll learn how to apply error mitigation techniques to help minimize the effects of noise, based on the measurement characteristics analyzed by the test circuit results.

Technical requirements

In this chapter, it is expected that you have some understanding of the effects of noise on electronic systems and how to simulate them on a quantum computer. This chapter will cover some refreshers on simulating noise; however, the recommendation for you is to review *Chapter 10, Executing Circuits Using Qiskit Aer*, to get an understanding of how to simulate noise on a simulator from the configuration information of a quantum computer. This will help you understand an end-to-end scenario to simulate and mitigate errors on a simulator based on a quantum computer. The results of the simulation will provide information that will be leveraged to mitigate your circuit results after executing your circuit on a quantum computer.

Here is the source code we'll be using throughout this book: `https://github. com/PacktPublishing/Learn-Quantum-Computing-with-Python-and- IBM-Quantum-Experience`. Here is the link for the CiA videos: `https://bit. ly/35o5M8o`

Generating noise effects of relaxation

We learned in *Chapter 10, Executing Circuits Using Qiskit Aer*, that we can generate various noise models that are based on the configuration of a specified quantum computer. After the configuration information is extracted, we can then apply any one of an array of error functions to a simulator, which will reproduce similar error effects to what we would get from a quantum computer.

In this section, we will expand on that to learn how to execute test circuits and visualize the results from those tests. This will help us to understand how various noise models affect the results over time. The two effects we will review here are the two most common issues found in near-term quantum systems: **relaxation** and **dephasing**. These are critical errors as they can affect the quantum state information, which would result in erroneous responses.

Later on in this chapter, we will also look at **readout errors**, which is another common source that originates when the system is applying a measurement pulse, while in parallel, listening in on the acquisition channel. The results and conversion from analog to digital can introduce many errors as well.

Generating noise models and test circuits

We will start by testing one of the most common and important effects of noise in quantum systems: **decoherence**. The three main types of decoherence are T_1, T_2, and T_2^*. Each of these represents a type of decoherence effect on the qubit. In order to analyze the effects of **relaxation** (T_1) and **dephasing** (T_2/T_2^*), we will first need to create the test circuits for each of the three. These test circuits will help us run experiments to analyze the characterization of the device. We will begin by looking at each one of these individually so as to understand the differences between them and how to mitigate them when they are run on a real quantum device.

In order to properly analyze the decoherence effects, we will need to run various circuits with a specific number and types of gates. Lucky for us, Qiskit Ignis includes a method to generate these test circuits for us. For decoherence testing, we will use `t1_circuits`, `t2_circuits`, and `t2star_circuits`, which will generate the T_1, T_2, and T_2^* circuits, respectively. Let's take a quick moment to review what the decoherence of each one means as we create the test circuits.

Generating and executing T_1 test circuits

T_1, as we covered in *Chapter 10, Executing Circuits Using Qiskit Aer*, is often referred to as the **relaxation time**. Relaxation time refers to the time it takes the energy of a qubit to decay from the **excited state** ($|1\rangle$) back down to its **ground state** ($|0\rangle$) as illustrated in the following graph, where *P(1)* indicates the probability of 1, and *P(0)* is the probability of 0. The T_1 time is defined as the value when **P(t) = 1/e** (refer to the following diagram):

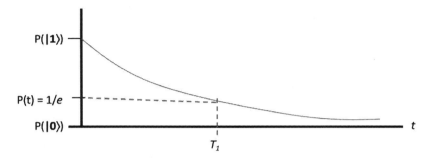

Figure 11.1 – T_1 defined as the decay time where the probability of the energy state reaches 1/e

In order to determine the amount of time to reach T_1 for any qubit, we will need to create a test circuit that places the qubit in an excited state, $|1\rangle$. This we know how to do by simply applying an X gate to the qubit.

Next, we will need to wait a certain amount of time before measuring the qubit. One way to do this is to insert an identity gate with a fixed gate time. This is a simple circuit to create manually; however, the challenge is to determine how many identity gates you need to include and how scalable that process is. Lucky for us, we have the t1_circuits method!

This method allows us to define how many gates to include in each circuit and the gate time for each identity gate, as well as list which qubits to apply to these gates. In the following code sample, we will generate an array of quantum circuits, each with an X gate and the number of identity gates we specified. We will also provide the gate times for the identity gates. Let's create a new **IQX Qiskit notebook** and insert the following code, which will load in additional helper math, plot, Aer, and Ignis libraries:

```
# Import plot and math libraries
import numpy as np
import matplotlib.pyplot as plt


# Import the noise models and some standard error methods
from qiskit.providers.aer.noise import NoiseModel
```

```
from qiskit.providers.aer.noise.errors.standard_errors import
amplitude_damping_error, phase_damping_error


# Import all three coherence circuits generators and fitters
from qiskit.ignis.characterization.coherence import t1_
circuits, t2_circuits, t2star_circuits
from qiskit.ignis.characterization.coherence import T1Fitter,
T2Fitter, T2StarFitter
```

Now that we have our Ignis libraries loaded, we can use them to generate the test circuits, as illustrated in the following cell. We will generate a list of the number of identity gates to include in each test circuit and include the gate time for each identity gate. The qubit we will measure for T_1 will be the first qubit.

We will use the same name of the parameters listed in the t1_circuits API documentation – num_of_gates, gate_time, and qubits – where the array length of the number of gates relates to the number of test circuits we will create, which in this case is 18, where out of which 12 are linearly spaced and 6 are manually defined entries. In the following code, we will define the variables to generate an array of test circuits:

```
# Generate the T₁ test circuits


# Generate a list of number of gates to add to each circuit
# using np.linspace so that the number of gates increases
# linearly
# and append with a large span at the end of the list (200-
# 4000)
num_of_gates = np.append((np.linspace(1, 100, 12)).astype(int),
np.array([200, 400, 800, 1000, 2000, 4000]))


#Define the gate time for each Identity gate
gate_time = 0.1


# Select the first qubit as the one we wish to measure T₁
qubits = [0]


# Generate the test circuits given the above parameters
test_circuits, delay_times = t1_circuits(num_of_gates,
gate_time, qubits)
```

```
# The number of I gates appended for each circuit
print('Number of gates per test circuit: \n', num_of_gates,
'\n')


# The gate time of each circuit (number of I gates * gate_time)
print('Delay times for each test circuit created,
respectively:\n', delay_times)
```

After generating an array of test circuits and their respective delay times, this will print out the number of gates that will be appended to each test circuit and the delay times for each circuit, respectively, as follows:

```
Number of gates per test circuit:
 [   1    10    19    28    37    46    55    64    73    82    91   100
 200   400  800  1000  2000  4000]


Delay times for each test circuit created, respectively:
 [1.0e-01 1.0e+00 1.9e+00 2.8e+00 3.7e+00 4.6e+00 5.5e+00
 6.4e+00 7.3e+00 8.2e+00 9.1e+00 1.0e+01 2.0e+01 4.0e+01
 8.0e+01 1.0e+02 2.0e+02 4.0e+02]
```

Let's confirm a few things about the test circuits we created. We know that in total, the number of test circuits created should be 18. Then, we will draw the first circuit, which should include the X gate to set the qubit in the excited state, followed by one identity gate before the measurement:

```
print('Total test circuits created: ', len(test_circuits))
print('Test circuit 1 with 1 Identity gate:')
test_circuits[0].draw()
```

The results confirm our expectation of 18 test circuits and a single identity gate:

```
Total test circuits created: 18
```

The following circuit diagram shows test circuit 1 with one identity gate:

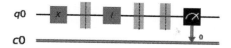

Figure 11.2 – Test circuit 1, with an X gate and a single identity gate

With the gate time of the identity gate set to 0.1, we know that this is a fairly quick result. Let's look at the next test circuit to see how it increases:

```
print('Test circuit 2 with 10 Identity gates:')
test_circuits[1].draw()
```

In the second test circuit, we see that we now have 10 identity gates, which increases our delay time from 0.1 in the first circuit to 1.0 in the second circuit. The following circuit diagram shows you test circuit 2 with 10 identity gates:

Figure 11.3 – Test circuit 2, with an X gate and 10 identity gates

Next, we will generate a simulator with an amplitude damping error applied to the identity gate on qubit 0:

```
# Set the simulator with amplitude damping noise

# Set the amplitude damping noise channel parameters T₁ and
# Lambda
t1 = 20
lam = np.exp(-gate_time/t1)

# Generate the amplitude dampling error channel
error = amplitude_damping_error(1 - lam)
noise_model = NoiseModel()

# Set the dampling error to the ID gate on qubit 0.
noise_model.add_quantum_error(error, 'id', [0])
```

Next, we will execute all our test circuits on the simulator with the generated noise model:

```
# Run the simulator with the generated noise model
backend = Aer.get_backend('qasm_simulator')
shots = 200
backend_result = execute(test_circuits, backend, shots=shots,
noise_model=noise_model).result()
```

Let's review our results. The first test circuit, which comprised only one identity gate, should, along with the noise model effects, display a very small error in our results:

```
# Plot the noisy results of the largest (last in the list)
# circuit
plot_histogram(backend_result.get_counts(test_circuits[0]))
```

As expected, we observe a very small, almost insignificant result of the amplitude decay down to the ground state:

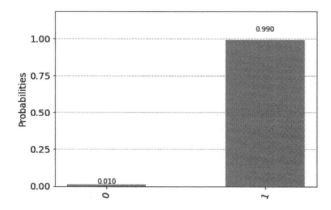

Figure 11.4 – The results from the first test circuit, with an insignificant error rate

Now, let's take a look at the other side and view the results from the last test circuit. Here, we have a total of 4,000 gates; the results, as we will see, are quite significant:

```
# Plot the noisy results of the largest (last in the list)
# circuit
plot_histogram(backend_result.get_counts(test_
    circuits[len(test_circuits)-1]))
```

As you can see in the histogram, the results are entirely back to the ground state, indicating that we have surpassed the T_1 time and that the execution of our last test circuit has resulted in every count being reverted back down to the ground state:

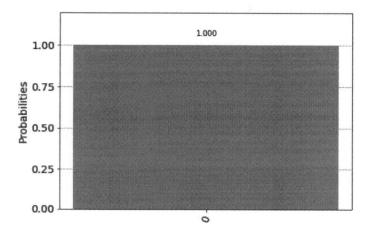

Figure 11.5 – Results from test circuit 18 with 4,000 identity gates, with significant errors

Now that we have created and executed our test circuits for T_1, we can analyze and use *fitters* to estimate the T_1 time based on the results of our test circuits.

Estimating T_1 decoherence times

Fitters are used to estimate the T_1 time based on experiment results from `t1_circuits` executed on noisy devices. The estimate is based on the probability formula of measuring 1 from the following equation, where A, T_1, and B are unknown parameters:

$$f(t) = A\,e^{-t/T_1} + B$$

Since we set the T_1 value earlier when we defined the noise model of the qubit as 20, let's assume for now that we do not know that and initialize the value to some percentage value away from the actual value. The `T1Fitter` class has a few parameters that it needs in order to characterize the qubit. We will start by initializing the values for a, t1, and b:

```
# Initialize the parameters for the T1Fitter, A, T₁, and B
param_t1 = t1*1.2
param_a = 1.0
param_b = 0.0
```

This will initialize our t1, a, and b parameters, which we will use to generate `T1Fitter`.

Next, we will generate `T1Fitter` by providing the following parameters:

- `backend_result`: The results from our test circuits on the backend
- `Xdata`: The delay times for the test circuits
- `qubits`: The qubits that we wish to use to measure T_1
- `fit_p0`: The initial values to set A, T_1, and B, respectively (*these must be entered in order*)
- `fit_bounds`: The tuple representing the lower and upper bounds for the parameters to fit
- `time_unit`: The unit of the delay time in `xdata`

Referencing the parameters from the test circuits, we can generate and plot the results of `T1Fitter`, as follows:

```
# Generate the T1Fitter for our test circuit results
fit = T1Fitter(backend_result, delay_times, qubits,
               fit_p0=[param_a, param_t1, param_b],
               fit_bounds=([0, 0, -1], [2, param_t1*2, 1]))

# Plot the fitter results for T₁ over each test circuit's delay
# time
fit.plot(0)
```

The result will plot the relaxation decay of the qubit over the delay times of each test circuit. You can see the decay results as follows:

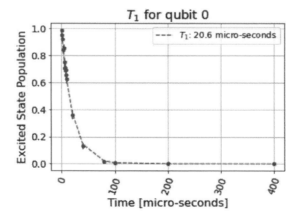

Figure 11.6 – T1Fitter estimated results, where T_1 is estimated to be at 20.6 microseconds for qubit 0

In this section, you have generated T_1 test circuits, executed them with amplitude dampening noise models on a backend device, and characterized the results to estimate T_1. Characterizing other qubits can be done as well by simply listing the other qubit indices; in this example, we chose to characterize qubit [0]. Let's now characterize T_2 and $T_2{}^*$ on a qubit. The steps you will see are very similar.

Generating the noise effects of dephasing

T_2 and $T_2{}^*$ are similar in that they are both representing the dephasing of a qubit. The difference is in the experimental process they conduct to measure each circuit. Determining the decay time of $T_2{}^*$ is conducted by placing the qubit in a superposition state using a *Hadamard gate*, then after some delay time, you apply another Hadamard gate and measure. This should result in the qubit returning to the originating state – in this case, the grounded state. This experiment is referred to as the **Ramsey experiment**.

To determine the decay time of T_2, we will perform a similar experiment as we did for $T_2{}^*$, by first placing the qubit in a superposition state. The difference is that rather than waiting for some delay time before applying another *Hadamard gate* before measuring, you instead wait until half the delay time and then apply either an X or Y rotation, then wait until the second half delay time is complete before taking the measurement. This experiment is referred to as the **Hahn echo experiment**.

In all, both experiments will measure the decay time of the dephasing where the expectation of the result is random. In the next section, we will generate the T_2 circuits based on the Ramsey experiment.

Generating and executing T_2 circuits

T_2 is often referred to as the dephasing time. Rather than looking at the relaxation of a qubit from the excited state to the ground state, the dephasing of a qubit has more to do when the state is in a linear combination of the two states. Let's step through what is meant here by dephasing:

1. When a qubit transitions from the ground state, $|0\rangle$, to the superposition state, $|+\rangle$, after we run a Hadamard gate on the qubit, we expect that by adding another Hadamard gate, the qubit will then return to the ground state, $|0\rangle$.

2. However, while the qubit is in the $|+\rangle$ state, this is where dephasing could be a problem. The problem lies in that over time, the qubit may or may not be in the $|+\rangle$ or $|-\rangle$ state, but rather in some angle around the Z axis away from the $|+\rangle$ state.

3. This would then render the qubit unpredictable when applying another *Hadamard gate* if our expectation is for the qubit to return to the ground state but instead is found in the excited state, $|1\rangle$.

In order to test this, we will need a test circuit that will first place the qubit from the initial state, $|0\rangle$, into the superposition state, $|+\rangle$. This, as we know, can be done with a Hadamard gate. Then, we can place an identity gate to increase the delay time between each step. Just as before, we will import a few libraries and define the parameters for the `t2_circuits` generator method by entering the following:

```
# Import the thermal relaxation error we will use to create our
# error
from qiskit.providers.aer.noise.errors.standard_errors import
thermal_relaxation_error


# Import the T2Fitter Class and t2_circuits method
from qiskit.ignis.characterization.coherence import T2Fitter
from qiskit.ignis.characterization.coherence import t2_circuits
```

Now that we have the necessary classes and method, we'll define our `t2_circuits` parameters in the next cell:

```
num_of_gates = (np.linspace(1, 300, 50)).astype(int)
gate_time = 0.1


# Note that it is possible to measure several qubits in
# parallel
qubits = [0]


t2echo_test_circuits, t2echo_delay_times = t2_circuits(
num_of_gates, gate_time, qubits)


# The number of I gates appended for each circuit
print('Number of gates per test circuit: \n', num_of_gates,
'\n')


# The gate time of each circuit (number of I gates * gate_time)
print('Delay times for T2 echo test circuits:\n',
t2echo_delay_times)
```

Running the preceding cell results in the following number of gates and delay times to generate our T_2 test circuits:

```
Number of gates per test circuit:
 [  1    7   13   19   25   31   37   43   49   55   62   68   74   80   86
   92   98  104  110  116  123  129  135  141  147  153  159  165  171  177  184
  190  196  202  208  214  220  226  232  238  245  251  257  263  269  275
  281  287  293  300]
Delay times for T2 echo test circuits:
 [ 0.2   1.4    2.6   3.8   5.    6.2   7.4   8.6   9.8  11.   12.4 13.6
  14.8 16.
  17.2 18.4 19.6 20.8 22.   23.2 24.6 25.8 27.   28.2 29.4 30.6
  31.8 33.
  34.2 35.4 36.8 38.   39.2 40.4 41.6 42.8 44.   45.2 46.4 47.6
  49.  50.2
  51.4 52.6 53.8 55.   56.2 57.4 58.6 60. ]
```

As in the previous test circuit example, let's examine the first test circuit to confirm that the gates are where we expect to see them:

```
# Draw the first T₂ test circuit
t2echo_test_circuits[0].draw()
```

This naturally results in the following test circuit. Note that the **Y** rotation gate is located in the middle:

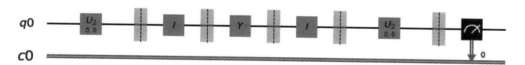

Figure 11.7 – T_2 test circuit with Hadamard rotations on each end
and a Y rotation in the middle of the identity gates

This is the Ramsey experiment test circuit we will be running. The other 49 test circuits we generated are increasing in size and will eventually surpass the T_2 time, which produces random results.

Let's now generate our T_2 noise model to include in the simulator. This will allow us to include only a `thermal_relaxation_error` model in the circuit, so when we execute our circuit, this is the only noise effect. We will then store our noise results in the `t2_echo_backend_result` variable:

```
# We'll create a noise model on the backend simulator
backend = Aer.get_backend('qasm_simulator')
shots = 400


# set the t2 decay time
t2 = 25.0


# Define the T2 noise model based on the thermal relaxation
# error model
t2_noise_model = NoiseModel()
t2_noise_model.add_quantum_error(thermal_relaxation_error(np.
inf, t2, gate_time, 0.5), 'id', [0])


# Execute the circuit on the noisy backend
t2echo_backend_result = execute(t2echo_test_circuits, backend,
                        shots=shots,
                        noise_model=t2_noise_model,
                        optimization_level=0).result()
```

Next, let's plot our results, starting with the first test circuit with the shortest delay time, and then the last test circuit with most delay time:

```
plot_histogram(t2echo_backend_result.get_counts(t2echo_test_
    circuits[0]))
```

This results in an expected ground state, which is denoted as follows, where we have a 99% probability of measuring 0 (very minimal effects of dephasing time):

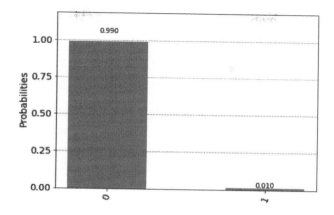

Figure 11.8 – The first T$_2$ test circuit executed on the noisy backend

Now, let's see the last test circuit's results:

```
plot_histogram(t2echo_backend_result.get_counts(t2echo_test_
    circuits[len(t2echo_test_circuits)-1]))
```

This, as we can see, has a fairly equal probability of either of the two basis states, which indicates that we have far exceeded the dephasing time, T$_2$ (exceeds the T$_2$ dephasing time):

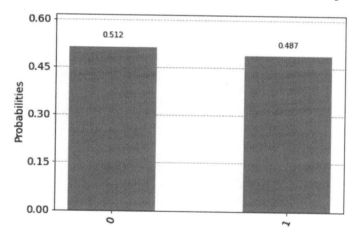

Figure 11.9 – The last T$_2$ test circuit executed on the noisy backend

What we saw here is how, over time, we can see that the dephasing time greatly affects our results. This dephasing time gets very problematic if not mitigated. Mitigating errors will be described later in this section, *Mitigating readout errors.*

Estimating T$_2$ decoherence times

We estimate the T$_2$ time based on experiment results from `t2_circuits` executed on noisy devices. The estimate is based on the probability formula of measuring 0 from the following equation, where A, T_2, and B are unknown parameters:

$$f(t) = A\,e^{-t/T_2} + B$$

Finally, to estimate T$_2$* and characterize the qubit with respect to the results, we will leverage `T2Fitter`. To generate the `T2Fitter` class, we will use similar parameter definitions as `T1Fitter` in the previous section, only this time, we will use the results from the T$_2$ test circuits:

```
# Generate the T2Fitter class using similar parameters as the
# T1Fitter
t2echo_fit = T2Fitter(t2echo_backend_result,
t2echo_delay_times, qubits, fit_p0=[0.5, t2, 0.5],
fit_bounds=([-0.5, 0, -0.5], [1.5, 40, 1.5]))

# Print and plot the results
print(t2echo_fit.params)
t2echo_fit.plot(0)
plt.show()
```

The preceding code prints out the estimate values for A, T_2, and B for qubit 0:

```
{'0': [array([ 0.52397653, 27.06685838, 0.47677457])]}
```

The previous code also plots the characterization of qubit 0, with an estimated value for T_2 at 27.1 ms:

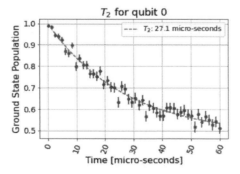

Figure 11.10 – Plot T2Fitter characterization of qubit 0, where T$_2$ is estimated to be at 27.1 ms

Now, that we have completed characterizing T_2 on qubit 0, let's look at the last characterization example of T_2^*.

Generating and executing T_2^* test circuits

T_2^* is also referred to as the dephasing time of a qubit. As mentioned earlier, the difference is in the experiment, where in the previous experiment for T_2, we added an array of identity gates before rotating the state of the qubit with a Y gate.

For T_2^*, we will generate test circuits that place the qubit in a superposition state and then after some delay time, it will apply a linear phase gate, immediately followed by a reversing the superposition back to the initial state. The test circuit will also include the induced oscillation frequency on the phase gate. We'll create the test circuits using the `t2star_circuits` method by creating it as described in the following cell:

```
# 50 total linearly spaced number of gates
# 30 from 10->150, 20 from 160->450
num_of_gates = np.append((np.linspace(1, 150, 30)).astype(int),
(np.linspace(160,450,20)).astype(int))

# Set the Identity gate delay time
gate_time = 0.1

# Select the qubit to measure T_2*
qubits = [0]

# Generate the 50 test circuits with number of oscillations set
# to 4
test_circuits, delay_times, osc_freq = t2star_circuits(
num_of_gates, gate_time, qubits, nosc=4)
print('Circuits generated: ', len(test_circuits))
print('Delay times: ', delay_times)
print('Oscillating frequency: ', osc_freq)
```

This will produce the 50 test circuits, with the specified delay time for each identity gate and the oscillating frequency for the phase gate:

```
Circuits generated:    50
Delay times:    [  0.1    0.6    1.1    1.6    2.1    2.6    3.1    3.6    4.2
4.7    5.2    5.7    6.2    6.7
  7.2    7.8    8.3    8.8    9.3    9.8 10.3 10.8 11.4 11.9 12.4 12.9
 13.4 13.9
 14.4 15.    16.    17.5 19.    20.5 22.1 23.6 25.1 26.6 28.2 29.7
 31.2 32.7
 34.3 35.8 37.3 38.8 40.4 41.9 43.4 45. ]
Oscillating frequency:    0.0888888888888889
```

Let's confirm the first test circuit and see how many identity gates are generated:

```
print(test_circuits[0].count_ops())
test_circuits[0].draw()
```

As we can see, this generates one identity gate, followed by a phase gate, surrounded by Hadamard gates:

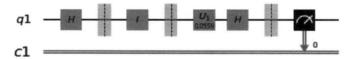

Figure 11.11 – The first test circuit, comprising an H, I, Phase, and then another H gate

If we look at the second test circuit, we should expect to see six identity gates followed by a phase gate, also surrounded by Hadamard gates:

```
print(test_circuits[1].count_ops())
test_circuits[1].draw()
```

We can now confirm that the T_2^* test circuits have been generated according to our parameters:

```
OrderedDict([('barrier', 8), ('id', 6), ('h', 2), ('u1', 1),
('measure', 1)])
```

We can also confirm that we have the six expected identity gates, followed by a phase gate, all of which are surrounded by Hadamard gates:

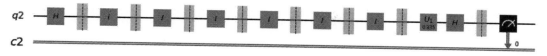

Figure 11.12 – The second test circuit, comprising an H, 6 Is, a Phase, and an H gate

These test circuits implement the Hahn echo experiment. Let's now execute these test circuits on a noisy backend; this time we will use a phase damping error to generate our noise model:

```
# Get the backend to execute the test circuits
backend = Aer.get_backend('qasm_simulator')

# Set the T_2* value to 10
t2Star = 10

# Set the phase damping error and add it to the noise model to
# the Identity gates
error = phase_damping_error(1 - np.exp(-2*gate_time/t2Star))
noise_model = NoiseModel()
noise_model.add_quantum_error(error, 'id', [0])

# Run the simulator
shots = 1024
backend_result = execute(test_circuits, backend, shots=shots,
noise_model=noise_model).result()
```

Let's view the first test circuit, which should have minimal effects of T_2^*:

```
# Plot the noisy results of the shortest (first in the list)
# circuit
plot_histogram(backend_result.get_counts(test_circuits[0]))
```

As expected, this illustrates very minimal effects of T_2^*. As you can see, we have a 99% probability of measuring 0, which is the expected result from this test circuit:

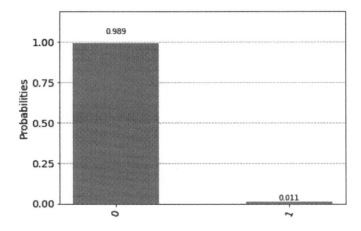

Figure 11.13 – Results of the first test circuit, with minimal T_2^* effects

We will review the results from the last test circuit. Due to the fact that this has the longest delay time, we should see the maximum effect of T_2^*:

```
# Plot the noisy results of the largest (last in the list)
# circuit
plot_histogram(backend_result.get_counts(
test_circuits[len(test_circuits)-1]))
```

As expected, the results are now completely random:

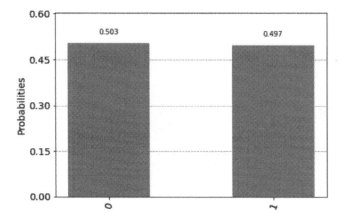

Figure 11.14 – Results of the last test circuit, with maximum T_2^* effects

We've successfully completed generating the T_2^* test circuits and obtained their results from executing them on a noisy backend. Next, we will estimate the T_2^* dephasing time and characterize the effects on qubit 0.

Estimating the T₂* dephasing time

We will estimate the T_2^* dephasing time based on the experiment results from t2star_ circuits executed on a noisy device. We will use the *probability formula* of measuring 0 from the following equation, where A, T_2^*, f, Φ, and B are unknown parameters:

$$f(t) = Ae^{-\frac{t}{T_2*}}\cos(2\pi ft + \phi) + B$$

The T2StarFitter parameters are the same, with the exception of the following:

- fit_p0: The initial values to the fit parameters – in order, A, T_2^*, f, Φ, B.

- fit_bounds: The lower and upper bounds, respectively. Parameters in order: A, T_2^*, f, Φ, B

The following code will set the initial parameter values so that we can generate our T2StarFitter and bounds:

```
# Set the initial values of the T2StarFitter parameters
param_T2Star = t2Star*1.1
param_A = 0.5
param_B = 0.5


# Generate the T2StarFitter with the given parameters and
# bounds
fit = T2StarFitter(backend_result, delay_times, qubits,
                   fit_p0=[0.5, t2Star, osc_freq, 0, 0.5],
                   fit_bounds=([-0.5, 0, 0, -np.pi, -0.5],
                               [1.5, 40, 2*osc_freq,
                                np.pi, 1.5]))


# Plot the qubit characterization from the T2StarFitter
fit.plot(0)
```

The result from `T2StarFitter` is as we expected, where the oscillations seem to de-phase down into an equal probability of 0 and 1 after 10.3 ms:

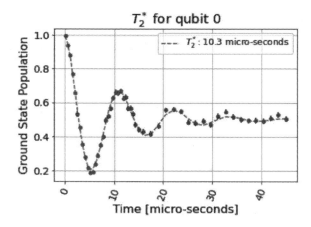

Figure 11.15 – T_2^* characterization of qubit 0, where T_2^* is estimated at 10.3 ms

Congratulations! You have just successfully characterized all three decoherence effects on a qubit. Of course, we're not done yet! Characterizing the decoherence of a qubit is important, but equally important is mitigating the errors. In the final section of this chapter, we will review readout errors, which are errors based on the effects of measuring and acquiring the results from the qubits. These readout errors are fairly common on near-term quantum systems, so it is a good tool to have in your development toolbox.

Mitigating readout errors

Ignis has measurement filters that can be used to mitigate various types of errors, such as *measurements* and *tensors*.

The **measurement calibration** is what we will use to mitigate measurement errors in this section. The process begins by first generating a list of circuits, where each circuit represents each of all the possible states of the qubits specified, then executing the circuits on an ideal simulator, the results of which we will then pass into a **measurement filter**. The measurement filter will then be used to mitigate the measurement errors. In the following example, we will first run the circuits on a simulator without any noise models. Then, we will create a noise model that will be applied to all the qubits of the simulator. Then we will execute the circuits on the noisy backend device, where we will then apply the measurement filter to mitigate the errors as best we can. Finally, we will view the results of the measurement filter and compare them to the original noisy results.

We'll begin by importing the necessary methods and classes from the Ignis mitigation library, specifically the `complete_meas_cal` method and the `CompleteMeasFitter` class. The first method, *measurement calibration circuits*, returns a list of circuits that cover the full Hilbert space of the system. What this means is that if you have *n* qubits, then all 2^n basis states will generate a list of quantum circuits. The second is the *complete measurement fitter* class, which initializes a measurement calibration matrix based on the list of quantum circuits returned from executing the measurement calibration circuits to generate a measurement correction fitter:

```
# Import Qiskit classes
from qiskit.providers.aer import noise
from qiskit.tools.visualization import plot_histogram


# Import measurement calibration functions
from qiskit.ignis.mitigation.measurement import
complete_meas_cal, CompleteMeasFitter
```

The parameters for each are as follows:

- `complete_meas_cal`:

  `qubit_list`: The list of qubits to execute the measurement correction onto. If no list is provided, then it will execute the measurement correction over all the qubits.

  `qr`: Quantum registers or the size of the quantum register. If none is specified, then it will create one.

  `cr`: Classical registers or the size of the classical register. If none is specified, then it will create one.

  `circlabel`: A label to prefix the circuit name so as to uniquely identify it.

  `Returns`: This returns two lists. The first is a list of calibration `QuantumCircuits.`, while the second is a list of state labels for each calibration circuit.

- `CompleteMeasFitter`:

  `Results`: The list of quantum circuits returned from running the `complete_meas_cal` method. The class allows you to set the calibration matrix later, so it is not required to construct.

  `state_labels`: The list of state labels returned from the `complete_meas_cal` method. The ordering of the state labels will be followed when generating the measurement fitter.

`qubit_list`: The list of qubits to apply. If none are specified, then the qubit list will be generated based on the first state label entry, `state_labels[0]`.

`Circlabel`: If the qubits had a prefix label in the `complete_meas_cal` method.

The complete measurement fitter also includes some methods we can use that will allow us to be a bit more flexible when generating our fitter, such as the following:

- `add_data(new_results[,…])`: This is to add the quantum circuit list results from the complete measurement calibration.

- `subset_fitter([qubit_sublist])`: Generates a fitter object of a subset from the original qubit list.

- `readout_fidelity([label_list])`: Generates the readout fidelity of the calibration matrix based on the results from the complete measurement calibration method.

Next, we will generate the complete measurement calibration circuits. We will generate a five-qubit set so that we can use it on any of the five-qubit quantum computers. Then, we will generate the calibration circuits using the `complete_meas_cal` method with a prefix circuit label, `mcal`, followed by printing out the number of circuits, which should equal 2^n circuits, where n is equal to 5, in this case. Finally, we will draw any of the calibration circuits returned. In this example, we will draw the last one, which represents the value `11111`:

```
# Generate the calibration circuits
# Set the number of qubits
num_qubits = 5
# Set the qubit list to generate the measurement calibration
# circuits
qubit_list = [0,1,2,3,4]


# Generate the measurement calibrations circuits and state
# labels
meas_calibs, state_labels = complete_meas_cal(qubit_list=qubit_
    list, qr=num_qubits, circlabel='mcal')
# Print the number of measurement calibration circuits
# generated
print(len(meas_calibs))
# Draw any of the generated calibration circuits, 0-31.
# In this example we will draw the last one.
meas_calibs[31].draw()
```

The printed result is the total number of calibration circuits, 32, which the `complete_meas_cal` method produces. This will create 32 circuits where each is initialized according to the state levels, which would run from `00000` through `11111`. The following circuit diagram pertains to the last circuit, `11111`, as follows:

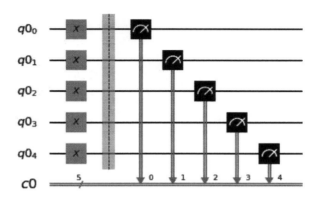

Figure 11.16 – The last calibration circuit, representing value 11111

If you wish to see all the state labels, simply print them out, as follows:

```
state_labels
```

This results in listing out all the state labels from `00000` through `11111`, which matches the calibration circuit results.

Now that we have our calibration circuits, let's start by first executing it on a simulator so that we can see what an ideal result is, meaning no noise effects or errors. Once we get our results, we will generate the measurement fitter and print out the calibration matrix:

```
# Execute the calibration circuits without noise on the qasm
# simulator
backend = Aer.get_backend('qasm_simulator')
job = execute(meas_calibs, backend=backend, shots=1000)

# Obtain the measurement calibration results
cal_results = job.result()

# The calibration matrix without noise is the identity matrix
meas_fitter = CompleteMeasFitter(cal_results, state_labels,
circlabel='mcal')
print(meas_fitter.cal_matrix)
```

The result is the following calibration matrix, where the rows and columns represent the *measured states* and the *prepared states*, respectively:

```
[[1. 0. 0. ... 0. 0. 0.]
 [0. 1. 0. ... 0. 0. 0.]
 [0. 0. 1. ... 0. 0. 0.]
 ...
 [0. 0. 0. ... 1. 0. 0.]
 [0. 0. 0. ... 0. 1. 0.]
 [0. 0. 0. ... 0. 0. 1.]]
```

Here, the diagonal values are all 1, and all the other fields are 0. This indicates that the measured states correctly match the prepared states.

The measure fitter also includes a nice plot method to visualize the accuracy of the results. To plot the calibration matrix, simply run the following:

```
meas_fitter.plot_calibration()
```

The results have a grayscale-based shading, where the darker cells indicate that the accuracy is closer to 1, and the lighter cells indicate accuracy closer to 0, where 1 indicates a 100% match between the measured and prepared states . Due to the default width of the following figure, the states listed across the top of the rendered calibration matrix are difficult to read. However, what it indicates are the prepared states starting with 00000 on the left-most column, increasing along each column towards the final prepared state, 11111:

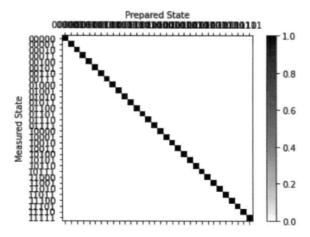

Figure 11.17 – Plot representation of the measured and prepared state results

Now let's run the same steps, but rather than using a simulator, let's run through an actual quantum device. We will start by creating a circuit with five qubits and we'll place one qubit in superposition and entangle it with all the other qubits:

```
# Create a 5 qubit circuit
qc = QuantumCircuit(5,5)
# Place the first qubit in superposition
qc.h(0)
# Entangle all other qubits together
qc.cx(0, 1)
qc.cx(1, 2)
qc.cx(2, 3)
qc.cx(3, 4)
# Include a barrier just to ease visualization of the circuit
qc.barrier()
# Measure and draw the final circuit
qc.measure([0,1,2,3,4], [0,1,2,3,4])
qc.draw()
```

This results in the following circuit:

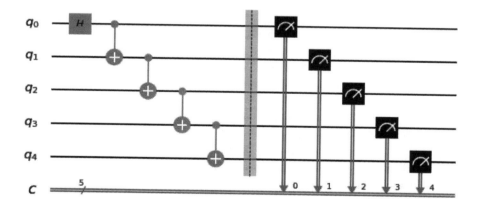

Figure 11.18 – A five-qubit test quantum circuit where all the qubits are entangled with a qubit in superposition

Next, we will get the least busy backend to execute our circuit. We will filter the results to include only backend systems that have greater than or equal to five qubits, not a simulator, and are in operational mode:

```
# Obtain the least busy backend device, not a simulator
from qiskit.providers.ibmq import least_busy
# Find the least busy operational quantum device with 5 or more
# qubits
backend = least_busy(provider.backends(filters=lambda x:
x.configuration().n_qubits >= 4 and not x.configuration().
simulator and x.status().operational==True))
# Print the least busy backend
print("least busy backend: ", backend)
```

This results in the least busy device available at the time it was executed. The results will vary based on the devices available to you and their operational state. At the time of writing, the backend result was ibmqx2.

Now that we have our backend, we can execute our circuit as follows:

```
# Execute the quantum circuit on the backend
job = execute(qc, backend=backend, shots=1024)
results = job.result()
```

Next, we will extract the result counts from the noisy backend results, which have not yet been mitigated. We will accomplish this by generating the measurement fitter filter, and then we will apply the filter to our backend results. Finally, we will capture the filtered result counts and compare the results between the filtered and non-filtered result counts:

```
# Results from backend without mitigating the noise
noisy_counts = results.get_counts()

# Obtain the measurement fitter object
measurement_filter = meas_fitter.filter

# Mitigate the results by applying the measurement fitter
filtered_results = measurement_filter.apply(results)

# Get the mitigated result counts
filtered_counts = filtered_results.get_counts(0)
```

Now, let's plot the noisy results from the backend:

```
plot_histogram(noisy_counts)
```

The result of this is the following; you can observe that we have the expected high probability for `00000` and `11111`. However, note that there are some very small results that are not part of what is expected. These little results are due to the readout errors from the quantum system:

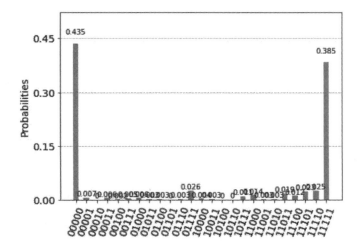

Figure 11.19 – Results without readout error mitigation

Finally, let's plot the mitigated results from the backend:

```
plot_histogram(filtered_counts)
```

The results illustrate how the filters have significantly decreased the errors from the previous noisy results such that only the expected values of 00000 and 11111 are probable, and all the other values have diminished:

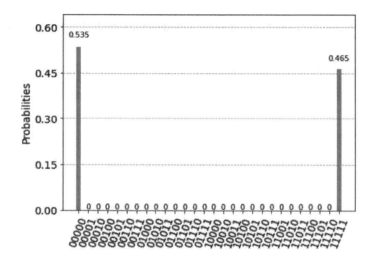

Figure 11.20 – Mitigated results from the backend

Congratulations! You have successfully mitigated noise from a quantum device. Furthermore, you were able to also generate a list of calibration circuits that can be fitted to any number of backend devices.

Summary

In this chapter, we covered some of the many effects that noise has on a quantum computing system. We discovered how we can measure decoherence effects using fitters to help visualize and test the quantum systems and calibrate the readout errors so as to apply error mitigation to the noisy results of a system. Finally, we leveraged the filter to mitigate the noisy results from a quantum device, which significantly reduced the errors.

In the next chapter, we will learn how to create quantum applications using the many features available in Aqua, where we can then look at creating quantum algorithms, and ultimately provide you with all the tools to create your own quantum algorithms and quantum applications.

Questions

1. List the various characterizations of a qubit.

2. Which decoherence is analyzed using the Ramsey experiment?

3. What is the difference between relaxation and dephasing decoherence?

4. Which of the following is not a value for dephasing – T_1, T_2, or T_2^*?

5. What is the maximum number of qubits you can apply to a measurement filter?

6. What is the difference between T_2 and T_2^*?

7. What do the rows and columns of a calibration matrix relate to?

8. What is the name of the effect when a qubit decays from the excited state to the ground state?

Further reading

- Sutor, B., *Dancing with Qubits*, Packt Publishing: `https://www.packtpub.com/data/dancing-with-qubits`

- Nielsen, M. & Chuang, I., *Quantum Computation and Quantum Information*, Cambridge University Press: `https://www.cambridge.org/us/academic/subjects/physics/quantum-physics-quantum-information-and-quantum-computation/quantum-computation-and-quantum-information-10th-anniversary-edition`

- Qiskit Textbook: `https://qiskit.org/textbook`

12
Learning about Qiskit Aqua

All the Qiskit elements that we have covered so far have dealt with foundational circuits that implement various quantum algorithms. Others covered simulators, generating noise models, and mitigating errors. For researchers, it's a lot to ask them to learn all the inner workings just to generate a quantum algorithm to use in their application. In fact, it is rare to find those who want to wander down into the *nuts and bolts* of the quantum algorithm they want to use. Generally, they would like to just get their data loaded into an algorithm, execute it on a quantum system, obtain the results, and just continue with their experiments. This is where **Aqua**, short for **Algorithms for Quantum Applications**, comes into the big picture.

The following topics will be covered in this chapter:

- Understanding the components and their usability
- Using Aqua Utilities to simplify your work
- Familiarizing yourself with the quantum algorithms in Aqua
- Creating your first classical/quantum application

In this chapter, you will learn about the various modules available within Qiskit Aqua, such as the quantum algorithms and components available to use with your projects. You'll also learn about the various utilities that are available within Aqua to simplify creating and integrating your quantum algorithms into your classical applications. Finally, you will put all these resources together to build a classical/quantum application using Aqua.

Let's start off this chapter by understanding what the various Aqua sub-modules are and their functionality with respect to creating quantum applications. At the time of writing, there are five sub-modules within Aqua: **Algorithms**, **Components**, **Circuits**, **Operators**, and **Utilities (Utils)**.

Each of these submodules has a distinct purpose, but they are not all always dependent of each other. What this means is you do not have to use the Circuits submodule in order to use the Algorithms or Components submodules. These submodules can be used independently or alongside each other – it all depends on the needs of your application and how you wish to combine them to adhere to your application requirements. We'll begin by covering the components and their functionality, as well as how they can be leveraged to construct quantum algorithms.

Technical requirements

For this chapter, it is expected that you have an understanding of creating quantum circuits and general application development using Python.

The following is the source code we'll be using throughout this book: https://github.com/PacktPublishing/Learn-Quantum-Computing-with-Python-and-IBM-Quantum-Experience.

Please visit the following link to check the CiA videos: https://bit.ly/35o5M80

Understanding the components and their usability

Components in Aqua are generally parts of an algorithm that can be used interchangeably in order to vary construction based on your needs and requirements. A simple analogy, being a foodie myself, is cooking a bowl of pasta and meatballs.

To prepare this dish, you will need three components: *pasta*, *meatballs*, and *sauce*. Of course, if you were to invite the top three chefs in the world to prepare a bowl of their signature version of this dish, you would most likely get three distinct servings. For example, there are a variety of pastas to choose from, such as *angel hair*, *linguine*, *fettucine*, *spaghetti*, and more.

Then, you have the meatballs, which can be of varying cuts of meat or sausages. And finally, the sauce itself can contain an incredible number of varying spices and herbs. And this doesn't even include other varieties, such as vegetarian or gluten-free selections. Each of these varying pastas, meats, and spices are the components of your meal, and the amount of the ingredients that are added to the dish and how it's prepared, cooked, and garnished are unique.

How these varieties are prepared affect the taste, texture, and time to prepare of the dish. The same can be said about the components of a quantum algorithm. Many components are used to prepare or initialize states, and generating an algorithm could vary based on the problem or performance required.

In this section, we will cover a few of the many components available in Aqua so that you can become familiar with their varying usage and then leverage them as the building blocks for your quantum algorithms. We'll begin with the **initialize states** component.

Initializing a fixed quantum state

Initializing states are generally used when a part of your algorithm expects a specific state as a starting point, or in some cases a continuation from a pre-defined state, such as a quantum circuit. So far, all the quantum states that have been used in this book had the same zero/ground state as the initialized state.

This is where all the qubits are initialized to the $|0\rangle$ state. This is automatically done for us when we first create a quantum circuit. However, if your algorithm is of the variational form or iterates where the initialized state needs to be in a state other than the zero/ground state, this is where the initialized state component comes in handy.

There are three initial state classes:

- `Zero`: This is the zero/ground state, where all states are initialized to the $|0\rangle$ state.

- `VarFormBased`: This is the variational form-based initial state.

- `Custom`: This is a customized initial state.

The `Custom` initial state class has the following parameters:

- `num_qubits`: This is an `int` value representing the number of qubits of the initial state. The default is 1.

- `state_vector`: This is a `complex` or `float` valued vector that represents the state that you wish to set. The vector size must be 2^n, where n is the number of qubits.

- state: This is a predefined state where the options are 'zero', 'random', and 'uniform', where 'zero' indicates you wish to prepare a zero/ground state, 'random' indicates a random state, and 'uniform' creates an equal uniform probability distribution.

- circuit: This is a QuantumCircuit that represents the initial state. When this is set, it will take precedence over both state and state_vector.

Let's create a custom initial state as this one has the most options and provides more freedom, should you need more variety in your algorithm. Start by creating a new notebook from the **Quantum Lab**. Now, follow these steps:

1. We'll begin by creating Custom states by using the predefined states of zero, random, and uniform by setting the state parameter for each:

```
from qiskit.aqua.components.initial_states import Custom
init_state_0 = Custom(num_qubits=3, state='zero')
init_state_uniform = Custom(num_qubits=3,
state='uniform')
init_state_random = Custom(num_qubits=3, state='random')
```

2. This creates each initial state with three qubits each. Let's confirm this by calling the construct_circuit method and drawing the results of each. We'll proceed in order and start with the zero initial state:

```
qc0 = init_state_0.construct_circuit(mode='circuit')
qc0.draw()
```

This will render a three-qubit circuit initialized to zero as there are no operations in the circuit at all, as shown in the following diagram:

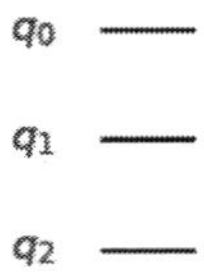

q_0 ———

q_1 ———

q_2 ———

Figure 12.1 – Custom initial state, zero

3. Now, let's repeat this process for the uniform initial state and construct and draw the circuit:

```
qc1 = init_state_uniform.construct_circuit(mode='circuit')
qc1.draw()
```

As shown in the following diagram, each qubit has a Hadamard gate, represented by the U_2 basis gate, which initializes the state to a uniform superposition state of uniform probability:

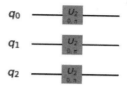

Figure 12.2 – Custom initial state, uniform

4. Finally, let's construct the circuit with the random initial state. This, of course, will vary each time you run it, so the results shown here may be different, though the number of qubits should be the same:

```
qc2 = init_state_random.construct_circuit(mode='circuit')
qc2.draw()
```

As shown in the following diagram, this results in a three-qubit circuit with the basis gates necessary to represent a random state:

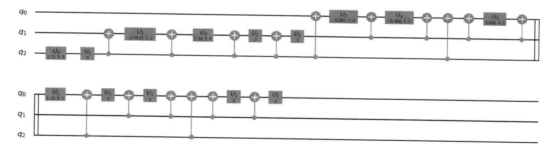

Figure 12.3 – Custom initial state, random

5. Finally, we can create a custom initial state from a quantum circuit. In this example, we'll create our usual quantum circuit. Here, we can see that our Custom initial state is created using circuit and not the state parameter, which could then be reused as an initial state. This is very helpful if you need to initialize your algorithms frequently:

```
# Create the quantum circuit
num_qubits = 2
qc = QuantumCircuit(num_qubits)
qc.h(0)
```

```
qc.cx(0,1)
# Construct the Custom class based on the built quantum
# circuit
q_component = Custom(num_qubits=num_qubits, circuit=qc)
q_component.construct_circuit().draw()
```

At the end, the `Custom` initialized state is based on the quantum circuit we created. We confirmed this via the resulting circuit. As you can see, it is composed of the basis gate, representing a Hadamard, followed by the Controlled-Not gate between the first (control) and second (Target) qubit:

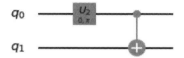

Figure 12.4 – Custom initial state, circuit

Initializing a state is good, should you need to use a quantum circuit as an initial state, as you can very easily construct one without having to recreate a circuit each time. The same can be derived using state vectors and variational forms. I have included some questions in the *Questions* section for you to try out.

Aqua has many facets that allow you to easily work in other areas of research, such as chemistry, finance, and optimization, to name a few. In the next section, we will look into **neural networks** – neural network discriminators in particular.

Creating a neural network discriminator

Machine learning is a growing area in quantum computing. Researchers have been looking at ways to leverage quantum computational techniques in various areas of machine learning, such as **generative adversarial networks** and supervised learning for regression and classification.

In this section, we will focus on the **discriminator model** as opposed to the **generative model**. As a reminder, the discriminator model learns by using conditional probability distribution, whereas the generative model learns via joint probability distribution.

In this section, we will create a PyTorchDiscriminator class based on **PyTorch**. This class contains various methods that will allow you to load your model and perform a training step, based on the parameters of your discriminator. Let's get started:

1. First, we'll create a PyTorchDiscriminator class by specifying the number of features (the dimension of the input data vector) and the dimension of the discriminator's output vector. This prepares the discriminator class so that it can load and provide other methods to simplify the connection between PyTorch components and your quantum algorithm:

```
# Import and create the PyTorchDiscriminator class
from qiskit.aqua.components.neural_networks import
PyTorchDiscriminator
# Set the number data input and output dimension to 2.
py_torch_disc = PyTorchDiscriminator(n_features = 2,
n_out=2)
```

    Now that you have created your PyTorchDisciminator class, you can load your discriminator model.

2. To load your PyTorch discriminator model, simply point to the directory where you have stored the model; PyTorchDiscriminator will do the rest:

```
# Load the discriminator model, implements the
# torch.load(dir)
discriminator_model = '/discriminator_model_directory'
py_torch_disc.load_model(discriminator_model)
```

    The PyTorchDiscriminator class works as a wrapper that implements the torch.model(directory) method.

3. Finally, if you wish to run a training step based on the discriminator parameters, you can do so by simply mapping the parameters to the content of your training data. Note that QuantumInstance is deprecated at the time of writing. *Ensure you read the latest information provided in the Qiskit API documentation* (https://qiskit.org/documentation/) *to avoid warnings or errors*:

```
# Parameters are defined in the Qiskit API as follows:
###
# data (tuple) - real_batch: torch.Tensor, Training data
# batch.
# generated_batch: numpy array, Generated data batch.
```

```
# weights (tuple) - real problem, generated problem
# penalty (bool) - Indicate whether or not penalty
# function is applied to the loss function.
# quantum_instance (QuantumInstance) - Quantum Instance
#(depreciated)
# shots (int) - Number of shots for hardware or qasm
# execution.
# Not used for classical network (only quantum ones)
###
result_dict = PyTorchDiscriminator.train(data, weights,
penalty, quantum_instance=quantum_instance, shots=None)
```

The preceding code will return the discriminator loss as a `dict` type, as well as updated parameters.

`PyTorchDiscriminator` is not the only discriminator available – you also have a **NumPy**-based discriminator, `NumPyDiscriminator`, that uses the same methods as `PyTorchDiscriminator`, such as loading and training data. For those interested in generators, don't feel like you're being left out. There is a `QuantumGenerator` class that is a parameterized quantum circuit that's trained using the **quantum generative adversarial network** (**QGAN**).

Now that we've looked at the various neural network components, we'll move on and look at **operators**.

Implementing state function operators

State function operators, as defined in the Qiskit API, *"are complex functions over a single binary string (as compared to an operator, which is defined as a function over two binary strings, or a function taking a binary function to another binary function)."* There are currently five state functions where each is defined by varying components:

- `StateFn`: This is the class used to represent state functions and measurements.

- `CircuitStateFn`: This is the class used to represent state functions and measurements based on a `QuantumCircuit` initialized from the ground state $|0\rangle$, which is stored in the `QuantumCircuit` class.

- `DictStateFn`: This is the class that's used to represent state functions and measurements based on a lookup table stored in a `Dict` object.

- VectorStateFn: This is the class that's used to represent state functions and measurements based on a vector representation stored in a StateVector class.

- OperatorStateFn: This is the class that's used to represent state functions and measurements based on a density operator stored in an OperatorBase class.

In this section, first, we'll implement CircuitStateFn, which we will define from a quantum circuit. We'll then implement a few of the operator methods to illustrate the various available functionalities:

1. Let's begin by defining a quantum circuit and importing the CircuitStateFn class:

```
# Import the CircuitStateFn class
from qiskit.aqua.operators.state_fns import
CircuitStateFn
# Create the quantum circuit
qc = QuantumCircuit(2)
qc.h(0)
qc.cx(0,1)
```

2. Now, let's construct and print CircuitStateFn by using the quantum circuit we created and setting the coefficient to 1. Since the state function is not a measurement operator, we will set it to False:

```
# Create the CircuitStateFn class with the quantum
# circuit
csf = CircuitStateFn(primitive=qc, coeff=1,
is_measurement=False)
print(csf)
```

This prints out the circuit state function, as follows:

CircuitStateFn(

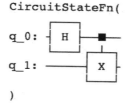

)

Figure 12.5 – Circuit state function generated by a quantum circuit

3. Now that we have a circuit state function, we can run a few operators on it. Let's try out the equal operator to determine whether the two state function circuits are equal. We'll create a second state function with a quantum circuit that is equal to the first and compare the two:

```
# Create a second quantum circuit with same width and
# operators
qc2 = QuantumCircuit(2)
qc2.h(0)
qc2.cx(0,1)


# Create the second circuit state function
csf2 = CircuitStateFn(primitive=qc2, coeff=1,
is_measurement=False)


# Compare both circuit state functions using the equals
# operator
print(csf.equals(csf2))
```

The preceding code will print out True, indicating the equality between operators.

4. Next, let's add this circuit state function to the first using the add operator:

```
# Add the two circuit state functions together
added_csf = csf.add(csf2)
print(added_csf)
```

Since both circuit functions, cf1 and cf2, are the same, this will print out the following circuit state functions using the multiplier:

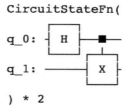

Figure 12.6 – Adding two circuit state functions

5. We'll now create a third distinct quantum circuit and append it to the given circuit state function:

```
# Create a quantum circuit
qc3 = QuantumCircuit(2)
qc3.h(0)
qc3.cx(1,0)
# Create a circuit state function from the quantum
# circuit
csf3 = CircuitStateFn(primitive=qc3, coeff=1,
is_measurement=False)
print(added_csf.add(csf3))
```

This will print the following circuit, adding the three added functions:

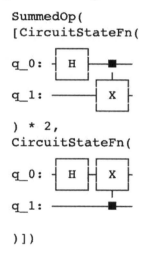

Figure 12.7 – Adding three circuit state functions

The state function representation of the three circuit state functions shown in the preceding diagram can be used to perform various operations such as tensor products, scalar multiplication, and assign/bind circuit parameters.

In this section, we reviewed just a handful of the many components available to you via Aqua to help you piece your quantum algorithm together. But of course, components, like pasta ingredients, aren't all you need – you also need some cooking utensils to cook up your dish. It's these utilities that we will cover in the next section.

Using Aqua utilities to simplify your work

Aqua comes with a sizeable set of utilities that offer some great functionality that simplifies generating your applications. In this section, we will implement a few utilities that may be useful, particularly when integrating your quantum applications with classical applications. We'll start with a simple converter from decimal into binary:

1. First, we'll import the `utils` module and convert the decimal number 6 into binary:

```
# Import the utils module
from qiskit.aqua import utils
# convert the number 6 from decimal to binary
binary_value = utils.decimal_to_binary(6,
max_num_digits=0)
print('Binary result: ', binary_value)
```

The preceding code will print out the binary result of the value 6:

```
Binary result: 110
```

2. Next, we need to create some random unitary values. This will take the specified dimension value, N, as its argument to create a random $N \times N$ unitary matrix. This can be especially useful if you want to apply filters to random data or generate some ad hoc matrix to apply operators:

```
#Random Unitary matrix
random_unitary = utils.random_unitary(N=3)
print('Random Unitary result: \n', random_unitary)
```

The preceding code returns a random unitary matrix of dimension 3 x 3. The values returned will vary from those illustrated in the following output, of course, as the values are randomly generated:

```
Random Unitary result:
 [[ 0.64678233+0.02j   0.13467893+0.71j   0.03385166+0.22j]
 [ 0.26698073+0.35j   0.21738899-0.02j   0.15455118-0.85j]
 [ 0.24741634+0.56j   0.45574316-0.46j  -0.05112698+0.43j]]
```

When creating large circuits, often, you will want to get a summary of the quantum circuit that provides information about the circuit, particularly if you have more than one quantum circuit to evaluate.

3. To simplify this, we can summarize circuits with a simple utility method. Let's create an array of random quantum circuits and obtain the summary of each with a single line of code:

```
# Create an array of random quantum circuits
from qiskit.circuit.random import random_circuit
quantum_circuits = []
# Append a group of random circuits
for x in range(2):
    quantum_circuits.append(random_circuit(3, 5,
    measure=True))
```

4. Now that we have an array of random quantum circuits, let's obtain a summary of each circuit:

```
# Obtain and print a summary of all the quantum circuits
circuits_summary = utils.summarize_circuits(quantum_
    circuits)
print(circuits_summary)
```

The preceding code results in the following summary. As stated earlier, keep in mind that as these are random circuits, the summary will vary based on the circuits that are generated:

```
Submitting 2 circuits.
================================================================
===================
0-th circuit: 3 qubits, 3 classical bits and 11
operations with depth 6
op_counts: OrderedDict([('measure', 3), ('ccx', 2),
('cu1', 1), ('t', 1), ('cu3', 1), ('ry', 1), ('h', 1),
('cy', 1)])
1-th circuit: 3 qubits, 3 classical bits and 14
operations with depth 6
op_counts: OrderedDict([('measure', 3), ('rzz', 2), ('x',
2), ('u3', 2), ('s', 1), ('swap', 1), ('crz', 1), ('y',
1), ('t', 1)])
Average: 3.00 qubits, 3.00 classical bits and 12.50
operations with depth 6.00
================================================================
===================
```

Information about circuits and converting data types is not all that you get with the `utils` module.

5. There are also methods that can help you configure backend simulations. For example, you can generate both a full and linear coupling map of qubits. Let's start with a fully entangled set of five qubits:

```
# Fully entangled coupling map
full_coupling_map = utils.get_entangler_map(map_
    type="full", num_qubits=5)
print('Full coupling map: ', full_coupling_map)
```

The result here is a fully entangled coupling map of five qubits, which creates a topology where every qubit is connected directly to all the other qubits:

```
Full coupling map: [[0, 1], [0, 2], [0, 3], [0, 4], [1,
2], [1, 3], [1, 4], [2, 3], [2, 4], [3, 4]]
```

6. We can also create a linear coupling map of all the qubits by simply updating the `map_type` parameter:

```
# Linearly entangled coupling map
lin_coupling_map = utils.get_entangler_map(map_
    type="linear", num_qubits=5)
print('Linear coupling map: ', lin_coupling_map)
```

As shown in the previous example, this creates a coupling map where each qubit is only connected to its adjacent qubit:

```
Linear coupling map: [[0, 1], [1, 2], [2, 3], [3, 4]]
```

7. Finally, you can also validate your coupling map by setting the parameters based on the constraints you specify. In this example, we will constrain the coupling map to five qubits and allow double entanglement, which means that each qubit can be entangled by more than one qubit:

```
# Validate entangled coupling maps
result = utils.validate_entangler_map(
    entangler_map=full_coupling_map, num_qubits=5,
    allow_double_entanglement=True)
print(result)
```

If the validation process is a success, it will return a list of integers, indicating the validated coupling map, as follows:

```
[[0, 1], [0, 2], [0, 3], [0, 4], [1, 2], [1, 3], [1, 4],
[2, 3], [2, 4], [3, 4]]
```

If any of the constraints are not valid, such as an incorrect number of qubits, if the entangler map is not a list type or list of lists, or if the qubits are flagged as not to be double entangled, then an error will be raised.

8.   Finally, a utility that can be very useful, particularly for any projects you're working on that require more feature dimensions than available qubits, is the **Principle Component Analysis (PCA)** utility. What the PCA utility provides is a way to reduce the number of dimensions via principle component analysis. This method will reduce the dimension by simply providing the original $N x D$ (ndarray) and the target dimension value, which will be reduced as follows:

```python
# Import NumPy to create the array
import numpy as np


# Generate a 2x3 (NxD) array
dim_map = np.array( [[ 0,1,0], [ 1,0,1]])
# Reduce the D from 3 to 2, resulting in a 2x2
# dimensional array
reduced_dim = utils.reduce_dim_to_via_pca(x=dim_map,
dim=2)
print(reduced_dim)
```

This reduces the original *2 x 3 (N x D)* array down to a *2 x 2* array, as follows:

```
[[ 8.66025404e-01   7.83243505e-18]
 [-8.66025404e-01   7.83243505e-18]]
```

The reduction in dimension from 3 to 2 is the result of principle component analysis and is often used to minimize a feature set so that you can, for example, run them on near-term devices such as a 5-, 15-, or 20-qubit quantum computers.

This, of course, is just a subset of the available utilities in Aqua. As more features are added and released, the available utilities will grow as well. Be sure to keep yourself up to date on the latest releases as they could save you a lot of time – time that you can use to focus on the more technical work, such as creating quantum algorithms. With that, we'll move on to the next section of this chapter, which is all about quantum algorithms.

Familiarizing yourself with the quantum algorithms in Aqua

So far in this chapter, you have learned about the various components and utilities that will help you create quantum applications. In this section, we will become familiar with the many algorithms currently available in Aqua. Recently, Aqua has gone through a major update, particularly regarding how it allows you, the developer, to create and leverage quantum algorithms.

In the past, it had a black box style of implementation where each algorithm only provided you with parameters and nothing else. This limited the developer's ability to modify or update components without having to rewrite a lot of code. Instead, this new version is very modular and allows you to specify which components to piece together to create your quantum application. This includes the various algorithms that are available.

The following examples will piece together a few of these available algorithms in one of many ways. For starters, we will review the various Oracles that you can use to formulate the different Oracle-based algorithms. We'll use truth tables and quantum circuits to generate our Oracles. We will then use those that are part of the latest circuit library, such as the **Quantum Fourier Transform**. We'll start with the Oracles first and create them using a couple of different methods, starting with the **Logical Expression Oracle**.

Implementing the Logical Expression Oracle

Logical expressions are commonly used to describe problems, particularly those that have some constraints. These logical expressions can be used to construct a circuit and execute it on various algorithms. Let's begin with a simple problem.

Imagine that you're a music producer and have been tasked to put together the next big rock band, based on the musicians you currently have on contract for your record company. The following musicians are available:

- **Sofia** is a singer who has a great voice and is available to tour as soon as possible.

- **Angelina** is also a singer with a great voice and is also available to tour right away.

- **Lex** is a guitar player that can play any genre and has his own tour bus.

- **Leo** is a drummer that gets along with everyone and is very liked in the industry.

Now, here is the problem you have been asked to solve: Sofia and Angelina tend to not get along on tour and have been known to have creative differences when writing music. Lex and Leo, however, get along fine together. However, Sofia and Lex broke up after the last time they toured together.

What you need to do is determine which combination of these four musicians is best for you to put together as a band, and then have them tour with minimal issues based on their history together.

To solve this, let's write this out as a logical expression:

1.   We'll map each musician as A = Sofia, B = Angelina, C = Lex, and D = Leo.

2.   Next, we'll create a logical expression using logical operators to illustrate the constraints. To start, we know that Sofia and Angelina do not get along, so this we can represent as follows, where ^ indicates XOR:

$$(A \wedge B)$$

3.   Next, we know that Lex and Leo get along fine together, so we can represent them as follows:

$$(C \text{ \& } D)$$

4.   Finally, we know that Sofia and Leo have just ended their relationship, so they might not be open to work together and tour, so we will represent them as follows:

$$\sim(A \text{ \& } C)$$

5.   By putting these all together, our complete logical expression for this example is as follows:

$$(A \wedge B) \text{ \& } (C \text{ \& } D) \text{ \& } \sim(A \text{ \& } C)$$

Now that we have defined our logical expression, let's create an Oracle on the logical expression so that we can use **Grover's algorithm** (described in *Chapter 14, Applying Quantum Algorithms*) to search for the optimal result:

1.   We'll begin by importing all the necessary modules and classes needed for the rest of these steps and defining our logical expression:

```
# Import the necessary modules and classes
from qiskit import BasicAer
from qiskit.aqua import QuantumInstance
from qiskit.aqua.algorithms import Grover, DeutschJozsa,
BernsteinVazirani, Simon
from qiskit.aqua.components.oracles import
    LogicalExpressionOracle, TruthTableOracle,
    CustomCircuitOracle
```

```
# State the SAT problem into a logical expression
# A = Sophia, B = Angelina, C = Leo, D = Lex
expression = '((A ^ B) & (C & D) & ~(A & C))'
```

2. Now that we have defined our problem as a logical expression, let's use this logical expression to create our `oracle`:

```
# Create an Oracle based on the Logical Expression
oracle = LogicalExpressionOracle(expression)
```

3. Now that we have created an `oracle` from the logical expression, we can create the quantum circuit by simply calling the `construct_circuit()` method:

```
# Construct the circuit from the oracle
quantum_circuit = oracle.construct_circuit()
quantum_circuit.draw('mpl')
```

The preceding code generates the quantum circuit representation of the oracle. This can be illustrated as follows:

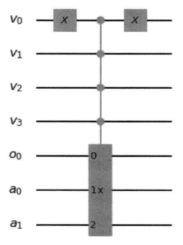

Figure 12.8 – Quantum circuit representing the Logical Expression Oracle

Note that this creates the variable quantum register v_x and the ancilla quantum register a_x, where x indicates the qubit index.

4. We can now use this Oracle on any Oracle-based algorithm. Since we are searching for the solution to this rock band problem, let's use Grover's algorithm. First, we will create the quantum instance, which will specify which backend will run the algorithm. In this example, we will use the `BasicAer` qasm simulator and set the number of `shots` to `1024`:

```
# Generate a quantum instance from a simulator
quantum_instance = QuantumInstance(BasicAer.get_backend(
    'qasm_simulator'), shots=1024)
```

5. Next, we will instantiate the `Grover` algorithm class by passing in the `oracle` we created as its argument:

```
# Create the Grover algorithm with the Logical Expression
# Oracle
grover = Grover(oracle)
```

6. Now that we have successfully constructed the Grover class, let's use the `run` method to execute the algorithm on the quantum instance we defined earlier, then `print` and `plot` the results:

```
# Run the Grover algorithm
result = grover.run(quantum_instance)

# Print the top measured result
print('Top result:', result['top_measurement'])
# Plot all measured results
plot_histogram(result['measurement'])
```

The preceding code results in the following output. Keep in mind that the qubit at position 0 is represented by the least significant bit (far right). This means that the result, `1110`, is equal to D=1, C=1, B=1, A=0:

```
Top result: 1110
```

We also obtain the following histogram:

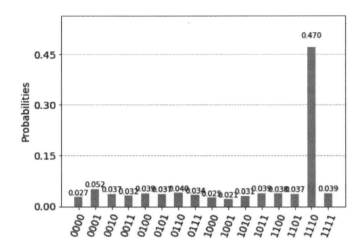

Figure 12.9 – Grover solution results based on the Logical Expression Oracle

As shown by the preceding results, the algorithm indicates our solution is **1110**. This states that Angelina, Leo, and Lex are the three ideal musicians to recruit into the next band project. Sofia can be recruited as a solo career singer.

This, of course, is a simple example. As you can imagine, if your logical expression is more complex, then the Grover search would help determine that in just a few lines of code. In the next section, we'll look at using truth tables to generate an Oracle.

Implementing a truth table Oracle

Truth tables are something you learn very early on when studying computer science or engineering. Truth tables can identify patterns or define conditions based on input and output values. We can use them here as well to define an Oracle.

In this example, we will use a truth table that will be used to determine whether the function is constant or balanced. What this means is that we are given a set of inputs where the results (output) are guaranteed to be either constant, in that all the results are the same; that is, all zeros (0) or all ones (1).

Alternatively, they can be balanced, where exactly half the results are zeros (0) and the other half are ones (1). To do this, we will use the **Deutsch-Jozsa algorithm**. You will learn about the specifics and the quantum advantage of this algorithm in *Chapter 13, Understanding Quantum Algorithms*.

In the following example, we will create a constant function, defined by the truth table, and run it through the **Deutsch-Jozsa** algorithm to determine this answer for us. First, let's create our truth table:

1. The truth table can be created in a variety of ways. It constructs the Oracle using the exclusive sum of products. You can also specify the truth table by providing the output values as a single bit-string; for example, a 2-qubit truth table can represent the results, such as *1001*, to indicate that the output to the input values of *00* and *11* are set to 1, while the other input values, *01* and *10*, are set to 0.

    In this case, since we are specifying that the function is constant, we will set the truth table expression to '1111', which indicates that all combinations 00, 01, 10, and 11 will result in a 1 as the output:

    ```
    # Create the truth table expression for constant
    truth_table = '1111'


    # Create the truth table Oracle from the expression
    constant_oracle = TruthTableOracle(truth_table)
    ```

2. Now that we have the constant `oracle`, we can create the `DeutschJozsa` object and construct the circuit representing it:

    ```
    # Create Deutsch-Jozsa algorithm
    dj = DeutschJozsa(oracle=constant_oracle,
    quantum_instance=quantum_instance)
    # Construct the circuit and draw the result
    dj_circuit = dj.construct_circuit(measurement=True)
    dj_circuit.draw('mpl')
    ```

    This will result in the following quantum circuit representing the Deutsch-Jozsa algorithm:

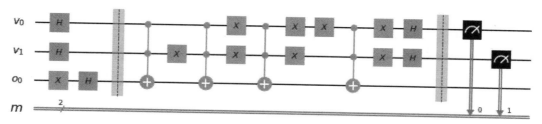

Figure 12.10 – Deutsch-Jozsa quantum circuit with a constant oracle

3.   Next, we can run the algorithm and output the results:

```
# Run the algorithm on the quantum instance
results = dj.run(quantum_instance)
# Print the results that determines constant or balanced
print(results)
```

Here, we can see that the results are as we expected – `constant`:

```
{'measurement': {'00': 1024}, 'result': 'constant'}
```

These were both good examples of defining Oracles and running them on quantum algorithms to solve problems.

In this section, one thing you will have noticed is that all the work of creating a circuit and executing is done without having to manually construct a circuit, or having to dig down into the specifics of the gates, optimizing the circuit, and so on. You simply defined your problem as an expression or truth table to create an Oracle and then ran it on a quantum instance. This is the essence of what Aqua can provide you with, as a researcher.

Rather than having to learn the deep details of the quantum circuit, you can define your problem in such a way that it can be represented and leveraged by the components in an existing algorithm.

To prove this, in the next section, we will create a simple classical/quantum application to solve a problem known as **Simon's problem**. This problem and its solution will put everything you've learned about in this chapter together.

Creating your first classical/quantum application (Simon's)

In this section, we will incorporate a lot of what we have learned so far to create a classical/quantum application to solve a problem using Simon's algorithm. The problem is provided in the next section.

Stating Simon's problem

Consider a two-to-one function that connects the results of two input values by **XORing** each input with a secret string, *s*. This can be represented as $x_1 \oplus s = x_2$.

We can define this problem using a truth table expression and constructing an Oracle and then leverage Simon's algorithm to solve the problem as *0110*. Now, let's implement Simon's algorithm to solve the value, `s`.

Implementing Simon's algorithm

Simon's algorithm allows us to search for the secret string that connects the results via a two-to-many function. In this example, the values are **XORed** with s, where s will be set to 11. Let's work on solving this using Qiskit Aqua's built-in components and algorithms:

1. First, we'll define the problem using the truth table expression. Here, we are still working in the classical portion of this application:

```
# Create the expression for secret value s:
# (This ties x1=01, x2=10 XOR with s=11)
s = '0110'


# Create the truth table Oracle from the expression
oracle_simon = TruthTableOracle(s)
```

2. Now that we have created the Oracle based on the truth table expression, which is based on the value s, we can construct Simon's algorithm and generate the quantum circuit:

```
# Create Simon algorithm
simon = Simon(oracle=oracle_simon,
quantum_instance=quantum_instance)
simon_circuit = simon.construct_circuit(measurement=True)
simon_circuit.draw()
```

This will render the following circuit based on the Oracle's description. Note that the construction of the quantum circuit includes padding the circuit with the Hadamard gates, adding the measurement operators, and including the ancilla qubits:

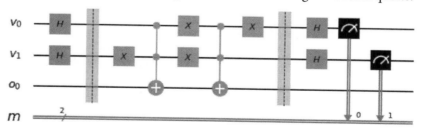

Figure 12.11 – Quantum circuit representation of Simon's algorithm

3. Finally, we run Simon's algorithm and obtain the results. Note that when we call the `run()` method, we are then executing it in a quantum system, which is the classical/quantum connection in that the circuit will run on a quantum computer:

```
# Run the Simon algorithm to determine s,
# where x1 XOR s = x2
results = simon.run(quantum_instance)
print('Secret string s = ', results['result'])
```

The results show that the secret string is 11, which is exactly what we expected it to be:

```
Secret string s = 11
```

Confirm this for yourself by running the dot product across all the input values with `s=11`.

As you can see from this and the previous examples, you can take a problem that's defined by a logical expression on a classical system and then, by leveraging Aqua, prepare the problem in a variety of ways, all of which can be executed on a quantum system. All of this can be done without having to delve into the specifics.

As Aqua continues to add many more components, algorithms, utilities, and other artifacts, this will help you create flexible yet modular quantum algorithms that suit all your needs.

Summary

In this chapter, we covered the various artifacts available to you via Qiskit Aqua. You learned about just a few of the many components available to you, including Oracles and circuit state functions. You also learned about some of the utilities and how they can take away some of the tedious work so that you can focus on the more interesting parts of your quantum application.

You now have the skills to easily create your own quantum applications in a way that simplifies the creation process. You can do this by piecing the applications together based on available algorithms, components, and utilities.

Finally, we looked at various problems that we needed to solve using a variety of quantum algorithms, without having to really understand how they are constructed. The focus was on how to represent the problem and apply it via a combination of available components and algorithms.

In the next chapter, we will cover the various quantum algorithms we've looked at in this chapter in detail and build them manually, rather than focusing much on their high-level usage.

Questions

1. Using the Quantum Circuit from the example shown in *Figure 12.4*, create a custom initialized state using the state_vector parameter.

2. Construct a Circuit State function from a state vector.

3. Construct a balanced Oracle and verify it using the **Deutsch-Jozsa** algorithm.

4. Implement the **Bernstein-Vazirani** algorithm to find the secret value, 170. (Hint: use the decimal to binary utility).

5. How many Oracle functions are there?

6. Does Aqua also include classical algorithms?

7. Leveraging the qiskit.aqua.circuits.StateVectorCircuit class, construct a circuit that represents an X gate.

8. Change the backend on QuantumInstance to a quantum computer backend that is available and rerun any of the quantum algorithms. Describe what differences, if any, you were able to observe.

13
Understanding Quantum Algorithms

If you've been reading the news around quantum computing, you would have noticed many articles from various companies, both large and small, all working on different projects related to quantum computing. The reason is largely based on the potential computing power that quantum systems offer when compared to classical systems. The potential to provide speedup or scalability are the two main areas of interest that most companies and research institutes are looking heavily into at the moment.

A good thing to keep in mind is that, at the time of writing this chapter, there are no quantum systems that are capable of solving any real-world problems. Currently, most of the work being done centers on understanding and creating quantum computation algorithms, which are usually focused on smaller **toy problems**, as they are commonly referred to.

By grasping the intricacies of the various quantum algorithms and learning to apply them to a specific problem set or industry, researchers and developers can then look at extending what they learned on the smaller problems and apply them to larger real-world enterprise solutions. This era of solving real-world problems using quantum computers that are intractable to classic computers is referred to as **quantum advantage**.

It's this quantum advantage phase that everyone is racing to achieve. Of course, this will vary as some problems might require more quantum computational power than others, but, over time, different industries will eventually achieve it soon enough. In order to get yourselves suited up and in the race, you'll need to understand some of the foundational quantum algorithms and how they are applied to solve general problems.

The following topics will be covered in this chapter:

- Understanding the meaning of outperforming classical systems
- Understanding the Bell states algorithm
- Learning about Deutsch's algorithm
- Understanding the Deutsch-Jozsa algorithm
- Learning about the foundational oracle-based quantum algorithm

In this chapter, we will review the various quantum algorithms in use today. One of the most difficult hurdles to overcome while learning quantum algorithms is that it is not a lift and shift from classical to quantum. By simply implementing a classical algorithm's steps from a classic system onto a quantum system, such as a simple adder, this will not automatically make it a quantum speedup algorithm. There's a bit more to it than that.

In *Chapter 5, Understanding the Quantum Bits (Qubit)*, we discussed how quantum states are stored and manipulated, and in *Chapter 8, Programming with Qiskit Terra*, we covered how to program on a quantum system. We will now put all those pieces together to learn and create quantum algorithms, and illustrate how they can outperform classical algorithms in this chapter. We will begin by providing an example of a quantum algorithm that is foundational and illustrate how quantum systems perform operations much faster by reviewing both the **Deutsch** and **Deutsch-Jozsa** algorithms. We'll follow that up with more generalized algorithms that focus on solving simple problems with the **Bernstein-Vazirani** algorithm.

This is by no means an exhaustive list of quantum algorithms, but this chapter will provide you with the foundational algorithms that will help you understand the advanced algorithms, and how they compare to classical algorithms. Should you want to see a more complete algorithm list, refer to *Appendix A, Resources*, for some links to sites that keep track of quantum algorithms and research.

Technical requirements

In this chapter, it is expected that you have a basic understanding of linear algebra in order to understand the equations of each algorithm. You should also have some experience programming basic circuits and executing them on both a simulator and a quantum device available on the **IBM Quantum Experience**. Finally, you should be familiar with both classical bit notation and logic, quantum Dirac notation, and have an understanding of the basic quantum computing principles such as superposition, entanglement, and interference, that were covered in the previous chapters.

Here is the full source code used throughout this book: `https://github.com/PacktPublishing/Learn-Quantum-Computing-with-Python-and-IBM-Quantum-Experience`.

Please visit the following link to check the CiA videos: `https://bit.ly/3o5M8O`

Understanding the meaning of outperforming classical systems

If you've been reading the news about quantum computing recently, then it's possible you have read many articles discussing the potential advantages that quantum computing can offer over classical computing.

In this section, we will learn about the advantages that a quantum system has over classical systems by studying some of the early examples that illustrate quantum speed up versus classical systems, albeit some of the examples are simple illustrations of the advantages that, in themselves, do not have any practical usage.

Claims such as quantum systems potentially solving equations at rapid speeds over classical systems or having the capability of a larger computation space all sound fascinating. However, recall that, at the time of writing this chapter, there are still no quantum systems available that can outperform current classical systems in solving real-world commercial problems. *So why all the chatter you ask?*

The answer is fairly simple – potential. Theoretically speaking, there are quantum algorithms that describe solutions to problems that illustrate quantum speedup, algorithms such as Shor's algorithm. However, to implement these algorithms, we will require systems with a large quantum volume in order to ensure error correction and accurate results. A good analogy to this is **video streaming**.

Multimedia compression has been around for decades, with video streaming discovered in the early 1990's. When video compression was first made commercially available, internet bandwidth had increased and was more widely available, albeit the quality of the video and the audio was not as rich as it is today, resolution was around 150 x 76 pixels, with a refresh rate of around 8-12 frames per second with poor audio quality. The limitation back then was both the compression technique to decrease the quality of the multimedia and the bandwidth to stream the multimedia content to multiple viewers simultaneously.

The infrastructure to ensure proper decompression and minimize information loss was dependent on error correction, and a proper protocol to avoid low quality often **jittery resolution**. Now, of course, just a little over two decades later, we can see the progress where we can stream live multimedia events with low errors and high resolution. Streaming to your home theater system with a large 4K high definition screen is something of a norm nowadays where you don't have to worry too much about the quality of the video.

Quantum systems share this same *roadmap*, where we have the hardware (quantum systems), and the algorithms to do things at a *low resolution* at the moment. The difference here is that we have something we did not have back then, a global infrastructure to which anyone, anywhere, has access to a quantum system via the cloud. Since the **IBM Quantum Experience (IQX)** is hosted on the IBM Cloud, anyone can access it by simply registering a free account.

In the early days of video streaming, very few had access to bandwidth. Those who did were limited by the infrastructure to collaborate. By having cloud accessible systems, many industries and academic institutions are doing more research on quantum hardware and algorithms. Of course, back in the early days of multimedia streaming, the solutions being solved were classified as toy problems. However, don't let the name fool you. These toy problems are far from just something to play with and show off to your colleagues. They are the stepping-stones to real-world solutions.

For example, if you find a solution that illustrates quantum speedup vis-à-vis classical, with just a handful of qubits and very little quantum volume, then that might not be useful in solving many of today's commercial or real-world problems.

> **Important Note**
>
> It's important to note that when mentioning the term *advantage*, this should not be confused with the term **quantum advantage**, which refers to the quantum era where a quantum computer can solve a real-world problem that is intractable for any classical system.

What it does provide is the foundational information needed to scale your solution to a system with the necessary quantum volume to solve a real-world problem. In order to understand what that roadmap to quantum advantage is, where a quantum solution exists that can outperform a classical system in solving a real-world problem, it's important to first understand the foundational quantum algorithms and how they not only differ from classical algorithms, but how they provide an advantage over them. This will simplify your understanding of other, more complex, algorithms and how they are used to solve solutions in various industries.

In this section, we will discuss the various different types of foundational quantum algorithms, starting with the original algorithms that demonstrate an advantage over classical systems. Before we begin, we will review an algorithm, which we have been using throughout this book as an example, to understand the very foundation of all quantum algorithms, the **Bell states** algorithm.

Understanding the Bell states algorithm

For most of the examples in this book, you may have noticed that we reused a simple 2-qubit quantum circuit to run many of our experiments. This circuit contained 2 gates, a single qubit gate, and a multi-qubit gate, a **Hadamard (H)** and **Control-Not (CNOT)**, respectively.

The reason for choosing this was not random. In fact, this particular type of circuit has a name, the Bell state. The Bell state, made by John Bell in 1964, describes how there are four maximally entangled quantum states between two qubits that are in a superposition state with a maximal value of $2\sqrt{2}$.

Each of these four states are most commonly referred to as the **Bell states**. *At this point, you may be wondering why this is so important?* Before we get into its importance, let's first prepare the four Bell states and perhaps, along the way, you might see its importance and understand the significance to some use cases such as quantum teleportation or super dense coding.

Preparing the Bell states

We'll begin by first preparing the Bell state that we have been using throughout this book.

We'll label each of these states as we create them, this first one being labeled as $|\Phi^+\rangle$. Preparing the Bell state entails three simple steps:

1. Prepare your 2-qubit input values. For this first state $|\Phi^+\rangle$, we will use the initialized state of $|00\rangle$:

$$|\Phi^+\rangle = |00\rangle$$

2. Next, add a Hadamard to the first qubit. This will place the first qubit in a superposition state:

$$|\phi^+\rangle = \frac{(|0\rangle + |1\rangle)\,|0\rangle}{\sqrt{2}}$$

3. Finally, we add a CNOT gate, where the control is set to the qubit in superposition. In this case, the first qubit and the target are set to the second qubit. By doing so, this will ensure that when the first qubit is 1, this will trigger the target qubit to rotate about the x-axis from the $|0\rangle$ state to the $|1\rangle$ state, or else it will remain in the $|0\rangle$ state. This gives us our final state:

$$|\phi^+\rangle = \frac{(|00\rangle + |11\rangle)}{\sqrt{2}}$$

This final state is the first Bell state, $|\Phi^+\rangle$, which will result in equal probability of either $|00\rangle$ or $|11\rangle$.

The only difference between preparing the first Bell state and the others is just in *step 1*, where you need to prepare your inputs. *Step 2* and *step 3* are the same for all. What this means is that for a two-qubit circuit, the remaining input states in *step 1* to prepare are $|01\rangle$, $|10\rangle$, and $|11\rangle$. Luckily for us, the following formula can be used to help us identify the remaining Bell states:

$$|q_0, q_1\rangle = \left(\frac{|0, q_1\rangle + (-1)^{q_0}|0, \overline{q_1}\rangle}{\sqrt{2}} \right)$$

By using this formula, we can calculate that all four Bell states are as follows:

- For the input state $|00\rangle$, we get the following equation:

$$|\phi^+\rangle = \frac{(|00\rangle + |11\rangle)}{\sqrt{2}}$$

- For the input state $|01\rangle$, we get the following equation:

$$|\phi^-\rangle = \frac{(|00\rangle - |11\rangle)}{\sqrt{2}}$$

- For the input state $|10\rangle$, we get the following equation:

$$|\Psi^+\rangle = \frac{(|01\rangle + |10\rangle)}{\sqrt{2}}$$

- For the input state $|11\rangle$, we get the following equation:

$$|\Psi^-\rangle = \frac{(|01\rangle - |10\rangle)}{\sqrt{2}}$$

Now, let's create these circuits by executing all the Bell states on both a simulator and quantum computer.

Implementing the Bell states

In this section, we will create the first two Bell states, $|00\rangle$ and $|10\rangle$, and leave you to create the remaining ones:

1. We'll begin by first creating a nice helper function to simplify the execution of all these circuits on either a simulator or quantum computer. After creating a new Qiskit Notebook, enter the following code that will take QuantumCircuit (qc), and a Boolean (simulator) as arguments. This will indicate whether to execute the circuit on a simulator if set to True, or a quantum computer if set to false. If selecting a quantum computer, the function will find the least busy quantum system with at least 2 qubits:

```
# Helper function to execute circuits
from qiskit.providers.ibmq import least_busy

# qc = QuantumCircuit to execute,
# simulator = boolean, if True then run on qasm
# simulator, else run on the least busy quantum system
def execute_circuit(qc, simulator):
    if(simulator):
        backend = Aer.get_backend('qasm_simulator')
    else:
```

```
            backend = provider.backends(filters=lambda x:
                      x.configuration().n_qubits > 2
                      and not x.configuration().
                      simulator)
            result = execute(qc, backend, shots=1024).result()
            return result
```

2. Now we are ready to create the first Bell state, $|00\rangle$. Let's create a 2-qubit `QuantumCircuit` circuit, and prepare the input state, $|00\rangle$. Since all quantum circuits are initialized to the state $|00\rangle$, we do not need to do anything to the circuit. We'll add a barrier to indicate the separation between steps:

```
# State 1: |Φ+>
state1 = QuantumCircuit(2)
# Initialize input to |0,0>
state1.barrier()
```

3. Then, add a Hadamard to the first qubit:

```
# Prepare the Bell state
state1.h(0)
```

4. Add a CNOT gate where the control is the first qubit, and the target is the second qubit:

```
state1.cx(0,1)
```

5. Finally, add measurements to all qubits and draw the circuit:

```
state1.measure_all()
state1.draw()
```

This will render the final circuit for our first Bell state, $|00\rangle$, as follows:

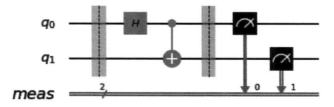

Figure 13.1 – Prepared Bell state, $|\Phi^+\rangle = |00\rangle$

6. Now let's execute this circuit with our helper function. Set the `simulator` argument to specify whether you want to execute it on a simulator or quantum system. To avoid any noise in our results, in this example, we will run the circuit on a quantum simulator to verify that our results are as expected:

```
# Execute the Bell state |Φ+>
result = execute_circuit(state1, True)
plot_histogram(result.get_counts(state1))
```

The results of this experiment render the following familiar output, which confirms the first Bell state, 00:

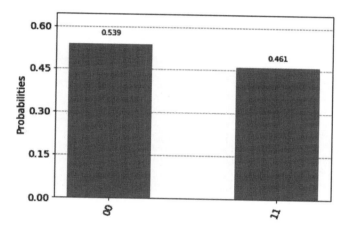

Figure 13.2 – Results of the Bell state, $|\Phi^+\rangle = |00\rangle$

7. We'll now continue on to the next Bell state, $|\Psi^+\rangle = |10\rangle$, and confirm the results as we did previously.

As mentioned earlier, the only difference between the four Bell states is in the first step, which is to prepare the input states. In this case, our input state is $|10\rangle$. We can follow the same steps as before after adding an X gate to the second qubit:

```
# State 2: |Ψ+>
state2 = QuantumCircuit(2)


# Initialize input state to |1,0>
state2.x(1)
state2.barrier()
```

```
# Prepare the Bell state
state2.h(0)
state2.cx(0,1)
state2.measure_all()
state2.draw()
```

This will result in the following circuit, which is very similar to the first except for the added **X** gate in the preparation step:

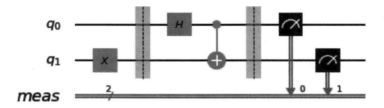

Figure 13.3 – Prepared Bell state, $|\Psi^+\rangle = |10\rangle$

8. As with the first Bell state, let's execute this circuit and observe the results:

```
# Execute the Bell state |Ψ+>
result = execute_circuit(state2, True)
plot_histogram(result.get_counts(state2))
```

The results from executing the preceding circuit are as follows:

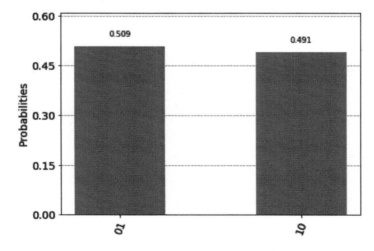

Figure 13.4 – Results of the Bell state, $|\Psi^+\rangle = |10\rangle$

After reviewing both results, we should note a couple of things. The first is that we can see from the first Bell state that both qubits are equally entangled, in that if you were to measure one qubit, let's say the first one, then you would know that the second qubit should be in the same state. Hence, if you measure the first qubit and the result is 0, then without measuring, you know the state of the second qubit.

Whether you measure the second qubit at the same time, or at a later juncture, the same can be said about the second Bell state, the only difference in that case being if you measure one qubit, then you know that the other will result in the opposite basis state value. Hence, if the first qubit results in 0, then the second qubit will result in 1, or vice versa.

This correlation between two qubits is the basis for two famous quantum applications—**quantum teleportation** and **super dense coding**, where, in each, there are two qubits that are prepared in an entangled state. This preparation of the two qubits is represented by the Bell states, where the preparation can be in either of the four Bell states we have just described.

When reading about use cases that describe quantum teleportation, you will hear a similar example to this: *Eve prepares a pair of entangled qubits and sends one to Alice and the other to Bob*; you'll now know how Eve prepares the pair of entangled qubits.

Now that we have an understanding of the Bell states and how they can be applied in applications such as quantum teleportation and super dense coding, we'll continue on our journey to understand quantum algorithms with the simplest algorithm of all, which illustrates how quantum algorithms offer computational advantages over classical systems. We'll then follow up those algorithms by looking at more complex offerings. We'll begin with Deutsch's algorithm.

Learning about Deutsch's algorithm

David Deutsch, a physicist at the **University of Oxford**, first discovered a solution that could be solved by a quantum computer faster than a classical computer. The problem itself has no importance or use in any computer problems, but it did serve as a way to illustrate the advantage that quantum computation has over classical computation. Let's understand that problem in the next section.

Understanding the problem

The problem is very simple. We'll use a simple analogy to explain it. Imagine someone is hiding a coin in each hand. The coin, when revealed, will either be heads or tails. Since there are two coins, one in each hand, there are four possible results, as shown in the following table:

Events	Left hand	Right hand
1	Heads	Heads
2	Heads	Tails
3	Tails	Heads
4	Tails	Tails

Table 13.1 – All four possible outcomes

From the preceding list of events, we can see there are two categories. The first and fourth events are an example of a constant outcome, where both the left and right produce the same result of either heads or tails. The second and third events are examples of balanced outcomes.

Here, the event results are the opposite of one another, indicating that if one is heads, then the other will be tails, or vice versa. Using this same analogy, if I were to reveal one hand at a time, let's say the left hand, then by just viewing the results of the left hand, you would not have enough information to determine whether the result will be constant or balanced because you still need to know what is in the other hand.

Now imagine if there were 100 hands in front of you and you had to examine each hand one at a time. At best case you would get it on the first two tries, meaning if the first hand had heads and the second had tails, you can conclude that the results of the other hands will be balanced. On the other hand (pun intended), if the first two hands revealed the same, either heads or tails, then you cannot conclude that it is balanced or constant.

You would have to, in a worst-case scenario, continue until the 51st hand is revealed, 51 because if the first 50 hands are heads, then the 51st would indicate whether it is constant (heads) or balanced (tails). This equates to $2^{n-1} + 1$ tries in the worst case. However, we are jumping ahead a little bit, so let's stick to the current scope of the problem of just two events.

Using a quantum algorithm, which is what Deutsch proposed here, to solve this problem is the same as opening all the hands at once and determining whether it is constant or balanced. *Interesting isn't it?* Let's see how this works!

We'll begin by migrating the analogy of the problem to a mathematical equation. This will simplify the description of the solution later on:

1. First, substitute heads and tails with binary notations of 0 and 1, respectively.

2. Next, we'll refer to the result of each hand as a function f, where the argument can refer to left or right, $f(0)$, $f(1)$, respectively.

   Therefore, the results are as follows:

Events	$f(0)$	$f(1)$
1	0	0
2	0	1
3	1	0
4	1	1

Table 13.2 – Mathematical representation of outcomes

As you can see from the preceding table, now we can restate our problem as a function f, that maps a single bit {0,1} to a result of either {0,1}, the results of which would be constant if the results for both $f(0)$ and $f(1)$ are the same, such as *Event 1* and *Event 3* (from the preceding table), or the results would be balanced otherwise. Now that we understand the problem, let's figure out the solution.

Defining the problem

We now know that if $f(0) = f(1)$, then we say f is *constant*, otherwise f is *balanced*.

The problem becomes interesting if we were to introduce a **black box**, sometimes referred to as an oracle, that is hidden from us. We don't know whether the function, hidden in the black box, is either constant or balanced, which is the problem we are asked to solve. The following diagram is a graphical example of our input value **x**, going into the black box function f, and outputting the result value $f(\mathbf{x})$, denoted here as **y**:

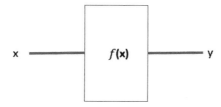

Figure 13.5 – Black box representation of our problem

As you can see in the preceding diagram, this problem can be solved classically. However, it will need to have two queries in order to determine whether f is constant or balanced, where each query would view the results of both $f(0)$ and $f(1)$ in order to conclude whether it is constant or balanced. When using Deutsch's quantum algorithm, we will see whether we can determine f using just one query. Let's see how in the next section.

Describing the problem as a quantum problem

Since we are working with quantum computations, we'll have to first switch to representing our functions and values using vectors. Therefore, our constant function can be represented in matrix form as follows:

$$f(0) = 0 = \begin{bmatrix} 1 \\ 0 \end{bmatrix}$$

The other function can be represented as:

$$f(1) = 0 = \begin{bmatrix} 1 \\ 0 \end{bmatrix}$$

The function f can therefore be represented by the following matrix:

$$f = \begin{bmatrix} 1 & 1 \\ 0 & 0 \end{bmatrix}$$

Quantum functions have to be unitary, so we will need to convert our function f to be a unitary matrix, U_f. We need to ensure it is unitary in order to execute it on a quantum system. U_f will be our black box, or oracle function. In order to do this, we will need to extend our previous diagram to include the extra components necessary to create our oracle:

1. First, we will convert our input and output registers into **ket notation**, $|x\rangle$.

2. Next, we will create two input registers, $|x\rangle$ and $|y\rangle$, where the input registers will feed into our black box, or oracle function, U_f.

3. Finally, we'll define out two output registers, one that is just the same as the input $|x\rangle$, and the other that is the **XOR** of the input register x, and the input register x *XORed* with the function $f(x)$, as $|x, y \oplus f(x)\rangle$.

Therefore, we can now define the oracle function as follows:

$$U_f : |x\rangle, |y\rangle \rightarrow |x\rangle, \qquad |y \oplus f(x)\rangle$$

This is illustrated as follows:

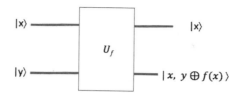

Figure 13.6 – Graphical representation of the Deutsch algorithm

Another requirement is that the function should be reversible, which we can see if we work it out in reverse:

$$U_f^{-1} : |x, y \oplus f(x)\rangle \rightarrow |x, y\rangle$$

Now that we have our function defined as a quantum function for our problem, we'll see how Deutsch's algorithm works.

Implementing Deutsch's algorithm

We'll examine the Deutsch algorithm and step through each task as we build the algorithm on IQX as follows:

1. Open a new Qiskit Notebook and run the first cell that loads our usual boilerplate libraries and modules.

2. Next, we will create a 2-qubit circuit and prepare each input, the first to $|0\rangle$ and the second to $|1\rangle$. We will use the Identity gate to represent the $|0\rangle$, which is the initial state, and an X-gate to represent the initial state of $|1\rangle$:

```
# Implement Deutsch's algorithm for a balanced function
qc = QuantumCircuit(2,1)

# Prepare the input qubits, where q0=0, q1=1
print('Step 1: Prepare the input qubits, where q0=0,
q1=1')
qc.i(0)
qc.x(1)
qc.barrier()
qc.draw()
```

This results in the following circuit diagram:

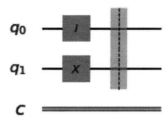

Figure 13.7 – Initializing the qubits to 0 and 1

As you can see from the preceding diagram, q_0 is set to $|0\rangle$ and q_1 is set to $|1\rangle$, which create the first state at the barrier (φ_0) as $|01\rangle$.

3. Now that our inputs are set, we will place them in a superposition state using Hadamard gates. This will allow us to iterate through once while leveraging all four states, rather than iterating through each of them one at a time:

```
# Place each qubit in superposition by applying a
# Hadamard
print('Step 2: Place each qubit in superposition by
    applying a Hadamard')
qc.h(0)
qc.h(1)
qc.barrier()
qc.draw()
```

The result of the preceding code is illustrated in the following diagram. The barriers are used to separate each step so as to simplify reading the circuit:

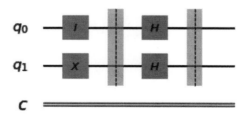

Figure 13.8 – Applying Hadamard to both qubits

As you can see from the preceding diagram, the Hadamard gate transforms the basis vectors for each qubit as follows:

$$H|0\rangle = \frac{1}{\sqrt{2}}|0\rangle + \frac{1}{\sqrt{2}}|1\rangle = \frac{1}{\sqrt{2}}(|0\rangle + |1\rangle)$$

This generates the following state at the second barrier as φ_1:

$$H|1\rangle = \frac{1}{\sqrt{2}}|0\rangle - \frac{1}{\sqrt{2}}|1\rangle = \frac{1}{\sqrt{2}}(|0\rangle - |1\rangle)$$

4. After the qubits have applied the preceding Hadamard gates, the resulting value for the quantum registers will be as follows:

$$\frac{1}{\sqrt{2}}(|00\rangle - |01\rangle + |01\rangle - |11\rangle)$$

One thing to note here is that we now have the second qubit in a negative superposition, $H|1\rangle$. This allows us to define the first and second qubit out of U_f, respectively, as follows:

$$\left(\frac{(-1)^{f(0)}|0\rangle + (-1)^{f(1)}|1\rangle}{\sqrt{2}}\right)\left(\frac{|0\rangle - |1\rangle}{\sqrt{2}}\right)$$

From the preceding equation, you can see that the second qubit, grouped in the second set of parentheses, has the same value, which is the negative superposition, $H|1\rangle$.

However, the first qubit we see has an interesting result. Let's dig a little deeper to understand what this means.

Here, we see that if f is constant, we'll have the following:

$$(\pm1)\left(\frac{|0\rangle + |1\rangle}{\sqrt{2}}\right)\left(\frac{|0\rangle - |1\rangle}{\sqrt{2}}\right)$$

If f is balanced, then we'll have the following:

$$(\pm1)\left(\frac{|0\rangle - |1\rangle}{\sqrt{2}}\right)\left(\frac{|0\rangle - |1\rangle}{\sqrt{2}}\right)$$

Note that the second qubit is always the same, but the first has a phase change from positive if constant, and negative if balanced.

5. Next, by applying a Hadamard gate to the first qubit, we can see something interesting as a result. Let's look at this one at a time.

    For a constant function, the first qubit is set to the following:

    $$\left(\frac{|0\rangle + |1\rangle}{\sqrt{2}}\right)$$

    We recall that applying a Hadamard gate to this superposition state will return us to the $|0\rangle$ state.

    For the balanced function, the first qubit is set to the following superposition state:

    $$\left(\frac{|0\rangle - |1\rangle}{\sqrt{2}}\right)$$

    We can also recall that applying a Hadamard gate to the previous superposition state will return us to the $|1\rangle$ state.

    This means that by measuring only the first qubit after applying a Hadamard gate to it, this will provide us with a result state of either $|0\rangle$ or $|1\rangle$, constant or balanced, respectively.

6. Let's implement this using our Qiskit Notebook.

    This is where we wish to set a quantum gate that would operate on q_1, which represents the y value, based on the value of q_0, which represents the x value. Therefore, this operator, which we'll call U_f, will have inputs (x, y). The gate we will use to represent this will be a **Control-Not (CNOT)** gate.

    In this case, we are working to create a balanced function, one-to-one, which equates to the following:

    $$f(0) = \tilde{f}(1)$$

    To accomplish this, we will need to define our state operator, U_f, as follows:

    $$U_f = \begin{bmatrix} 0 & 1 \\ 1 & 0 \end{bmatrix}$$

    Now, we will place a CNOT gate with the Control on the first qubit, $\mathbf{q}_0$ and the Target on the second qubit, $\mathbf{q}_1$:

```
# Add a CNOT gate with the Control on q0 and Target on q1
qc.cx(0,1)
# Draw the circuit
qc.draw()
```

This should now include the CNOT gate that generates the function type (balanced) and renders the following diagram:

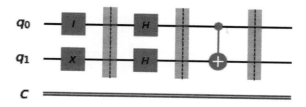

Figure 13.9 – Defining the function type (balanced)

7. Next, we'll add Hadamard gates to all qubits and a measurement operator to the first qubit:

```
# Add the Hadamard gates to all qubits
qc.h(0)
qc.h(1)
qc.barrier()
```

As we saw in our equation earlier, we only need to apply a Hadamard gate to the first qubit, as we will only be measuring the one qubit. However, we're just adding it here so you can see that it also does not disrupt the first qubit:

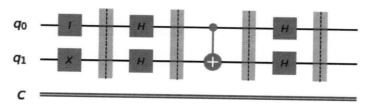

Figure 13.10 – Applying the Hadamard gate to the qubits before measuring

This results in the following state, $|y\rangle$:

$$|\psi\rangle = \frac{1}{2}\left(\frac{1}{\sqrt{2}}|0\rangle + \frac{1}{\sqrt{2}}|1\rangle\right)\left(\frac{1}{\sqrt{2}}|0\rangle + \frac{1}{\sqrt{2}}|1\rangle\right) - \left(\frac{1}{\sqrt{2}}|0\rangle + \frac{1}{\sqrt{2}}|1\rangle\right)\left(\frac{1}{\sqrt{2}}|0\rangle + \frac{1}{\sqrt{2}}|1\rangle\right)$$
$$+ \left(\frac{1}{\sqrt{2}}|0\rangle + \frac{1}{\sqrt{2}}|1\rangle\right)\left(\frac{1}{\sqrt{2}}|0\rangle + \frac{1}{\sqrt{2}}|1\rangle\right) - \left(\frac{1}{\sqrt{2}}|0\rangle + \frac{1}{\sqrt{2}}|1\rangle\right)\left(\frac{1}{\sqrt{2}}|0\rangle + \frac{1}{\sqrt{2}}|1\rangle\right)$$

Let's now apply some algebra to simplify our results:

$$|\psi\rangle = \frac{1}{2}\left(\frac{1}{2}\left(|00\rangle + |01\rangle + |10\rangle + |11\rangle\right) - \frac{1}{2}\left(|00\rangle + |10\rangle - |10\rangle - |11\rangle\right)\right.$$
$$\left. + \frac{1}{2}\left(|00\rangle - |01\rangle - |10\rangle + |11\rangle\right) - \frac{1}{2}\left(|00\rangle + |01\rangle - |10\rangle - |11\rangle\right)\right)$$

Next, we will multiply out our coefficients, so we only have our two qubit states:

$$|\psi\rangle = \frac{1}{4}(|00\rangle + |01\rangle + |10\rangle + |11\rangle - |00\rangle - |10\rangle + |10\rangle + |11\rangle + |00\rangle - |01\rangle - |10\rangle + |11\rangle$$
$$- |00\rangle - |10\rangle + |10\rangle + |11\rangle)$$

Finally, after adding up all the states, we are left with our results, where, as expected when we add across, we have 100% probability of the state $|11\rangle$:

$$|\psi\rangle = \frac{1}{4}(|11\rangle + |11\rangle + |11\rangle + |11\rangle) = 11$$

Since, we will only be measuring the first qubit, we can throw the second qubit away or just not measure it.

8. Let's take a measurement of the first qubit, shown as follows, the result of which would determine the category of the function as either balanced (1) or constant (0):

```
# Add measurement operator to the first qubit
qc.measure(0,0)
```

We already know that from the previous equation, this should equate to a balanced function:

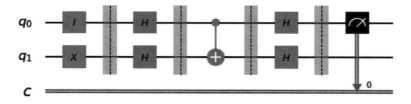

Figure 13.11 – Applying the measurement operator to just the first qubit

9. Now we can execute the preceding circuit and verify our results by using the following code:

```
# Execute the quantum circuit on the simulator first to
# confirm our results.
print('Step 6: Execute the quantum circuit to view
    results.')
backend = Aer.get_backend('qasm_simulator')
result = execute(qc, backend=backend,
shots=1024).result()
counts = result.get_counts(qc)


# Print and plot our results
print(counts)
plot_histogram(counts, title='Balanced function')
```

As calculated previously, the results of this experiment indicate a balanced function, as indicated by the result '1', rather than '0'.

This results in the following output:

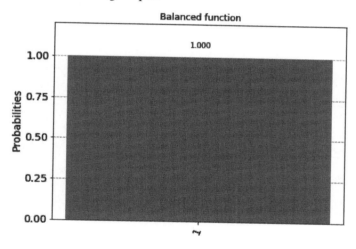

Figure 13.12 – Result of value 1, indicating a balanced function

As expected, we see that our result is a **1**, indicating a balanced function.

10. Let's now select a quantum device to execute the following code:

```
#Import the least_busy module and enable Qiskit job
#watcher
from qiskit.providers.ibmq import least_busy
%qiskit_job_watcher


#Identify the least busy devices
backend_devices = provider.backends(filters=lambda x:
                    x.configuration().n_qubits > 2
                    and not x.configuration().
                    simulator)
# Assign least busy device to backend
backend = least_busy(backend_devices)


#Print the least busy device
print('The least busy device: {}'.format(least_
busy(backend_devices)))
```

The preceding code will select the least busy backend to run our quantum circuit, where the minimum number of qubits is greater than 2, and it's not a simulator.

11. Now let's execute the circuit on the least busy quantum device and view our results:

```
# Execute the previous constant circuit on a quantum
# device
result = execute(qc, backend=backend,
shots=1024).result()
counts = result.get_counts(qc)
# Print and plot results
print(counts)
plot_histogram(counts, title='Balanced function')
```

The results plotted here show the same result, with some very insignificant error values, as shown in the following screenshot:

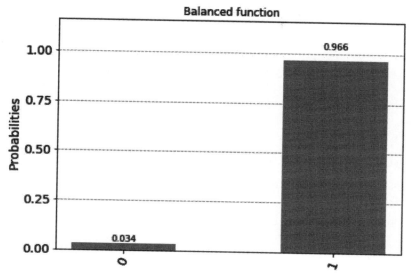

Figure 13.13 – Results from the quantum computer, with the same results and some minor errors due to noise

From the preceding screenshot, the result shows the same as what we expected for the given function we provided, which in this case is the balanced function. There is an exercise in the *Questions* section where you are required to create a constant function.

What we have shown here is an example of how a quantum computer can perform operations faster than a classical system. Naturally, this particular exercise does not offer any real-world solution, but it does help in understanding how these systems have speedup properties. In the next section, we will look at generalizing this example by applying it to more than one qubit.

Understanding the Deutsch-Jozsa algorithm

In the previous section, the Deutsch algorithm provided us with an example of quantum speedup with one qubit. Here, the **Deutsch-Jozsa** algorithm provides a more generalized form of the algorithm. It can be applied to more than one qubit. Originally proposed by David Deutsch and Richard Jozsa in 1992, with improvements by Richard Cleve, Artur Ekert, Chiara Macchiavello, and Michele Mosca in 1998, the problem is still the same, but as we mentioned at the end of the previous section, the problem is now extended to more than just a single qubit. The Deutsch-Jozsa algorithm will operate on multiple qubits at once, and, of course, will still provide a quantum speedup compared with classical, as we will see in the next section.

Understanding the Deutsch-Jozsa problem

In this example, we will extend the previous definition of the problem. Previously, we defined our problem on a single bit value function to determine whether a function was constant or balanced as follows:

$$f: \{0,1\} \rightarrow \{0,1\}$$

In this case, we will expand the problem to include more than one bit as an input, such that:

$$f: \{0,1\}^n \rightarrow \{0,1\}$$

You can see from the preceding equation that f is *constant*, if $f(x)$ is the same for all, that is, $x \in \{0,1\}^n$. Otherwise, f is *balanced*, if $f(x) = 0$ for half of x, and $f(x) = 1$ for the other half of x. For example, if we set n equal to 2 in our input values, $\{0,1\}^n$, then this will result in four different input values, that is, 00, 01, 10, and 11:

Based on these four possible input values of x, in order to create a balanced function, we can set the first half of the results to 0, such that:

$$\begin{Bmatrix} 0 & 0 \\ 0 & 1 \end{Bmatrix} \rightarrow 0$$

And we can set the second half of the results to 1:

$$\begin{Bmatrix} 1 & 0 \\ 1 & 1 \end{Bmatrix} \rightarrow 1$$

If we were to solve this classically, we would need $2^{n-1}+1$ queries to determine whether the results are constant or balanced.

Generating a quantum solution using the Deutsch-Jozsa algorithm

Just as in the Deutsch algorithm, the Deutsch-Jozsa algorithm will only require one query in order to determine whether the function is constant or balanced. In order to generate our quantum circuit to implement the Deutsch-Jozsa algorithm, we will use some of the same components as before:

1. Let's start with our inputs to our black box (oracle). The first input register is an n-bit string representing the input X. We denote this with a capital X, as most texts refer to single qubit or bit values with a lowercase variable such as $|x\rangle$, whereas multi-qubits are represented by uppercase variables such as $|X\rangle$.

    The second input register is a single bit string representing the input y, which, as before, is initialized to 1. This is commonly referred to as an **ancilla qubit**.

2. Next, we define the function of the oracle similar to how we did in the previous form. However, the difference here is that $|x\rangle$ is now a multi-qubit input, $|X\rangle$. U_f is then defined as follows:

$$U_f\colon |X\rangle|y\rangle \rightarrow |X\rangle|y \oplus f(X)\rangle$$

So, our output would similarly map to two outputs. The first is the same as the first input $|X\rangle$, and the second output is our function $|y \oplus f(X)\rangle$. This results in the following graphical representation:

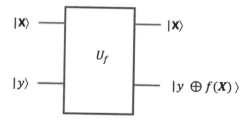

Figure 13.14 – Graphical representation of the Deutsch-Jozsa algorithm

Just as before, we will set the second qubit register, which is our 1-qubit $|y\rangle$, to $|1\rangle$, which will have the same effect as it did on the Deutsch algorithm implementation by helping us create the eigen value for $|y\rangle$ as $(-1)^{f(x)}$.

Now, that we have defined our components to the circuit, let's implement this on the IQX in the next section.

Implementing the Deutsch-Jozsa algorithm

In order to implement the Deutsch-Jozsa algorithm, let's create a new Qiskit Notebook and run the boilerplate cell to load up all our Qiskit modules. Once the setup is complete, let's create our circuit step by step and see how it resolves our problem as we go:

1. First, let's set our input values. We will start by creating a quantum circuit with two inputs, the first set to X, which we will create as a 4-qubit input, followed by a single qubit representing y, which we will initialize to 1. Then we will apply a Hadamard to all the input qubits:

```python
# Create the quantum circuit with both input registers X,
# and y
input_qubits = 4   # Refers to our X input register,
#4-qubits
ancilla_qubit = 1 # Refers to our y input register,
#1--qubit


# Total qubits in our quantum circuit
total_qubits = input_qubits + ancilla_qubit


# Generate the circuit
qc = QuantumCircuit(total_qubits, input_qubits)
# Set the X qubits in superposition
for idx in range(input_qubits):
    qc.h(idx)


# Set the y qubit to 1, then apply a Hadamard
qc.x(input_qubits)
qc.h(input_qubits)

qc.barrier()
qc.draw()
```

This will result in the following diagram:

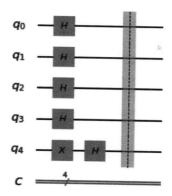

Figure 13.15 – Preparing the input values of our quantum circuit

The input state results in the following:

$$|\psi\rangle = |0\rangle^{\otimes n}|1\rangle$$

When we apply a Hadamard gate to the preceding equation, it breaks out to the following:

$$H|0\rangle^{\otimes n} = \frac{1}{\sqrt{2}}((|0\rangle + |1\rangle)^0 \otimes (|0\rangle + |1\rangle)^1 \otimes \ldots \otimes (|0\rangle + |1\rangle)^{n-1})$$

When we apply a Hadamard gate to the single qubit $|y\rangle$, this gives us the following equation:

$$H|1\rangle = \frac{1}{\sqrt{2}}(|0\rangle - |1\rangle)$$

Simplifying both $H|0\rangle^{\otimes n}$ and $H|1\rangle$ gives us the following equation:

$$|\psi\rangle = H^{\otimes n}|0\rangle^{\otimes n}H|1\rangle = \frac{1}{\sqrt{2}}\sum_{x\in\{0,1\}^n}|X\rangle\left(\frac{|0\rangle - |1\rangle}{\sqrt{2}}\right)$$

2. Next, we will create the oracle U_f function for our circuit similar to how we created it in the previous section on the Deutsch algorithm. We will use the same here, only this time we have the ket X, which is more than a single bit of information:

$$|\psi\rangle = \frac{1}{\sqrt{2^n}}\sum_{x\in\{0,1\}^n}(-1)^{f(x)}|x\rangle\left(\frac{|0\rangle - |1\rangle}{\sqrt{2}}\right)$$

The value of x is the bit representation of the bit string X of 0 or 1.

3. Let's now set our bit string, '1010', by placing an X gate with the set bits and Identity gates with the others. You can also just not add an I gate, but for now, we will add those just to visually indicate the '0' values of the bit string:

```
# Set the bit string which we wish to evaluate, in this
# case lets set '1010', where I indicates value 0, and x
# indicates value 1.
qc.i(0)
qc.x(1)
qc.i(2)
qc.x(3)


qc.barrier()
qc.draw()
```

This will render the following addition to our circuit, where the added section represents setting the input state $|1010\rangle$ based on the bit string 1010:

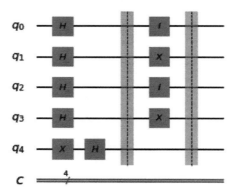

Figure 13.16 – State representation $|1010\rangle$ of bit string 1010

4. Next, we will apply our oracle. In this case, we will set it to a balanced output where all outputs should be 1s, with zero probability of 0s. We'll do so by adding CNOT gates, where the Control is applied to each qubit and the Target is set to the last qubit:

```
# Set oracle to either constant (output = 0s)
# or balanced (output = 1s)


# In this example we will choose a balanced function
for idx in range(input_qubits):
```

```
        qc.cx(idx, input_qubits)

qc.barrier()
qc.draw()
```

The result of this should be as follows, where we set each Control of the CNOT gate to all qubits and the Target to our ancilla qubit, q_4:

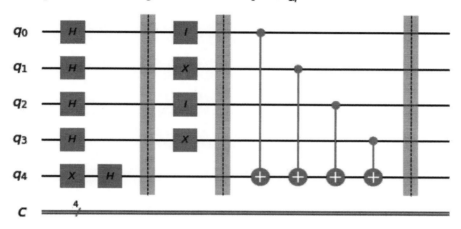

Figure 13.17 – Representation of the added balanced oracle

5. Next, we will set the closing bit string, which we use to wrap our oracle, in this case, '1010':

```
# Set the closing bit string we selected earlier to
# evaluate
qc.i(0)
qc.x(1)
qc.i(2)
qc.x(3)

qc.barrier()
qc.draw()
```

The preceding code will give us the following diagram, just as we expected, where the oracle is bound by the bit string:

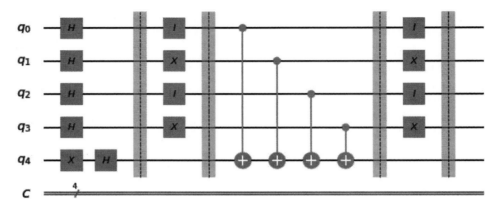

Figure 13.18 – Oracle bounded by bit string representation

6. Next, we will apply the Hadamard gates to all the qubits:

```
# Add the Hadamard gates to complete wrapping the oracle
for idx in range(4):
    qc.h(idx)

qc.barrier()
qc.draw()
```

The result of this is rendered as follows:

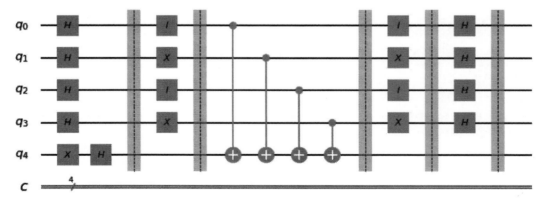

Figure 13.19 – Completed quantum circuit of the Deutsch-Jozsa algorithm for a balanced function

7. Finally, we will add our measurements so that we can read out the results. We will apply the measurements only to the first four qubits:

```
# Add measurements only to our inputs
qc.measure(range(4),range(4))


# Draw the circuit
qc.draw()
```

Therefore, our final quantum circuit should be as follows. Each step in creating the Deutsch Jozsa algorithm is separated by the barriers, where the first is the preparation, the second is to set the bit string 1010, the third is to set our oracle U_f, and then we reverse the first two steps, followed by our measurements:

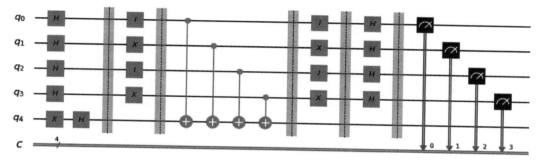

Figure 13.20 – Final circuit for the Deutsch-Jozsa algorithm

8. Now that we have created our quantum circuit for the Deutsch-Jozsa algorithm, let's execute the circuit on a simulator first to visualize what results we get back:

```
# Execute the circuit
backend = Aer.get_backend('qasm_simulator')
result = execute(qc, backend=backend,
shots=1024).result()
counts = result.get_counts(qc)


# Print and plot results
print(counts)
plot_histogram(counts)
```

As expected, our results returned a probability of 100% of 1s for a balanced circuit:

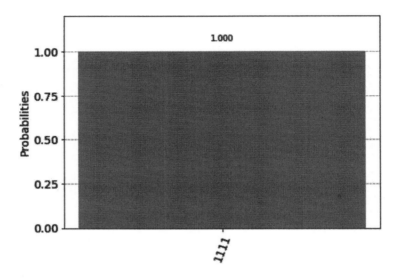

Figure 13.21 – Results from the simulator of a balanced function

9. Now, let's run this on a quantum computer and compare the results. We'll need to make sure we use a quantum computer that has the parameters we need to run our circuit, which is to say, it should have a sufficient number of qubits, not a simulator, and ensure that it is operational and not undergoing maintenance:

```
#Enable the job watcher widget
%qiskit_job_watcher

# Print all backends with at least 5 or more qubits
provider.backends(filters=lambda x: x.configuration().n_
    qubits >= total_qubits and not x.configuration().
    simulator and x.status().operational==True)
```

The preceding code will first launch the **Jupyter job watcher** widget, where you can monitor the status of your job on the screen. This will also output a list of available backends that qualify under the constraints of the filter we provided. Here is a list that was returned. Keep in mind that the results will vary depending on when you run this and the quantum devices available at that time:

```
[<IBMQBackend('ibmqx2') from IBMQ(hub='ibm-q',
 group='open', project='main')>,
 <IBMQBackend('ibmq_16_melbourne') from IBMQ(hub='ibm-q',
 group='open', project='main')>,
 <IBMQBackend('ibmq_vigo') from IBMQ(hub='ibm-q',
 group='open', project='main')>,
 <IBMQBackend('ibmq_ourense') from IBMQ(hub='ibm-q',
 group='open', project='main')>,
 <IBMQBackend('ibmq_london') from IBMQ(hub='ibm-q',
 group='open', project='main')>,
 <IBMQBackend('ibmq_burlington') from IBMQ(hub='ibm-q',
 group='open', project='main')>,
 <IBMQBackend('ibmq_essex') from IBMQ(hub='ibm-q',
 group='open', project='main')>]
```

10. Next, let's select either one from the list of backends and run our circuit on any system of your choice. In this example, we will run it on `ibmq_ourense`:

```
# Select any of the available backends previously you have
# listed,
# In this case we will pick 'ibmq_ourense'
backend = provider.get_backend('ibmq_ourense')

# Execute the previous circuit on a quantum device
result = execute(qc, backend=backend,
shots=1024).result()
counts = result.get_counts(qc)

# Print and plot results
print(counts)
plot_histogram(counts)
```

Once the preceding code completes execution, we should see the following results. Of course, they will vary based on the device and any noise that would affect the final measurement:

```
{'1001': 43, '1010': 34, '0011': 69, '1110': 65, '1100':
44, '1011': 56, '0111': 85, '1101': 78, '1000': 31,
'0100': 25, '0101': 64, '0001': 43, '0010': 42, '1111':
253, '0000': 51, '0110': 41}
```

We will also get the following output:

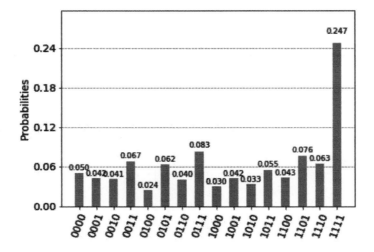

Figure 13.22 – Results after executing the circuit on the 'ibmq_ourense' quantum system

As expected, we see that we have a high probability of all 1s. We also see the effects of noise on our results, albeit fairly insignificant, when compared to our expected result.

Now that we have completed both the Deutsch and Deutsch-Jozsa algorithms, we can see that there is some speedup when compared to classical systems. However, we can also see that there are really no practical or real-world examples where we can apply these algorithms. That said, we have understood how the use of superposition and entanglement can speed up certain functions compared to classical techniques. We'll expand our understanding of algorithms into something that is a bit more of a generalized quantum algorithm, namely, Bernstein-Vazirani, in the next section.

Learning about the foundational oracle-based quantum algorithm

We learned in the previous section that the very early quantum algorithms illustrated quantum speedup vis-à-vis classical systems in relation to a simple problem. In this section, we will expand on this to look at a more complex problem, which we can speed up or increase the advantages over classical systems. To do this, we will learn about another oracle-based algorithm, **Bernstein-Vazirani**. The difference between this one and the previous foundational algorithms is that the Bernstein-Vazirani algorithm will identify a hidden bit string using an oracle function in a single query.

Learning about the Bernstein-Vazirani algorithm

Originally invented in 1992 by Ethan Bernstein and Umesh Vazirani, the Bernstein-Vazirani algorithm extends the Deutsch-Jozsa algorithm to a generalization to find an unknown or secret bit string. Where the Deutsch-Jozsa algorithm worked to solve the problem of determining whether a given function is constant or balanced, the Bernstein-Vazirani algorithm works to determine a secret number by applying a function that maps an input to its output.

Understanding the Bernstein-Vazirani problem

The problem that the Bernstein-Vazirani algorithm addresses is fairly straightforward and similar to the previous problem. Given an unknown function, or black box (oracle), similar to the Deutsch-Jozsa oracle, an input string of bits results in an output of either 0 or 1:

$$f: \{0,1\}^n \to \{0,1\}$$

For this function f, we are guaranteed that the following applies:

$$f(x) = s \cdot x \ (\text{mod } 2)$$

From the preceding equation, s is an unknown or secret string such that:

$$s \in \{0,1\}^n$$

The problem therefore is to find the secret value s.

Solving this classically is the same as the previous examples, where we would have to check each value one bit at a time to determine the secret value *s*. However, as we have seen in the previous examples, we can solve this with a quantum algorithm executing a single query. Let's walk through the example to see how we can solve this using the Bernstein-Vazirani algorithm.

Generating a quantum solution using the Bernstein-Vazirani algorithm

The Bernstein-Vazirani algorithm is very similar to that of Deutsch-Jozsa in that it performs the same steps to create the quantum circuit for the algorithm:

1. Initialize all *n* input qubits to the ground state $|0\rangle$.

2. Initialize the ancilla qubit to the excited state $|1\rangle$.

3. Apply a Hadamard gate to all input qubits and the ancilla qubit, $H^{n+1}|0\rangle^{\otimes n}|1\rangle$.

4. Query the oracle to apply a phase shift based on the secret string value using CNOT gates.

5. Apply another set of Hadamard gates to the input qubits.

6. Measure the input qubits to obtain the secret string.

As you can see from the preceding steps, the algorithm is very similar. However, the main differentiator here is *steps 4* and *5*. When a qubit hits the secret key, we then apply a phase shift, that is, when $s_i = 1$. Then, in *step 5*, when we apply the second set of Hadamard gates, the phase will return from $|-\rangle$ to $|1\rangle$, if $s_i = 1$, or from $|+\rangle$ to $|0\rangle$ if $s_i = 0$.

Let's implement these steps one at a time and review the changes to the state. As before, we will use barriers to separate each step so we can visualize each step along the way. We'll be doing this with all quantum algorithms in this chapter.

Implementing the Bernstein-Vazirani algorithm

The following steps will describe a step-by-step guide to create the **Bernstein-Vazirani (BV)** algorithm and describe the outcome of each step to help you understand how each step affects the state, which will eventually produce the secret string:

1. Let's start by creating a new Qiskit Notebook with the usual boilerplate cell that will load much of the base Qiskit modules and our account so we can execute the quantum circuit on an actual quantum computer.

First, we will create our quantum circuit, which will be made up of four qubits, and one ancilla qubit, and we will define our **secret bit string** (shh):

```
# Create your secret number
shh = '1010'


# Set the number of qubits to represent secret number and
# an ancilla qubit
input_qubits = len(shh)
ancilla_qubit = 1
total_qubits = input_qubits + ancilla_qubit


# Create the quantum circuit
qc = QuantumCircuit(total_qubits, input_qubits)
```

The preceding code creates our base quantum circuit, qc, which we will use to construct the Bernstein-Vazirani algorithm. The input qubits must be at least the length of our secret string, which in this case is the value 1010. Our input register will need to be at least these many qubits in length. We then added an ancilla qubit, which, in the previous examples, we referred to as the output qubit. Moving forward, we will start referring to this qubit as an ancilla qubit, in that it is more of a utility qubit that will not be measured or output to our results.

2. Next, we will add Hadamard gates to the input qubits, so as to ensure that all input qubits are set to a superposition state:

```
# Add Hadamard gates to the input qubits
for idx in range(input_qubits):
    qc.h(idx)


# Draw the input circuit
qc.draw()
```

This will render our quantum circuit as follows:

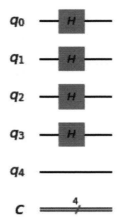

Figure 13.23 – Initializing the input qubits state from $|0\rangle$ to a superposition state, $|+\rangle$

3. Next, we will need to prepare our ancilla qubit, $\mathbf{q}_4$, just as we did before, by first initializing it to the state $|1\rangle$, followed by a Hadamard gate, which will prepare the state of the ancilla qubit to $|-\rangle$:

```
# Prepare the ancilla qubit of the circuit
qc.x(total_qubits-1)
qc.h(total_qubits-1)

qc.barrier()

# Draw the prepared circuit
qc.draw()
```

The preceding code will render the following circuit, which we see is the same initialization of our circuit as before. This is how most quantum algorithms are initialized, which allows working with all possible combinations of qubit states. The barrier is added simply to view the various state changes:

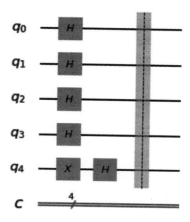

Figure 13.24 – Initialization of all qubits

The state at the first barrier is now set to the following, where the input qubits are as follows:

$$|0\rangle^n \rightarrow \frac{1}{\sqrt{2^n}} \sum_{x \in \{0,1\}^n} |x\rangle$$

The ancilla qubit is set to:

$$|1\rangle \rightarrow \frac{|0\rangle - |1\rangle}{\sqrt{2}}$$

4. Next, we need to make a quick bit order adjustment before we apply our oracle function. Since the qubits are ordered from left to right, we will need to reverse the order of our secret number:

```
# Before creating the oracle, we need to adjust the
# qubits
# Since they are ordered from left to right, we will
# reverse the secret number


# Current secret value
```

```
print('Secret before reverse: ', shh)


# Reverse order
shh = shh[::-1]
print('Secret after reverse: ', shh)
```

As you can see from the following output, the order is now `0101`, so we can now apply our oracle function:

```
Secret before reverse:   1010
Secret after reverse:    0101
```

5. To apply the oracle function, we want to trigger a phase shift each time we hit a `'1'` in the secret string. To do that, we will apply a CNOT gate to each qubit, where the Control is set to each qubit and the Target is linked to the ancilla. In our case, the secret string has `'1'` set on **qubit 1** (q_1) and **qubit 3** (q_3):

```
# Now that we have the right order, let's create the
# oracle
# by applying a CNOT, where the qubits set to '1' are the
# source
# and the target would be the ancilla qubit
for idx in range(input_qubits):
    if shh[idx] == '1':
        qc.cx(idx, input_qubits)


qc.barrier()
qc.draw()
```

The preceding code renders the quantum circuit up to the oracle:

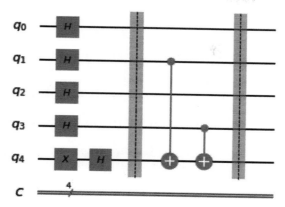

Figure 13.25 – Oracle applying CNOT where the secret string is set to '1'

Since all our qubits are in a superposition state, by applying the phase shift based on the secret string $|S\rangle$, we get the following equation:

$$|S\rangle = \left(\frac{|0\rangle + (-1)^{s0}\,|1\rangle}{\sqrt{2}}\right) \otimes \left(\frac{|0\rangle + (-1)^{s1}\,|1\rangle}{\sqrt{2}}\right) \otimes \cdots \otimes \left(\frac{|0\rangle + (-1)^{sn}\,|1\rangle}{\sqrt{2}}\right)$$

Therefore, from the preceding equation, our secret string $|S\rangle$ will apply a phase shift to each qubit where the string is set. This will shift the $|+\rangle$ to $|-\rangle$, whenever the input bit x and the secret string s is equal to 1. We can then represent the previous equation as follows:

$$\frac{1}{\sqrt{2^n}} \sum_{x\in\{0,1\}} (-1)^{s*x}\,|x\rangle = \left(\frac{|0\rangle + (-1)^{s*0}\,|1\rangle}{\sqrt{2}}\right) \otimes \left(\frac{|0\rangle + (-1)^{s*1}\,|1\rangle}{\sqrt{2}}\right) \otimes \cdots \otimes \left(\frac{|0\rangle + (-1)^{s*n}\,|1\rangle}{\sqrt{2}}\right)$$

6. And finally, in our last step before applying measurements to the input qubits, we apply another set of Hadamard gates. What this set of Hadamard gates achieves is that it will return the state of each qubit back to either the $|0\rangle$ or $|1\rangle$ state.

This is entirely dependent on whether the qubit experienced a phase shift while passing through the oracle. If it did not, then the state would change from $|+\rangle$ to $|0\rangle$, or from $|-\rangle$ to $|1\rangle$:

```
# Now let's close up our circuit with Hadamard gates
# applied to the input qubits
for idx in range(input_qubits):
```

```
        qc.h(idx)

    qc.barrier()

    # Finally, let's add measurements to our input qubits
    qc.measure(range(input_qubits), range(input_qubits))

    qc.draw()
```

This will render the following circuit diagram, which completes the steps to implement the Bernstein-Vazirani algorithm along with the measurement operators:

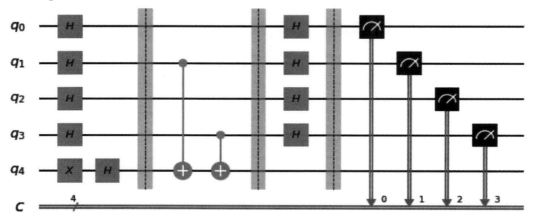

Figure 13.26 – Final circuit that implements the Bernstein-Vazirani algorithm

7. Now that the circuit is complete and ready to go, we can execute the circuit on a simulator and then on a real quantum device:

```
# Execute the circuit and plot the results
backend = Aer.get_backend('qasm_simulator')
result = execute(qc, backend, shots=1024).result()
counts = result.get_counts(qc)
plot_histogram(counts)
```

The results should have 100% probability for the value of our secret string, as illustrated in the following histogram:

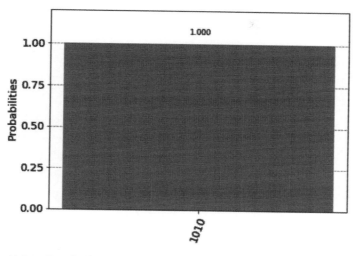

Figure 13.27 – Result identifies with 100% probability the value of our secret string

8. Now, let's run it on a quantum computer. As we have done in the previous example, let's launch the job watcher widget and get a list of backends that have the number of qubits we need, and ensure that it is operational:

```
#Enable the job watcher widget
%qiskit_job_watcher


# Print all backends with at least 5 or more qubits
provider.backends(filters=lambda x: x.configuration().n_
    qubits >= 5 and not x.configuration().simulator
    and x.status().operational==True)
```

9. From the output list that is returned, select any of the following. I will select ibmq_ourense from the list to execute the circuit:

```
# Choose whichever backend you wish from the list,
# For this example, we will use 'ibmq_ourense'
backend = provider.get_backend('ibmq_ourense')


# Execute the previous circuit on a quantum device
result = execute(qc, backend=backend,
shots=1024).result()
counts = result.get_counts(qc)


# Print and plot results
print(counts)
plot_histogram(counts)
```

This results in the following counts and histogram, which we can see also identifies our secret string, including, of course, a little noise:

```
{'0010': 39, '1000': 60, '0110': 3, '1001': 140, '1010':
602, '0001': 14, '1101': 11, '1111': 3, '1011': 93,
'0000': 18, '0100': 4, '1110': 18, '0011': 19}
```

We also get the following output:

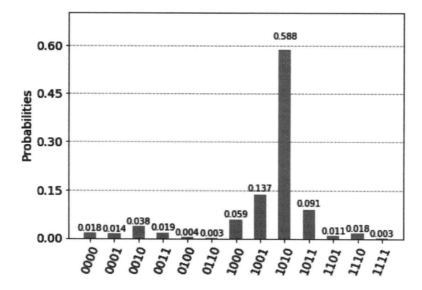

Figure 13.28 – Results from running the circuit on the ibmq_ourense quantum system

As you can see from the preceding diagram, similar to the earlier quantum algorithms, we can solve certain problems in a single query, where it would take classical systems a few queries to solve. These problems leveraged a feature called **phase kickback**, where we used the phase to solve the question of whether the function was balanced or constant.

Looking back at the step where we applied the last layer of Hadamard gates, it appears as if the control qubit got flipped instead of the other qubit.

In this section, we learned about the foundational oracle-based algorithms and how they illustrate quantum advantage over classical systems to solve problems. We also learned about how oracles and ancilla qubits are leveraged to obtain some of the solutions, which will, in turn, help you understand the more complex algorithms as you expand your knowledge and research. Although these were simple problems that have no commercial value by themselves, they did, however, manage to trigger an interest in the quantum information science field that is still growing to this day.

Summary

In this chapter, we covered some of the many quantum algorithms that employ common techniques that are used in a variety of other quantum algorithms.

The goal of this chapter was to explore each of them systematically so you can have a good combination of understanding of the problem each algorithm is solving. Also, now you have an understanding of how to implement them on both a simulator and a quantum computer. The topics here are, of course, foundational and oracle-based, although the techniques are commonly found in many other quantum algorithms.

In the next chapter, we will step away from the oracle-based foundational algorithms and look at another form of algorithm that solves similar problems. However, rather than using phases to identify the solution, it will instead leverage periodicity, which is primarily why they are called **periodic algorithms**.

Questions

1. Create a circuit that implements Deutsch's algorithm for a constant function and verify your results.

2. Which algorithm would you use to determine whether an n-bit string is balanced?

3. Would phase kickback work if the ancilla qubit was not set to the state $|1\rangle$? Explain your answer.

4. Implement the Bernstein-Vazirani algorithm to find the state $|11010\rangle$.

5. What would happen if you set the ancilla qubit in either of the algorithms by first placing a Hadamard gate, followed by an X gate? Explain the reason for the results.

6. Program and create an automated oracle generator for the Bernstein-Vazirani algorithm that randomly generates the secret state. Can you determine the value by just running the circuit and reviewing the results?

14
Applying Quantum Algorithms

In this chapter, we will focus on algorithms that have the potential to solve more applicable problems, such as periodicity and searching. These algorithms differ from the earlier algorithms as these are used in various domains and are included in many modern quantum algorithms. A few examples of these modern quantum algorithms are the **quantum amplitude estimation, variational quantum Eigensolvers**, and **quantum support vector machines** algorithms. Having a good understanding of these will help you when learning about or creating your own algorithms as the techniques used can be applied in many industries.

Period algorithms can be used to solve factorization or phase estimation problems. **Search algorithms** can also provide some speed-up over classical algorithms on how they leverage amplitude amplification to find a specified entry.

The following topics will be covered in this chapter:

- Understanding periodic quantum algorithms
- Learning about Simon's algorithm
- Learning about the Quantum Fourier Transform algorithm
- Learning about Shor's algorithm
- Learning about Grover's search algorithm

After completing this chapter, you will be able to grasp the concepts of these algorithms and leverage the algorithms already provided in **Qiskit Aqua**, so you can use them without having to *reinvent the wheel*.

Technical requirements

This chapter assumes that you are familiar with some of the basic quantum algorithm components, such as superposition, oracles, phase kickback, and programming, on the Qiskit notebook. You are also expected to have an understanding of basic linear algebra, such as multiplying matrices, the complex conjugation of a matrix, and inner products. Some advanced mathematics, such as an understanding of the **Fourier transform**, is also assumed.

Here is the source code used throughout this book: `https://github.com/PacktPublishing/Learn-Quantum-Computing-with-Python-and-IBM-Quantum-Experience`. Here is the link for the CiA videos: `https://bit.ly/35o5M8O`

Understanding periodic quantum algorithms

In *Chapter 13, Understanding Quantum Algorithms*, we covered algorithms that use phase kickback to solve various problems.

In this section, we will move away from phase kickback and into periodic quantum algorithms. Periodic functions are those where values are repeated over time. Your watch, for example, is periodic in that each minute has 60 seconds, each hour has 60 minutes, and each day has 24 hours.

If you have your watch set up with the hours from 1 to 12, then your watch has a period of 2 per day, in that your watch will repeat the numbers 1 to 12 twice in one day. Of course, this is separate from the AM and PM indicators, whether it is day or evening hours. Periodic functions occur all around us in many ways, so understanding how to relate these to a quantum circuit is key to understanding many of the quantum algorithms, including the most famous one of all, **Shor's algorithm**.

But for now, we will learn about **Simon's algorithm** in the next section.

Learning Simon's algorithm

In the previous chapter—*Chapter 13, Understanding Quantum Algorithms*—we used algorithms that involved an additional qubit, an **ancilla qubit**, to determine whether functions were balanced or constant. As interesting as they are, by proving that there is some advantage to quantum over classical computation, the truth is that there isn't much that you can do with those algorithms.

At least that is what Daniel Simon believed as he worked on a problem that would prove that there is some **black box** (as it is often referred to when describing an oracle) problem that can provide *exponential* quantum speed-up over classical algorithms. The algorithm that he discovered was one that is commonly referred to as a **periodic quantum algorithm**. Let's start by understanding the problem.

Understanding the problem

The problem that Simon proposed involves determining whether a function is a **one-to-one** or **two-to-one** function. *What do we mean by that?* Let's look at each of them side-by-side and see what this means.

A one-to-one (or injective) function, as it is known, is quite simply a function that maps one input value to a single output value, such that no other input value in the domain would resolve to an output value that has already been assigned. The following table shows a simple example of a one-to-one function where the input, x, maps to an output, $f(x)$, that is not the same for any other input x:

x	$f(x)$
00	01
01	10
10	11
11	00

Table 14.1 – One-to-one function example

A two-to-one function is, as it is titled, a function, f, that maps two inputs, x, to the same output, $f(x)$. The following table shows an example of a two-to-one function, where the two inputs are mapped to either 00 or 11:

X	$f(x)$
00	00
01	11
10	11
11	00

Table 14.2 – Two-to-one function example

Simon's problem asks whether we are given a function, f, such that the function satisfies the following condition:

$$f(x_1) = f(x_2)$$

In the preceding condition, x_1, and x_2 are two separate input values, and x_1 XORed with x_2 is a bit string, s, as shown in the following equation:

$$x_1 \oplus x_2 = s$$

Can we then find the solution for whether f is a one-to-one or two-to-one function, and also, can we find the value of s?

Classically, this can be solved by checking at least $2^{n-1} + 1$ values of x, where n is the number of inputs. This means we would have to iterate through at least half plus 1 of the inputs to determine whether the function, f, is one-to-one or two-to-one. This, of course, will increase in complexity as n grows larger and larger. What we need is a solution that can resolve this in less time and with perfect accuracy, which is what Simon's algorithm does for us. Let's get started.

Generating a quantum solution using Simon's algorithm

The solution to this using Simon's algorithm is very similar in the construction flow to the algorithms we learned about in previous chapters, in that we will be applying Hadamard gates to the input qubits both at the beginning of the algorithm and at the end just before we apply the measurement operator. There is also going to be an oracle in between the Hadamard gates; more specifically, our steps will be as follows:

1. Create a quantum circuit that has two qubit registers. The first register will be the size of our inputs, and the second quantum register will be of the same size as the first. Our quantum circuit will start with *2n* qubits, where *n* is the number of qubits of our input value.

2. Apply Hadamard gates to all the qubits of the first qubit register.

3. Apply our oracle function to all the qubits, which will serve as our black box housing the value s.

4. Apply another set of Hadamard gates to the qubits in the first quantum register.

5. Measure all the qubits in the quantum circuit.

As you can see from the preceding steps, this is fairly similar to the previous algorithms we covered in *Chapter 13, Understanding Quantum Algorithms*, except here, we have more than a single qubit in our second quantum register, and we are not initializing the second register to the state $|1\rangle$. By not setting the second register to the state $|1\rangle$, this algorithm will therefore not leverage phase kickback as in the previous algorithms from *Chapter 13, Understanding Quantum Algorithms*. Let's start by preparing our circuit while we discuss each step as we build out the algorithm in the next section.

Implementing Simon's algorithm

In this section, we will describe a step-by-step guide to creating a circuit that implements Simon's algorithm:

1. We will start by creating our quantum circuit based on the size of our input values; in this example, we will base the input size on the length of our secret string, *s*, which we will initialize to '011'. We'll begin by creating a new Qiskit notebook.

    We will initialize the circuit to a length of *s* = 011 and create a circuit that is twice the length of our secret string. This will ensure we have a sufficient sized quantum circuit for our two input registers. We'll use a light-hearted variable name to label our secret string:

    ```python
    # Set our secret string to '011'
    shh = '011'


    # Creating registers
    # Set the input qubit register size equal to the length
    # of s
    input_qubits = len(str(shh))
    # Set the total qubits equal to twice the size of input
    qubits
    total_qubits = 2*input_qubits


    # Create the quantum circuit
    qc = QuantumCircuit(total_qubits)
    ```

    The preceding code creates our quantum circuit where the secret string, *s*, is set to '011', and our input size is set to 3, which is the length of the secret string, *s*. Our quantum circuit size is twice that, with a total of 6 qubits.

2. Next, we'll add Hadamard gates only to the qubits in the first quantum register—that is, the input. Since we set the length of our secret string to the value `input_qubits`, we can use this to assign the Hadamard gates only to the qubits in the first quantum register:

```
# Apply Hadamard gates before querying the oracle
qc.h(range(input_qubits))
qc.barrier()
qc.draw()
```

The preceding code will render our quantum circuit as follows, and we'll continue using barriers to illustrate the different stages of Simon's algorithm:

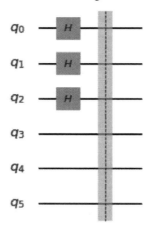

Figure 14.1 – Initializing the quantum circuit with Hadamard gates on the first register only

3. Next, we will implement our query function, which implements our secret string, `shh='011'`:

```
# Create the oracle function of our secret string
# Since we are only setting the last two qubits,
# we will only apply cx gates to the last two.
for idx in range(input_qubits):
    if(shh[idx] == '1'):
        for count in range(input_qubits):
            qc.cx(idx, input_qubits + count)

qc.barrier()
qc.draw()
```

The preceding code will add a Control-NOT gate between the qubit that is aligned with the input value set to `'1'`, and the Target to the second register qubits, respectively. This will render our quantum circuit up to our oracle, as follows:

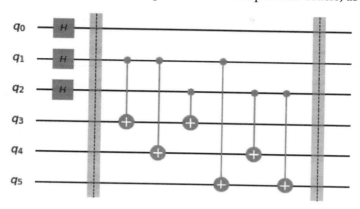

Figure 14.2 – Oracle implementing the 011 secret string

4. Finally, we will add our final set of Hadamard gates to the input registers and measure all the qubits:

```
# Apply Hadamard gates to the input register
qc.h(range(len(str(shh))))


# Measure ancilla qubits
qc.measure_all()
```

At this point, we should have the following circuit created, which includes an oracle that is wrapped on both sides by a set of Hadamard gates, before applying a measurement across all qubits:

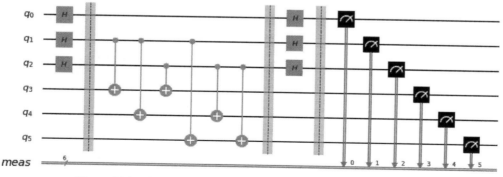

Figure 14.3 – Quantum circuit implementation of Simon's algorithm

5. Now that we have the circuit complete, let's execute this on a simulator first:

```
# Execute the quantum circuit on the simulator
backend = Aer.get_backend('qasm_simulator')
shots = 1024
results = execute(qc, backend=backend, shots=shots).
result()
counts = results.get_counts(qc)


# Print results
print('Counts: ', counts)
```

The preceding code will result in the following output:

```
Counts:   {'111000': 280, '111110': 223, '000110': 281,
'000000': 240}
```

Keep in mind that the bit order is from right to left, where the measurement from the first qubit, q_0, is the position on the far left and continues toward the right. By this convention, we can see that the first output, '111000', combines both the first and second registers, where the first register is '000' and the second register is '111' and its count is 280. Let's clean up our results and get the substring of the input register and their specific values. This will allow us to focus on just the register and the results we need.

6. We start off by looping through each count and reversing the count keys. This will allow us to visualize our registers listed from left to right, the first and second register, respectively. We follow this up by cropping out the input register and its count so that we can add up the totals:

```
# Create a new object to store the input register counts
sub_results = {}
# Loop through each of the count keys and extract the
# the input register and their respective counts.
for count in counts.keys():
    rev_count_key = count[::-1]
    input_count = count[input_qubits:]
    count_value = counts[count]
    if input_count in sub_results:
        sub_results[input_count] += count_value
    else:
```

```
        sub_results[input_count] = count_value

# Print and plot the results
print('sub results', sub_results)
plot_histogram(sub_results)
```

The preceding code will print and plot the results of only our input registers:

```
sub results {'000': 487, '110': 537}
```

Note that we now have two results: one has the value '000' and the other '110', as follows:

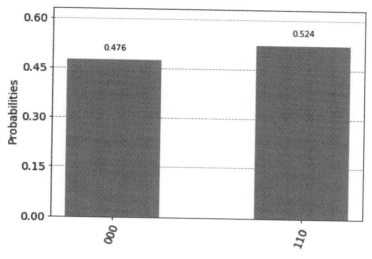

Figure 14.4 – Results of input register counts

As we can see in the preceding graph, we have two input register results—**000** and **110**—for our secret string. Recall from earlier that the string values are reversed, so **110** is actually '011', our secret string. Of course, if we only had '000' as the result, this would mean that f would be a one-to-one function. $x \oplus s$ is one-to-one when s='000', which therefore means since we also have s='011', we now know that this is a two-to-one function.

In this section, we learned about oracle-based and periodic quantum algorithms. We also learned about Simon's algorithm, its problem, and how to implement it for generating a quantum solution.

What we have seen is the first form of an oracle algorithm that can be used to solve a general problem. This algorithm has been said to serve as an inspiration for other algorithms, including **Shor's algorithm**. We'll press on and continue to the next algorithm, which moves us out of the oracle-based quantum algorithms to periodic-based quantum algorithms, namely, **Quantum Fourier Transform (QFT)**.

Learning about the Quantum Fourier Transform algorithm

QFT is related to **Discrete Fourier Transform (DFT)** in that it too can transform from one domain to another. DFT is used to transfer signals from the time domain to the frequency domain, or in a more generalized description; mapping one domain, x, to another domain, $F(\omega)$, with the following formula:

$$F(\omega) = \sum_{j=0}^{N-1} e^{\frac{2\pi i k j}{N}} x_j$$

Similarly, we can define a quantum transformation as a transformation from one basis to another. For example, all the computations we have done in this book so far have been measured according to the Z basis. This means our basis states have been set on the Z axis of the qubit with the states $|0\rangle$ and $|1\rangle$, referring to the positive and negative ends of the Z axis on the Bloch sphere, respectively.

There are, of course, other basis states that we can transition to if needed. One example would be the X axis of the qubit, where the basis states there are $|+\rangle$ and $|-\rangle$, which refers to the positive and negative ends of the X axis on the Bloch sphere, respectively. QFT would transform between these two basis states.

In this section, we will work through a simple example of a QFT algorithm to extend our understanding of it when we see it used in many other quantum algorithms.

We'll begin by applying QFT to a simple three-qubit quantum state.

Understanding the QFT algorithm

To transform our quantum function from one basis state to another, we need to apply QFT, as follows:

$$|Z - \text{basis}\rangle \xrightarrow{\text{QFT}} |X - \text{basis}\rangle$$

In the preceding equation, $Z - basis$ refers to the basis states on the Z axis, $|0\rangle$ and $|1\rangle$, and $X - basis$ refers to the basis states on the X axis, $|+\rangle$ and $|-\rangle$. The Qiskit documentation (https://qiskit.org/documentation/) refers to the Fourier basis with the tilde (~), where *QFT* is the Quantum Fourier Transform applied to the state $|1\rangle$, given as follows:

$$\text{QFT}\,|x\rangle = |\tilde{x}\rangle$$

This can be equated, where the transformation is represented by the QFT between the amplitudes of x_j and y_k, as follows:

$$\sum_{j=0}^{N-1} x_j\,|j\rangle \overset{QFT}{\longrightarrow} \sum_{k=0}^{N-1} y_k\,|k\rangle$$

Now, let's see how we can implement QFT in a quantum circuit.

Implementing the QFT algorithm

Let's begin by deriving our implementation based on an input state, $|\Psi\rangle$.

An alternative is to apply it sequentially to the following formula as we move from qubit to qubit. For this example, we will operate as follows; given a state $|\Psi\rangle = |j_{n-1}, j_{n-2}, \dots, j_1, j_0\rangle$, we will apply a Hadamard gate where we add the phase based on the state $|\Psi\rangle$, where each value, j_i, is appended to the phase, as follows:

$$|\Psi\rangle = \frac{\left(|0\rangle + e^{2\pi i(0.j_0)}|1\rangle\right)\dots\left(|0\rangle + e^{2\pi i(0.j_{n-2}\dots j_0)}|1\rangle\right)\left(|0\rangle + e^{2\pi i(0.j_{n-1}\dots j_0)}|1\rangle\right)}{\sqrt{2^n}}$$

In the following exercise, we will implement the QFT of $|\Psi\rangle = |110\rangle$, where $j_2 = 1, j_1 = 1, j_0 = 0$:

1. We'll begin by opening a new Qiskit notebook and create our quantum circuit with the width equal to the length of our state value, '110':

```
# Initialize the 3-qubit quantum circuit
# Set the state '110'
s = '110'
num_qubits = len(s)
qc = QuantumCircuit(num_qubits)
```

2. Now that we have our quantum circuit created, let's initialize the state, *s*, to $|110\rangle$. Since we write from the least significant position, we will reverse s accordingly as well:

```
# Set reverse ordering
s = s[::-1]

# Construct the state 110
for idx in range(num_qubits):
    if s[idx] == '1':
        qc.x(idx)

qc.barrier()
qc.draw()
```

The preceding code will initialize and render our circuit as follows:

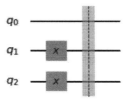

Figure 14.5 – Initializing the state, s, to $|110\rangle$

3. Now that we have our state prepared, we can begin transforming it using QFT.

Let's review our transformation equation with our state $|110\rangle$:

$$|\Psi\rangle = \frac{\left(|0\rangle + e^{2\pi i(0.0)}|1\rangle\right)\ldots\left(|0\rangle + e^{2\pi i(0.10)}|1\rangle\right)\left(|0\rangle + e^{2\pi i(0.110)}|1\rangle\right)}{\sqrt{8}}$$

This states that for each qubit where we apply a Hadamard gate, we will need to include rotations while traversing from the qubit down to the least significant qubit—hence, $j_n, \cdots, j_0$. As we traverse down, the qubit states decrease by each degree. This means each of the controlled phase rotations, **Control Rotation (CROT)**, is based on the following matrix representation:

$$\text{CROT}(\theta)_k = \begin{bmatrix} 1 & 0 & 0 & 0 \\ 0 & 1 & 0 & 0 \\ 0 & 0 & 1 & 0 \\ 0 & 0 & 0 & e^{i\theta} \end{bmatrix}$$

In the preceding equation, CROT(θ)$_k$ is the CU$_1$ gate, and the parameter θ is set as follows:

$$\theta = \frac{\pi}{2^{k-1}}$$

Therefore, we'll start with the most significant qubit, q$_2$, from our state $|\Psi\rangle$, as follows.

4. Starting at the most significant qubit, we'll add a Hadamard gate to the circuit:

```
# Import the value pi for our rotations
from numpy import pi


# Always start from the most significant qubit,
# in this case it's q2.
# Step 1, add a Hadamard gate
qc.h(2)
```

5. Now that we have our first step, the next step is to add CROT(θ) gates starting at *k=2*, which is the index of the most significant qubit position, q$_2$, and our parameter θ starts at the following:

$$\theta = \frac{\pi}{2^{k-1}} = \frac{\pi}{2^{2-1}} = \frac{\pi}{2}$$

We add the CROT gates from most significant to least significant, starting at pi/2, and doubling the denominator of the parameter as we move down each qubit:

```
# Step 2, add CROT gates from most significant qubit
qc.cu1(pi/2, 1, 2)
```

6. We then repeat this as we traverse from the current qubit down to the next qubit—in this case, q$_0$:

```
# Step 3, add another CROT from 2 to the next qubit down,
# while doubling the phase denominator
qc.cu1(pi/4, 0, 2)


# Draw the circuit
qc.draw()
```

As we are traversing down, the denominator on the parameter is doubling in size as well, such that the next parameter θ is as follows:

$$\theta = \frac{\pi}{2^2} = \frac{\pi}{4}$$

This renders the following circuit, which now includes the Hadamard gate and the two CROT gates:

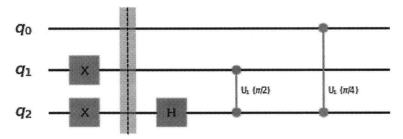

Figure 14.6 – The first set of transformations starting from the most significant qubit

7. That completes the first level, which dealt with the most significant qubit. We will now move down to the next qubit (the second most significant qubit) and repeat the process of adding a Hadamard gate, followed by CROT(θ) gates, where the phase rotations get smaller as we traverse down each qubit. Let's continue to the next qubit:

```
# Now that we finished from 2 down to 0
# We'll drop to the next least significant qubit and
# start again,
# Step 1, add a Hadamard gate
qc.h(1)
```

8. This is the same as *step 4* of adding a Hadamard gate; now we apply the control rotation gate in the same manner as we did earlier and then draw the circuit:

```
# Step 2, add Control Rotation (CROT) gates from most
# significant towards
# least significant starting a pi/2, and doubling the
# denominator
# as you go down each qubit.
qc.cu1(pi/2, 0, 1)


# Draw the circuit
```

```
qc.draw()

# Now that we finished from 1 down to 0
# We'll drop to the next least significant qubit and
# start again.
```

This will complete the second transformation, which will render the following circuit, which starts with a Hadamard gate and then appends the CROT gates afterward:

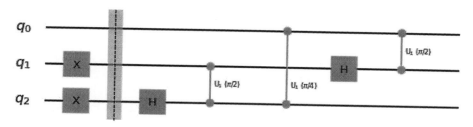

Figure 14.7 – The next transformation set starting at the next qubit down

9.   Next, we will run our transformation on the last qubit, and then draw the circuit:

```
# Step 1, add a Hadamard gate
qc.h(0)
# Since we are at the least significant qubit, we are
# done!

# Draw the circuit
qc.draw()
```

Since this is the last qubit and the least significant qubit, it has no lower levels, so we complete the CROT phase of the QFT. This renders the following circuit so far:

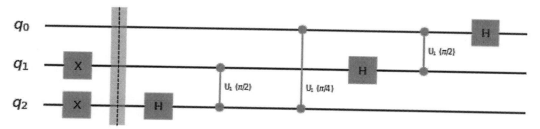

Figure 14.8 – The final transformation of our QFT circuit

10. Finally, once we have all rotations set, we need to apply swap gates in order to reverse our results. We need to do this to complete the QFT and set the values in the proper order. The swap is performed from the outermost qubits moving inward until you reach the last two qubits in the middle (if the total number of qubits is even), or until you reach the last two pairs with a single qubit in the middle (if the total number of qubits is odd).

To simplify this, we can create a function that will swap the outer qubits and work its way toward the middle. In this case, since we only have three qubits, we will only swap the outer two qubits, as follows:

```
# Define a function which will add the swap gates to the
# outer
# pair of qubits
def add_swap_gates(qc_swaps, qubits):
    for qubit in range(qubits//2):
        qc_swaps.swap(qubit, qubits-qubit-1)
    return qc_swaps
```

11. Now, we can run our quantum circuit through the add_swap_gates function and complete the circuit:

```
qft_circuit = add_swap_gates(qc, num_qubits)
qft_circuit.draw()
```

This will render our QFT circuit, which encodes our '110' value, as follows:

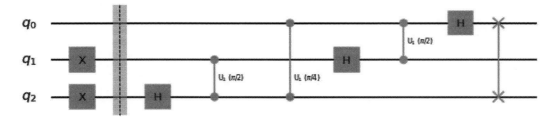

Figure 14.9 – The QFT circuit that encodes '110'

12. To visualize our QFT results, we can execute the preceding circuit using the state vector to see our final QFT encoding for each qubit:

```
# Get the state vector simulator to view our final QFT
# state
backend = Aer.get_backend("statevector_simulator")

# Execute the QFT circuit and visualize the results
statevector = execute(qft_circuit,
            backend=backend).result().get_statevector()
plot_bloch_multivector(statevector)
```

The preceding code results in the following encoding for each qubit:

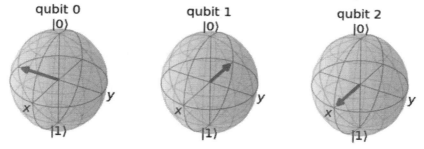

Figure 14.10 – A Bloch sphere representation of the '110' QFT encoded value

Note here that each qubit is in a superposition state and varies by phase based on the '110' encoded value. We can also represent this using the qsphere object, which will have the same information, only represented in a single sphere object:

```
plot_state_qsphere(statevector)
```

In the following diagram, we can see that the information is encoded into the QSphere and has its encoded representation in the phase and state vector indicated by the color wheel and QSphere, respectively:

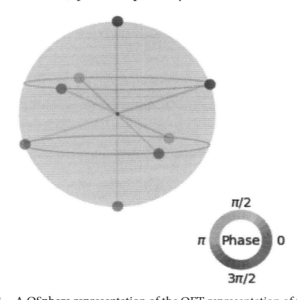

Figure 14.11 – A QSphere representation of the QFT representation of the '110' state

Congratulations! You have just completed encoding your first QFT! This is an algorithm that you will see in many other algorithms that depend on periodic functionality.

In this section, we learned about the QFT algorithm and implemented it as well. With an understanding of the basis of state transformation, you are now able to leverage this in many period functions and algorithms, such as estimating Eigenvalues or unitary matrices and factoring discrete logarithms.

Next, we will look at one of the more famous algorithms that leverages the QFT algorithm: **Shor's algorithm**.

Understanding Shor's algorithm

Probably one of the most discussed quantum algorithms, even for those who know very little of the numerical theory behind it, **Shor's algorithm** has gained popularity because of its ability to factor two numbers with some speed-up over classical systems. This might not seem too impressive for those who are not familiar with how factorization is used in various algorithms.

The most popular of these is the RSA algorithm, which is the algorithm used to encrypt much of today's data. Information such as bank records, passwords, health records, and pretty much any data that currently implements the RSA algorithm as part of its secure infrastructure is most likely leveraging factorization of prime numbers. The reason why this is so widely used is that it would take a very long time to determine two factored prime numbers of a product, particularly when the product is very large.

Shor's algorithm gained its popularity because of its ability to swiftly factor out integers, specifically its ability to solve period-finding problems in polynomial time. It's this period-finding algorithm that we will focus on in this section. We'll also leverage the built-in algorithms that are provided to us by Qiskit Aqua to implement Shor's algorithm. Before we do that, let's review the problem we are trying to solve.

Understanding a Shor's problem

The problem we are trying to find is actually very simple to describe. Imagine I provide you with a number, N, and I guarantee that the number N is a product of two prime integers. The problem is for you to find the two prime numbers that when multiplied, result in N. This can be represented as $a \times b = N$, where a and b are prime numbers, and N is the product.

This is a simple problem if the number is small, but gets exponentially complex as the prime numbers a and b get larger.

For example, if I were to give you the value $N = 15$, it would not take you too long to work out the problem. You'd just list out all prime numbers from 1 through 15, and multiply each out until you find the total, which in this case, would be 3 and 5.

Now imagine if I were to provide you with the following number for N:

$$N = 170,141,183,460,469,231,731,687,303,715,884,105,727$$

You can imagine how difficult this would be for you to do by hand. Just to give you an idea of the magnitude of the complexity, the current largest prime number, according to the Great Internet Mersenne Prime Search, has 24,862,048 digits!

RSA depends on this prime factorization complexity as part of its encryption process, which provides protection to our data as it's incredibly difficult to determine the factored prime numbers. That is until 1994, when Peter Shor published his paper *Algorithms for quantum computation: discrete logarithms and factoring*. In this ground-breaking paper, he discussed how to factor an integer in polynomial time, which works out to $\log N$.

In the next section, we'll review the process specifically, followed by implementing it using the Aqua built-in Shor algorithm to factor a number N.

Implementing Shor's algorithm

What Shor's algorithm describes is merely how to factor out a number N. We saw in the previous section how difficult a task this could be. We'll now review the process that Peter Shor developed into his now-famous algorithm. We'll start with a simple example: let's work on factoring out $N = 21$. The following is an outline of Shor's factoring algorithm:

1. The first step is to select our random base value a, such that $1 < a < N$.

2. Next, we want to confirm that the **greatest common denominator (gcd)** of a and N is not 1:

$$gcd(a, N) = 1$$

    If we chose a value a that is the gcd of N, then it will be equal to 1, then we can safely say we have found a factor of N. For example, if we choose a to be 5 and N to be 15, then we have chosen a as the gcd since there is no larger value to factor 15. Otherwise, we can conclude that a and N are co-prime values and can continue on to the next step.

3. Next, we will search for a value order r of a mod N, where $a^r = 1$ mod N. If we happen to find that r is an odd number, then we will need to go back and start again with another value of a. Otherwise, we move on when r is an even number. The reason for wanting r as an even number is so that we can apply it to the following formula:

$$\left(a^{\frac{r}{2}} + 1\right)\left(a^{\frac{r}{2}} - 1\right) = 0 \bmod N$$

4. If either of the two factors in the previous equation does not resolve to 1, then we can conclude that we have found one of the factors of N and we are done!

5. However, if both resolve to 1, then we must go back and restart with a new value for a.

Let's give this a try using the Qiskit Aqua implementation of Shor's algorithm and see whether we can find the factors of a number N:

1. Open a new Qiskit Notebook and let the autogenerated cell run. Once completed, we'll import the Aqua library modules we will be using to implement Shor's algorithm:

```
# Import Shor's algorithm library
from qiskit.aqua.algorithms import Shor
```

```
# Import the QuantumInstance module that will allow us to
# run the algorithm on a simulator and a quantum computer
from qiskit.aqua import QuantumInstance
```

Once you've successfully imported the modules, we'll define our values. We'll start with something simple by setting N to 21 and a to 3:

```
# Declare the product 'N', and our base 'a'
N = 21
a = 3
```

Now, we know by observation that when a = 3, gcd(3,21) is equal to 1 and we are done. We will nonetheless run this to confirm that the Aqua implementation of Shor's algorithm checks for the restriction of *step 2* from our outline (listed previously).

2.   Next, we will configure QuantumInstance by setting the backend to the simulator, and the number of shots to 1024:

```
# Configure backend simulator parameters
backend = Aer.get_backend('qasm_simulator')
shots = 1024


# Initialize the QuantumInstance object which will
# execute Shor's algorithm
qi = QuantumInstance(backend=backend, shots=shots)
```

3.   Now that we have set QuantumInstance, let's pass it in our parameters to Shor's algorithm and construct the Shor's algorithm object with the parameter values we provided:

```
shors_algorithm = Shor(N=N, a=a, quantum_instance = qi)
```

When constructing the Shor's algorithm object, you should expect to see the following ValueError exception:

```
ValueError: The integer a needs to satisfy a < N and
gcd(a, N) = 1.
```

This verifies that the Shor's algorithm object does in fact verify that *step 2* is satisfied before moving on.

4. So now, let's change our value of a to 2 and try again. Go back to the previous cell where we initialized our value for a and set it to 2, which would look like the following:

```
# Declare the product 'N', and our base 'a'
N = 21
a = 2
```

Once the previous cell has completed running with the new value of a, proceed back down to the cell that raised the `ValueError` exception and rerun that cell again. This time, you should not expect to see any exception raised.

5. After the construction of Shor's algorithm has completed, we can now run the algorithm on `QuantumInstance` we created:

```
results = shors_algorithm.run()
```

This will run Shor's algorithm based on the values we have provided. This may take a few moments based on the performance of the system at the time you executed it.

6. After the results are returned, we can simply print out the factors from our result object, as follows:

```
print(results['factors'])
```

This will print out the results, which we can see is the value we expected:

```
[[3, 7]]
```

Try experimenting with a few different values. However, keep in mind that Shor's algorithm itself is very complex and requires a very large quantum volume to factor larger numbers, so do not be too surprised if you see some errors raised.

This brings us to a very important factor to note here. There really shouldn't be any concern regarding your data security just yet from current near-term quantum computers, as they do not yet have sufficient quantum volume to break the current encryption systems due to the limited capacity. Once these machines expand, of course, this may be a different story. But, of course, there is so much research currently in progress using both classical and quantum solutions to help prevent these forms of potential risk. Research such as **post-quantum cryptography** will provide new techniques that can continue to keep our data safe.

In this section, we learned about periodic quantum algorithms and how they can be implemented into a quantum circuit. These algorithms were, namely, Simon's problem, the QFT algorithm, and Shor's algorithm.

This now brings us to another search algorithm. Where Shor's helped us search for factors of a number, Grover's algorithm will help us search for information using superposition, entanglement, and interference to find a hidden value by different means.

Learning about Grover's search algorithm

Search algorithms are unique in that they can be leveraged by various algorithms to find information, whether in a data repository or a list of values such as features in an image. The advantage to quantum, of course, is in the potential for the speed-up of the search. **Grover's algorithm** is one such example. It uses a well-known technique that allows the use of interference to amplify certain states in our quantum circuit in a way that will increase the amplitude of the value we are searching for and decrease those that we are not. Let's start, as always, by describing the problem, where each state is analogous to an entry in an unordered list.

Learning about the problem

The problem here is also very simple: we are given a set of states where all except one has a value set to 1 and all others are set to 0. We wish to identify which one of those states is set to 1.

Classically, this can be done in, in the best case, 1 step, if the first value is set. In the worst case, it would take N steps, where N is the total number of states and the last state is set. This means that on average, it will take $N/2$ steps to find the value as we would need to check each value individually.

Clearly, this is not ideal if our set is a very large list. We need to find a better way to find our value. This is where, in 1996, Lov Grover came in and discovered a way to solve this problem with his now-famous quantum algorithm. We'll step through the implementation of Grover's algorithm as we try to search for a value in a three-qubit circuit.

To describe this problem using functions, we can state the following, given a function:

$$f\{0,1\}^n \rightarrow \{0,1\}$$

From the preceding equation, $f(x) = 0$ for all cases of x except for a specific case, x^*, such that $f(x^*) = 1$. Find the value of x^*. Since we will be working with qubits, let's select a value N, such that $N = 2^n$.

Now that we have defined our problem, let's step through Grover's search algorithm.

Understanding Grover's search algorithm

Grover's algorithm is similar to the Deutsch-Jozsa and Bernstein-Vazirani algorithms, in that it too leverages an oracle. The difference is that it also leverages interference in a way that it will increase the amplitude of the state we are searching for while decreasing all other states, which in turn increases the speed by $\sqrt{N}$, where N is the number of states to search.

We'll begin by first explaining the Grover's search process in order to obtain an intuitive understanding of how it works. For a deeper description of the mathematics behind this, I would recommend the book *Dancing with Qubits* by Robert S. Sutor, which covers this in greater detail.

Grover's search algorithm can be broken down into two main components—perhaps three, if you count initializing all qubits into superposition and adding measurements at the end—but that is something that most quantum algorithms do, so we'll just stick to the two main points. The first is referred to as **Grover's oracle**, and the second is the **Grover diffusion operator**.

In this example, we will describe a two-qubit system that when placed in superposition by placing a Hadamard gate to each qubit, provides four possible states—**00**, **01**, **10**, and **11**—as follows:

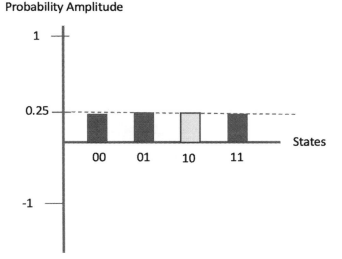

Figure 14.12 – Two qubits in a superposition state

When in this state, the average equals the probability amplitude, which in this case is **0.25**, as indicated by the dotted line across the top of each state.

For this example, we'll say the state that we wish to search for is the state '10'.

The first component is the **oracle**, U_f. This is where we generally tag the value we are searching for. By tagging, I mean we will signal that the state that we are searching for will be identified by simply changing the sign of the state from positive to negative. The transition would be as follows:

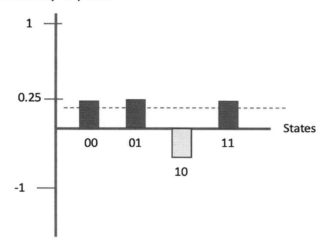

Figure 14.13 – Changing the sign of the state to negative

Now that we have changed the sign, we can't unfortunately just measure and go at this point—mainly because as we know, the probability amplitudes are squared, so our results would all still be equal, which does not provide us with any new information about what we are searching for. However, since we are working with amplitudes, we can leverage interference here by increasing the amplitude of the state we tagged and decreasing the amplitude of the other states. *How do we do this?* By incorporating the second component of Grover's search, the **diffusion operator**.

The second component of Grover's algorithm is the **Grover diffusion operator**. Here, we will be performing a mathematical step known as *inversion about the mean*. What this does is inverts the distance between the average and the peak of each state. This is analogous to having each state flip reflectively about the average mean. Visually, the transition will be as follows:

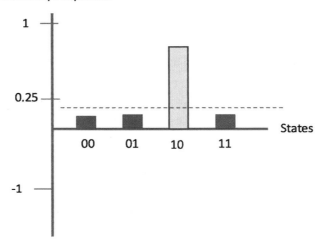

Figure 14.14 – Inversion about the mean amplifies the states constructively and destructively

As we can see from the results of performing the inversion about the mean, the amplification of the tagged state is now significantly higher than the other states. If we were to now take a measurement, we would see that the result with the higher probability is the state we are searching for. Keep in mind, of course, that this is all done with a single query to our quantum circuit!

One thing to note is that when the number of states, N, is large, this means we will need to repeat both steps more times. The number of times to optimize the results is $\sqrt{2^n}$, where n is the number of qubits.

Let's implement Grover's search algorithm next.

Implementing Grover's search algorithm

As usual, we'll explain each step described in the previous section while we work through the algorithm step by step. To start, create a new Qiskit Notebook for this example and work through the following:

1. We'll begin by declaring the value we want to set. Let's set the value to `110`, or `6`. This way, we can use a three-qubit circuit to implement Grover's algorithm and place all the qubits in superposition by adding a Hadamard gate to each qubit:

```
# Set the state we wish to search
N = '110'
num_qubits = len(N)


# Create the quantum circuit
qc = QuantumCircuit(num_qubits)


# Set all qubits in superposition
qc.h(range(num_qubits))
qc.barrier()


#Draw the circuit
qc.draw()
```

This will render our initialized circuit:

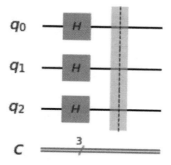

Figure 14.15 – Initialized quantum circuit in superposition

2. Next, we want to encode the state that we want to search—in this case, it is the state $|110\rangle$. Here, we will reverse the state and encode N in the circuit:

```
# Reverse the state so it's in proper qubit ordering
N = N[::-1]

# Encode N into our circuit
for idx in range(num_qubits):
    if N[idx] == '0':
        qc.x(idx)
qc.barrier()

# Draw the circuit
qc.draw()
```

For each step, we will add a barrier so that we can see the process rendered:

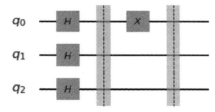

Figure 14.16 – Encoding our state '110', we mark the '0' qubits in the state with an X gate

3. Next, we will create Grover's oracle. What we will do here is first set the most significant qubit in a superposition state, followed by a CNOT gate where the target is the most significant qubit, and the source is all the other qubits. Then, place another Hadamard gate on the most significant qubit to complete the oracle. This will negate the state that we set in the previous source cell, $|110\rangle$:

```
# Create the Grover oracle for our 3-qubit quantum
# circuit
qc.h(2)
qc.ccx(0, 1, 2)
qc.h(2)
qc.barrier()

# Draw the circuit
qc.draw()
```

The preceding code renders the following circuit, which we see sets the two CNOT gates in our oracle surrounded by **H** gates on the most significant qubit:

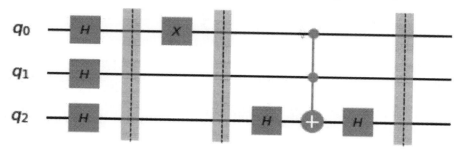

Figure 14.17 – Applying Grover's oracle to the circuit

4. Now, we want to reset the state that we are searching in the circuit so that it returns to the superposition value:

```
# Reset the value after the oracle
for idx in range(num_qubits):
    if N[idx] == '0':
        qc.x(idx)
qc.barrier()


# Draw the circuit
qc.draw()
```

The preceding code completes Grover's oracle, which we described earlier as the first component of Grover's search algorithm:

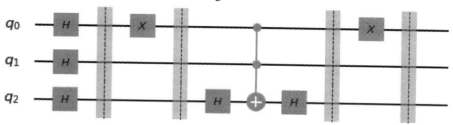

Figure 14.18 – The first component of Grover's search algorithm

5. Next, we will implement the second component, the Grover diffusion operator. We start by applying all the qubits in a superposition state:

```
# Set all qubits in superposition
qc.h(range(num_qubits))
qc.x(range(num_qubits))
qc.barrier()


# Draw the circuit
qc.draw()
```

This renders the following superposition state, followed by Grover's oracle:

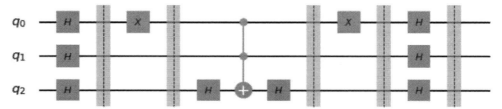

Figure 14.19 – The first step in the Grover diffusion operator: apply H gates to all qubits

6. Next, we will apply another oracle as we did previously across all qubits, where the most significant qubit is set as the target of the two CNOT gates:

```
# Apply another oracle, same as the previous,
qc.h(2)
qc.ccx(0, 1, 2)
qc.h(2)
qc.barrier()


# Draw the circuit
qc.draw()
```

This renders the next step in the diffusion operator—that is, invert about the mean:

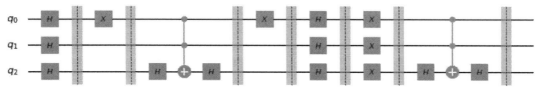

Figure 14.20 – The second step of the diffusion operator to invert about the mean

7. Finally, we wrap up the Grover diffusion operator by applying the first step in reverse. Since we applied a set of **H** gates across all qubits, followed by a set of **X** gates, also across all qubits, we will reverse this in the following manner. Apply **X** gates across all qubits, then apply **H** gates across all qubits:

```
# Reapply the X rotations on all qubits
qc.x(range(num_qubits))


qc.barrier()


# Reapply Hadamard gates to all qubits
qc.h(range(num_qubits))


# Draw the circuit
qc.draw()
```

The preceding code completes the Grover diffusion operator component of the quantum circuit:

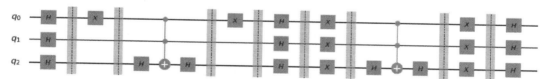

Figure 14.21 – The complete Grover's algorithm circuit

8. Now, we'll just add measurement operators and prepare to run the circuit on the backend, but first on a simulator:

```
# Add measurement operators
qc.measure_all()


# Draw the circuit
qc.draw()


# Run on the qasm simulator
backend = Aer.get_backend('qasm_simulator')
# Execute the circuit on the backend
job = execute(qc, backend, shots=1024)
```

```
# Extract the results
results = job.result()
counts = results.get_counts(qc)
```

The preceding code will prepare the following quantum circuit to run on either a simulator or quantum computer:

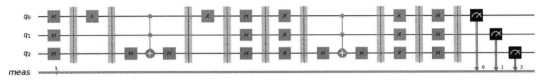

Figure 14.22 – The complete quantum circuit ready to run on a simulator or quantum system

9. We'll start by setting our backend to the Qasm simulator and execute our circuit:

```
# Run on the qasm simulator
backend = Aer.get_backend('qasm_simulator')

# Execute the circuit on the backend
job = execute(qc, backend, shots=1024)

# Extract the results
results = job.result()
counts = results.get_counts(qc)

# Print and plot results
print(counts)
plot_histogram(counts)
```

After executing the circuit, this will print and plot our results as follows:

```
{'001': 35, '011': 42, '010': 25, '101': 32, '110': 782,
'111': 37, '100': 38, '000': 33}
```

In the following histogram, we can see that the state we are searching has the higher probability, a probability of almost 80%, whereas all the other states have a significantly lower probability of around 3%:

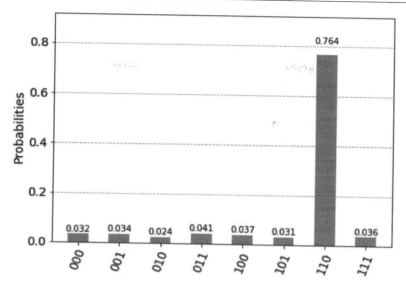

Figure 14.23 – Results of executing Grover's search of state 110 on a quantum simulator

Success! As expected, our Grover's algorithm implementation has found the state within a single query.

10. Now, let's try it on a quantum device. We'll select the quantum computer that is the least busy and operational and has the number of qubits necessary to run our quantum circuit. We'll include our job watcher widget just so that we can monitor our progress:

```
# Execute the circuit on the least busy quantum computer
from qiskit.providers.ibmq import least_busy

backend = least_busy(provider.backends(filters=lambda x:
    x.configuration().n_qubits >= (num_qubits) and
        not x.configuration().simulator and x.status().
        operational==True))
print("Set backend: ", backend)

# Launch the job watcher widget
%qiskit_job_watcher
```

The preceding code will print out the least-busy quantum computer and assign it to the backend variable.

11. We can now execute this as we did previously with the simulator, then print and plot the results:

```
# Execute the circuit on the backend
job = execute(qc, backend, shots=1024)

# Extract the results
results = job.result()
counts = results.get_counts(qc)

# Print and plot results
print(counts)
plot_histogram(counts)
```

Once completed, you should see something similar to the following output:

```
{'001': 132, '011': 127, '010': 147, '101': 97, '110':
238, '111': 88, '100': 101, '000': 94}
```

This, of course, depends on the device itself as each system is different from one another. However, the results should be clear that the state with the highest probability is the state that we are searching for—in this case, $|110\rangle$.

We also obtain the following histogram:

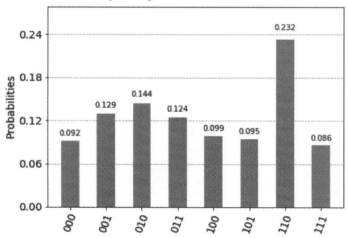

Figure 14.24 – Results of executing Grover's search of state 110 on a quantum computer

As we can see here, the result with the highest probability is the state we are searching for, and the other states have a lower probability. However, note that both the probabilities of the state we are searching for and those that we are not are not as spread out as compared to when we ran this on the quantum simulator. This is, of course, because of noise and low quantum volume. Luckily, you can remedy this by applying noise mitigation filters in **Qiskit Ignis**. But for now, we can see enough of a difference to observe that the Grover's search algorithm that we implemented does indeed identify the state we are searching for.

Congratulations! You have successfully implemented a variety of quantum algorithms, which are foundational to understanding how quantum computers are different in solving problems than classical systems and how they have the potential to solve real-world problems.

Summary

There are many algorithms that implement many of the techniques we covered in this chapter, such as amplitude amplification, oracles, phase kickbacks, and much more, which you will see used in many other algorithms, such as the **quantum amplitude estimation** and **variational quantum Eigensolver** algorithms.

I do strongly suggest trying variations of these algorithms yourself to get a better feel and understanding as to how they work.

We also used the algorithms that are built into Qiskit Aqua, which allows you as a researcher to leverage the algorithms. You have now gained the skills to integrate these algorithms into your existing research or applications without having to worry about developing circuits, mitigating against noise, or any of the other components that make up an algorithm in Aqua. This book has already done the heavy lifting for you, so you just have to implement the algorithm and process the results as you see fit.

Questions

1. What other problems can you solve using periodic functions?
2. Implement QFT on a five-qubit state—for example, `'10110'`.
3. Since quantum gates are reversible, how would you create an inverse QFT on the encoded value we created, `'110'`, or $|\tilde{6}\rangle$?

4. Using Grover's algorithm, find the following states: `'101'`, `'001'`, and `'010'`.

5. How many iterations of Grover's algorithm would you need to run to find the state $|10101\rangle$?

6. Rerun the Grover's search example. Only repeat Grover's oracle and the diffusion operator twice and note the difference in the result. What do you see that is different? What would you expect to change if you ran it three times?

7. Does Qiskit Aqua also include classical algorithms along with the quantum algorithms?

8. What other algorithms are included with Qiskit Aqua?

Appendix A
Resources

In addition to this book, there are many other resources available that you can leverage to get a deeper understanding of quantum computing and where to find the latest research. This appendix will include a non-exhaustive list of resources that will provide you with more details on the latest technological advances so you can put what you learned in this book into practice on the **IBM Quantum Experience**:

- **The Qiskit Community**: The website for this community is `https://qiskit.org/advocates`. This is where you can find out about joining the Qiskit community as a **Qiskit Advocate**, or find out about upcoming events that you can join or even host yourself. There are meetups, hackathons, Qiskit camps, and many other events are listed where you can meet with other quantum developers and researchers, and expand your learning by collaborating with others.

- **The Qiskit documentation**: The link for the full documentation is `https://qiskit.org/documentation/`. This is the main documentation page for all the Qiskit elements discussed in this book. It has references to all the code and links to the source code. Tutorials are also included in the documentation to assist your understanding of new features and how they are applied. You can also explore various tutorials for finance (`https://qiskit.org/documentation/tutorials/finance/index.html`), chemistry (`https://qiskit.org/documentation/tutorials/chemistry/index.html`), and optimization (`https://qiskit.org/documentation/tutorials/optimization/index.html`) here.

- **The Qiskit Interactive Textbook**: The link for this textbook is `https://qiskit.org/textbook/preface.html`. This is a living document containing many interactive exercises that build upon basic knowledge, such as linear algebra, and guide you through to the advanced topics of quantum computing. The interactive pages enable the user to work on the content in parallel with your project.

- **The Qiskit GitHub repo**: The GitHub repository link for Qiskit is `https://github.com/Qiskit`. This is the official Qiskit GitHub repository where you will find the code for all the Qiskit elements. Like most other open GitHub source projects, you can fork and contribute to the open source project by either mitigating any issues or implementing a design request. You can also submit requests for enhancements or issues you may find. If it is your first time, it is recommended to work on issues labeled *good first issue*.

- **Quantum Algorithm Zoo**: As the welcome page indicates, *this site is a comprehensive catalog of quantum algorithms*. It provides details about the algorithm type, speedup, and a description of the algorithm. They are grouped by type such as *algebraic and number theoretic, oracular, approximation and simulation*, and several others. This is very useful should you want to get a quick overview of an algorithm and how it works. The link for this page is `http://quantumalgorithmzoo.org/`.

- **Arxiv: Quantum Physics**: This is an open access documentation repository for scholarly papers and articles, at `https://arxiv.org/archive/quant-ph`. This resource is for articles that specifically cover the topic of quantum physics, a topic that also includes many quantum computation papers.

- **IBM Q Network quantum papers**: This resource provides a list of all research papers that were published by the IBM quantum research team in partnerships with **IBM Q Network** partners, and members. This resource's URL is `https://ibm.biz/q-network-arxiv`.

The link is an **AirTable**, an online hybrid spreadsheet-database, which lists the industry domains to which a given project is relevant, such as *finance, optimization, chemistry, machine learning*, and so on. It also lists the name of the company and which quantum computers or simulators they used in their research. Arxiv links to all the papers listed are also included. This is a great resource to have to ensure you keep up to speed on the latest research and the wider quantum research landscape.

- **The Qiskit YouTube channel**: The URL for this channel is `https://www.youtube.com/channel/UC1BNq7mCMf5xm8baE_VM13A`. This is the official Qiskit YouTube channel on which there are several series on research and development with frequently scheduled uploads to keep viewers up to date on the latest content and research from the IBM quantum research team, IBM Q Network partners, and of course the Qiskit community team.

- **SciRate**: This site (`https://scirate.com/`) gathers the top-rated Arxiv papers in each category, including quantum physics. It's a good resource should you have time to read what most people are reading about from Arxiv.

- **Qiskit Events**: Finally, Qiskit Events is the resource that will keep you up to date on any upcoming events hosted by the Qiskit community (`https://qiskit.org/events`). You can also filter this list by region and view previous events and playbacks, if available.

Assessments

Chapter 1 – Exploring the IBM Quantum Experience

Question 1

Which view contains your API token?

Answer

The **My Account** view has your API token available, and it is where you can also regenerate a different token if needed.

Question 2

Which device in your list has the fewest qubits?

Answer

The availability of the device with the fewest qubits will vary based on the quantum devices available. But at the time of writing, there is a device with just 1 qubit, **ibmq_armonk**, which is Pulse-enabled. The other devices with the fewest qubits are the various 5-qubit machines.

Question 3

How many connections are there in the device with the fewest qubits?

Answer

This may vary based on the available quantum devices, but you can determine this by selecting the quantum device from the list of backends and counting the number of edges between qubits. Currently, there are 4 to 5 connections based on the different qubit topologies.

Question 4

What are the two tools called that are used to generate quantum circuits?

Answer

Circuit Composer, which is a UI, and **Quantum Labs/Notebooks**, which are based on Jupyter Notebooks with Qiskit pre-installed.

Question 5

Which view would provide you with a list of basis gates for a selected device?

Answer

The backend list view, from the IBM Quantum Experience main landing page (dashboard), will provide you with a list of basis gates for a selected device.

Chapter 2 – Circuit Composer – Creating a Quantum Circuit

Question 1

Using the entangled coin-flip experiment, re-run the experiment. What is the state vector of the results?

Answer

This will vary each time you run the circuit, but the results will have roughly the same average of about 50% for 0 and 1.

Question 2

What are the result states if you were to add a NOT gate before the Hadamard gate in the entangled coin-flip experiment's circuit?

Answer

As you are now starting the second qubit in a state other than the initial state by adding a NOT gate, the results will be opposite from each other – that is, either **01** or **10**.

Question 3

Using the entangled coin-flip experiment from the circuit editor, switch the measurements so that the output of q_0 reads out to classic bit 1, and q_1 reads out to classic bit 0. What are the two states in the result and what are their probabilities?

Answer

Changing the readout location for the measurement operator can be done by the UI, as follows:

1. First, select one of the measurement operators, then select the **Edit** button, located at the top left of the measurement operator (the pencil icon).

2. Change the assigned bit from 0 to 1, or 1 to 0 if you selected the second measurement operator.

3. Repeat the preceding steps to change subsequent measurement operators.

Question 4

What would the result states be if you were to add a Hadamard gate to the second qubit before the CNOT gate in the entangled coin-flip experiment's circuit?

Answer

The results would be, for q_0 and q_1, an equal probability of 50% – that is, **00** and **11**.

Chapter 3 – Creating Quantum Circuits Using Quantum Lab Notebooks

Question 1

Quantum Lab notebooks are built upon which application editor?

Answer

Quantum Lab notebooks are built on Jupyter Notebook with the latest version of Qiskit installed.

Question 2

How would you create a five-qubit circuit, as we did in *Chapter 2, Circuit Composer – Creating a Quantum Circuit*?

Answer

The circuit contained a Hadamard gate (H), and a Control-NOT gate (cx) with q_0 as the control and q_1 as the target, followed by measurement operators on both qubits, represented as follows:

```
qc = QuantumCircuit(2,2)
qc.h(0)
qc.cx(0,1)
qc.measure([0,1],[0,1])
qc.draw()
```

Question 3

To run the experiment on another real device, which quantum computer would you select if your quantum circuit has more than 5 qubits?

Answer

Any of the quantum computers listed in the available backend quantum devices would be ideal to run a quantum circuit, as long as the number of qubits is 5 or more. Therefore, **ibmq_armonk** would not be a valid choice as it only has 1 qubit, and ibmq_qasm_simulator is a simulator and not an actual quantum computer.

Question 4

When you run on a real device, can you explain why you get extra values when compared to running on a simulator?

Answer

The other values displayed are due to the effect of noise on the quantum system. Simulators are ideal quantum systems that do not have the effects of noise.

Chapter 4 – Understanding Basic Quantum Computing Principles

Question 1

How would you create a circuit that entangles two qubits where each qubit is different (that is, **01, 10**)?

Answer

We can use the following code to create a circuit that entangles two qubits:

```
qc = QuantumCircuit(2,2)
qc.h(0)
qc.x(1)
qc.cx(0,1)
qc.measure([0,1], [0,1])
qc.draw()
```

Question 2

Which simulator is used to display the Bloch sphere?

Answer

As the Bloch sphere displays the state vector of the quantum circuit, the **statevector** simulator would be ideal.

Question 3

Execute the superposition experiment with the `shots=1` parameter, then `shots=1000`, and then `shots=8000`. What is the difference?

Answer

In your code, just change the argument for `shots` to the various options selected, as follows:

```
backend = execute(qc, backend, shots=1)
backend = execute(qc, backend, shots=1000)
backend = execute(qc, backend, shots=800)
```

Question 4

Run the quantum teleportation experiment on a real quantum device and describe the results compared to the simulator's results. What's different, if anything, and why? (*Hint*: noise affects near-term devices).

Answer

The results will be similar to that of the simulator. However, you will notice that some other results have small probabilities, which are due to the effects of noise.

Chapter 5 – Understanding the Quantum Bits (Qubit)

Question 1

What is the transpose of the single-qubit $|0\rangle$ state stated as a column vector?

Answer

The single-qubit $|0\rangle$ state is represented as a column vector, $\begin{bmatrix} 1 \\ 0 \end{bmatrix}$. Therefore the transpose of the single-qubit $|0\rangle$ state would be represented as a row vector, $[1,0]$.

Question 2

Which would provide visual information about the phase of a qubit—the Bloch sphere or the Qiskit sphere?

Answer

The Qiskit sphere (QSphere) includes a checkbox to visualize the phase information.

Question 3

Can you visualize multi-qubits on the Bloch sphere? If yes, then why? If no, then why not?

Answer

No, we can't visualize multi-qubits on the Bloch sphere, not as easily as the QSphere. The Bloch sphere is generally leveraged to illustrate a single qubit vector position for a given state, whereas the QSphere includes the phase.

Question 4

Write out the tensor product of three-qubit states in all forms.

Answer

The resulting basis states for a three-qubit system are $|000\rangle$, $|001\rangle$, $|010\rangle$, $|011\rangle$, $|100\rangle$, $|101\rangle$, $|110\rangle$, $|111\rangle$.

Question 5

What is the probability amplitude of a three-qubit system?

Answer

The amplitude of a three-qubit system is $\frac{1}{\sqrt{2^n}}$, where n is the number of qubits, which results in $\frac{1}{\sqrt{2^3}} = \frac{1}{\sqrt{8}}$.

Question 6

What material is used to create the capacitors of a qubit?

Answer

Superconducting capacitors of a qubit are made of niobium.

Question 7

What are Josephson junctions made of?

Answer

Josephson junctions are made of aluminum.

Question 8

At what approximate temperature do the qubits have to be in order to operate properly?

Answer

The qubits have to be at approximately 15 millikelvins to operate properly.

Chapter 6 – Understanding Quantum Logic Gates

Question 1

For the multi-qubit gates, try flipping the source and target. Do you see a difference when you decompose the circuit?

Answer

No, there is no difference that can be seen, only that the source is now assigned to the opposite qubits.

Question 2

Decompose all the gates for both single- and multi-qubit circuits. What do you notice about how the universal gates are constructed?

Answer

The single gates are now displayed by their respective basis gate, including rotation values, if any. Multi-qubit gates, such as the Toffoli gate, are also broken down to specific gates used to construct the operation of the Toffoli gate between the assigned qubits.

Question 3

Implement the Toffoli gate where the target is the center qubit of a three-qubit circuit.

Answer

We use the following code to implement the Toffoli gate where the target is the center qubit of a three-qubit circuit:

```
qc = QuantumCircuit(3)
qc.ccx(0,2,1)
qc.draw()
```

Question 4

Decompose the Toffoli gate. How many gates in total are used to construct it?

Answer

When decomposing the Toffoli gate down to Hadamard, T, T dagger, and CX gates, there are a total of 15 gates, and it runs 12 operations deep.

Question 5

Apply the Toffoli gate along with a Hadamard gate to a state vector simulator and compare the results to that from the Qasm simulator. What differences do you see and why?

Answer

The Qasm simulator, since it runs 1024 shots by default, will produce a result of approximately 50% 000 and 50% 001, assuming placement of the Hadamard gate is in the first qubit. Whereas the state vector simulator, which only runs a single shot, will either result in the state 000 or 001; the results of which will vary depending on the qubit in which you placed the Hadamard gate.

Question 6

If you wanted to sort three qubits in the opposite direction, which gates would you use and in which order?

Answer

You can use the `swap` gate to switch the value of each qubit from one qubit to another (for an example of two qubits):

```
qc = QuantumCircuit(2)
qc.x(0)
# current state is '01'
qc.swap(0,1)
# current state is reversed, '10'
```

Question 7

Given a three-qubit circuit, how would you go about swapping the first and third qubits?

Answer

```
qc = QuantumCircuit(3)
qc.swap(0,2)
```

Question 8

Given a three-qubit circuit, how would you set the second qubit as the target of a Toffoli gate?

Answer

```
qc = QuantumCircuit(3)
qc.ccx(0,2,1)
```

Chapter 7 – Introducing Qiskit and Its Elements

Question 1

Which of the four elements would financial analysts use to integrate their risk analysis applications into a quantum computer?

Answer

Ideally, they would use Qiskit Aqua, as that provides APIs to algorithms that have already been created for general-purpose use or to construct without having to worry about the underlying fundamentals, such as circuit design, optimal performance, error correction, or other facets.

Question 2

In your own words, describe what each element would provide to a quantum algorithm researcher.

Answer

These should, in general, capture the functionality of each element. For example, **Terra** provides the underlying connection to the hardware via circuit/pulse schedules to manipulate the qubits on quantum computers.

Aer provides high-performance simulators, such as state vector, Qasm, pulse, and unitary simulators, and availability to generate noise models based on actual quantum computer configuration and properties.

Ignis facilitates both noise and error correction. **Aqua** provides a high-level class of content to integrate with a classical application.

Question 3

If you wanted to run schedules on a quantum computer, which simulator would you need to use?

Answer

The Pulse simulator.

Question 4

If you wanted to obtain the unitary of a circuit, which element would provide the necessary simulator?

Answer

Aer is the element that contains all the various simulators, including the unitary simulator.

Question 5

If you wanted to analyze the computational power of a quantum system, which element would your application need?

Answer

As **Quantum Volume** is a method used to determine the computational power of a quantum computer, we would need to use Ignis.

Question 6

Can you name and describe each of the simulators that are provided by Aer?

Answer

There are four simulators: QasmSimulator, StatevectorSimulator, UnitarySimulator, and PulseSimulator.

Question 7

Which module would you need to import in order to plot a histogram?

Answer

To import the histogram plotter (`plot_histogram`), you would need the module from the Terra element named `qiskit.visualization`.

Chapter 8 – Programming with Qiskit Terra

Question 1

What are the four elements of Qiskit?

Answer

Terra, Aer, Ignis, and Aqua.

Question 2

Construct a random quantum circuit with a width of 4 and a depth of 9.

Answer

```
from qiskit.circuit.random import random_circuit
#Circuit with a width = 4, a depth = 9
qc = random_circuit(4, 9, measure=True)
```

Question 3

Create a quantum circuit with the same width as the circuit you created in *Question 2* and concatenate it so that it is added before the random quantum circuit you created.

Answer

```
qc1 = random_circuit(4,2)
qc_combined = qc1 + qc
```

Question 4

Print the circuit properties of the concatenated quantum circuit from *Question 3* and specify the total number of operators, not including any measurement operators.

Answer

```
qc_combined.draw()
qc_combined.count_ops()
```

Question 5

Create a circuit with a parameterized R^Y gate that would rotate by an angle of $\pi/2$.

Answer

```
import numpy as np
from qiskit.circuit import Parameter
param_theta = Parameter('θ')
qc = QuantumCircuit(2)
qc.rz(param_theta,0)
qc = qc.bind_parameters({param_theta: np.pi/2})
qc.draw()
```

Question 6

Create and draw a schedule with any of the available waveforms from the Pulse library.

Answer

```
from qiskit.pulse.library import Gaussian, Constant,
GaussianSquare, Drag
amp = 1
sigma = 10
samples = 128
duration = 128
# Gaussian sample
gaussian_sample = Gaussian(samples, amp, sigma)
gaussian_sample.draw()
# Constant sample
```

```
constant_sample = Constant(duration, amp)
constant_sample.draw()
# Gaussian square sample
gaussian_square = GaussianSquare(duration, amp, sigma,
width=100)
gaussian_square.draw()
# Drag sample
drag = Drag(duration, amp, sigma, beta=5.5)
drag.draw()
```

Question 7

Using the **Provider** object, how many quantum systems do you have access to that have 5 or more qubits?

Answer

```
num_of_qubits = 5
backend = provider.backends(filters=lambda x:
                x.configuration().n_qubits >= num_of_qubits)
backend
```

Chapter 9 – Monitoring and Optimizing Quantum Circuits

Question 1

Create a filter that will return the least busy backend to run a quantum circuit that includes any constraint other than those covered in this book (*Hint*: use the `backend.configuration()` function to view other backend configuration variables).

Answer

The following code will filter all available backends for a quantum computer with more than 2 qubits, and a Quantum Volume greater than 8:

```
backends = provider.backends(filters=lambda x:
                x.configuration().n_qubits >= (2) and not
```

```
                    x.configuration().simulator and
                    x.configuration().quantum_volume > 8)
backends
```

Question 2

Can you name two components of the transpiler?

Answer

Pass and **PassManager**.

Question 3

Which component allows you to specify the passes to use?

Answer

PassManager is used to specify which passes are used and which passes can communicate with other passes.

Question 4

What is the depth of a Toffoli gate when decomposed?

Answer

The following code will add a Toffoli gate to a quantum circuit and then decompose it down to its composed gates, and then you can use the depth() function to print out the depth of the decomposed circuit:

```
qc = QuantumCircuit(3)
qc.ccx(0,1,2)
print(qc.decompose().depth())
```

Question 5

Is there a difference between when decomposing a Toffoli gate using `decompose()` versus the transpiler?

Answer

The `decompose()` function expands the gate based on its decomposition rules, whereas the transpiler decomposes circuits to its basis gate set as defined by the backend that it will execute on.

Question 6

What are the basis gates on the `ibmq_santiago` device?

Answer

```
backend = provider.get_backend('ibmq_santiago')
basis_gates = backend.configuration().basis_gates
print('Basis gates for ibmq_santiago: ', basis_gates)
```

Question 7

What are the five pass types?

Answer

Layout Selection, Routing, Optimizations, Basis Change, and Synthesis.

Question 8

What is the default `optimization_level` value when running the `execute()` function?

Answer

Optimization level 1.

Question 9

What are the default `optimization_level` values set for `TrivialLayout` and `DenseLayout`?

Answer

The default optimization levels are set to 1 by default regardless of pass selection. The `optimization_level` parameter is set in the `transpile()` function.

Chapter 10 – Executing Circuits Using Qiskit Aer

Question 1

Can you list all the simulators found in the Aer library?

Answer

The list of simulators can be generated using the `Aer.backends()` function.

Question 2

How many simulators are there altogether in Qiskit? (*Hint*: this includes Basic Aer, Aer, and IBM Quantum Provider.)

Answer

You can extract them from each module and see for yourself, as follows:

```
Aer.backends()
BasicAer.backends()
```

Question 3

Create a QSphere representation of a qubit on the negative Y axis, creating the state $\frac{|0\rangle - i|1\rangle}{\sqrt{2}}$, using only a single Hadamard gate along with the phase gates.

Answer

In order to accomplish this, you will need to set the qubit in a superposition state. This can be done using the Hadamard gate (H), which will place the qubit in the state $\frac{|0\rangle + |1\rangle}{\sqrt{2}}$.

After that, we will have to run a phase shift from the $|+\rangle$ state to the $\frac{|0\rangle - i\,|1\rangle}{\sqrt{2}}$ state, which would mean we need a phase gate to shift the state by a phase of $-\pi/2$, as follows:

```
qc = QuantumCircuit(1)
qc.h(0)
qc.sdg(0)
simulator = Aer.get_backend('statevector_simulator')
result = execute(qc, simulator).result()
statevector = result.get_statevector(qc)
statevector
```

Question 4

What must the initialized probability value of a circuit be in order to be valid?

Answer

The sum of the squares of the total `param` values in the initialize function argument must add up to 1, as in the following example, where $\frac{1}{\sqrt{2}}$ is set twice. So, if you take the sum of the squares, it will be equal to 1:

```
import numpy as np
qc = QuantumCircuit(2, 2)
init_qubits = [0, 1]
qc.initialize([1, 0, 0, 1] / np.sqrt(2), init_qubits)
```

Question 5

Can you use the QSphere to visualize both the phase and probability information of a qubit?

Answer

Yes, where the phase is given by the color of the state vectors and the probability is visualized by the size of the tips of the state vectors. The larger the diameter, the higher the probability.

Question 6

How would you apply a noise function to qubits 2, 3, and 4 of a five-qubit system?

Answer

For a NoiseModel readout error, you would apply the instructions to the qubit in the argument as follows:

```
from qiskit.providers.aer.noise import ReadoutError
from qiskit.providers.aer.noise import NoiseModel

readout_error = ReadoutError([[p0, p0_1], [p1_0, p1]])
# Apply the readout error to qubit 2-4, remember it is zero-
# based.
noise_model.add_readout_error(readout_error, [1,2,3])
```

Question 7

What would happen if you set the depolarization error values close to 1?

Answer

This will set the λ value to 1, therefore completely depolarizing the channel.

Question 8

If you applied a readout error equally to all qubits, what results would you expect and why?

Answer

When running on a simulator, rather than resulting in an ideal condition (no errors), you will instead see errors, where the significance of the errors is based on the set ReadoutError() parameters.

Chapter 11 – Mitigating Quantum Errors Using Ignis

Question 1

List the various characterizations of a qubit.

Answer

Calibrations, coherence, gates, and Hamiltonians.

Question 2

Which decoherence is analyzed using the Ramsey experiment?

Answer

With respect to decoherence, the Ramsey experiment is generally used to measure T_2^* (T_2 Star). The Hahn echo is used to measure T_2.

Question 3

What is the difference between relaxation and dephasing decoherence?

Answer

Relaxation is the state of the qubit dropping over time from the excited state, $|1\rangle$, down to the ground state, $|0\rangle$.

Dephasing is the phase noise that affects the phase state of the qubit. For example, if the qubit is in a superposition state, then it would mean the difference between the qubit state moving from the $|+\rangle$ state to the $|-\rangle$ state, or vice versa, over time.

Question 4

Which of the following is not a value for dephasing – T_1, T_2, or $T_2{}^*$?

Answer

T_1, T_2, and $T_2{}^*$ are values that represent dephasing, where T_1 represents relaxation.

Question 5

What is the maximum number of qubits you can apply to a measurement filter?

Answer

There is no maximum; you can apply the measurement filter to as many qubits as you need.

Question 6

What is the difference between T_2 and $T_2{}^*$?

Answer

T_2 and $T_2{}^*$ are both dephasing; the difference is in the actions of each experiment to the qubit and what the expected results would be. For $T_2{}^*$ and T_2, you start by applying a Hadamard gate, which puts the qubit in a superposition state. Then, to calculate $T_2{}^*$, you wait a fixed amount of time and then apply a Hadamard gate again and take a measurement. Your results should have you back in the original state. However, if there is some dephasing, the results will then be in the opposite state. This is commonly referred to as a **Ramsey experiment**.

For T_2, you wait half the fixed amount of time, and then apply a NOT (X) gate, and then wait the remaining (last half) of the fixed amount of time, and then apply a measurement. This is commonly referred to as the **Hahn echo experiment**.

Question 7

What do the rows and columns of a calibration matrix relate to?

Answer

The column headers represent the prepared states, and the rows represent the measured values. In a noiseless (ideal) system, the two would be the same each time, which would represent the diagonal. However, if there is noise and the measured state is different than the prepared state, the results will highlight sections outside the diagonal. This calibration matrix represents the measured noise of the system.

Question 8

What is the name of the effect when a qubit decays from the excited state to the ground state?

Answer

Relaxation decoherence, often referred to as T_1.

Chapter 12 – Learning about Qiskit Aqua

Question 1

Using the quantum circuit from the example shown in *Figure 12.4*, create a custom initialized state using the `state_vector` parameter.

Answer

```
from qiskit.aqua.operators.state_fns import CircuitStateFn
num_qubits = 2
qc = QuantumCircuit(num_qubits)
qc.h(0)
qc.cx(0,1)
# Construct the Custom class based on the built quantum circuit
q_st_func = Custom(state_vector=csf, num_qubits=num_qubits)
```

Question 2

Construct a circuit state function from a state vector.

Answer

```
from qiskit.aqua.operators.state_fns import CircuitStateFn
qc = QuantumCircuit(2)
qc.h(0)
qc.cx(0,1)
csf = CircuitStateFn(primitive=qc, coeff=1,
is_measurement=False)
```

Question 3

Construct a balanced Oracle and verify it using the **Deutsch-Jozsa** algorithm.

Answer

To construct a balanced oracle, you need to first place a NOT (X) gate to each qubit where the binary string has a 1. Then you need to apply a Control-NOT (CX) gate to each qubit where each qubit is the source, and the target qubit is the ancilla qubit.

Question 4

Implement the **Bernstein-Vazirani** algorithm to find the secret value, 170. (*Hint*: use the decimal-to-binary utility.)

Answer

In order to create the circuit, you need to convert the value from decimal, 170, to the binary representation of 170. Then, after applying a Hadamard gate to all the qubits, except the ancilla qubit, to which you will first apply a NOT gate followed by a Hadamard, apply a CX gate to each qubit that is represented by the binary value 170, which is represented by the value 10101010. So, you would apply a CX gate to each of the odd qubits, where the control of each CX gate is set to qubit 1, 3, 5, and 7 and the target of each CX gate is the ancilla qubit. Then, apply a Hadamard gate followed by a measurement operator to all qubits, except the ancilla qubit.

Question 5

How many Oracle functions are there?

Answer

In general, most algorithms have one oracle function; however, there are some algorithms that require more than one, or multiple oracle functions, such as the Grover algorithm, which repeats the oracle function based on the number of qubits.

Question 6

Does Aqua also include classical algorithms?

Answer

Yes, there is currently a base class for `ClassicalAlgorithms` in Aqua.

Question 7

Leveraging the `qiskit.aqua.circuits.StateVectorCircuit` class, construct a circuit that represents an X gate.

Answer

```
state_vector = [0, 1]
state_vector_qc = StateVectorCircuit(state_vector)
qc_sv = state_vector_qc.construct_circuit()
qc_sv.draw()
```

Question 8

Change the backend on `QuantumInstance` to a quantum computer backend that is available and rerun any of the quantum algorithms. Describe what differences, if any, you were able to observe.

Answer

Based on the quantum computer and its Quantum Volume, you would see similar results with some noise. You can run some error mitigation, such as the measurement calibration fitters, to correct those as well so as to get more precise results.

Chapter 13 – Understanding Quantum Algorithms

Question 1

Create a circuit that implements Deutsch's algorithm for a constant function and verify your results.

Answer

Deutsch's algorithm is used to determine whether a function f(x) is balanced or constant for a single bit input. In order to solve this using a quantum computer, your 2-qubit circuit should include an oracle function with a Control-Not (CX) gate between the 2-qubits, where the input is the Control and the other qubit is the Target. Prior to the oracle function and similar to the Deutsch-Jozsa algorithm, your ancilla qubit (the second qubit) should have a NOT (x) gate prior to placing it in superposition.

Question 2

Which algorithm would you use to determine whether an n-bit string is balanced?

Answer

The Deutsch-Jozsa algorithm.

Question 3

Would phase kickback work if the ancilla qubit was not set to the state $|1\rangle$? Explain your answer.

Answer

No, it would offset the results. Remove the X gate in your circuit and run the experiment to see the difference in both the measured results and in the state vector.

Question 4

Implement the Bernstein-Vazirani algorithm to find the state $|11010\rangle$.

Answer

Simply follow the same setup of adding Hadamard gates to all input qubits, and an X followed by a Hadamard gate to the ancilla qubit, then include the CX gate to qubits 1, 3, and 4, followed by Hadamard and measurements to all the qubits except the ancilla qubit.

Question 5

What would happen if you set the ancilla qubit in either of the algorithms by first placing a Hadamard gate, followed by an X gate? Explain the reason for the results.

Answer

The results would be incorrect. The X gate prior to the Hadamard prepares the state with a negative phase, whereas if the X is on the other side of the H gate, it has a different effect that prepares a different state prior to applying the CX gates.

Question 6

Program and create an automated oracle generator for the Bernstein-Vazirani algorithm that randomly generates the secret state. Can you determine the value by just running the circuit and reviewing the results?

Answer

This can be done by reading the binary representation of the secret state and creating the oracle using CX gates to apply to each qubit where the binary value 1 is present.

Chapter 14 – Applying Quantum Algorithms

Question 1

What other problems can you solve using periodic functions?

Answer

Quantum phase estimation and Shor's algorithm are two of the more well-known ones.

Question 2

Implement QFT on a five-qubit state—for example, `10110`.

Answer

To create a QFT, simply set a variable to the value `10110`. Then, apply an X gate to each qubit that has a `1` assigned. Then, follow the pattern to generate the QFT by applying an H gate to the most significant qubit, then followed by Control-Rot gates starting at $\pi/2$ and dividing in half as you traverse across each C-Rot, $\pi/4$, $\pi/8$, $\pi/16$, and more. Then, repeat as you progress down each qubit. Finally, apply swap gates from the extreme qubits – in this case, qubit 0, qubit 4, qubit 1, and qubit 3.

Question 3

Since quantum gates are reversible, how would you create an inverse QFT on the encoded value we created, `'110'`, or $|\tilde{6}\rangle$?

Answer

You would simply reverse the operations you performed in creating the QFT of the value 6.

Question 4

Using Grover's algorithm, find the following states: `'101'`, `'001'`, and `'010'`.

Answer

Generate an oracle for each state by applying an X gate for each qubit that is represented by a `0` followed by a Control-Control-NOT gate, and then followed by repeating the X gate on the same qubit. Since it is only 3 qubits in length, you would only need to create the oracle and the Grover diffusion operator once.

Question 5

How many iterations of Grover's algorithm would you need to run to find the state $|10101\rangle$?

Answer

Twice (two times), as the repetition is based on $\sqrt{N}$, where N is the number of qubits. Since we will need 5 qubits, $\sqrt{5}$ is greater than $\sqrt{4}$, which is 2.

Question 6

Rerun the Grover's search example. Only repeat Grover's oracle and the diffusion operator twice and note the difference in the result. What do you see that is different? What would you expect to change if you ran it three times?

Answer

The amplification of the expected answer will begin to decrease as the difference between the two is calculated across for each iteration.

Question 7

Does Qiskit Aqua also include classical algorithms along with quantum algorithms?

Answer

Yes.

Question 8

What other algorithms are included with Qiskit Aqua?

Answer

There are many, and there will be many more by the time you are reading this. The full list can be found in the Qiskit documentation under **qiskit.aqua.algorithms**. At the time of writing, there are over 20 quantum algorithms in Aqua, including Berstein-Vazirani, HHL, Deutsch-Jozsa, Simon, VQE, QAOA, NumPyEigensolver, and Shor's.

Other Books You May Enjoy

If you enjoyed this book, you may be interested in these other books by Packt:

Dancing with Qubits

Robert S. Sutor

ISBN: 978-1-83882-736-6

- See how quantum computing works, delve into the math behind it, what makes it different, and why it is so powerful with this quantum computing textbook
- Discover the complex, mind-bending mechanics that underpin quantum systems
- Understand the necessary concepts behind classical and quantum computing
- Refresh and extend your grasp of essential mathematics, computing, and quantum theory
- Explore the main applications of quantum computing to the fields of scientific computing, AI, and elsewhere
- Examine a detailed overview of qubits, quantum circuits, and quantum algorithm

Quantum Computing and Blockchain in Business

Arunkumar Krishnakumar

ISBN: 978-1-83864-776-6

- Understand the fundamentals of quantum computing and Blockchain
- Gain insights from the experts who are using quantum computing and Blockchain
- Discover the implications of these technologies for governance and healthcare
- Learn how Blockchain and quantum computing may influence logistics and finance
- Understand how these technologies are impacting research in areas such as chemistry
- Find out how these technologies may help the environment and influence smart city development
- Understand the implications for cybersecurity as these technologies evolve

Leave a review - let other readers know what you think

Please share your thoughts on this book with others by leaving a review on the site that you bought it from. If you purchased the book from Amazon, please leave us an honest review on this book's Amazon page. This is vital so that other potential readers can see and use your unbiased opinion to make purchasing decisions, we can understand what our customers think about our products, and our authors can see your feedback on the title that they have worked with Packt to create. It will only take a few minutes of your time, but is valuable to other potential customers, our authors, and Packt. Thank you!

Index